THE BIGGEST PICTURE

Wendy Curtis

From the Big Bang to the Development
of the Big Bang Theory

by Wendy Curtis

To my mother, Roberta Wesley Hillman for her immediate encouragement and unwavering support. I wish my father could have seen the release of this book.

Contributors:
Evan Penn Serio

and Lee Bouse, Arianna Bruno, Carl Caivano, Ernie Carbone, Grace Dickinson, Alan Fleming, Chris Gaudreau, Norman Johnson, David Kelley, Michael Kelley, Katie Knutson, Michelle Kroll, Jim MacAllister, Billy Mantzios, Patrick McAllister, Titus Neijens, David Ng, Dan O'Neil, Jay Rathaus, Navit Reid, Jingyu Rhine Caroline Romedenne, Jason Root, Melisha Santiago, Steffani Scheer, Jared Snider, Dennis Spencer, Dan Taibbi, Michael Thorn, and Robert Wilfong

MW00387742

ABOUT THIS BOOK

This book presents the scientific community's current best theories about major events from the Big Bang until present times, in chronological order. Alternative theories and previous theories that have been superseded are included when notable.

The immense scope of this book and its limited number of pages allow only the most important ideas and events to be included. The resulting *Big Picture* view is designed to help the reader to keep the principal ideas in mind. The main idea on each page is presented in large sized type, and supporting facts and details are included in smaller type. Other material, including additional footnotes and references, is available from our website at **www.GeobookStudio.org**.

Paragraphs of supporting detail are labeled by topic with icons to help the reader identify the ones they may be most interested in reading. Here are some of those topics and their icons:

Animals

Class & Social Stratification

Conflicting Paradigms

Core vs Periphery

Currency

Drugs / Illicit Substances

Emergence

Energy

Foods

Global Systems

Information & Thought

Justice, Equality, & Governance

Language, Music, & Art

Life

Nationalism

Natural Resources

Oil / Fossil Fuels

Population Growth

Science / Principles of Science

Technology

Date Tag

GeoBook Studio

Thank you for your interest in this book. Feedback and suggestions are welcomed and may be included with proper acknowledgement, in subsequent editions. E-mail us at team@ Geobookstudio. org. or contact us through our website with any comments or to order additional copies or other products:

www.GeoBookStudio.org.

Version 2.5 © Wendy Curtis • June 30, 2016

An interactive version of this book is also available as an Apple iBook.

Get it on iBooks

CONTENTS

We look outward and marvel at the
expansive beauty of the heavens.

We evolved within an evolving Universe.

We quest to understand it.

Is this the nature of the Universe- that
intelligent life arises within it, and intelligent
beings try to understand the Universe itself?

Are we thus an embodiment of the consciousness of the Universe?

We observe and then try to explain what we have seen. We
develop stories, myths, and theories. Observation and logic are
our two primary tools. Our explanations become a paradigm;
a model of the Universe- what it is and how it works.

This world view explains what we already know
and guides our journey of discovery as we try to
understand more. Our explanations satisfy us for a
while, but as we discover new things and attempt to
explain ever more about the world, we sometimes find
our old explanations inadequate or even inconsistent.

If an inconsistency is minor, the theory can be
modified to be more coherent. If the inconsistency
becomes ever more troublesome, and no satisfactory
modification of the theory can be envisioned, then
the whole theory must be replaced with a new one.
Paradigm shifts can be politically tumultuous.

People have an innate curiosity about origins: the origin
of oneself, the origin of the Earth, the origin of all
things. Every human culture has had a creation myth.

Thousands of generations of humans have walked
upon the Earth and wondered. The earliest humans
watched the Sun rise, felt its warmth and watched
it set. Did they know that the Sun brought warmth?
Did they expect it to rise tomorrow?

Humans have always marveled at the heavens.
This is the first time in history when an average
fourteen year old has never seen the Milky Way
because city lights now obscure the view.

As humans attempt to understand the world around us and try
to correlate causes and effects, we sometimes make mistakes.
To help us in our quest, we invented guidelines, called 'science.'

Chapter 1: The Big Bang Creates the Simplest Elements

In the beginning, according to the **Big Bang Theory**, the **Universe** was not immense and spread out, as it is today.

According to the theory, the Universe was in a compact state, called a **Singularity**.

Everything that is in the Universe today- all of the matter and energy that make up stars, black holes, planets, and everything else in all the galaxies- was present at the beginning but it was in a different form. Instead of being dispersed throughout unfathomable expanses of space, it was crammed together in a very small space.

The Singularity was a peculiar and paradoxical thing; it was 'large' in the sense that it contained everything in the whole Universe but it was small in size. Because the Singularity contained everything in the Universe, its gravity was so strong that it crushed itself small.

Atoms of matter could not have existed; their constituent parts, protons, neutrons and electrons, would have been pulled so close together by gravity that they would have merged and unraveled into waves of energy. So there was no matter but only just energy, pure energy.

Because the singularity contained everything in the Universe, it *was* the Universe. Even though it was small, smaller than an atom, it was the whole Universe. There was nothing around it; anything around it would have been pulled into it by its immense gravity.

The Big Bang Theory has been around for many decades. It is still the most accurate and comprehensive model of the Universe that we have to describe the evidence astronomers observe. It started out as a hypothesis, as all theories do, and was later upgraded to the status of 'theory' when it gained the support of many scientists. The theory was developed in response to logical implications stemming from Einstein's equations of relativity and to observational evidence that the universe is expanding. Both of these topics are discussed in detail in the last two chapters of this book.

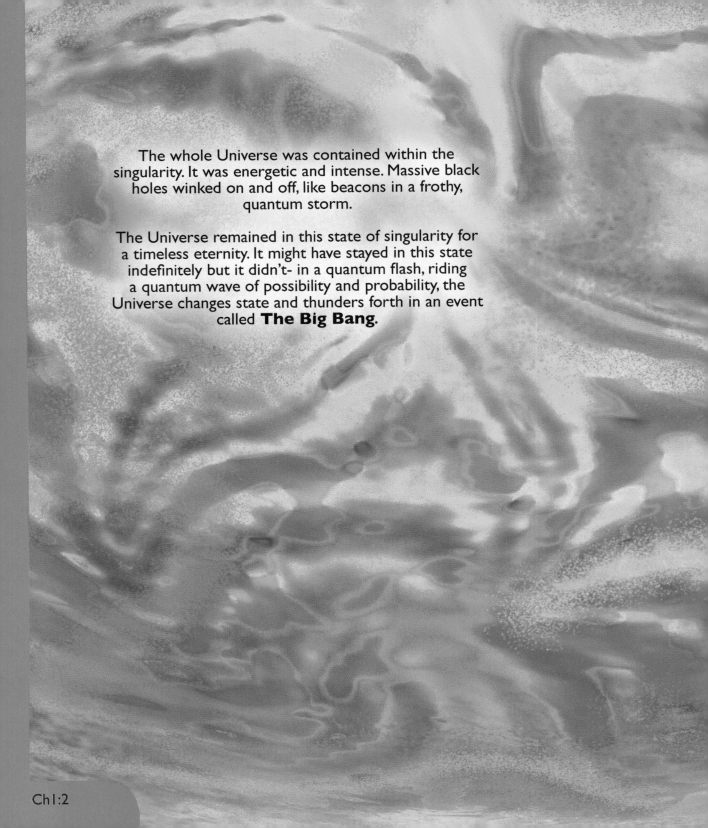

The whole Universe was contained within the singularity. It was energetic and intense. Massive black holes winked on and off, like beacons in a frothy, quantum storm.

The Universe remained in this state of singularity for a timeless eternity. It might have stayed in this state indefinitely but it didn't- in a quantum flash, riding a quantum wave of possibility and probability, the Universe changes state and thunders forth in an event called **The Big Bang**.

The peculiarities of a **Singularity** are paradoxical.

A singularity is beyond massive but contains no matter.

Time and space do not even exist in a singularity. In the Universe today, time marches forward and space has dimension; but in the crazy, quantum, micro realm of a singularity, time is bent around itself and space has no meaning. Einstein's theory of special relativity defines space and time in relation with gravity but these terms do not seem to apply to a singularity.

The quirky laws of quantum mechanics govern the hyper-dense, micro-world of a singularity. These laws of physics are not the same rules that operate at larger scales.

There seem to be two sets of rules in physics; one for the small scale and one for the large. This is upsetting for physicists and they would prefer to have a single, unified theory. But for now, scientists recognize two forces at work in the micro realm (the strong and the weak nuclear forces) and two that operate at larger scales (gravity and electromagnetism).

The search to find one grand theory to unify and replace what are currently considered four separate forces is the quest of physicists of our era. There is hope and precedent; the forces of electricity and magnetism were once considered distinct until it was shown, in the 1800's, that a single set of equations could describe them both. More on this in the final chapters of this book.

There is nothing outside the singularity. There are no stars or planets. There is not even empty space around it.

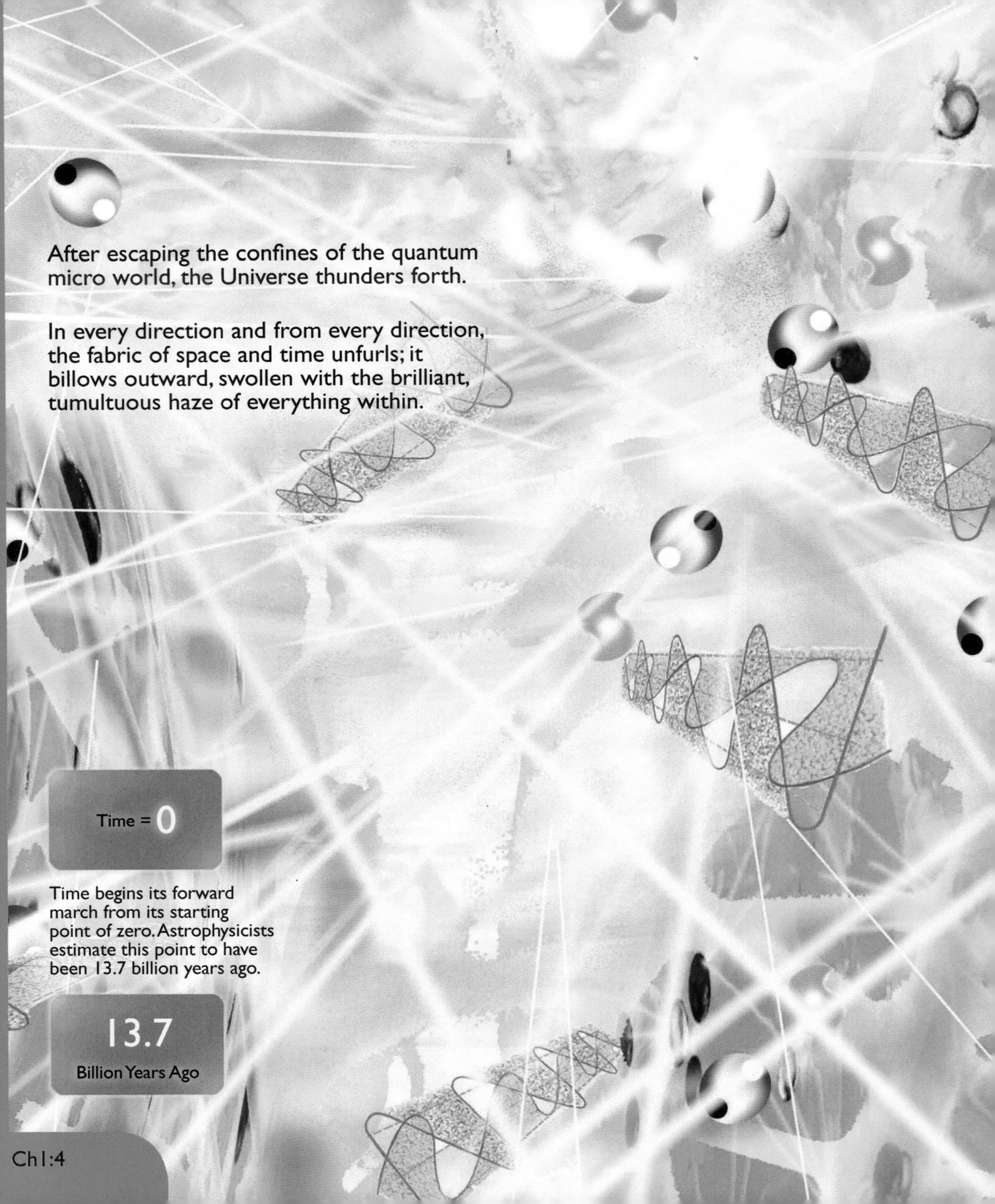

After escaping the confines of the quantum micro world, the Universe thunders forth.

In every direction and from every direction, the fabric of space and time unfurls; it billows outward, swollen with the brilliant, tumultuous haze of everything within.

Time = 0

Time begins its forward march from its starting point of zero. Astrophysicists estimate this point to have been 13.7 billion years ago.

13.7

Billion Years Ago

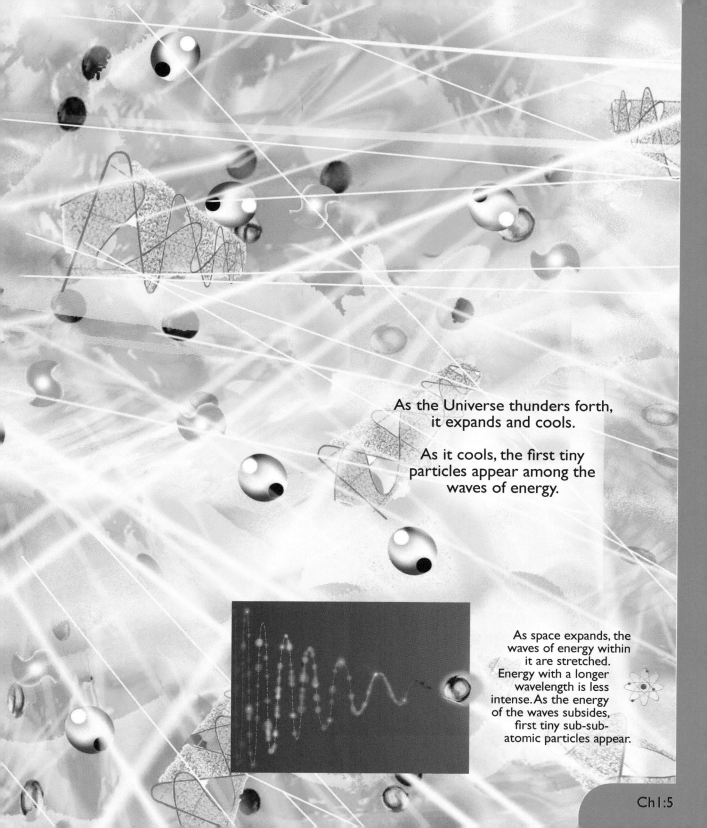

As the Universe thunders forth,
it expands and cools.

As it cools, the first tiny
particles appear among the
waves of energy.

As space expands, the
waves of energy within
it are stretched.
Energy with a longer
wavelength is less
intense. As the energy
of the waves subsides,
first tiny sub-sub-
atomic particles appear.

As the cooling continues, particles move slower and are able to bond together into larger particles, and then ultimately into **atoms**.

During these early stages of expansion, the Universe is a brilliant fog. A light ray cannot go far without colliding with a small particle and bouncing off in a different direction. With light rays bouncing this way and that; the Universe remains opaque, rather than transparent.

The brilliant fog of the early stages of the Big Bang is giving way to transparency as light rays travel ever farther before bouncing off in some random direction.

When **quarks** (an early forming, very small particle) join up into teams of three, protons are born. Protons are the nuclei of atoms of matter. As each proton forms, it soaks up a great store of energy from the quantum soup and locks that energy away in its sub-atomic bonds. The protons condense out, like dew drops forming on a lawn; and because $E = mc^2$, as each atomic nucleus forms, it takes away an amount of energy equivalent to its mass multiplied by the speed of light squared.

Electrons are very small particles which had formed at an early stage. They are negatively charged and are still ricocheting around in the haze. The protons, which have just formed, are larger particles with a positive charge. When the temperature drops low enough, the particles will lose speed; and then, by virtue of their complementary charges, the electrons and protons will settle in with one another. Together they make whole atoms that have a neutral charge.

13.3

Billion Years Ago

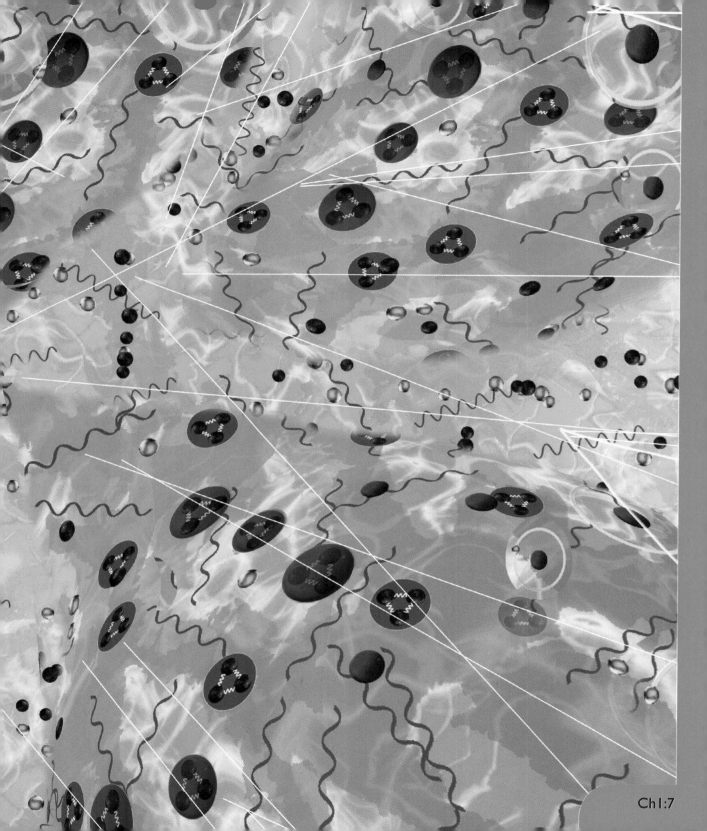

Once atoms form and there are not so many small particles around, **light rays** can travel further without bumping into something. The haze clears and the Universe becomes transparent.

The light rays run off. Each keeps going in whatever direction it happens to be heading.

Scientists call this the time of **The Last Scatter**.

The distance between obstacles that the light rays can collide with, increases primarily because the multitude of sub-atomic particles joined together into a fewer number of larger particles (atoms). But the continuing expansion of space also increases the distance between particles. For both reasons, light rays are able to traverse ever increasing distances before ricocheting off the next particle. Once the light rays stop bouncing around and travel straight, the Universe becomes transparent and would have been visible, if anyone with eyes had been there to see it.

These light waves that were released at this time, still run free in the universe today. When they were released, they were more energetic and had shorter wavelengths than they do now but because the universe continued to expand, these waves have been stretched out. Today they form the faintly detectable Cosmic Background Radiation. The CBR is also known as the *Afterglow of the Big Bang*. Finding the CBR was one of the great accomplishments of the 20th century and provides some of the most convincing proof of the Big Bang Theory.

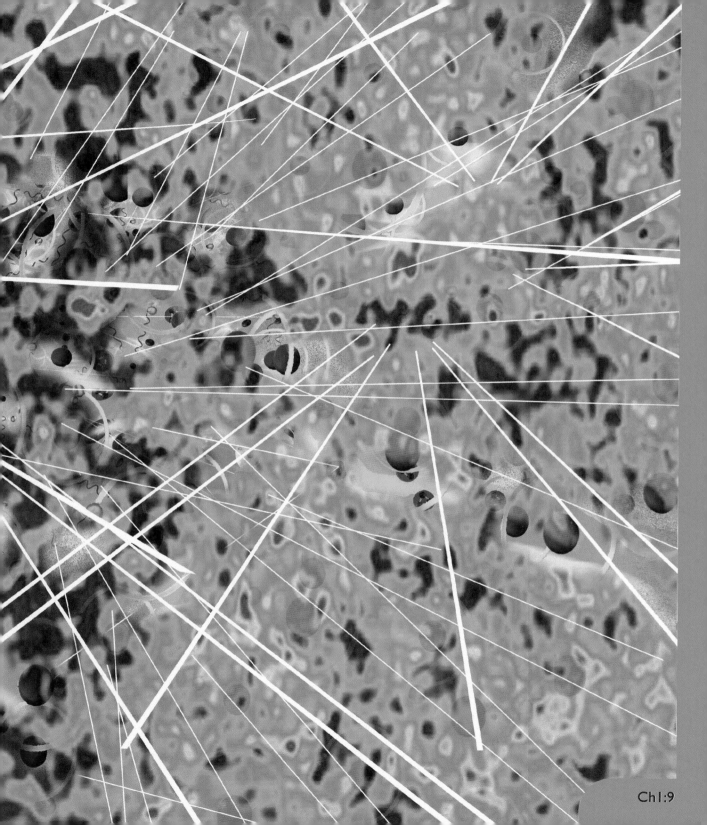

Chapter 2: Stars Forge the Rest of the Elements

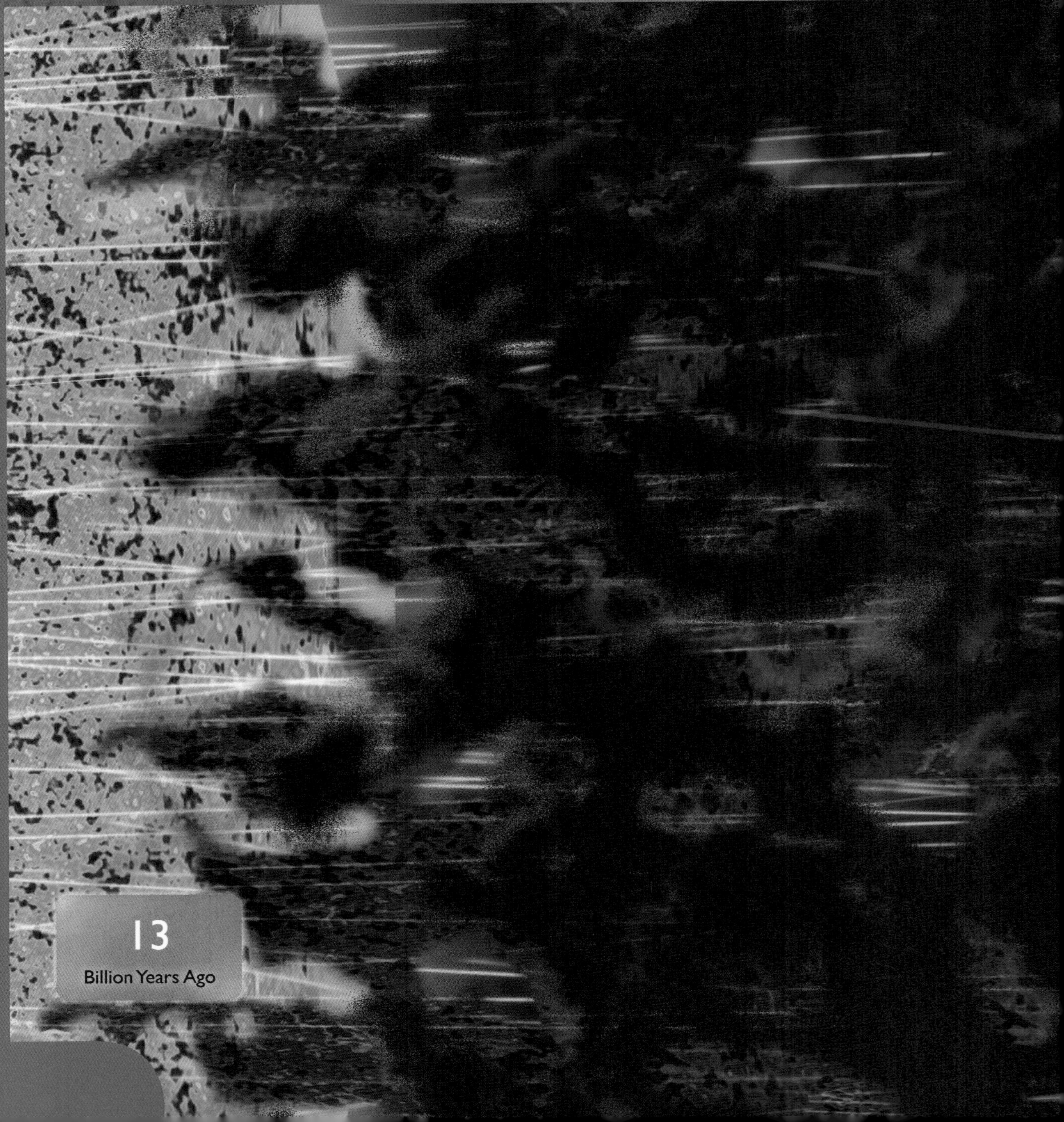
13
Billion Years Ago

Almost as soon as the Universe becomes transparent, the brightness of the Universe fades and space begins to darken.

In the developing darkness, are the atoms that have recently formed- there are no stars yet. Each atom is just a tiny thing, separate from every other atom and all somewhat evenly dispersed, throughout all of space. Each atom silently responds to the other atoms because each atom feels the gravitational effect of the others.

Each separate atom, as tiny as it is, has its own minuscule, gravitational effect on the space around it. Each atom floats and travels alone through the fabric of space and makes a slight distortion to that fabric. Since each atom is effecting the fabric of space and each atom is in space, the whole thing is intrinsically dynamic and connected.

Even in the developing darkness, the isolated atoms are moving about, sliding down the slightest inclines in the fabric, falling toward nearby atoms and gathering together.

Each atom is its own spinning system of sub-atomic particles -its own island of trapped energy- and although each atom is separate and isolated from the others, they respond to each other through gravity. Even though atoms are tiny, each one has some mass, some weight to it, and so each atom affects the space around it by making a very slight indentation in it. The idea that particles of matter affect the fabric of space is part of Einstein's idea that E=mc2; energy and matter are interchangeable via an equation that involves the speed of light through seemingly empty space. More on this in the final chapters of this book where the development of the Theory of Relativity is explored.

In the darkness, the simple atoms that have formed, silently respond to each other's gravity which attracts them toward each other. They gather slowly into loose associations that begin to resemble gigantic clouds.

Regions of space with a lesser density of atoms become ever-emptier as the atoms that they do contain drift toward areas that already have a higher density of atoms. In this way, empty voids develop between the gigantic clouds of atoms.

The cloudy regions are actually not very dense either - not by earthly standards. Even though they contain a lot of atoms, the amount of space is so expansive that the distribution of atoms is thin.

The original distribution of atoms was only roughly even with some regions of space having slightly higher densities of atoms in them. This is because the Big Bang began with a quantum wave which left a quantum signature; almost uniform but not quite.

These small differences in regional density will later be amplified by the ongoing expansion of the Universe. Denser areas will become galaxies and sparser areas will become immense voids.

There are only simple atoms; no large atoms like carbon or oxygen exist yet.

The simplest kind of atom is the **hydrogen** atom. It has only one proton and one electron. This is all that had condensed out of the cooling energy of The Big Bang. Some of the hydrogen atoms had then collided and joined together to make the slightly larger atom called **helium**. At this point in time, the variety of atoms in the Universe is restricted to just these smallest atoms.

The Periodic Table of the Elements, which is a roster of every kind of atom, now contains only its first two members.

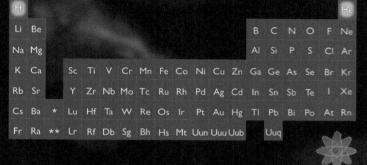

In the late stages of the Big Bang, the universe had cooled enough for hydrogen to condense out. Then some of the hydrogen atoms had run into each other and merged into a fewer number of larger helium atoms. The merging of atoms is called **nuclear fusion**. The fusion process requires that the colliding atoms be moving at great speeds which requires high temperatures. Luckily for us, the temperature of the universe soon dropped enough so that no more fusion could happen (besides making a minuscule amount of lithium, the third smallest atom).

If fusion had been able to continue, all the atoms would have continued to fuse together until each one had become part of an atom of iron. **Iron** atoms are matter in its lowest energy state. If fusion had continued and all atoms were in their lowest possible energy state, there would be no energy differentials with which to drive chemical reactions and life could never have developed.

The **Dark Era** continues and the enormous, amorphous clouds, which are just loose collections of simple atoms, become **proto-galaxies** as gravity draws their atoms ever closer together. In the darkness of the rapidly expanding young Universe, suddenly in every proto-galaxy, clumps of atoms become **stars** which light up and shine forth and begin to illuminate the Universe.

The first stars form in the centers of the cloudiest sections of every cloudy region. In the center of a cloudy section, the atoms are crammed close together under immense pressure. The atoms ricochet around and when they happen to collide head on, they fuse. Nuclear fusion releases energy and so stars not only shine but the energy generated counters gravity and keeps the star from imploding. Nuclear fusion releases energy but at the cost of some mass. The hydrogen atoms that fuse into a fewer number of helium atoms, weigh a little bit less than the resultant helium atoms. So stars actually get lighter as they shine. The lost mass is the sunshine.

Within each proto-galaxy a multitude of separate clumps of atoms form rather than just a single clump at the proto-galaxy's center. This is because gravity gets exponentially weaker with distance so atoms are pulled most strongly toward the atoms nearest themselves and only weakly to the center of the cloud. Gravity shapes the galaxies and the structures within them.

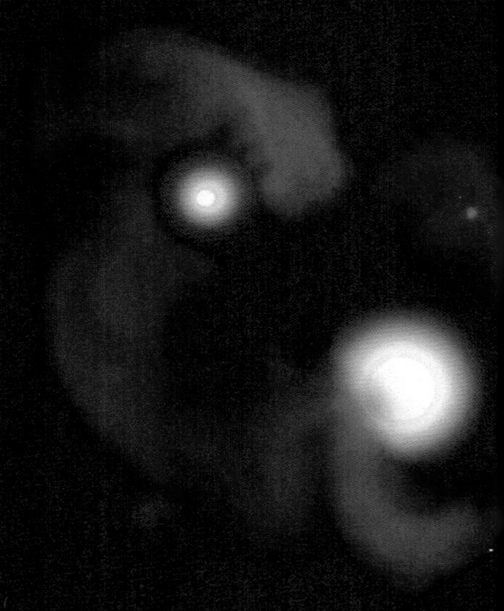

From a multitude of simple elements, a single star emerges and from a star, complex atoms are born. **Emergence** is the concept that complex structures are born from the interactions of a large number of simple components, under the influence of an energy source, preferably a cyclic or reiterating one. A star emerges from a multitude of separate hydrogen atoms, all interacting under the influence of gravity. Emergence is actively being studied as a new science but as yet no defining mathematical equation to describe it has been discovered. Emergent systems are all around us; the interaction of separate automobiles forms traffic patterns, the internet has enabled new ways of organizing political protest.

Stars fuse some of the many small atoms into a fewer number of larger atoms. This is called nuclear fusion, a process which liberates energy and so stars shine.
Stars can form atoms as large as **iron**.

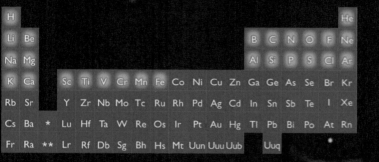

Carbon, the atom that living things are made of, comes into existence.

Iron is the largest atom that can be produced by stellar nuclear fusion. It is the most stable atom in the lowest energy state. Unlike all previously made elements which release energy when they fuse, making an element larger than iron requires energy.

The first generation of stars run on, forging
carbon, oxygen and other mid-sized elements.
But stars can only forge elements as large as iron.

A star's progress through the stages of
nuclear fusion depends upon its mass.

Each star begins its life cycle by forging hydrogen
into helium, but when the supply of hydrogen in the
core runs low, its nuclear furnace dims. Without the
outward pressure supplied by the nuclear fusion
reactions, gravity is unopposed and the star contracts.
As the star contracts, pressure and temperature in
its center increase and if the pressure is enough, the
helium atoms fuse into carbon atoms and the star
shines anew and regains gravitational stability.

After the carbon runs out, the nuclear furnace dims
again, allowing gravity to contract the star, causing
the pressure to rise. If the star is not large enough to
have enough pressure to fuse the carbon atoms, the
nuclear furnace will go out. The star will then contract
until the carbon atoms become so closely packed
that the electrons of one atom bump up against those
of a neighboring atom, at which point the electron
repulsion force (like charges repel) keeps gravity from
proceeding further and the expiring star has become
a cloudy region with a carbon core.

If the star is more massive, it will generate enough
pressure to force the carbon atoms to fuse into
oxygen. After oxygen runs out, the atoms will fuse
into silicon and so on, up to iron. If a star is so
massive that the pressure within its core forces the
iron in the core to converge, the star can explode.
In this glorious explosion as a star goes *supernova*,
elements larger than iron are created. In fact, all kinds
of atoms are created, even strange combinations of
particles that are so unstable that they soon lose
pieces, until reaching a stable configuration in a
process known as radioactive decay. Our periodic
table is a chart of all the stable elements.

If the massive star manages not to explode,
it can become a **black hole**.

If a star expires after reaching the carbon
fusion stage, it becomes a cloud of hydrogen
and helium gas surrounding a diamond
core. This is because carbon atoms can be
arranged in different solid forms; as the
mineral graphite (pencil lead) or when
very closely packed, as diamonds.

After forging iron, a star reaches the end of the nuclear fusion cycle. If a star is large enough, it will then explode in a **supernova** explosion. Only in these explosions, are the rest of the elements finally created.

Finally all of the different kinds of atoms form.

Some atoms are more abundant than others. The Big Bang produced only hydrogen and helium which still make up 98 % of all the (non-dark) matter of the universe. The next most abundant atoms are the ones which are forged in stars. Elements larger than iron are rare indeed.

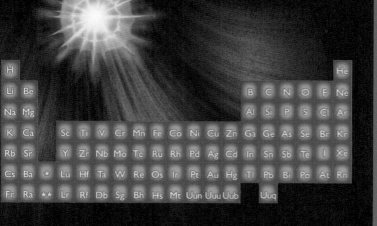

Chapter 3: Our Galactic Neighborhood

New stars keep firing up in each of the proto-galaxies which are evolving from faint, shapeless forms into structured spirals. The clouds of hydrogen and helium also contain **Dark Matter** but we can only detect the 'normal,' visible matter.

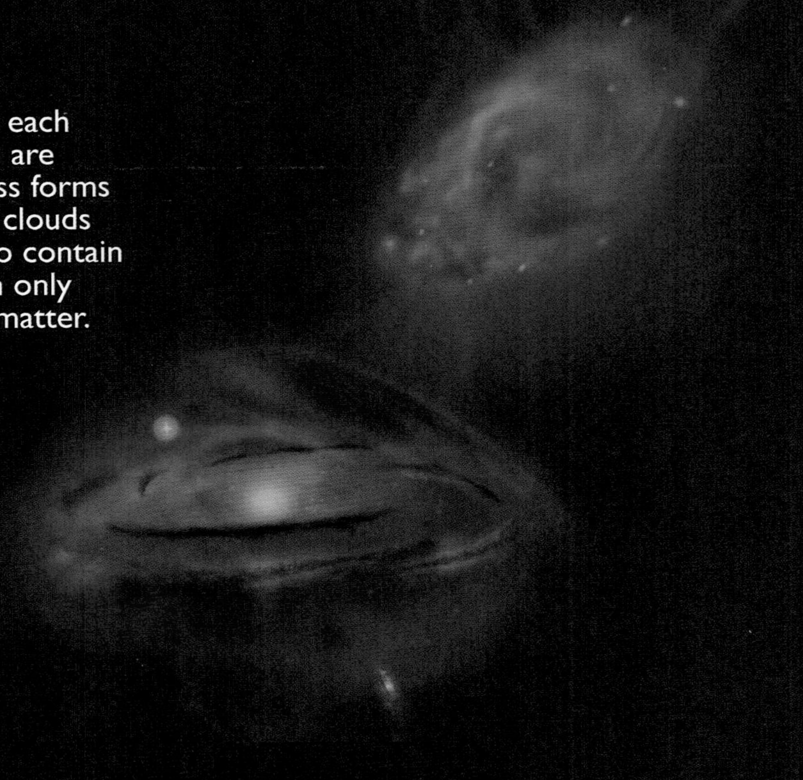

Gravity shapes and defines the structures of the Universe.

Structure in the Universe is defined and written by gravity. Young galaxies are relatively shapeless and relatively evenly distributed but will eventually develop their whirling, sweeping spiral shapes and individual galaxies will gather into clusters or become arrayed in lines called filaments. The structures that gravity builds later interact with each other which builds structure at a larger scale; atoms gather into stars and stars interact with other stars and galaxies jostle with other galaxies as gravity continues its weak but persistent effect. Complex structure in the Universe emerges out of initially dispersed matter by gravitational collapse.

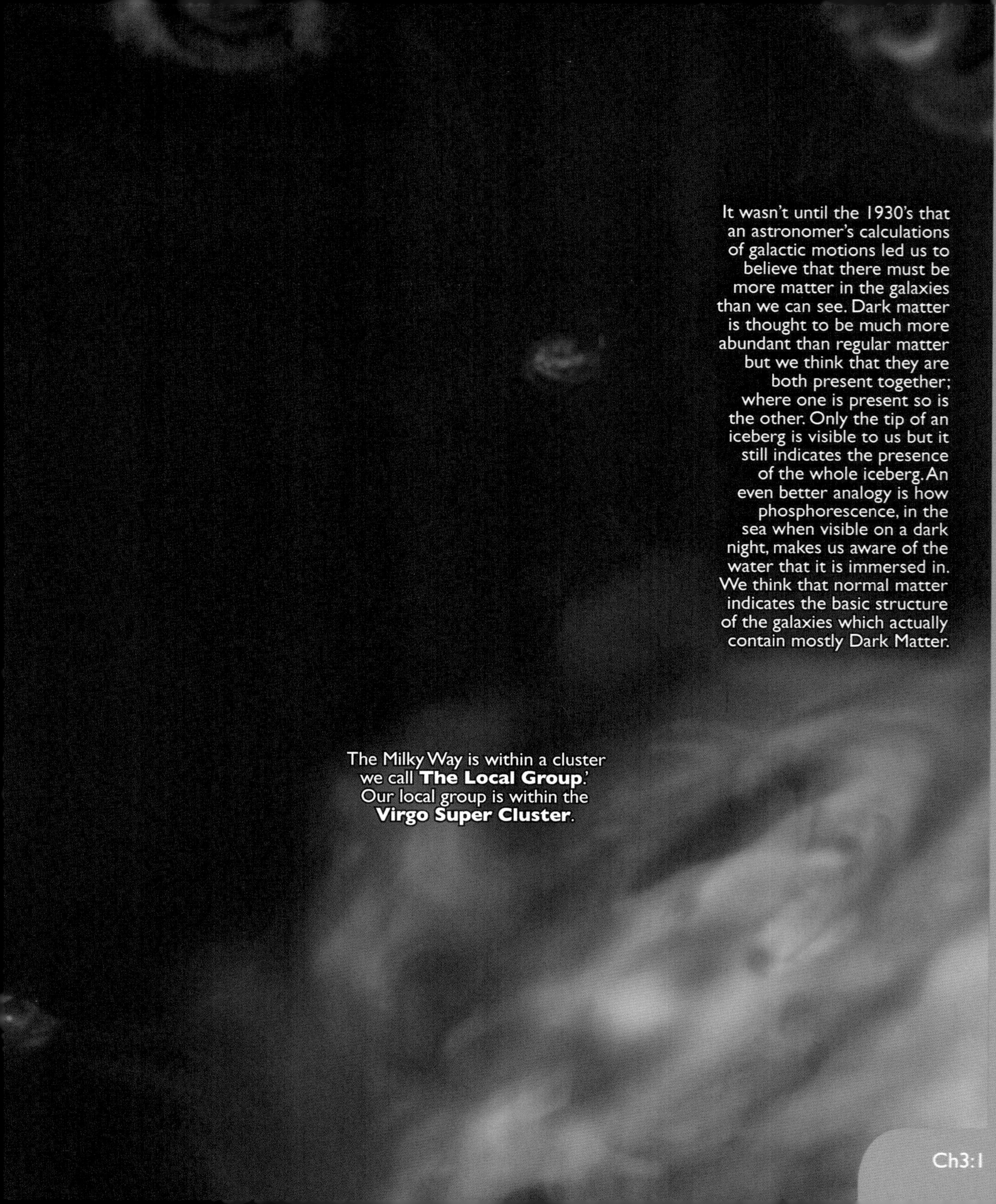

It wasn't until the 1930's that an astronomer's calculations of galactic motions led us to believe that there must be more matter in the galaxies than we can see. Dark matter is thought to be much more abundant than regular matter but we think that they are both present together; where one is present so is the other. Only the tip of an iceberg is visible to us but it still indicates the presence of the whole iceberg. An even better analogy is how phosphorescence, in the sea when visible on a dark night, makes us aware of the water that it is immersed in. We think that normal matter indicates the basic structure of the galaxies which actually contain mostly Dark Matter.

The Milky Way is within a cluster we call '**The Local Group**.' Our local group is within the **Virgo Super Cluster**.

10

Billion Years Ago

The galaxies become separated by great voids of empty space and are gathered into clusters and along linear bands.

The galaxies stay the same size even though space continues to expand. As the galaxies continue to evolve, their own mass keeps them gravitationally bound together preventing them from expanding even as the Universe as a whole continues to expand. This causes the galaxies to become separated from each other by the growing expanses of empty space.

The spaces between galaxies expand fully, blowing up like soap bubbles to form vast voids. The galaxies remain between the voids and thus come to be arranged in clusters or arrayed in linear swaths known as filaments at the intersections of voids.

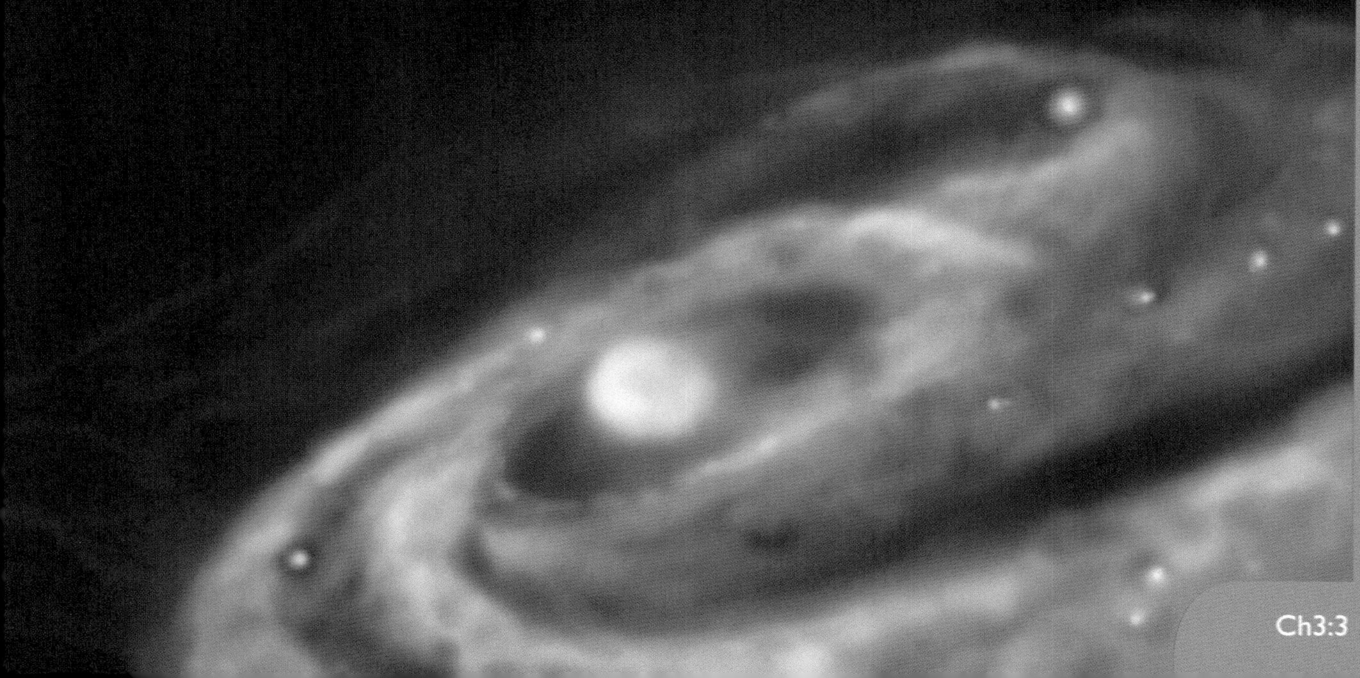

The galaxies continue to evolve. In each galaxy, successive generations of new stars form, shine forth, and then expire. Each generation contributes to the growing quantity of old enriched stardust which gathers into vast clouds that drift between the stars but stay within the confines of the galaxy. The enriched dust within these giant clouds is the raw material from which planets can be made. From this gas and dust, a new generation of stars will be born and some will have planets around them.

Atoms can join together to make molecules which can exist as gasses, liquids or solids. In gasses, the molecules drift around separately with much space between them. In liquids, the molecules are closer together but can still slide past each other. In solids, atoms are arranged in specific three dimensional arrangements and are locked in place. Solids with highly ordered repeating arrangements are called **minerals**.

Dozens of different kinds of molecules including amino acids, which are the building blocks of life, can be detected in the giant clouds.

5

Billion Years Ago

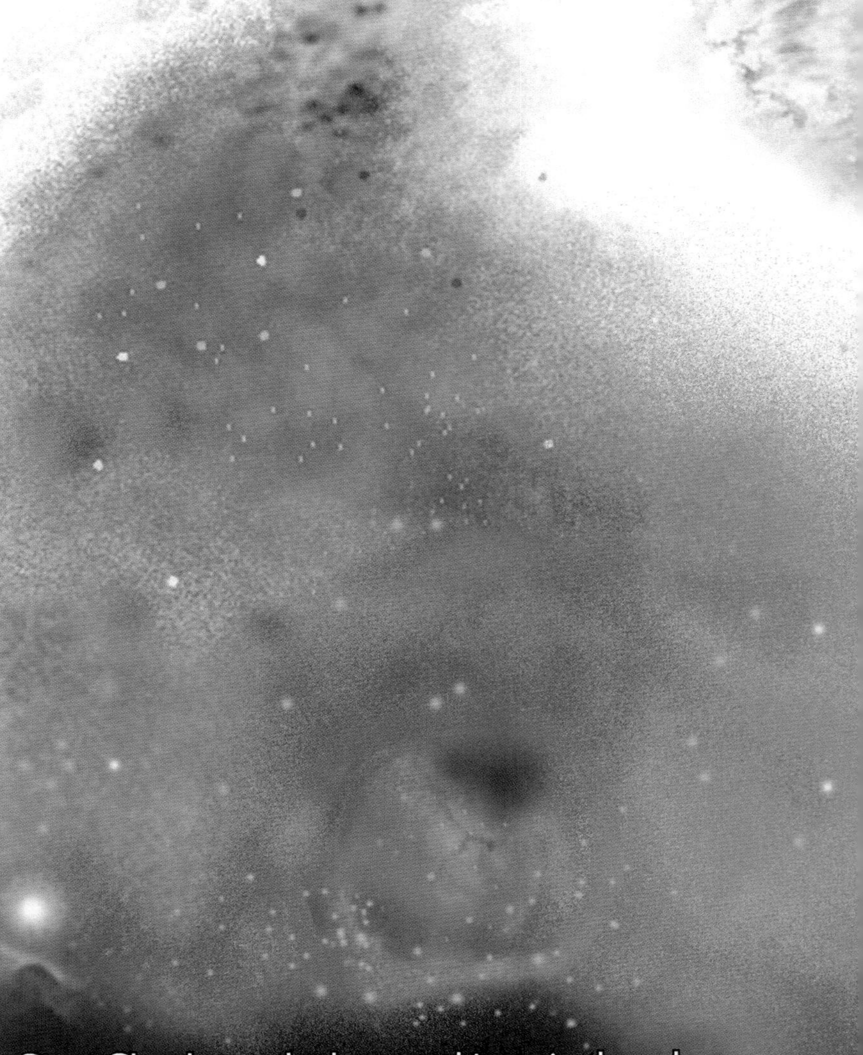

Giant Clouds are the largest objects in the galaxy.

They typically extend across a hundred light years of space.

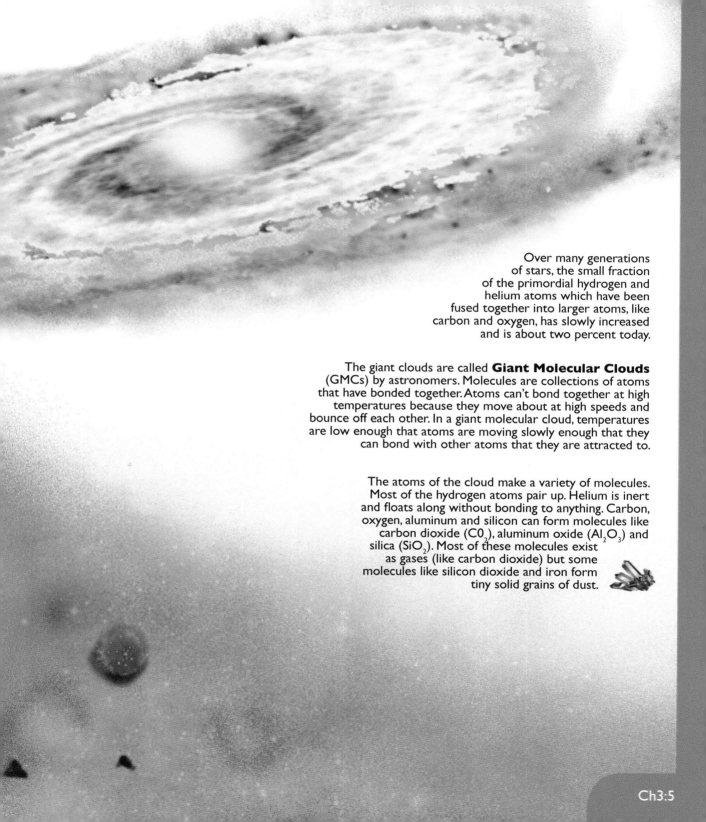

Over many generations of stars, the small fraction of the primordial hydrogen and helium atoms which have been fused together into larger atoms, like carbon and oxygen, has slowly increased and is about two percent today.

The giant clouds are called **Giant Molecular Clouds** (GMCs) by astronomers. Molecules are collections of atoms that have bonded together. Atoms can't bond together at high temperatures because they move about at high speeds and bounce off each other. In a giant molecular cloud, temperatures are low enough that atoms are moving slowly enough that they can bond with other atoms that they are attracted to.

The atoms of the cloud make a variety of molecules. Most of the hydrogen atoms pair up. Helium is inert and floats along without bonding to anything. Carbon, oxygen, aluminum and silicon can form molecules like carbon dioxide (CO_2), aluminum oxide (Al_2O_3) and silica (SiO_2). Most of these molecules exist as gases (like carbon dioxide) but some molecules like silicon dioxide and iron form tiny solid grains of dust.

Chapter 4: Formation of the Sun

Not all regions of the galaxy foster cloud growth and thus the formation of new stars and planets.

In the distant regions of the galaxy, stars are so widely spaced that old stardust builds up very slowly. In the central hub, stars are so closely packed that any stray gas or dust is soon swallowed up by a nearby star. But within the spiral arms of a galaxy, old stardust lingers and can be consolidated into the **giant galactic clouds** that give birth to new stars.

Giant galactic clouds are not easily transformed into new stars. A giant cloud must first contract and when it does it will be transformed into a cluster of smaller denser cloudlets each of which can become a solar system.

A shock wave from an exploding star can trigger the process of star formation.

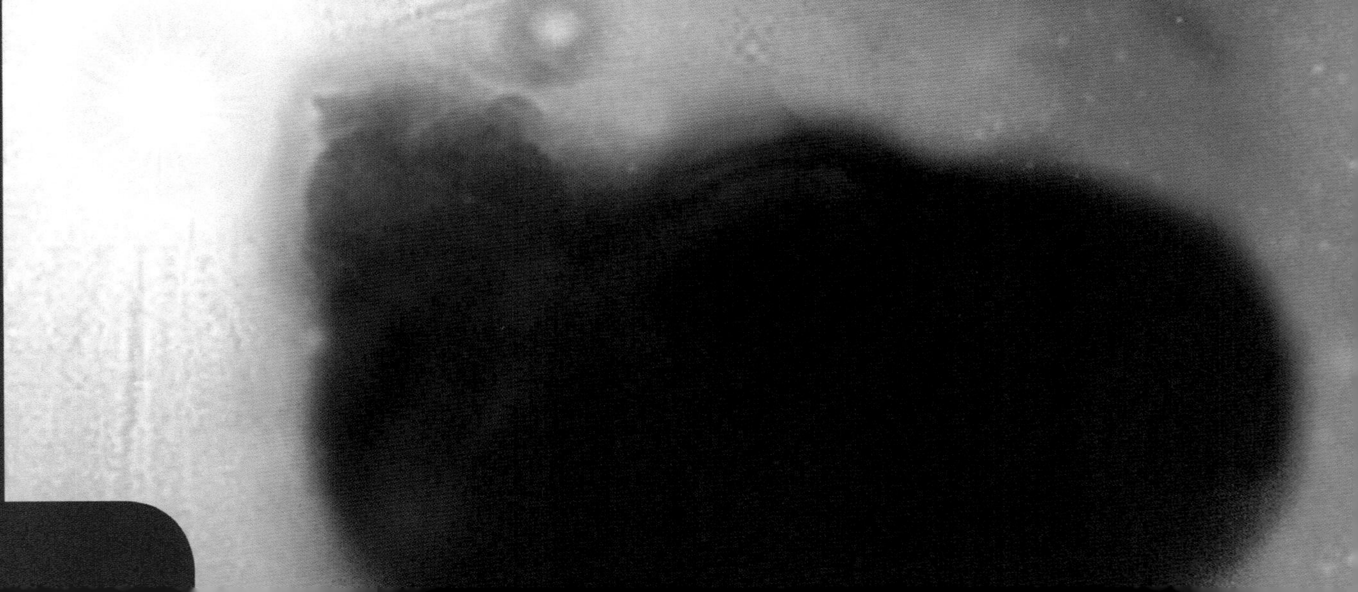

The whole galaxy rotates around itself. Stars close to the center swing fast around the central hub. Farther away stars orbit at slower speeds. The positions of the stars, clouds and other galactic objects change relative to each other as the galaxy rotates, which changes the gravitational fields between them. These gravitational field disruptions create density waves, which propagate through the spiral arms. Without these waves the spiral arms would soon wind themselves up around the hub but the disruptive waves slows that process down.

While there are some tiny mineral grains in giant clouds, there are not very many different kinds. On Earth today there are about 4500 different kinds of minerals; like quartz, topaz and calcite. Long ago there were fewer kinds of minerals. One of the tiny mineral grains present in galactic clouds is diamond. Diamond is pure carbon. Graphite is also a mineral form of pure carbon. But pencil lead is soft and diamond is super dense. The diamond grains were compressed into the diamond crystal structure in the core of a long since expired star.

Giant stars arise, run their course and explode in just tens of millions of years. The life expectancy of smaller stars like our Sun is about 10 billion years. In star forming regions, supernova explosions are not uncommon.

Astronomers find supernovas by comparing images made at different times. They identify bright stars in one photo and then see if any of those bright stars are absent in another photo of the same region taken at a later date.

As a shock wave impacts a giant cloud, it temporarily upsets the weak forces that have been preventing the cloud from contracting under its own gravity. In the wake of the shock wave, thousands of small dense cloudlets form.

The gravitational force of the cloud is weak because the atoms in the cloud are spread so thin. It is so weak that it is easily countered by other forces within the cloud. Even the turbulence created by temperature differences in the cloud is enough to stave off gravity.

In a cool cloud there is some turbulence: parcels of gas move relative to each other. The parcels move in an order of magnitude faster than the atoms within them do. Weak magnetic fields within a cloud also hamper the efforts of gravity to contract it.

We think it was a supernova explosion that triggered the giant galactic cloud that spawned our sun and Solar System. During a supernova explosion, all kinds of elements form. Most of these are so unstable that they quickly lose some particles and thus radioactively decay until they reach a stable form. Some of the daughter products of some of these unstable elements are found in our solar system implying that our solar system formed soon after a supernova explosion or that another star went nova during our formation.

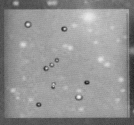

Clusters of new stars still form today. The stellar nursery closest to us is in the constellation of Orion and is visible with hand held binoculars.

The cloud's gravity is weak but relentless. Once gravity gets the upper hand, the process of contraction intensifies and transforms the cloud into a stellar nursery, where thousands of new stars will develop.

Young stars are found in groups because they all developed from the same giant cloud

It is not only supernova shock waves that can provide a trigger. Spiral density waves propagating through the galaxy or the slight shock waves produced when clouds collide can also initiate the metamorphosing process. And if a giant cloud simply grows unusually large and drifts far away from any star or heat source, it can contract under its own gravity without any catalyzing event.

Every giant cloud could break up into clumps, each of which could become a bright new star, but in the absence of a trigger, clouds can continue to hang together loosely and drift along almost indefinitely.

Each of the thousands of cloudlets
that form has its own center
of gravity. Within each cloudlet,
matter will migrate toward that
center, forming a core that will
eventually become a star.

Each cloudlet begins to rotate slowly as the weak random turbulent currents within it organize into a single direction. The rate of spin increases as the cloudlet contracts.

The core grows as more of the atoms that make up the cloudlet fall to the center. Nearby atoms migrate toward the core before more distant atoms because gravity pulls more strongly on closer objects. Thus, the growing core is surrounded by a vacated region. The empty region grows as the core becomes denser. Astronomers call this process 'Inside Out Collapse'.

A multitude of small clumps form rather than just one big clump in the center of the original Giant Molecular Cloud. This is because gravity gets exponentially weaker with distance so atoms are pulled most strongly toward the atoms nearest themselves and only weakly to the center of the cloud.

As the core of each cloudlet continues to contract, it rotates faster- just as a spinning figure skater picks up speed as she pulls her arms in.

As it spins faster, the core loses its spherical shape and begins to flatten out.

If the core were not spinning, it would stay in a spherical shape but as the spinning increases, it starts to flatten into a disc. Spinning material has a tendency to keep on going straight and fly outward. This is sometimes called centrifugal force but it is not really a separate force. The core spins on an axis and material is being flung outward away from this axis. Although gravity squeezes from every direction toward the center, it is opposed by this outward 'centrifugal force' except along the axis. Gravity is able to pull the material at the poles toward the center more effectively thus flattening the sphere. Another example of this principle can be seen in the less than spherical shape of Neptune's atmosphere.

The temperature of the core rises.

The core continues to gain material as more atoms from further out in the cloudlet continue to rain in. The core continues to contract as its gravity increases. The impacts of the in-falling atoms and the contraction both cause the temperature to rise.

Finally, the flattening sphere collapses all the way down into a spinning disc. So much heat is generated that jets of matter explode out from the center, relieving some of the pressure.

The escaping material is released out along the axis of rotation. The pressure of the system is greatest at the central hub of the disc, and matter explodes outward from that center. It cannot escape in the plane of the disc because of resistance from all the matter that is already there.

All spinning clouds can collapse into discs. For example, galaxies also form discs. Bipolar jets are common to any rotating system that is over-pressurized.

4.57

Billion Years Ago

Young stars and the discs around them are difficult to observe because normal, optical telescopes are unable to see beyond the dust that enshrouds them. Infrared heat sensing devices can penetrate haze. The first crude photographs showing a proto-stellar disc were taken in the 1980's.

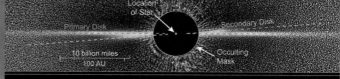

Location of Star

Primary Disk   Secondary Disk

10 billion miles
100 AU

Occulting
Mask

Beta Pictoris
Hubble Space Telescope • ACS/HRC

A new generation of more advanced infrared telescopes have recently been launched on satellites, we hope that their photographs will soon reveal new information.

The **bipolar jets** blast out from the center of the nascent star. They reach out into the remnants of the original cloudlet.

Gravity pulls matter from the disc toward the center and it spirals into the developing star.

The disc could completely disappear but new material from the outer regions of the cloudlet keeps falling in replenishing the disc.

The matter that is raining in from distant reaches of the original cloudlet falls such a long way that it generates a great deal of heat as it strikes the disc, so the disc continues to heat up.

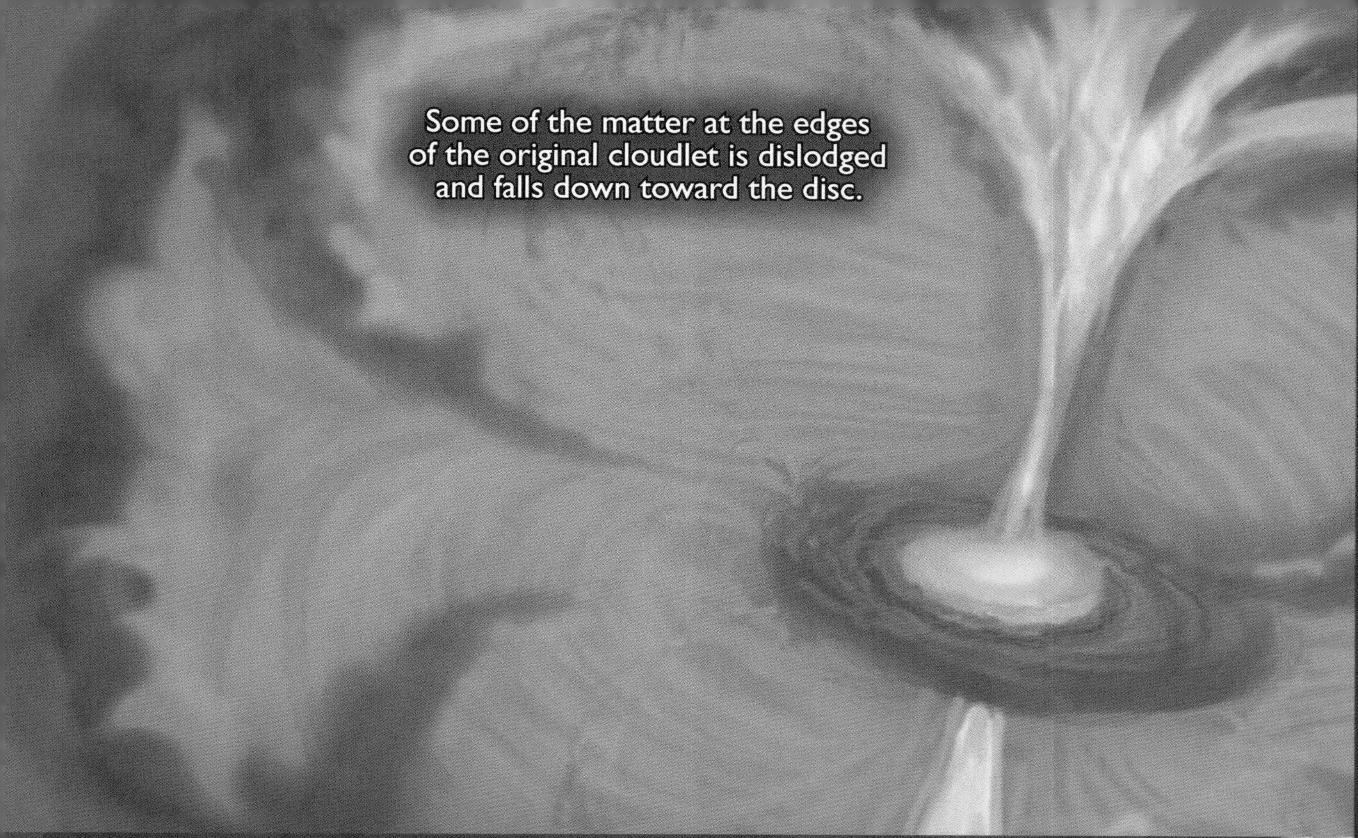

Some of the matter at the edges of the original cloudlet is dislodged and falls down toward the disc.

The center of the disc is not yet a real star. Its glow is due only to heating by gravitational compaction. The fires of nuclear fusion are only just igniting.

Deep in the core of the disc, the Sun is born. Its nuclear furnace produces not only light but a radiant wind of charged particles. This **solar wind** pushes outward and prevents any more material in the disc from falling into the Sun. The Sun stabilizes and the bipolar jets collapse, never to fire up again.

It takes a long time for the energy produced at the center of the Sun to work its way outward to the surface. Finally, visible light shines forth.

Nuclear reactions liberate energy which is why stars shine.

The hydrogen atoms that fuel the reactions in a young star weigh a tiny bit more than the fewer number of larger helium atoms that are produced from them. This very slight difference in mass is converted to energy, to sunshine. Thus a star gets ever so slightly less massive as it shines, in accordance with $E = mc^2$.

There have been several different theories about the origin of the sun and Solar System. Any theory must explain the broad features of the system.

First, those features must be identified and described. All of the planets orbit the Sun in the same direction and the Sun spins in that same direction. Thus the sun and all the objects of the solar system share a common sense of motion. The planets are arranged in a flat, frisbee like plane aligned on the Sun's equator. Another feature that the theory must explain is the compositional gradient of the planets with distance from the sun. The inner planets contain relatively large iron cores blanketed by aluminum silicate rock mantles, while those farther from the sun contain huge gaseous atmospheres of hydrogen and helium over relatively small rocky icy cores. There is also a size gradient: the inner planets are small but the outer planets are enormous.

A scientific theory can have minor problems but all major, broad scale properties must be explained satisfactorily. Small problems or inconsistencies are tolerated but kept under a watchful eye. Further research will bring new information that will either resolve the problems or the small inconsistencies will grow into ever widening fissures that will eventually bring down the whole edifice.

Light from the sun cannot shine forth very far because of the gas and dust that still enshrouds the nascent solar system. The solar wind begins to blow the gas away.

The temperature within the disc is so hot that most materials are in a gaseous form. Only a few substances, like iron and compounds of silica, take a solid form. Although these solid grains are tiny, they will not be pushed away by the solar wind but will remain behind. Eventually, they will gather together to form clumps called **planetesimals**, the building blocks of planets.

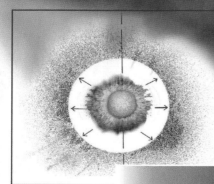

The solar wind begins to push the gases away.

The solar disc is hottest near the sun and cooler farther out.

Chapter 5: Building the Planets

The solar wind of light and charged particles that emanates from the young Sun blows the enshrouding fog of gas ever further out.

The solid particles that had been able to condense from the hot haze aggregate together into clumps called **planetesimals**.

The planetesimals that form in the inner Solar System are made from substances that can take the form of solids at high temperatures. The most common materials that are solid at these high temperatures are compounds of iron, oxygen, silicon, aluminum and calcium. These refractory compounds make an array of new minerals.

The temperature is still so hot that water and carbon, which are essential to life, exist as gases that the sun's radiant wind pushes away. Even in the area where Earth will eventually form, the precious water and carbon are swept away- out to the farther reaches of the Solar System.

Even materials like lead, which we are used to seeing in the solid from, are in a gaseous state; at high temperature, lead forms lead oxide vapor.

The **solar system** will develop as a whole, processes that operate on the system will shape the development of its parts.

The planets that we know today will eventually emerge. The similarities and differences between them are systematic and are consequences of processes that operated on the solar system as a whole.

As the front of the solar wind moves ever further outward, it moves into ever cooler regions where more of the gases have condensed into solids. The increasing abundance of solid grains allows ever larger planetesimals to form with increasing distance from the sun.

The first solid particles of dust that condensed formed tiny grains that could only stick together if they actually happened to collide with each other. Therefore it takes a long time for the first large clumps to finally assemble. But once they do the pace of growth dramatically increases as their own gravity begins to attract them to each other. Once gravity plays a role, the clumps aggregate together at ever increasing rates because their gravity grows as they grow. The pace of growth is fast as the clumps become planetesimals, the building blocks of **proto-planets**.

The planetesimals in the inner solar
system keep getting larger, although
fewer, as gravity pulls them together.

Planetesimals can be meters to kilometers in
size. Planetesimals become **spherical** as they
become larger because each planetesimal's
gravity pulls its own atoms to its center.

None of the inner planetesimals were able to
incorporate the abundant hydrogen gas that
had been around because they did not have
enough gravity to attract and hold onto the
elusive hydrogen atoms. Therefore they grew
to only moderate sizes. Later on, when they
are large enough to hold onto
vapors, there aren't any left.

The solar wind continues to push the gas that enshrouds the solar system outward into cooler regions.

The wind acts like a snowplow and pushes up a wall of gas at its leading edge. When the wind reaches the Frost Line, the place in the disc where water vapor is cool enough to become ice, there is a huge increase in the amount of solid material available for making planets.

As the front of the solar wind passes the Frost Line, the largest of all the proto-planets, **Jupiter**, is already waiting.

Jupiter had already grown large by feeding on the ice crystals which gives it enough gravity to retain gases. The solar wind pushes the wall of gas right to it and Jupiter sucks it all in.

The gas is composed mostly of hydrogen atoms and Jupiter gathers so much of it that Jupiter comes to consist of primarily just hydrogen.

As ice crystals form, they also entrap grains of dust within them, which then are delivered to Jupiter as well. Carbon is present in this area as ices of carbon dioxide and other carbon compounds.

This process separates the solar system into different zones.

The composition of the solar system is largely similar to that of the Universe but the structure of the solar system concentrates some of the rarer elements in different parts of the solar disc.

Hydrogen is the most common element in the Universe because it condensed directly from the cooling energy in the aftermath of the Big Bang. It is the most common element in the solar system too, comprising three quarters of all material in the universe. Because hydrogen is such a small element, it makes a light gas that only a large planet has enough gravity to hold onto.

Of the elements that make up the remainder, oxygen is one of the most common because it is made more easily in the nuclear furnaces of stars than are most other elements. Atoms larger than iron are rare indeed-being created only in stellar explosions.

Ch5:4

After Jupiter becomes gigantic its immense gravity upsets the orbits of other planetesimals that had formed near it. Some of these fall into Jupiter while others fall toward the Sun.

The front of the solar wind now continues on past Jupiter, but Jupiter was able to grab most of the gas and dust as it was passing by. The proto-planets outboard of Jupiter (Saturn, Uranus and Neptune) will not grow as large.

Once planetesimals reach large sizes, collisions between them can be destructive, fragmenting rather than aggregating the bodies, depending on the speed and angle of the collision. Planetesimals that continue to increase in size become proto-planets. Fragments of proto-planets that get smashed are called asteroids. Small planetesimals that never get incorporated into larger bodies are also called **asteroids**.

Some of the disrupted planetesimals are sent off on really wild trajectories and leave the plane of the disc to wind up in the **Oort Cloud**, a far away shell of debris surrounding the solar system.

Eventually only Mercury, Venus, Earth and Mars will remain in the inner Solar System but at this stage, the proto-planets are smaller and more numerous.

Planetesimals that have been dislodged from their once stable orbits out near Jupiter continue to fall toward the sun.

The asteroids and proto-planets sailing in from the outer regions carry frozen water, which they deliver to any of the proto-planets of the inner solar system they collide with.

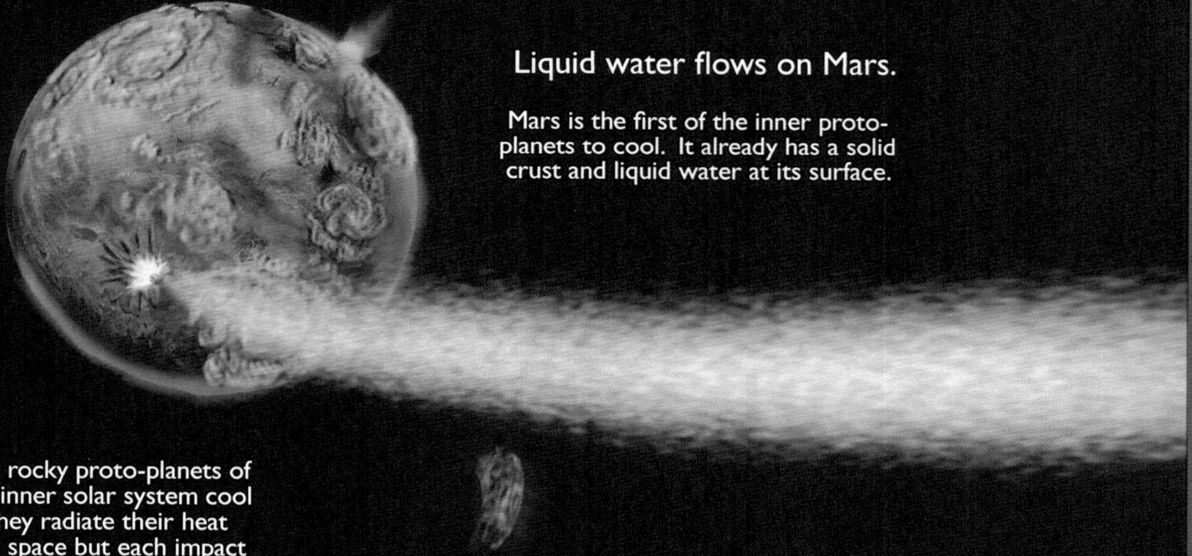

Liquid water flows on Mars.

Mars is the first of the inner proto-planets to cool. It already has a solid crust and liquid water at its surface.

The rocky proto-planets of the inner solar system cool as they radiate their heat into space but each impact heats them up anew.

Some of the planetesimals that formed outboard of Mars, in the neighborhood of the original Frost Line, escaped the extreme temperatures that would have made them molten. These bodies, which we now call primitive asteroids or **carbonaceous chondrites**, retain a record of the conditions of the primordial solar disc and are a treasure trove of information for us today. All the planetesimals that did melt completely were metamorphosed and had this original information erased.

No new proto-planets will be able to form in the gap between Mars and Jupiter because of Jupiter's immense gravity, however there is still some matter left in this area- we call it the **asteroid belt**.

Comets are asteroids composed mostly of ice with minor rocky parts and are some-times referred to as 'dirty snowballs.'

The proto-planets of the inner solar system, including Earth, become full fledged planets as they differentiate and develop **magnetic fields**.

When a proto-planet heats up enough to become molten, it stratifies into layers; heavy droplets of iron migrate to its center and lighter materials are buoyed upward.

The iron core that forms gives rise to a magnetic field.

This protects the planet by deflecting incoming charged particles and thus shields Earth from the continuing siege of the solar wind.

Once protected by a magnetic field, water vapor and other volatile gases are no longer so easily pushed away and the **atmosphere** grows.

The iron in the most central portion of the core is under immense pressure, which confines it to a solid state, even though the center of the Earth is hottest. The iron atoms of the outer part of the core move more freely, as a hot liquid. The liquid iron circulating around the solid inner core is what gives rise to this field. This two part system is somewhat analogous to a generator where a magnet is moved around stationary wires (or done the other way; the stator is rotated around the magnet).

Earth's composition can be calculated by weight. Iron atoms are much heavier than oxygen, silicon or magnesium atoms. By weight the bulk Earth consists of 35% iron, 30% oxygen, 15% silicon and 10% magnesium. The other 10% is made up of everything else including copper and carbon, hydrogen and gold.

Earth consists almost entirely of just 4 elements: oxygen, iron, silicon and magnesium. These 4 elements constitute over 90 percent of the matter that makes up the Earth. Of these, oxygen atoms are the most numerous. Most of us think of oxygen simply as the air we breathe- but it is also the major constituent of most rocks. Earth could aptly be called **The Oxygen Planet**.

Oxygen combines with other elements to make oxides. A familiar one is rust, which is iron oxide.

Water and carbon compounds are scarce on the young Earth but most of the incoming asteroids are from cooler regions and they continue to deliver these precious substances to our developing planet. The amount of water will soon increase to modern levels but the amount of water relative to the whole Earth will remain minuscule- only a slight portion of the whole Earth.

The water on the early Earth is present in different states. Vapor exists in the atmosphere and small amounts are dissolved in the molten oceans of rock. There are also some solid crystals of rock that incorporate a minor fraction of O-H in their structures.

Earlier theories of planetary development assumed that water had always existed on Earth and had been stored deep inside, later to be released by volcanoes.

The current theory, favored by the most scientists, is that Earth developed in a region where water vapor and other gases had been blown away by the solar wind but were delivered back by asteroids. Recently, a blend of the two theories is becoming popular with scientists because some evidence suggests that the isotopic signature of Earth's oceans is not identical to that of asteroids.

It has been proposed that asteroids delivered not only water and carbon compounds -including amino acids- to Earth, but also living cells of bacteria which seeded Earth with life. Life evolving elsewhere and being transported here is a hypothesis called **Panspermia**. Not many scientists adhered to this idea in the past, not just because transportation would be difficult but because there is no reason to assume that life assembled from its building blocks in another place more easily than it could have here. But if life had begun on Mars, some issues that puzzle scientists might be resolved. It would have given life the head start that would resolve new evidence that life may have started earlier than once thought. It would also explain why life here on Earth is all so similar, always using nucleic acids for genetic transcription and always preferring left-handed molecules over right-handed versions, even though both are usually equally prevalent in inorganic settings. Handedness of a molecular level is known as **Chirality**.

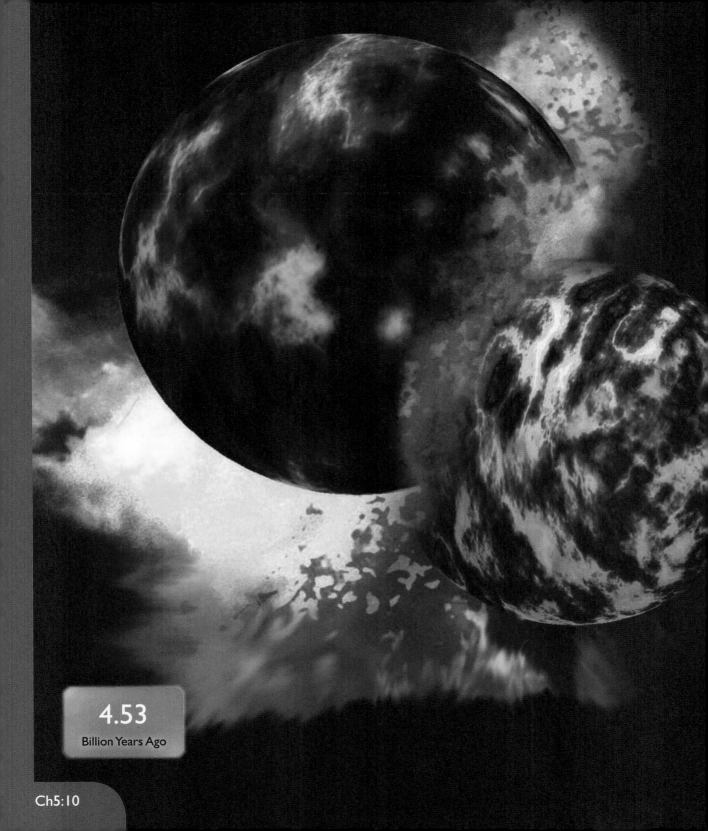

4.53

Billion Years Ago

A small planet strikes Earth in an event that will give birth to the **Moon**.

Scientists call the impacting proto-planet Theia or sometimes Orpheus. **Theia** had been orbiting the Sun on an orbital path not far from Earth's. The collision is not head on but a glancing blow.

The collision plows off a piece of the Earth's mantle. The heat generated by the impact melts that chunk of mantle as it is pushed away. Theia is also vaporized and cast into space. The heaviest parts of the orbiting debris, the iron portion, falls back to Earth, increasing the size of Earth's core. The lighter portion reassembles into the moon.

The moon will not be able to hold onto much of its water vapor. It is too small to have enough gravity to hold elusive gases close; and because it loses the iron that it had, it will not develop a strong magnetic field to shield itself against the relentless solar wind.

During of the great collision with Theia, some of the water the Earth had is vaporized and then lost to space. Luckily, asteroids will continue to impact the Earth delivering more water ice. Earth might have already cooled off and had an ocean before the impact with Theia, but in any case, it is definitely made molten afterwards. The continuing bombardment of asteroids will eventually increase the size of the Earth by about 10%.

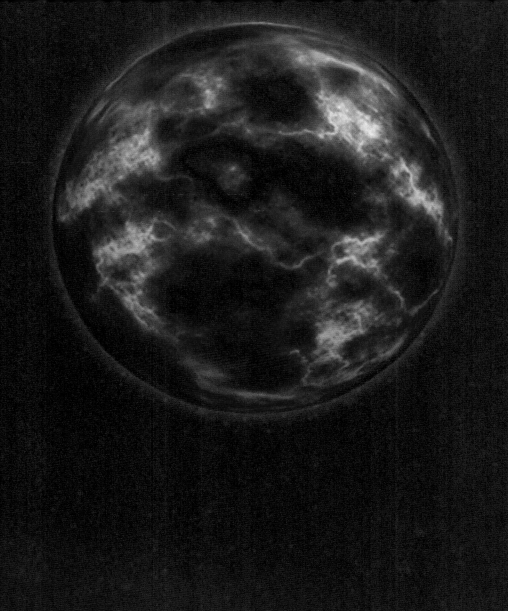

Energy can neither be created nor destroyed but can only be converted from one form to another, according to the first law of thermodynamics. Theia had been traveling on its orbital path and therefore possessed kinetic energy, the energy of motion. Some of this kinetic energy is converted into heat during the impact; in the immediate aftermath of the collision, the mantles of both the Earth and the moon are both molten. Some of the kinetic energy is used up jostling Earth on its axis; Earth now has an inclination of 23 1/2 degrees.

The moon forms as the orbiting
dust and debris coalesces. The Earth
will never be alone again. Because
of its moon, Earth will experience
rhythmic daily tides whose tempo
makes the planet more dynamic.

Earth has only one moon and its diameter
is more than 1/4 the diameter of Earth.

Other planets in our solar system
have many moons; Mars has two
and Saturn sixty. But those moons
are tiny relative to their mother
planets. Some of Jupiter's moons are
larger than our own but compared
to Jupiter, they are mere ornaments,
like a necklace of exotic beads.

The Moon is so large relative
to Earth, that the Earth and
the moon are technically a
double-planet system.

There are other models for the formation of the moon. Any model must explain the facts about the Earth and Moon as we observe them today; the Moon's composition is similar to Earth's but the moon lacks a well defined iron core. The **Impactor Model** is the favored theory today. This is the model shown in the previous pages. It provides an explanation for the compositions being similar because the outer portions of the Earth and its impactor, Theia were both blown off and then mixed together before resettling. The distribution of iron is explained by the iron that Theia had being transferred to earth during the impact, due to Earth having the greater gravity; Earth's core grew when it acquired Theia's iron.

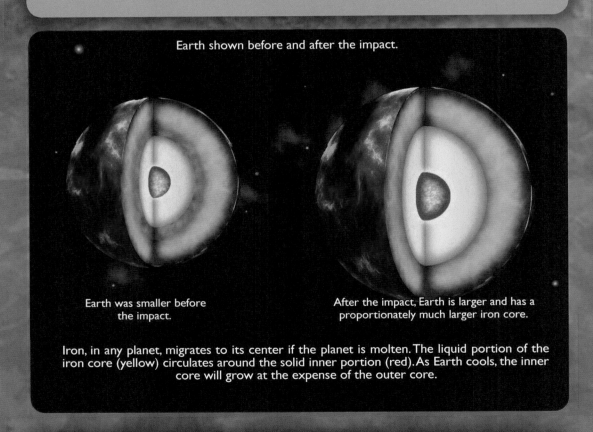

Earth shown before and after the impact.

Earth was smaller before the impact.

After the impact, Earth is larger and has a proportionately much larger iron core.

Iron, in any planet, migrates to its center if the planet is molten. The liquid portion of the iron core (yellow) circulates around the solid inner portion (red). As Earth cools, the inner core will grow at the expense of the outer core.

A detraction of the impactor model is that Theia would have to have struck Earth with a glancing blow at a fairly specific angle. Such a specific requirement reduces the likelihood of it having happened.

An alternative theory of the formation of the moon is the older, but still possibly viable, **Fission Model** in which the moon is spawned from Earth's molten mantle. This model would also explain the similarity of the mantles and the lacking of a core in the moon.

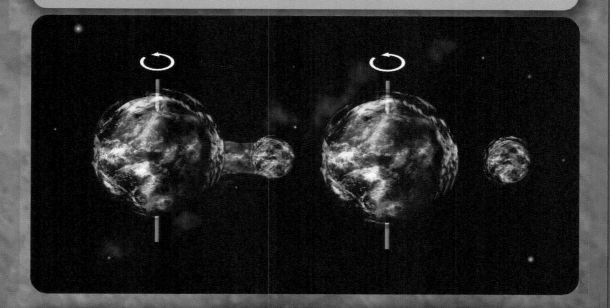

In the Fission Model, a portion of Earth's mantle flings off, like a water balloon. This would have required a sudden, unstable spin up of a very hot Earth. Earth's spin rate would have increased when its iron core formed, as heavy droplets of iron sank to its center- just as a skater spins faster when she pulls her arms in. Also, when the iron sank, heat would have been released.

Some of the problems that were leveled against the fission theory might have been resolved if the drag of the heavy vaporized silicate atmospheres had been taken into account; the drag would have stopped the moon from being flung too far away.

When the Fission Theory was displaced in favor of the Impactor Theory, craters on the moon were being studied in detail and with great enthusiasm in order to plan the Apollo landings. Scientists were amazed at how many impacts had occurred and started considering the implications of all the impacts on other issues. It is possible, that in their enthusiasm, scientists might have prematurely dismissed the Fission Theory.

A third model for the moon's formation is the **Capture Model**. According to the capture model, the moon formed elsewhere and only afterward came close enough to be pulled into Earth's orbit. There is a major problem with this theory- the moon would have impacted Earth, or not been pulled in at all due to the gravitational field. Additionally, the theory doesn't explain the Moon's similar but iron deficient composition.

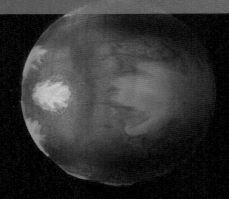

The moon doesn't spin. It is locked in synchronous orbit and always shows the same face toward Earth.

Shortly after the formation of the moon, both orbs of the resulting double planet system are molten. On each orb, heat from the interior pours forth, convected by giant plumes of effusing magma.

The side of the moon that always faces Earth stays warmer than the far side, which faces into the cold of space.

Earth will cool off more slowly than will the moon.

Both are spheres radiating heat from their surfaces out into space, and smaller spheres cool more quickly as they have a higher ratio of surface area per unit volume.

Earth's atmosphere will also slow the radiant flow of heat, but the moon doesn't have enough gravity to hold onto its atmosphere. The Earth also contains more dense elements, like iron, and these have more heat energy stored in them. Some of the heavy elements are also radioactive, like uranium, and release heat as they decay.

Because the Earth is spinning, currents in its roiling magma ocean circulate in particular patterns.

According to recent computer models (by Zhong et al.) several, symmetrically arrayed, large plumes (shown in yellow) convect a molten planet's heat up from the core/mantle boundary to the surface. As the fresh, hot magma moves away from the center of each plume head, it cools a bit before sinking back down. The return flow of sinking magma collects in linear belts (shown in blue) before dropping back down to be reheated by contact with the hot core.

In a cooling magma ocean, some minerals form before others

Minerals are solid crystalline arrangements of atoms. Different kinds of minerals form at different temperatures. As liquid magma progressively cools, a series of minerals form in sequence (geology texts call this Bowen's Reaction Series). The first mineral to form is olivine. Olivine is heavier than the liquid soup of molten rock that it is solidifying out of, therefore, it sinks away, down to the bottom of the magma ocean where is builds up a floor. The next mineral to begin to form in the hot, thousand plus degree liquid, is a whitish, calcium-rich feldspar mineral which forms long, shiny, prismatic crystals as it grows These white crystals are less dense than the magma and so they float to the surface of the molten sea of rock. When the temperature drops a bit

further, pyroxene minerals also form. All three minerals form concurrently for a while, and then the production of olivine ceases.

A white crust of rock forms on the cooling surface of the moon.

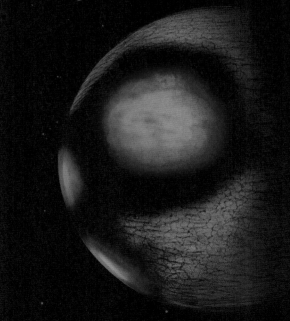

On the Moon, unseen **olivine** crystals form and sink away while calcium feldspar crystals form and rise to its surface.

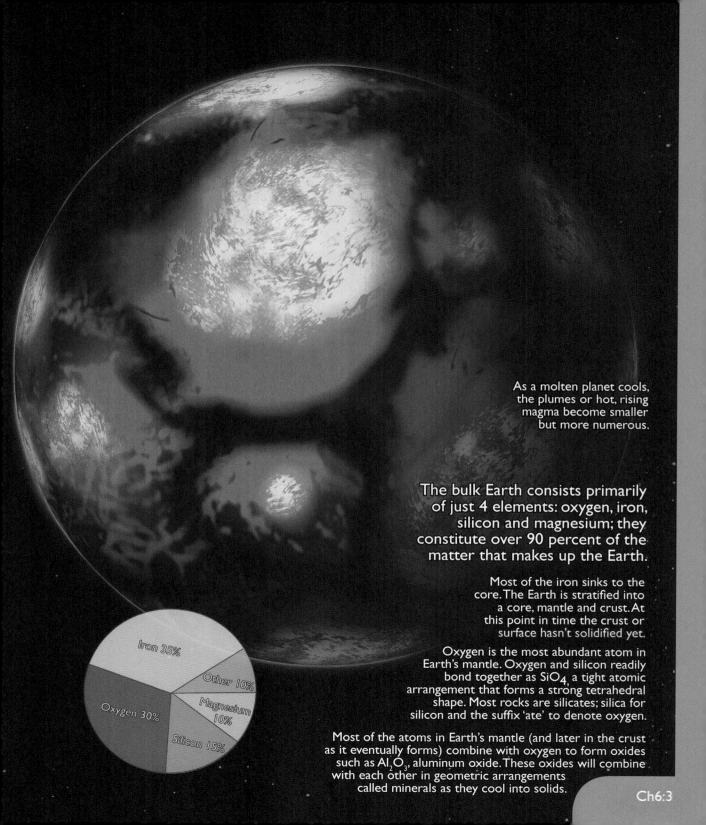

As a molten planet cools, the plumes or hot, rising magma become smaller but more numerous.

The bulk Earth consists primarily of just 4 elements: oxygen, iron, silicon and magnesium; they constitute over 90 percent of the matter that makes up the Earth.

Most of the iron sinks to the core. The Earth is stratified into a core, mantle and crust. At this point in time the crust or surface hasn't solidified yet.

Oxygen is the most abundant atom in Earth's mantle. Oxygen and silicon readily bond together as SiO_4 a tight atomic arrangement that forms a strong tetrahedral shape. Most rocks are silicates; silica for silicon and the suffix 'ate' to denote oxygen.

Most of the atoms in Earth's mantle (and later in the crust as it eventually forms) combine with oxygen to form oxides such as Al_2O_3, aluminum oxide. These oxides will combine with each other in geometric arrangements called minerals as they cool into solids.

Iron 35%

Other 10%

Oxygen 30%

Magnesium 10%

Silicon 15%

On the moon, the crust of white crystals has grown like a shell, covering much of the surface, including the entirety of the far side.

The shiny white mineral that rises to the surface of the magma ocean is calcium feldspar, also called plagioclase or anorthite, has the chemical composition: $CaAl_2Si_2O_8$.

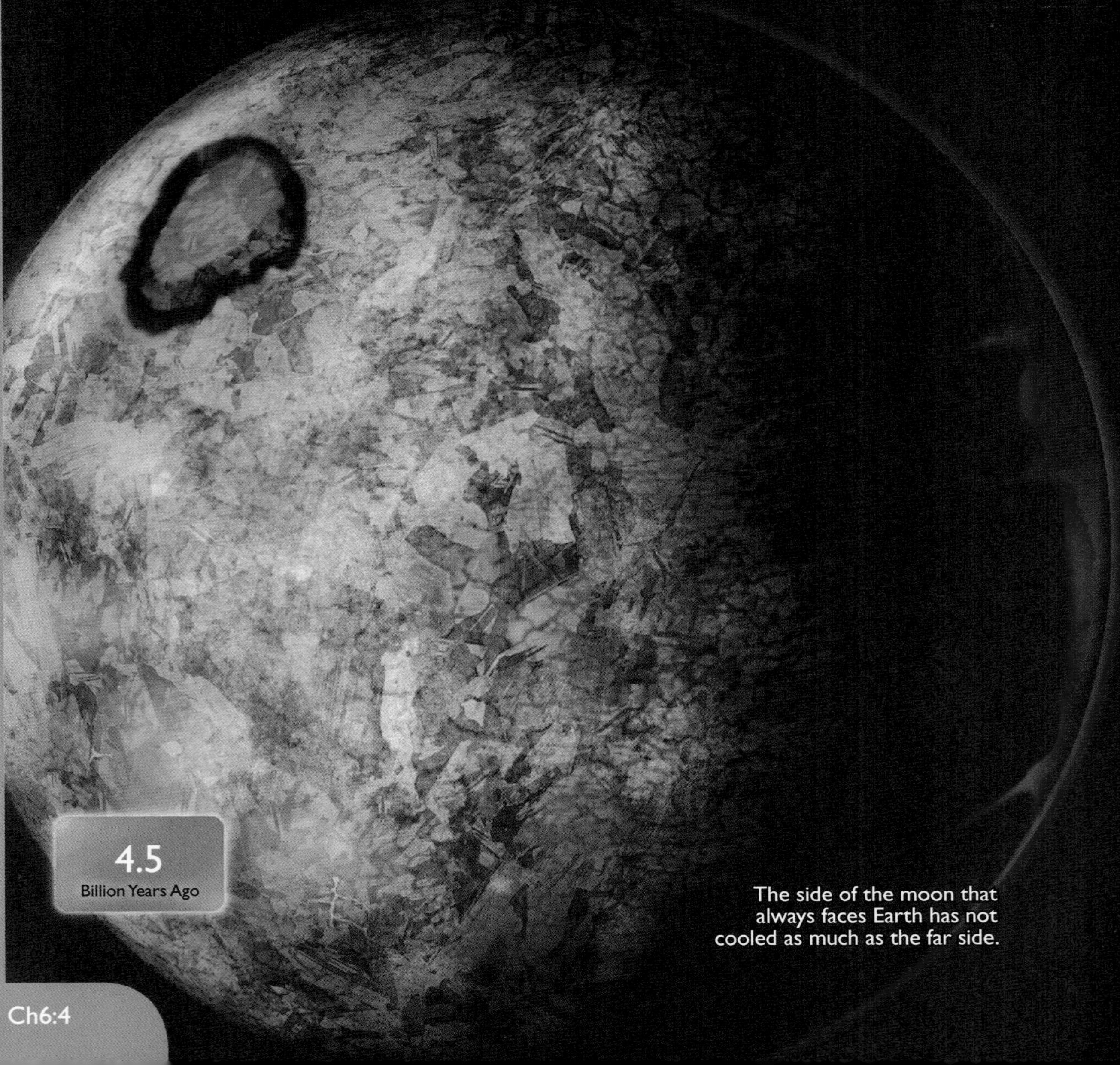

4.5
Billion Years Ago

The side of the moon that always faces Earth has not cooled as much as the far side.

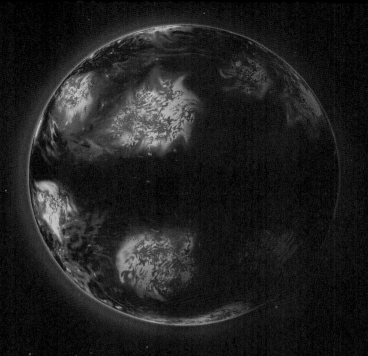

Earth is slowly cooling. Although not much crust has formed yet, solidification of minerals is occurring but this is happening far beneath the orange waves.

The white crystals do not float to the surface of Earth's deeper magma ocean. Pressure affects the formation of minerals. as does temperature and the composition of the magma.

At great depth in Earth's magma ocean, olivine is forming and sinking. Although the temperature is so hot that these minerals would liquefy at surface pressures, at depth the atoms are confined by pressure into crystal lattices. Olivine forms in massive quantities and sinks to the floor of the magma sea. With so many olivine crystals removed, the composition of the remaining liquid becomes less dense. White crystals of calcium rich feldspar form, but they do not float in the now less viscous magma.

Earth begins to
develop a thin brown
crust of solidified rock.

Currents of molten magma
flow from the hot interior to
the cooler surface above.

Heat always flows from hot to cold
and never the other way. This is the
First Law of Thermodynamics.

The currents are affected by the Earth's spin,
as are ocean currents today; surface currents
veer to the right in the Northern hemisphere
and to the left in the south, which is known as
the **Coriolis effect**. The currents are also
influenced by the tides caused by the moon.

Hot spots of magma still erupt
the surface but they are separate
by extensive pavements of roc

The magma ocean is solidifying fro
the bottom up as crystals form at dep
and either stay suspended or sink. Th
ocean is growing shallower as the pile
crystalline mush builds up from belo

Hot spots develop in patterr

According to geophysical models, an ideal molten planet shou
have 6 plumes that circulate its heat up from the interior; and
the planet cools, the plumes should decrease in size but increa
in number. Thus, Earth probably started with 6 plumes and
this time in its cooling history, it likely had more than 20 plume
Today, we have more than a dozen hot spots on Earth; underneat
such places as Hawaii, Yellowstone and Iceland. These hotspots a
much smaller than the hot plumes that churned in the primev
Earth's magma ocean but they are still conduits of heat th
come from great depths all the way to the surface. Modern h
spots are estimated to measure approximately 100 kilometers
diameter. Most geophysicists think that hot spots extend from t
surface to the core/mantle boundary but others think that t
mantle has two layers of convective cells and that the hot spo
source the top of the lower cell. During Earth's early evolutio
the plumes are probably sourcing the core/mantle bounda

As the Moon and the Earth continue
their orbital dance, tidal forces
between them act on the system.

One effect is to slow Earth's rate of spin.
At this time, the Earth completes its
daily rotation in about 6 hours. Another
effect is that the Moon slips farther away
from Earth as time goes by.

When the Moon formed it was only
a few Earth diameters away. Today
it is 30. At this time, the Moon was
perhaps 10 Earth diameters away.

The Moon is completely
encased in its shiny
white crust.

Asteroids continue to strike, carving
out craters and pulverizing some of the
crust. The Moon begins to lose its glassy
appearance as dust and debris build up.

Lacking a magnetosphere, the Moon's
atmosphere is pushed away by the solar wind.

An alternative theory is that as at Earth cooled, it developed a crust of shiny white crystals of calcium feldspar, similar to the one that formed on the moon.

Although scientists do agree that the moon developed a white crust composed of calcium feldspar crystals which floated to the surface of its magma ocean, as shown in the previous pages, few of them think that the cooling Earth ever developed a similar white crust. It is simply assumed by most people that the young Earth had a thin, dark brown crustal skin, similar to images they have seen of lava flows on Hawaii and in other places.

Some petrology texts do briefly discuss the possibility of an Earthly feldspar crust, (for example, Petrology: Igneous, Sedimentary, and Metamorphic. Blatt, H., R.J. Tracy, B.E. Owens. 3rd Edition. NY: W.H. Freeman, 2006. Page 206). But a more recent textbook, from the less Earth centric field of planetary geology (Introduction to Planetary Science (Springer Publishing The Netherlands 2007 page 68) states: 'minerals were crystallizing in a global ocean of molten silicate as the Earth differentiated into a core composed of liquid iron and nickel, a mantle consisting of olivine and pyroxene crystals, and a primordial crust of anorthite crystals that floated in the magma ocean'.

The following is a description of this alternative hypothesis.

When plumes of molten magma still cover most of Earth's surface, crystals of white calcium feldspar float in the ocean of liquid rock and collect in linear bands between the plumes. Or alternatively, the crystals form and rise only from the shallower parts of the ocean but once on the surface, the crystals can drift anywhere. Asteroids strike frequently, creating shallow pockets of very hot magma which are soon covered by a white slag of the crystals.

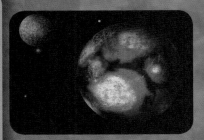

Earth's heat continues to pour out; hotter magma rises from below in plumes and is carried along in currents caused by Earth's rotation and the lunar tides. The islands of the white crystals of calcium feldspar are jostled by the currents. The white crust insulates the magma below.

The white crust may or may not have been completely encasing; Earth's magma ocean is subjected to currents caused by its spinning that may have prevented the rafts from joining up, whereas the moon doesn't spin.

As the temperature of the magma drops further, more kinds of minerals form. Most of the remaining expanses of open magma ocean soon skin over with a dark brown crust containing a suite of minerals, including olivine, pyroxene, and feldspar minerals, which geologists call **basalt**.

Insulated beneath the pieces of white crust, pockets of primevally hot molten magma still exist. These magmas erupt through or around the edges of the rafts of white crust. These especially hot magmas, pour out dense, dark lavas; today, geologists call these old, enigmatic pavements 'Komatiite flows.' The komatiites weigh down some of the anorthosite platforms, which gradually sink isostatically, to slightly lower depths where they remain until later tectonic disturbances.

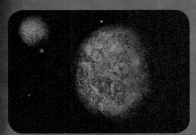

There are reasons to think that the first crust that formed on Earth was a flotation crust of white feldspar similar to the Moon's, despite specific obstacles to this hypothesis. Supporting the idea of a feldspar crust is that calcium feldspar crystals do float in molten magma under a variety of circumstances, and that province-sized platforms of calcium feldspar crust, called anorthosites, exist in the oldest regions of every continent. Obstacles to the possibility of a flotation crust include the effects of the greater pressure in Earth's deeper magma ocean, and the age dates of Earth's anorthosite-covered regions.

The deeper depth of Earth's magma ocean would have created pressures that might have prevented calcium feldspar crystals from being buoyant, according to some scientists (L. Elkins-Tanton 2012). In such a deep magma ocean, most of the minerals would form at mid levels -not at the surface- and at this level, with a magma of this viscosity, the crystals would not be much less dense than the liquid that they are forming in. The highly pressurized magma also allows other kinds of minerals, like pyroxenes, to crystallize as well, even before the temperature drops radically; as more other kinds of crystals form, the ocean soon becomes too slushy to allow buoyant crystals to rise. A rebuttal to this argument is that Earth's magma ocean is circulating and the crystals that are piling up unevenly on the ocean floor creating deeper and less deep areas. Also, the magma ocean will likely overturn when it is partially solidified due to the layers of crystals having been deposited in a gravitationally unstable way; the early forming crystals of olivine were magnesium rich and the later ones were iron rich, (Solomatov 2000). When some kind of turbulence triggers the system, the denser, iron rich layers will displace the lighter ones and this mixing will reheat the magma ocean (as gravitational potential energy is converted to kinetic energy). The reheated ocean will not be as deep as it had been. A final argument is that asteroid strikes are common while the magma ocean is solidifying; each strike imparts heat, creating locally hot puddles and seas, some of which would be the correct depths in which to allow calcium feldspar crystals to float.

As more scientists learn to look at Earth from a planetary geology perspective, and new data comes in, this debate might be resolved. Someday, as telescopes improve, we may eventually witness young planets cooling in around some distant star.

Calcium rich feldspar crystals are known to float to the top of molten bodies of magma under a variety of circumstances. Extremely calcium-rich feldspar crystals, also called anorthite crystals, solidify out of liquid magma at very high temperatures (1500°C) and are less dense that the melt they form in. A crust that forms from aggregations of these crystals is called anorthosite. While the moon's crust is the only known example of an anorthosite crust that completely covered a planetary body, anorthosite layers are found in many magmatic intrusions, such as the Stillwater or Kiglaplait. The Barberton Greenstone Belt in the Kaapvaal Craton in South Africa contains anorthosite and is thought to be created or influenced by the impact of a giant asteroid(AGU 9April2014). Extensive Anorthosite platforms exist worldwide, one of the largest is in Canada (part of the Nain Plutonic Suite) and covers thousands of square kilometers.

Age-dates of Earth's surviving anothosite-covered regions are the greatest obstacle to the possibility that these provinces are coeval with the cooling of the whole Earth as a molten body. Historically, geologists trying to calculate formation dates of large anorthosite bodies have determined them all to have been formed either in the Proterozoic, between 1.7 and 1.4 billion years ago or from the Archean about 3.8 billion years ago. Even the Archean group, which is by far the smaller of the groups, would not be old enough to be primeval- at least 4.3 billion years ago would be required. The rebuttal to this argument has 2 points: that primeval anorthosites would not include datable crystals and that tectonic activity reworked the primeval anorthosites and this metamorphism is the source of the determined dates. Calcium rich feldspar forms early in the cooling of a magma ocean and elements like zircon, which can be dated due to their eventual radioactive decay, are not easily incorporated into a crystal lattice and would stay in the liquid part of the system until later in the cooling process. Most anorthosites were involved in tectonic collisions that happened at the times the anorthosites have been dated to.

The atmosphere is dense and thick.

As the temperature drops, water vapor condenses out of the atmosphere and it rains.

Some of the rain falls on red hot lava and steams back into the atmosphere. But some rain falls on cooler rocks and gathers into puddles.

It rains and it rains. Pools of water grow into shallow seas.

Some scientist think that it might have rained for more than a million years.

The oldest minerals that we have ever found are **zircon crystals** that date to this age (from Jack Hills Australia).

4.4
Billion Years Ago

The temperature is still hot and the seas are just beginning to fill.

Where puddles of water meet molten magma, complex molecules form.

The complex molecules interact in a system of naturally occurring patterns and associations. Most scientists think that it is from the associations and patterns of reaction among inanimate, pre-biotic molecules that life will eventually emerge.

Emergence is when numerous simple items interact under the influence of a cyclic energy source to produce a new, complex structure whose properties are more than the sum of the parts. The emergence of life from inanimate molecules is the quintessential example of such a process.

Emergence is a relatively new concept and scientists have not yet found a way to define it mathematically. An energy source that acts on a system of numerous simple components, preferably repeatedly in some cyclic manner, seems to be required. Scientists and engineers struggled for more than 50 years to discover the laws of thermodynamics. The first law basically states that heat flows from hot to cold and never the other way around. The second states that systems tend to become disordered; entropy increases. Life seems, at least in some ways, to defy the second law. It has even been postulated (by Robert Hazen for example) that there might be an additional, yet undiscovered law of thermodynamics that is related to emergence.

Sea level rises. The sea is green and the sky is red.

The frequency of meteor strikes increases again in a spike called **The Late Heavy Bombardment**.

The late heavy bombardment, or LBH, is thought to be unleashed as the giant planets (Jupiter, Saturn, Uranus and Neptune) adjust to orbital resonances between them and resettle in their orbits. This change upsets the orbits of comets and asteroids in the vicinity of those planets and some of them bombard Earth as they fall toward the Sun. Alternatively, there was no LBH, and the apparent spike is only an illusion caused by the better preservation of the more recent and final strikes.

Some of the meteors that are raining in may be enriched in organic compounds. A minority of these meteors are fragments of Mars because some of the asteroids that strike Mars cast pieces of Mars into space and some of these pieces eventually make it to Earth.

Earth's atmosphere is rich in carbon dioxide and methane which are powerful greenhouse gases. The warm sea is green with dissolved iron.

Sea level rises as water vapor continues to fall out of the cooling atmosphere, volcanos continue to belch out gasses that contain steam that had been locked away in hydrous minerals, and comets and meteors continue to bring in ices from cooler regions of the solar system.

4.2
Billion Years Ago

Although covered with water, Earth is still very hot.

Convection currents continue to bring heat from the core and mantle to the surface; new plumes of molten magma keep erupting in numerous places across the globe.

Some of the magma erupts from volcanos.

Volcanos form as sequential layers of lava pile up on the sea floor, and more lava pushes its way up through those already solidified layers.

Most of the magma erupts out of cracks in the crust that are now covered by the oceans.

At these deep sea vents, the sulphur, iron and manganese dissolved in the magma precipitates out. The precipitating minerals build strange, pillar-like chimneys around the hot gases that pour out.

Large complex molecules are known to form on the mineral surfaces of vents today.

The chimneys have a porous, pumice like texture which provides small chambers in which groups of molecules can be contained. The surfaces of these cell like chambers are coated with iron and sulphur and other chemical residues which can act as catalysts.

At the magma / water interface, minerals and compounds are brought into contact but are not yet in equilibrium. As they react with each other and form new substances hydrogen gas, H_2 is produced. This is the source of energy that early life will use. Life requires energy because living organisms rearrange atoms and molecules in ways that would otherwise not occur. Life will power itself with an organized flow of electrons and the hydrogen gas is the source of the original donor electrons.

Organized systems of complex molecules develop at the Deep Sea Vents.

Complexity requires an appropriately sized energy source. The complex molecules forming at the underwater vents are protected from the damaging ultra-violet rays of the sun which could otherwise break these big molecules up into smaller ones. While UV Rays can be an energy source that builds up complex molecules, it can also then degrade those molecules even as they are forming. For another example of an energy source being appropriate to a system, consider a shore environment; the ripples in the sand, the slope of the beach, the dunes along the beach are all complex structures emerging from the interaction of the tides and winds with innumerable grains of sand but all of these complex architectures can be erased by an over-sized energy source like a hurricane.

An alternative theory about the location for the Origin of Life, has life developing *near* but not *at* the vents. A dozen or so kilometers on either side of a magmatic vent, the underlying rock is riddled with cracks and fissures that formed as the rock shrank while solidifying. Seawater circulating through these cracks warms to moderate temperatures and becomes alkaline. White, calcium rich chimneys of porous rock form where the warmed waters exit the cracks.

As geologic processes continue to evolve, new rock types do as well. **Granite** emerges as the building block of continents.

Most scientists think that granite is formed by the partial melting of basalt, the most typical volcanic rock. When a rock is heated, some of the minerals in it melt before others. If the melt portion flows away, resolidifies and is partially remelted again, and the process repeated, eventually granite might be produced from basalt.

Erosion of the volcanoes produces sediment that builds a shelf that shallows the shoreline. The weight of the accumulating sediments keeps increasing. The heavy areas gradually sink down into the warm mantle, which is not far below.

If large enough, meteors can puncture the crust, exposing very hot mantle to atmospheric pressure. With the pressure reduced the hot mantle rock liquefies and magma pours forth. This is called **Pressure Release Melting**. Rock at great depths does not usually liquefy because the pressure is high enough to keep even very hot rock confined to a solid state.

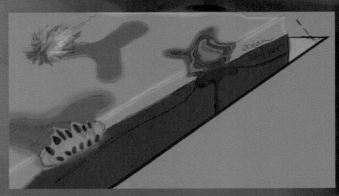

Several geologic processes are happening. Meteors are hitting Earth frequently. Old, cold volcanic ridges are sinking in the warm mantle. Mantle plumes are injecting magma into existing volcanic rock and partially melting it. Weathered rock is building up as sediment along the margins of ridges. Ridges are forced together and rock is metamorphosed. Microbial life may have been an influence in some of these processes, but this is a new and unproven idea.

The moon is pocked with craters where asteroid strikes have punctured, pulverized and cracked the white crust.

Life is emerging.

The leading theory for the origin of life is that it arises from inanimate, pre-biotic molecular associations and systems in a series of emergent steps.

Exactly when and in what order these steps occur is a matter of great debate

Life requires an energy source and the ability to make use of it (metabolism), the ability to replicate itself (ie. RNA), and the ability to keep itself separate from the rest of the world (cell wall). Once these three necessities are met, natural selection will act definitively on the system.

Larger and larger chains of carbon atoms are being formed - one carbon at a time - through a process of naturally occurring chemical reactions. These reactions occur sequentially, and together are known as the **Krebs Cycle**. Substances created by this sequence will be metabolized by early life forms.

Extensive land masses containing large amounts of granite merge to form **protocontinents**. Because Granite is so much less dense than the other rock types, the protocontinents ride high on Earth's mantle.

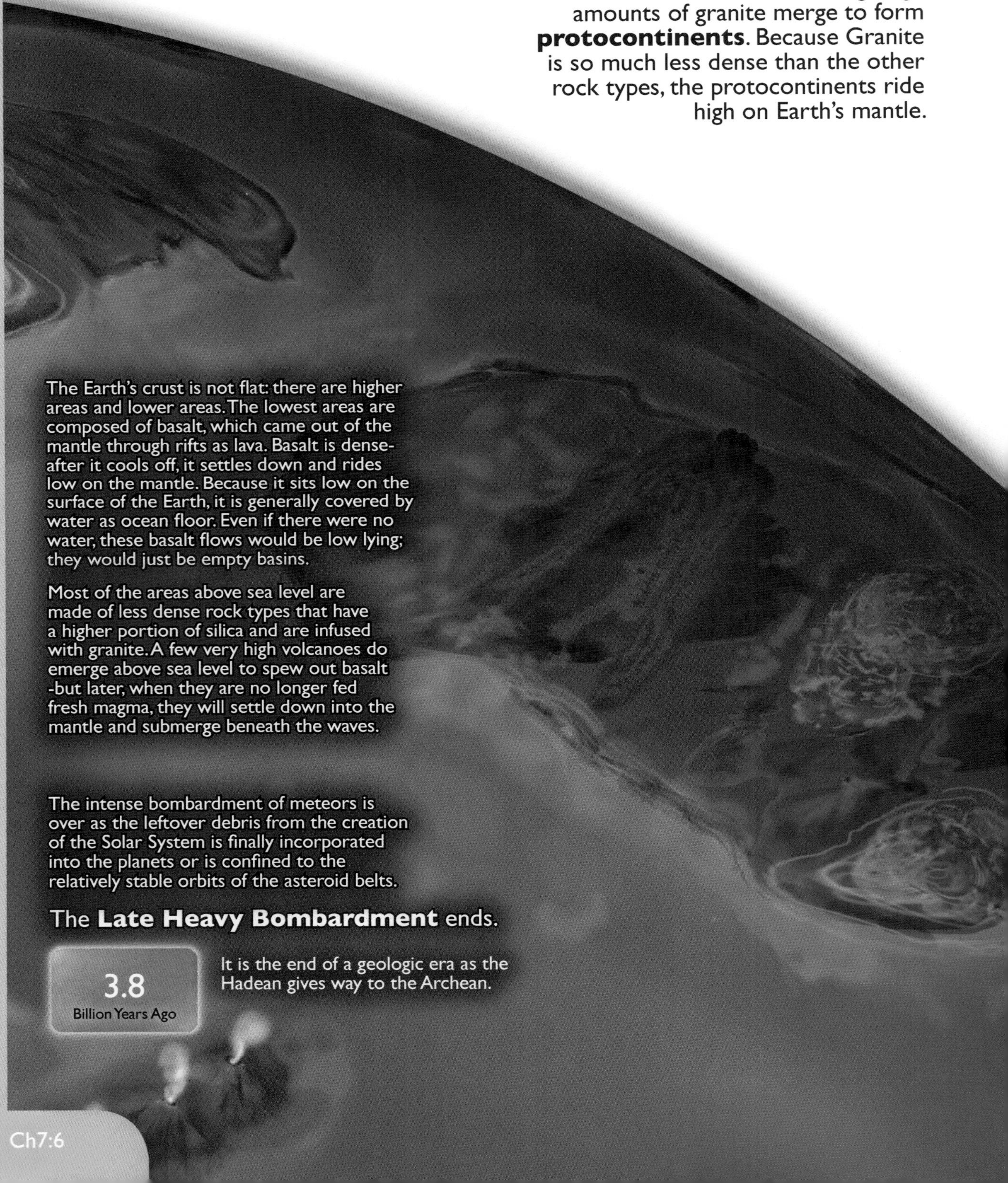

The Earth's crust is not flat: there are higher areas and lower areas. The lowest areas are composed of basalt, which came out of the mantle through rifts as lava. Basalt is dense- after it cools off, it settles down and rides low on the mantle. Because it sits low on the surface of the Earth, it is generally covered by water as ocean floor. Even if there were no water, these basalt flows would be low lying; they would just be empty basins.

Most of the areas above sea level are made of less dense rock types that have a higher portion of silica and are infused with granite. A few very high volcanoes do emerge above sea level to spew out basalt -but later, when they are no longer fed fresh magma, they will settle down into the mantle and submerge beneath the waves.

The intense bombardment of meteors is over as the leftover debris from the creation of the Solar System is finally incorporated into the planets or is confined to the relatively stable orbits of the asteroid belts.

The **Late Heavy Bombardment** ends.

3.8
Billion Years Ago

It is the end of a geologic era as the Hadean gives way to the Archean.

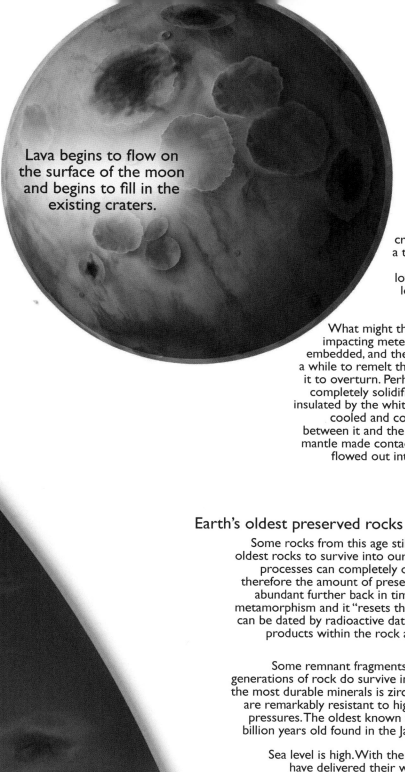

Lava begins to flow on the surface of the moon and begins to fill in the existing craters.

Why does the lava begin to flow now, so long after the craters formed? One hypothesis is that the mantle had stratified in a gravitationally unstable pattern; the first crystals that had formed and sank were magnesium rich olivine crystals which are less dense than the later forming iron rich olivine crystals. So with any kind of a trigger, the denser crystals on the top will fall to a lower level and displace the less dense crystals and the mantle will overturn.

What might the trigger be? Some of the impacting meteors may have been deeply embedded, and the heat they imparted took a while to remelt the mantle enough to allow it to overturn. Perhaps the mantle had never completely solidified because it was so well insulated by the white crust, and as the mantle cooled and contracted, a gap developed between it and the crust. Then, the crust and mantle made contact in one spot and magma flowed out into the craters of this area.

Earth's oldest preserved rocks date from this time.

Some rocks from this age still exist today. They are the oldest rocks to survive into our geologic record. Tectonic processes can completely or partially melt rocks and therefore the amount of preserved rock evidence is less abundant further back in time. Partial melting is called metamorphism and it "resets the clock" for any rock that can be dated by radioactive dating because the 'daughter' products within the rock are released when heated.

Some remnant fragments of even older earlier generations of rock do survive in the record. One of the most durable minerals is zircon. **Zircon** crystals are remarkably resistant to high temperatures and pressures. The oldest known zircon grains are 4.4 billion years old found in the Jack Hills of Australia.

Sea level is high. With the LHB over, meteors have delivered their water and no longer create heat by their impacts allowing the atmosphere to cool and more rain to fall.

Relentless winds raise giant waves which pound the shores of the protocontinents. The moon, still much closer to the Earth, pulls strong tides and Earth spins fast on its axis. The raging waves will soon soften the shoreline by breaking up the edges of continents and the sediment generated by this process will create continental shelves.

High tide follows low in just a few hours. The strong tides will soon spread the increasing abundance of sediment into shallow slopes.

There are yet no trees and forests on the land to help slow down the winds.

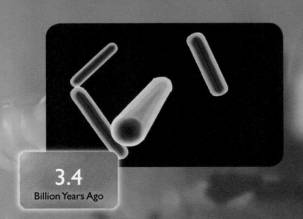

Life has emerged.

Single cells, bounded by a membrane exist in the form of **bacteria**.

3.4
Billion Years Ago

These fossils of early bacteria are preserved in marine sediments. Life probably came into existence earlier, but there is definite evidence by this time. These are the oldest known fossils, but they are only visible with a microscope.

For an energy source, these cells use the chemical disequilibrium between sulphur or iron compounds and sea water. Some single cells at this time may have already evolved the ability to utilize the energy of the sun. But the first photosynthesizing bacteria do not subject the same starting materials to the sun's rays as most photo synthesizers do today. Instead early photo synthesizers reactions use sulphur or iron compounds which require only a small amount of energy to initiate a productive reaction- but the reaction only yields a small surplus.

Our moon is no mere ornament. Its gravity rhythmically rocks the massive tides back and forth and stabilizes the biorhythms of Earth's evolving creatures.

Single celled organisms, each bounded by a membrane that separates the "self" from the outside world and with a functioning metabolism and ability to reproduce have emerged. Now natural selection will continue to evolve the system.

Single celled organisms were the first living organisms on Earth and are still the dominant life form in terms of biomass. Today, bacteria make up roughly 50% of the biomass on Earth.

Stromatolites, living mats of bacteria and sand, form mounds and structures that emerge in shallow waters. They use the energy of the sun to photosynthesize and give off free oxygen as a by-product.

Photosynthesis does not *create* oxygen. The same number of oxygen atoms remain in the Earth system. Photosynthesis uses sunlight as an energy source to break the carbon-to-oxygen bonds of carbon dioxide molecules and then allows the freed oxygen atoms to combine together into molecules of oxygen. Two oxygen atoms combine together forming one oxygen molecule, O_2. We call these molecules, oxygen, free oxygen or diatomic oxygen and this is the form of oxygen that our lungs remove from the air as we breathe.

Stromatolites are the oldest fossils that can be seen with the naked eye, although the stromatolite is a colony of single celled organisms, each one of which is microscopic.

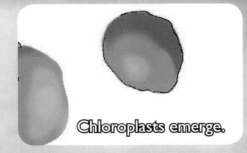

Chloroplasts emerge.

The cells that make up stromatolites contain **chloroplasts**, the structures in which photosynthesis occurs.

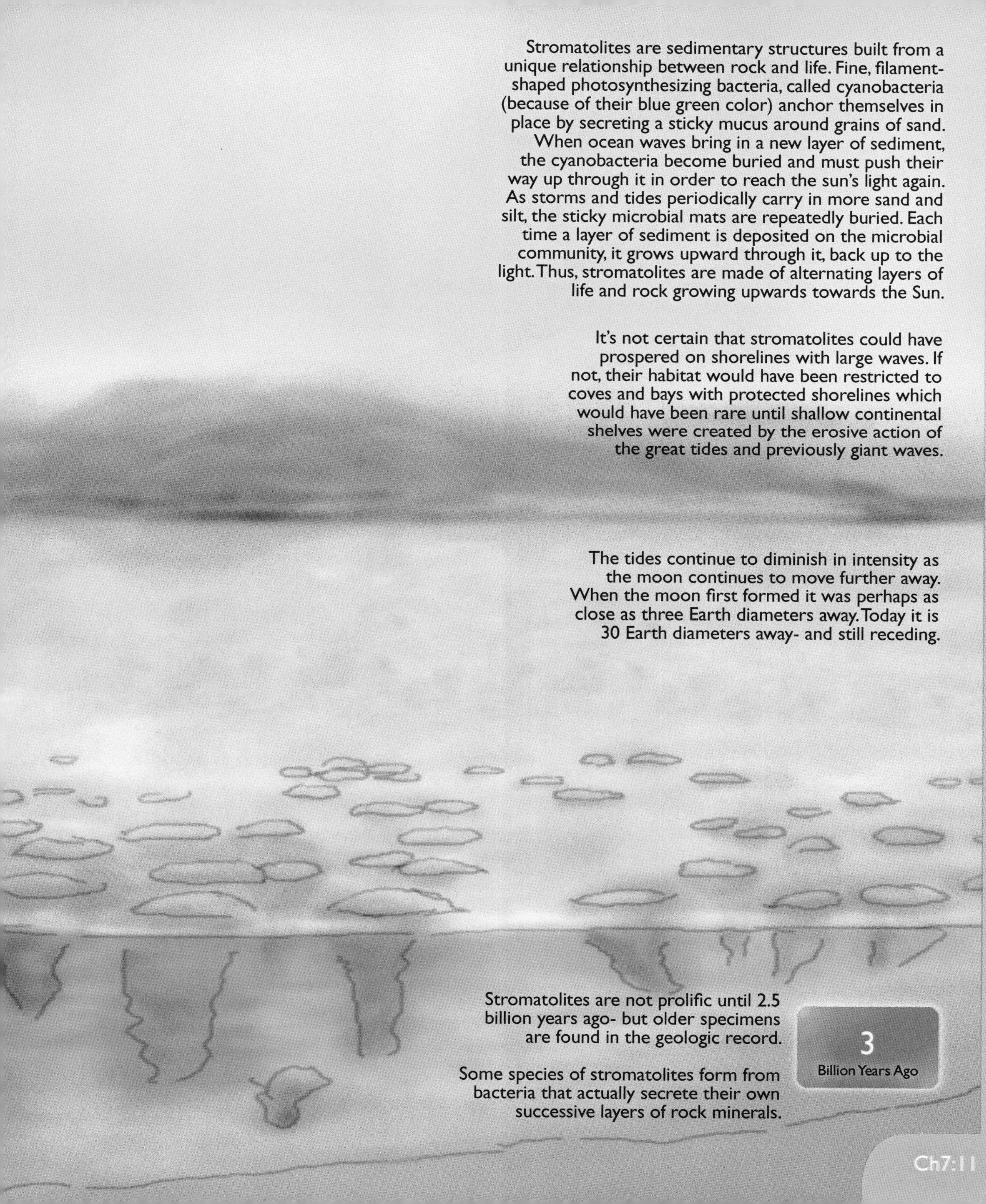

Stromatolites are sedimentary structures built from a unique relationship between rock and life. Fine, filament-shaped photosynthesizing bacteria, called cyanobacteria (because of their blue green color) anchor themselves in place by secreting a sticky mucus around grains of sand. When ocean waves bring in a new layer of sediment, the cyanobacteria become buried and must push their way up through it in order to reach the sun's light again. As storms and tides periodically carry in more sand and silt, the sticky microbial mats are repeatedly buried. Each time a layer of sediment is deposited on the microbial community, it grows upward through it, back up to the light. Thus, stromatolites are made of alternating layers of life and rock growing upwards towards the Sun.

It's not certain that stromatolites could have prospered on shorelines with large waves. If not, their habitat would have been restricted to coves and bays with protected shorelines which would have been rare until shallow continental shelves were created by the erosive action of the great tides and previously giant waves.

The tides continue to diminish in intensity as the moon continues to move further away. When the moon first formed it was perhaps as close as three Earth diameters away. Today it is 30 Earth diameters away- and still receding.

Stromatolites are not prolific until 2.5 billion years ago- but older specimens are found in the geologic record.

Some species of stromatolites form from bacteria that actually secrete their own successive layers of rock minerals.

3
Billion Years Ago

2.4
Billion Years Ago

The moon looms large in the sky. It is still close to the Earth and Earth spins fast on its axis.

Day follows night, then day appears again in only 6 short hours.

The proliferation of photosynthesizing bacteria produces more free oxygen. The oxygen reacts with the iron that is dissolved in the sea water. As the iron begins to rust, it falls out of solution and the sea turns from green to blue.

It is an **Oxygen Catastrophe** as the increasing oxygen level poisons the existing organisms that are dependent upon a low-oxygen environment.

Most of the early life forms evolved in a low oxygen environment and cannot adapt fast enough to the change, and a **mass extinction** occurs.

The many layers of rust accumulate into thick sedimentary sequences called banded iron formations. They will become the source of almost all the iron we mine today.

Once most of the iron has rusted, free oxygen levels in the ocean increase leading to the creation of many new mineral forms, not just iron oxide.

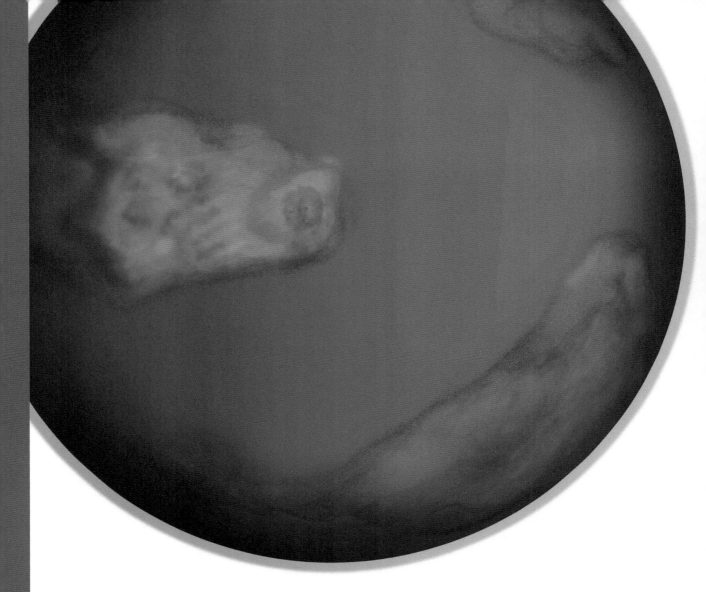

Soon after the oceans turn blue, so does the sky.

Once all the iron in the oceans is oxidized,
free oxygen starts to build up in the
oceans and then, finally, in the atmosphere.
The sea and sky become blue.

1.5
Billion Years Ago

Complex cells evolve as simple cells incorporate other simple cells inside themselves. The incorporated cells become **organelles** within the larger complex cell they helped create.

For example, photosynthesizing bacteria become chloroplasts within a larger cell.

Complex cells are called **eukaryotes** and are much more complicated than the simple prokaryote cells they evolve from. All plants, fungi and animals evolve from the first complex cells. Some scientists think that there is a greater gulf between simple cells and complex cells than there are differences between plants and animals.

In complex cells, most of the DNA is enclosed in the cell's nucleus, which is bounded by its own membrane. Simple cells have only an outer membrane enclosing everything within the cell -all the compounds required for metabolism and the strands of RNA or DNA.

Not all the DNA of a complex cell resides in the nucleus. Mitochondria, the engines of metabolism within each cell, still have a bit of their own DNA, further evidence that mitochondria, like other organelles, were once separate, independent cells.

Single celled eucaryotic organisms probably predated multi-cellular eucaryotic organisms. An amoeba is a modern example of a single celled eukaryote. All multi-cellular organisms are eukaryotes.

Prokaryotes, organisms that consist of a single simple cell, can form colonies, such as a stromatolite, coral reef or colony of mold. The members of the colony benefit from living and working together as a group. We do not consider them to be a multi-cellular organism but there is no clear cut distinction except that we define it as so. Many colonial prokaryotes can live independently if separated from the rest of the colony but this is not true for all cases.

Early eukaryotes were single-celled and colonial but multi-cellular forms likely evolved soon thereafter.

All multi-celled organisms are made of complex cells.

Eucaryotic cells emerge.

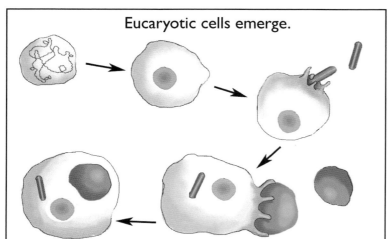

The supercontinent **Rodinia** forms.

Algae evolve that can exist on land, at least in moist areas such as shorelines. They form crusts and scums but the land is otherwise devoid of vegetation.

The distribution of the continents around the globe is always changing.

Sometimes the continents are evenly distributed across the planet but at other times, they collide and merge into larger conglomerations- sometimes they all merge together into a single, giant **supercontinent**. A supercontinent, once assembled, persists until convection currents within the Earth's mantle rift it apart again. One complete round of assembly followed by disassembly is known as a **supercontinent cycle**.

When continents collide, mountains ranges rise up between them at the suture zones. The mountains are made from the sediments that had been lying on the continental shelves of each continent. These sediments are thrust upwards as the continents come together and the ocean that had been between them disappears. When a supercontinent forms, all of the new mountain ranges are of similar age. The mountains that formed on the edge of the North American craton are known as **The Grenville Mountains**.

Remnants of Rodinia's mountains are still recognizable today, although they have eroded so much that only the roots of the mountains still remain. Most of these relics have been eroded down to a flat, basement surface and covered by later sediments or obscured by subsequent tectonic activity. You can see the roots of the Grenville Mountains today in New York State, where they have been uplifted and exposed; they are know as the Adirondack Mountains.

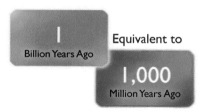

I	Equivalent to
Billion Years Ago	
1,000	
	Million Years Ago

There were other supercontinents before Rodinia. The further back in time one goes, the harder it becomes to reconstruct the tectonic history of the old terrains. Geologists are relatively certain of the positions of the continents that formed Rodinia but less so of Nuna, Kenoraland or Ur, which dates back to 3 bya. Rodinia assembles at I billion years ago but it too will break apart. The next supercontinent to assemble, **Pangaea**, is more likely to be familiar to the reader.

The supercontinent
Rodinia drifts toward the
South Pole, creating the
perfect platform for ice.

The ice sheets advance
and keep on growing.

There are several possible factors that could have interplayed to cause the runaway formation of ice.

First, there is the albedo effect: white ice reflects a much higher proportion of the Sun's light back into space than does open sea or land. Once ice sheets grow, even more sunlight is reflected away and the temperature drops further causing more ice to grow in an intensifying process.

The great landmass is a barrier to ocean currents. If the warm waters at the equator can't easily flow pole ward, more ice can form at high latitudes.

The photosynthetic bacteria could have used up most of the CO_2 (which is a greenhouse gas) from the atmosphere.

Photosynthesis converts atmospheric CO_2 to carbon containing organic matter and releases free oxygen, O_2. As dead organic matter rots, it oxidizes and forms CO_2. A lack of ocean currents could have allowed dead bacteria to settles to the bottom of the ocean without rotting, thus sequestering the carbon they contained in the stagnant ocean.

The orbital distance of the Earth from the Sun could have reached a cyclic maximum. Although, these cycles occur regularly at intervals of slightly more than 100,000 years, if this one occurred just as the other processes were happening, it could have allowed for a runaway albedo effect.

We have good evidence that snowball Earth did occur. Ice sheets leave signatures such as the scratch marks that rocks (carried by the ice) carve into the bedrock below.

Sea level falls as the ice builds.

700
Million Years Ago

The snowball Earth episode may have
happened in pulses. Ice sheets would
advance, retreat and advance again. Some
scientists debate whether the entire planet
was covered in ice or if some portions of
ocean were clear of ice at the equator.

Earth becomes entombed as the ice
sheets continue to advance.

Life dies during this extrem episode that
geologists call **Snowball Earth**.

The supercontinent Rodinia finally rifts apart, releasing volcanic gases which cause a greenhouse effect that allows Earth to break out of its icy shell. Life suddenly flourishes in what geologists now call **The Garden of Ediacara**.

The supercontinent had acted like a blanket trapping heat from the interior. This heat caused the supercontinent to swell and rift apart. As magma poured from the rifts, CO_2 was released causing a greenhouse effect which warmed the planet.

The supercontinent broke apart mostly along previous continental borders. Places already riddled with faults gave way first. The areas with the faults were underneath the mountain ranges that had formed when the continents had collided to form the supercontinent.

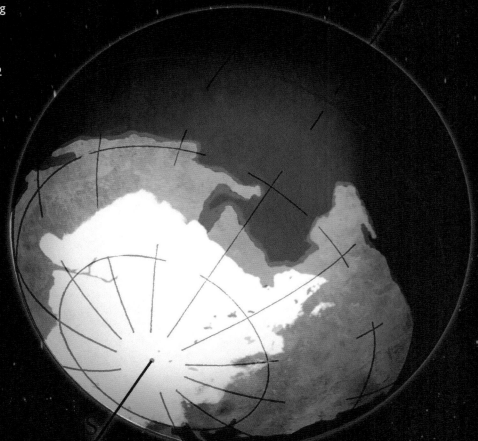

600
Million Years Ago

With some water still tied up in ice, sea levels are low. The seas between continents near the equator flourish with new, multi-cellular forms of life.

The Cambrian period (discussed on the next page) was once thought to be the time of the origin of large organisms. That date was dialed back another 40 million years when well preserved fossils of soft bodied organisms were found in the Ediacaran Hills of Australia. Because life in those long ago times was soft bodied and had no hard parts, preservation was rare. After the fossils in Australia were discovered, diligent searching revealed other Ediacaran era fossils in the rock strata of the relic shorelines of other continents from this time. Since the time of Darwin, scientists had suspected that there were some precursor organisms before the sudden arrival of sophisticated animals in the Cambrian.

The Ediacaran fossils have been difficult to categorize as plant or animal and are perhaps even their own Kingdom.

Life continues to evolve.
Animals with hard parts and
complicated body plans emerge.

Anything goes- even clumsy methods of
locomotion allow the animals to filter
feed planktonic material in the water
column. Other animals evolve higher on
the food chain to feed on these life forms.

This extraordinarily rapid evolution
of the first animals large enough
to be visible is known as the
Cambrian Explosion.

The first animals rapidly evolve and diversify in a race of ever-increasing predatory and defensive designs, as the struggle for survival ratchets up. Strange body plans and strategies for survival typify these first animals that flourish in the warm open waters of the Cambrian seas.

Cambrian
525
Million Years Ago

The earliest land plants evolve by 450 million years ago.

Plants on the land, once confined to the wettest areas and restricted to crusty slimes of algae, have evolved ways to stall dessication and have evolved vascular systems that allow them to pull up water and grow to heights of a meter tall.

Larger, more sophisticated predators evolve.

The first **vertebrates** are evolving from their pre-Cambrian ancestors.

These animals have a backbone of articulating vertebrae protecting a spinal nerve.

All fish are vertebrates and are thus of the order Chordata, animals with a backbone.

600 Million years ago

The continents have been drifting away from each other since the breakup of Rodinia. They are becoming more isolated as they reach their maximum separation.

540 Mya

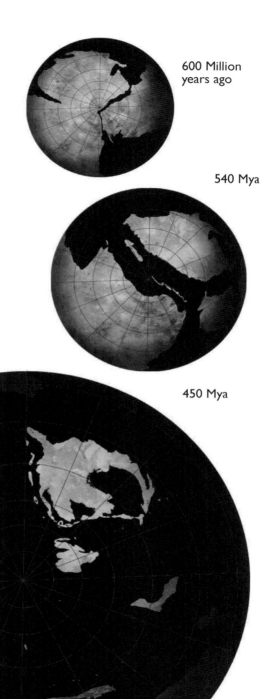

450 Mya

The first animals to venture from the sea onto land are the six-legged **Arthropods**.

Arthropods have 6 legs and an exoskeletal shell. The most abundant arthropod species have been the trilobites and they still swim these Silurian seas. The new landlubbing arthropods will later evolve into insects, spiders and crabs.

Animals face new challenges to survive on land; they must stand up without the buoyant aid of water, they must resist drying out and they must find a new way to absorb oxygen.

So, what was the lure of the land? Did the aquatic life, teeming in the sea just spill out over the banks into the vacant realm? Perhaps, animals came out to avoid predators in the sea or to graze on the crusts of algae and the new, albeit small, plants that were now growing on the land.

To conserve their moisture, the earliest land animals might have avoided the scorching sun by only coming out of the water at night.

The fossil record preserves arthropod skeletons in land sediments dating back to 419 million years ago. Tracks that apparently show the movement of arthropods across beaches exist from 450 million years ago.

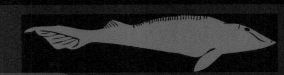

Sea level rises to an usually high level, flooding large areas of most continents. Two thirds of proto North America, called **Laurentia**, is flooded.

A few factors affect sea level. One is the amount of water tied up in glaciers at polar latitudes. Another is how thick the continents are. The continents were compressed and thickened after colliding with each other and forming the supercontinent but as Rodinia rifted, the continents were stretched and thinned. Bigger land masses displace more water causing sea level to rise.

Vertebrate animals step out of the water and onto dry land as lungs develop and fins turn to limbs. They have a body plan which we are quite familiar with; called **tetrapods,** they have four legs.

Some fish had evolved sturdier fins, which allowed them to 'walk' about in the mud. This skill likely becomes more useful for fish in drying lagoons as they are able to waddle to the next lake or puddle to swim again.

These evolving fishes develop lungs from their gills, then develop thicker skin, and their sturdy fins evolve into legs.

Fishes fill the niches of the Devonian seas as they diversify into many new and sophisticated species. Although the first fish appeared earlier, this period is sometimes called 'The Age of the Fish' because of this spectacular radiation, . The development of the **Tetrapod** from a fish ancestor is truly significant for us!

Devonian
375
Million Years Ago

Plants are also making the necessary adjustments to life on land.

Plants grow ever taller as their vascular systems develop to keep their tops supplied with water.

It takes a lot of strength to stand on dry land. Without the support of the water, a strong skeleton and muscles are required just to raise the head and support the internal organs.

These new land animals must still return to the water to breed.

The continents have been drifting closer to one another. Soon they will merge into a new supercontinent.

Vegetation grows tall as soon as plants evolve that can produce **lignin**, a molecule that gives them the strength to stand up. Taller plants are able to gather more sunlight and therefore rapidly become prolific. The atmosphere becomes richer in oxygen because free oxygen is a by-product of photosynthesis. Leaf litter and vegetative debris pile up on an unprecedented scale. Micro organisms and Fungi have not yet evolved to rapidly process the tough lignin and so vegetative matter accumulates without decomposing. This carbon rich debris is buried and will eventually be turned into **coal**.

Swamps flood the land. Shallow waters swallow the vegetative debris, further retarding its decomposition.

At the end of this geologic epoch, called the Carboniferous period, the carbon dioxide content of the atmosphere and the temperature are similar to today's climate.

Carboniferous
330
Million Years Ago

The development of the hard shelled egg allows previously amphibious animals to stay on the land instead of returning to the water to breed.

These new animals are called **reptiles**.

The ability to venture far from shore is particularly helpful because the continents have been coming together, creating larger inland areas and reducing the percentage of shoreline.

The **amniotic egg** encloses a miniature ocean and a nutritious yolk sac for the developing embryo.

The enclosed egg, also called an amniotic egg, requires that fertilization take place within the female's body. While female fish and amphibians lay eggs in water and afterwards males deposit sperm over the eggs, amniotes require penetrative sex to fertilize the eggs inside the females body before the eggs are laid.

Which came first- the chicken or the egg?

The egg paves the way for animals to complete the transition to land, but chickens will not evolve for another couple of hundred million years. The chicken will descend from dinosaurs, who are about to appear on the world stage.

Permian
290
Million Years Ago

As sea level drops, more land is exposed creating more habitat for land dwelling animals.

A continent can be seen approaching in the distance.
The supercontinent **Pangaea** is forming.

As tectonic plates converge, the ocean crust
between the plates is subducted and a line of
volcanoes forms over the subduction zone.

Giant insects fly in an
atmosphere rich in
oxygen and low in CO_2.

The vegetative debris
that had been recently
sequestered, has reduced
the amount of CO2, a
greenhouse gas.

High levels of
atmospheric
oxygen allow for
energetic flight.

High oxygen levels also make
forests vulnerable to fires
caused by lightning strikes.

Temperatures
fall and ice caps
form at the poles
dropping sea levels.

Oxygen levels reach their highest levels
in Earth's history, about 30 %. Today
oxygen makes up about 20% of the air.

A sinister fog of choking fumes envelopes the planet. At the same time, the continents merge into a supercontinent.

Life on Earth had been thriving; a diverse biosphere that included multi-cellular creatures had evolved. But now this pleasant era is ending. Volcanic activity on a massive scale pours out extensive new pavements of rock, called **flood basalts**, in Siberia and transforms the atmosphere into a suffocating shroud. At the same time, Earth's loses many of its coastal environments as the continents merge into the more compact supercontinent; a supercontinent has less perimeter than do multiple continents. Earth's oceans become stagnant as ocean currents are disrupted by the new continental configuration. Entire marine ecosystems perish in the dying oceans.

P/T Extinction
250
Million Years Ago

As the continents merge into the supercontinent **Pangaea,** another supercontinent cycle is completed.

Life on Earth suffers one of its worst extinction events. It is the time of **The Great Dying**.

Beneath the polluted skies, more than 75% of all land species wither to extinction.

Most scientist attribute the cause of this extinction event to have been due to the extensive amount of lava pouring out in Siberia; it paves over an area the size of Western Europe. A plume of magma rising up from the mantle erupts underneath a continent. To make matters worse, it erupts under layers of peat and coal which release more toxic gasses that add to the load of sulphur dioxide and particulates. These aerosols likely plunge the planet into freezing temperatures which also reduces the amount of coastline.

Many causes for this extinction event have been proposed

It has also been proposed that an asteroid struck, but no conclusive evidence of one has been found, despite much searching by scientists. Another version of the asteroid hypothesis is that the impact of a giant asteroid *caused* the eruption of the Siberian Traps. The culprit would have been giant and struck on the other side of the globe; the Wilkes Land Crater, also called the Wilkes Mass Concentration lies beneath the Antarctic ice sheet and is therefore hard to study. It is a 300 km wide area of unusually high density surrounded by a concentric rings visible in satellite radar images. So far the date of this impact, if it was an impact, is not precise but only bracketed to have been between 500 and 100 mya.

Perhaps, the disruption of deep ocean currents starves the sea floor of oxygen and dead sea life no longer decomposes but simply accumulates. When new deep ocean currents are established, they churn up this load of undecomposed biomass. As it rots, this anoxic load sucks the oxygen out of surface waters, suffocating marine life.

Another hypothesis, championed by Peter Ward, is that anaerobic bacteria, that had once been the dominant life forms on Earth, proliferate again and out compete multi-cellular organisms.

Earth becomes almost uninhabitable for plants and animals.

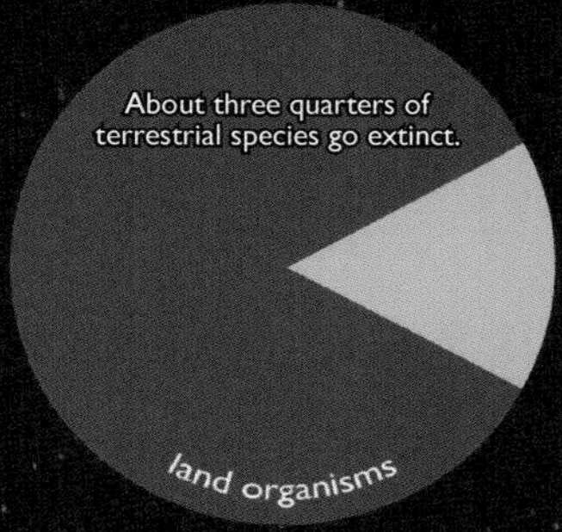

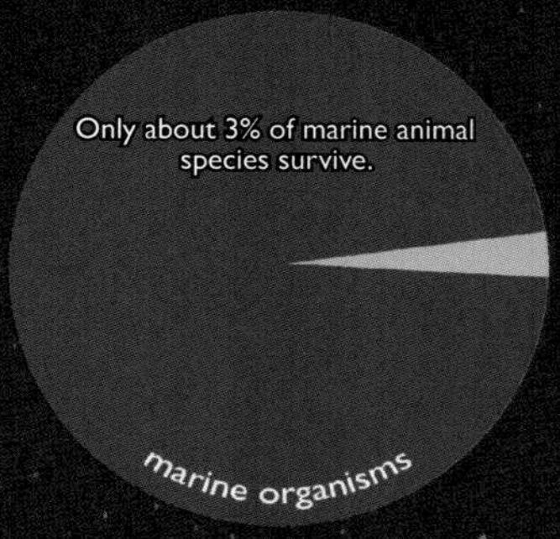

In the anoxic waters of the stagnant seas, marine life is all but obliterated.

About three quarters of terrestrial species go extinct.

Only about 3% of marine animal species survive.

land organisms

marine organisms

Multi-cellular life on Earth begins to recover from the great extinction event, and the ragtag survivors organize into new ecosystems, which will soon flourish.

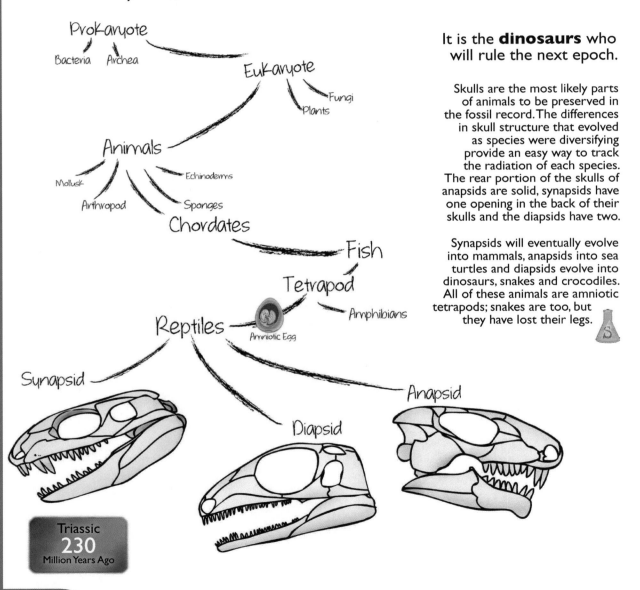

It is the **dinosaurs** who will rule the next epoch.

Skulls are the most likely parts of animals to be preserved in the fossil record. The differences in skull structure that evolved as species were diversifying provide an easy way to track the radiation of each species. The rear portion of the skulls of anapsids are solid, synapsids have one opening in the back of their skulls and the diapsids have two.

Synapsids will eventually evolve into mammals, anapsids into sea turtles and diapsids evolve into dinosaurs, snakes and crocodiles. All of these animals are amniotic tetrapods; snakes are too, but they have lost their legs.

Prokaryote
Bacteria   Archea
Eukaryote
Fungi
Plants
Animals
Echinoderms
Mollusk
Arthropod   Sponges
Chordates
Fish
Tetrapod
Amphibians
Reptiles
Amniotic Egg
Synapsid
Diapsid
Anapsid

Triassic
230
Million Years Ago

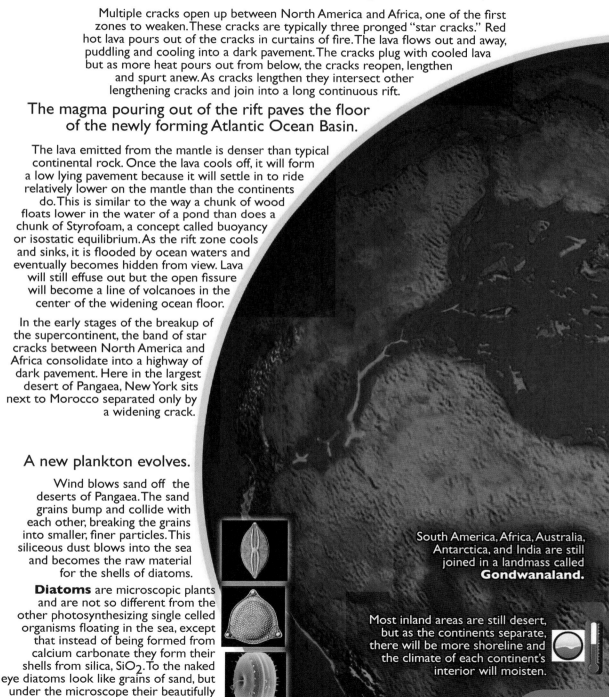

Pangaea begins to break up as heat from Earth's mantle builds up beneath the blanketing land mass, causing the crust to expand and crack.

Multiple cracks open up between North America and Africa, one of the first zones to weaken. These cracks are typically three pronged "star cracks." Red hot lava pours out of the cracks in curtains of fire. The lava flows out and away, puddling and cooling into a dark pavement. The cracks plug with cooled lava but as more heat pours out from below, the cracks reopen, lengthen and spurt anew. As cracks lengthen they intersect other lengthening cracks and join into a long continuous rift.

The magma pouring out of the rift paves the floor of the newly forming Atlantic Ocean Basin.

The lava emitted from the mantle is denser than typical continental rock. Once the lava cools off, it will form a low lying pavement because it will settle in to ride relatively lower on the mantle than the continents do. This is similar to the way a chunk of wood floats lower in the water of a pond than does a chunk of Styrofoam, a concept called buoyancy or isostatic equilibrium. As the rift zone cools and sinks, it is flooded by ocean waters and eventually becomes hidden from view. Lava will still effuse out but the open fissure will become a line of volcanoes in the center of the widening ocean floor.

In the early stages of the breakup of the supercontinent, the band of star cracks between North America and Africa consolidate into a highway of dark pavement. Here in the largest desert of Pangaea, New York sits next to Morocco separated only by a widening crack.

A new plankton evolves.

Wind blows sand off the deserts of Pangaea. The sand grains bump and collide with each other, breaking the grains into smaller, finer particles. This siliceous dust blows into the sea and becomes the raw material for the shells of diatoms.

Diatoms are microscopic plants and are not so different from the other photosynthesizing single celled organisms floating in the sea, except that instead of being formed from calcium carbonate they form their shells from silica, SiO_2. To the naked eye diatoms look like grains of sand, but under the microscope their beautifully intricate geometric forms are revealed.

South America, Africa, Australia, Antarctica, and India are still joined in a landmass called **Gondwanaland.**

Most inland areas are still desert, but as the continents separate, there will be more shoreline and the climate of each continent's interior will moisten.

Dinosaurs are evolving.

Their hind legs are situated beneath their hips, giving them a more upright stance than their sprawling reptilian ancestors. This allows them to move on dry land with more speed and agility, and to out-compete other reptiles.

Pterosaurs rule the skies but these reptiles are not dinosaurs.

Ornithischians

Sauropods

Saurischians

Theropods

Dinosaurs diverge into two sister families, the Ornithischians and the Saurischians. The Saurischians will further divide into Sauropods and Theropods. Most Sauropods are vegetarians.

Pangaea continues to break apart.

During the breakup of Pangaea, star cracks formed along zones of weakness in the swollen crust and lava poured forth from them. The cracks lengthened and some of them joined up with neighboring ones forming a long, continuous rift zone which became the dominant rift, now called The Mid-Atlantic Rift. The other arms of the star cracks which didn't join up became failed rift zones. A sequence of these failed rifts decorate the Eastern edge of North America and the western edges of Europe and Africa and are today low lying linear tracks. One of the most famous of these is now a trough in which the Hudson River of New York flows, after it is later exposed by glacial erosion; it sides are lined by basaltic cliffs called the palisades.

Continents can be billions of years old, but no sea floor is more than 200 million years old because it eventually gets recycled in a subduction zone. The lava coming out of rifts forms a dense rock called basalt. Because basalt is dense, it will eventually settle to form low lying areas.

Due to plate tectonics, new crust is made in rift zones and old crust travels to subduction zones where it is carried back down into the mantle. When basalt plains eventually settle to lower elevations, they become inundated by the sea and come to be ocean floors. They would still be low lying plains even if there were no oceans. At subduction zones, pavements of basalt go down but the lighter continents manage to resist subduction. The basalts emitted at this point in time are among the oldest ocean tracks in the world today.

Jurassic
200
Million Years Ago

The North Atlantic ocean
continues to widen.

At the same time, Alaska
and other terranes are
being accreted to western
North America.

Jurassic
150
Million Years Ago

The failed rift zones are filling in.

These low-lying troughs fill in with sediment that
erodes off the nearby highlands. The troughs are
denser than the highlands, which are made of
continental rock. The highlands become even lighter
as they erode and the troughs become even heavier
as sediment accumulates. The system is not in isostatic
equilibrium. With every earthquake, the troughs sink
and the highlands rise.

Dinosaurs evolve feathers for insulation to aid thermal regulation. The feathers will facilitate flight.

One of the earliest birds, **Archaeopteryx**, appears.

The famous fossil of Archaeopteryx dates to 149 million years ago and is found in Germany

Sea turtles evolve.

They swim in the narrow sea that develops between North America and the African and South American continents. They return to the beaches they were born on to reproduce but forage throughout the narrow sea. Over time, the continents get further apart and the sea widens. The sea turtles will evolve ever stronger, muscular flippers and become long distance swimmers. The size of their flippers can increase as the ocean widens; because the ocean widens at a slow enough pace for animal evolution to keep up.

Super organisms evolve.

Cockroaches that had been feeding on rotted wood evolve into termites whose large colonies are the first **Super Organisms**. Individuals have different roles, like forager, soldier and queen. Reproduction is a role limited to few. Colonies contain thousands of members but individuals are not autonomous and can only survive as part of the group.

The individual members of a super organism colony do not work to further their own personal reproductive success. Although evolution has been typically envisioned - even by most scientists - as ruthless competition between individuals, this is not the case with super organisms.

The working members of the colony are sisters who are genetically almost identical and are daughters of the queen, who is still reproducing. They are willing to forgo individual reproduction and instead work together for the continuation of the queen's genes, which are similar to their own. The queen mates once with a single male and stores the sperm for both immediate and later use. All members and future members have the same parents and are thus genetically very similar. Insects that organize themselves this way are also known as **Eusocial Insects**.

Flying reptiles must share their airborne niche with flying dinosaurs that are becoming ever more sophisticated.

The first flowers bloom.

The first flowers bloom as new kinds of plants called **Angiosperms** evolve new strategies to spread their seed. They are just getting started and conifers and ferns are still the dominant vegetation.

archaefructus liaoningensis

A medium-sized asteroid strikes the Moon and will create the **Tycho Crater** which is still easy to see today.

108
Million Years Ago

Globe image with permission © C.R. Scotese 2014

Mammals become ever more clever and cunning.

Dinosaurs rule but mammals are right at their feet. The mammals are not only surviving, but evolving keen eyesight and sharp teeth. They are very small, because the only mammals that can exist among the dinosaurs are small, fleet-footed, furtively dodging creatures.

The volcano depicted here, in what is now Liaoning Province, China, periodically erupts. The noxious fumes and choking ash devastate the ecosystem, killing some animals, even as they sleep. The fine ash preserves fossils in exquisite detail, feathers and even skin are still visible today. The volcano has been nicknamed the Mesozoic Pompeii.

This site has been extensively excavated since the 1990s, greatly expanding the world's library of evidence.

The climate is warm and shallow seas swamp portions of the continents.

Marine reptiles and fish swim the inland waterways.

Colorado and other western states are flooded and marine reptiles can swim from the Arctic Ocean to the Gulf of Mexico. Over the next few million years, the middle of the waterway will begin to dry out and it will no longer be a swim-through, impeding the migration paths of animals. As species are separated into isolated populations there will be a sudden burst of evolutionary diversification and new speciation.

As the continents separated, the dinosaurs from one continent could no longer interbreed with those on another.

As time and evolution continue, isolated populations diverge and new species emerge.

Africa and South America were late to separate and their populations are more closely related.

Paleo globe courtesy Scotese.

In Africa, an aquatically adapted dinosaur, Spinosaurus, evolves to hunts fish and marine reptiles.

Cretaceous
80
Million Years Ago

Dinosaurs are everywhere, having diversified into every conceivable niche on land, in the sky and finally in the water.

Flowering trees begin to supplant ferns and conifers as the dominant vegetation.

Instead of needles, flowering trees have leaves, and are called deciduous.

Insects and flowering plants evolve a self-reinforcing cycle, of symbiosis. The insects aid the plants' abilities to reproduce through pollination, and the insects are fed by an increasing number of plants.

Other insects besides termites. like wasps, ants and bees evolve **eusocialablity**. The social organization of the insects as a colony is so successful that eusocial insects soon have the dominant share of total insect biomass.

Plants evolve fruit which rewards animals with a sweet morsel for transporting their seeds, just as insects were rewarded earlier with sugary nectar.

Unfortunately for the plants, animals sometimes eat the plant's leaves. A plant needs its leaves for photosynthesis so plants evolve various defense mechanisms, such as thorns, waxy coatings, and indigestible or toxic compounds.

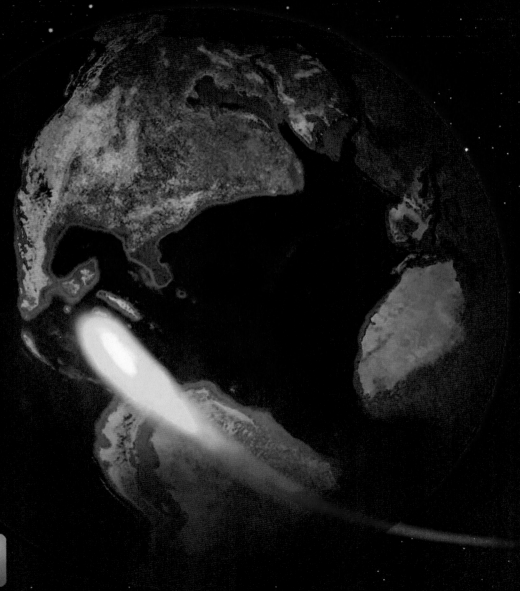

Unfortunately for the dinosaurs, a very large asteroid is heading toward Earth.

K/T Boundary
65
Million Years Ago

The asteroid strikes Mexico at an angle.
North America is the first casualty but the
damage will soon be worldwide.

The heat of the impact melts the rock where
it lands and flings molten glass **sphericules**
across North America, setting forests aflame.

The Chixalub Crater on the Yucatan
Peninsula of Mexico still remains today. The
deposition of glass sphericules is arrayed
outward from it, in a northerly direction.

This closes the chapter on the dinosaur age.

It comes just when life on Earth is flourishing; dinosaurs
abundantly fill the niches on every continent, highly evolved
mammals manage to coexist at their feet, flowers are in full
bloom and had become ever more beautiful in order to
attract their beneficial animals that co-evolved with them. It
was a beautiful world but all that is about to change abruptly.

Ironically, the beauty of flowers is not to impress
their own kind, but to entice insects and animals.

Flowers are molded by selection to be beautiful to animals;
the most attractive flowers reproduce most successfully.

Flowering plants will, of course, survive this
extinction event and continue to further evolve.

Chapter 11: Mammals Embrace the New Era

The survivors of the apocalypse are delighted to discover that there are no more big dinosaurs.

The mammals are ready. The long years of surviving alongside the dinosaurs selected them for sharp senses, hardy metabolisms and the habit of burrowing. They soon scamper out of their underground refuges into a vacated landscape.

Their burrows protected have them from the scorching rain of vaporized rock and the forest fires that followed. Their snug homes will also insulate them from the cold temperatures that are soon to come; sunlight will be unable to penetrate the ash and dust in the atmosphere for several months.

Some dinosaurs actually do survive but only small, feathered ones; the birds. Birds are well insulated and able to fly to the least devastated areas.

All large land animals die. Only the small straggle into the new era.

Some species of animals that feed on dead plant matter survive while all of those that depend exclusively on living plants go extinct. This is consistent with dust, resulting from the impact, obscuring the sun and preventing photosynthesis for several months

Large animals not only require large amounts of food but also can have difficulty in regulating their body temperatures..

According to the eloquent scientist, Neil deGrasse Tyson, no species of land animal 'larger than a bread box' survives.

65
Million Years Ago

Mammals prosper and will soon evolve to fill all of the vacant niches with a variety of well adapted, specialized forms.

Some mammals will even evolve to fly in the sky - bats - and some, such as whales, will return to the sea.

Mammals are a class of animals named for their sucking behavior. Infant mammals drink the nutritious milk of their mother's mammary glands.

Mammals give birth to live young after a period of gestation within their mother's womb. Like reptiles, the eggs of mammals are fertilized internally but then the fetus continues to develop within the female whereas reptiles must lay their eggs and then either leave them to hatch and fend for themselves or at most, guard the eggs and then bring the hatchlings food to eat. This food can even be partially digested and regurgitated for the young but the food that baby mammals suck from their mother's teats is manufactured to be exceptionally nutritions. Immediately after birth, the first milk that a mother produces also contains anti bodies that prime the infant's immune system.

Flightless birds prosper on the Southern continents.

Super organisms of insects continue to evolve.

The willingness of the individuals in a colony to work together, even when most of them do not reproduce, seems to depend on their being closely related. Greater genetic diversity is generally better for a species because it allows natural selection to proceed more rapidly. Since these super organisms are becoming more prolific, the gains of working together must outweigh the disadvantage of less genetic diversity.

Early colonies had almost no diversity (the queen mated once and sisters were identical), but wasps eventually develop methods of cohesion that allow more diversity to be tolerated. Now the queen mates with different males and the less related sisters still cooperate.

The ancestor to the horse is small and browses on brushy vegetation.

They can travel intermittently between North America and Eurasia as sea level rises and falls. This allows them to sometimes evolve separately and later interbreed and exchange beneficial new genes. It has an odd number of toes.

Andrewsarcus, a huge carnivorous mammal, roams the reaches of Mongolia.

The ancestor of whales. pakicetus, is an elongated dog-sized mammal that scavenges the shorelines of Southern Asia. It has an even number of toes.

Ambulocetus is the next step in the evolution of whales. It wades in the water waiting to ambush animals on the bank. Its limbs are enlarged like paddles and it has a muscular tail,

India is a separate continent, drifting northward at an fast rate.

As India and Asia converge, volcanoes erupt on the Asian coast.

India had been nestled in with Madagascar, Australia and Antarctica when the supercontinent Pangaea was still assembled, but now a mantle plume has come up from underneath and pours out lava both on the continent and on the ocean floor that is forming behind it.

India, like all continents is part of a tectonic plate. The Indian plate includes some of the ocean floor around the continent. As the oceanic portion of the plate subducts beneath the Asian plate, volcanoes rise.

Continents might drift partly because the deeper layers of rock they are riding on move in response to convective currents in the mantle. Scientists do not agree on why India moved so quickly. Most think that the prime mechanism of continental drift is slab pull, the tug on the rest of the plate caused by the leading edge of the plate that is gravitationally falling down a subduction zone. Today most continents are moving at around the same rate that your fingernails grow, about an inch a year.

Eocene
45
Million Years Ago

As Africa and Europe approach each other, another line of volcanoes rises.

The volcanos in Europe form as the leading edge of the African plate which is not the continent of Africa itself but the dense slab of the ocean floor ahead of it, dives beneath the European plate.

It was once thought that the subducting plate melted as it entered the mantle providing the lava but we now know through seismic imaging that the down going slab is too cold to readily melt.

As the slab descends, pressure increases and minerals change into denser more compact forms. Hydrous minerals like amphiboles and micas contain some atoms of hydrogen in their crystal lattices and as they metamorphose into higher grade minerals such as garnet, they release H_2O which rises as a vaporous curtain toward the surface. Water lowers the melting temperature of rock and when the vapors near the surface, the rock that was there all along melts and the resulting lava spews out of volcanos.

Termites help to stabilize climate.

Wild swings of climate change are dampened by fluctuating levels of termite populations, which respond to changes in sea level. Termites produce prodigious amounts of methane, a powerful greenhouse gas. When global temperatures rise, so does sea level, which reduces the amount of land available for termites to live on, and their populations decline causing the atmospheric concentration of methane to decline. As the climate cools, ocean level falls, exposing more land and allowing termite populations to increase.

Oligocene
30
Million Years Ago

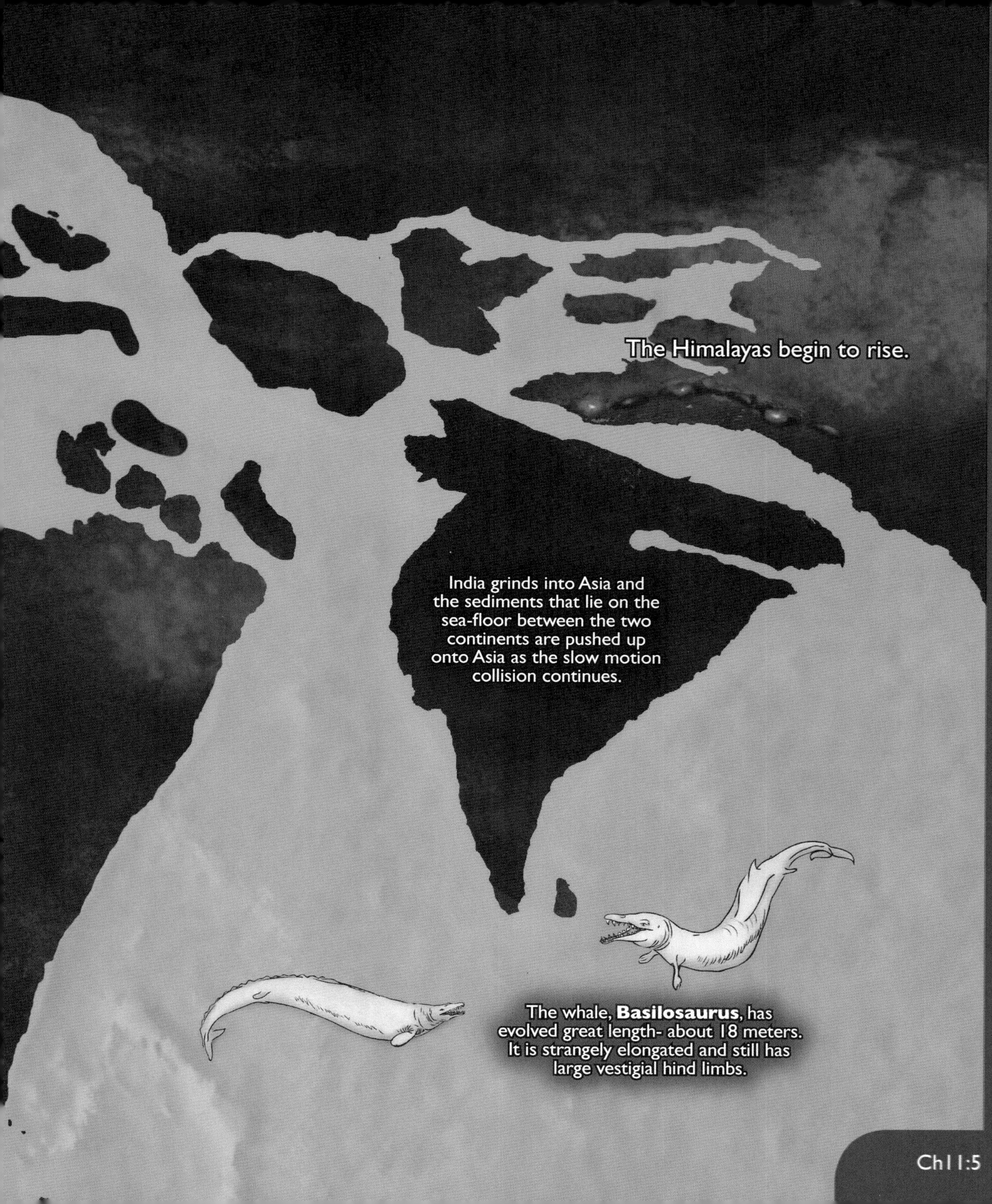

The Himalayas begin to rise.

India grinds into Asia and the sediments that lie on the sea-floor between the two continents are pushed up onto Asia as the slow motion collision continues.

The whale, **Basilosaurus**, has evolved great length- about 18 meters. It is strangely elongated and still has large vestigial hind limbs.

The Alps rise.

Life, for the primates living in the canopy, is dangerous; the threat of falling is ever present.

Primates, an order within the class of mammals, inhabit the forest canopy and have been evolving to move with agility through the trees.

The digits of their hands and feet are limber, their thumbs opposable and nails have replaced claws to allow for sensitive grasping of vines and branches.

They have forward facing eyes that give them stereoscopic vision which helps them to judge distances precisely

Prosimians
Lemur, Tarsier, Bushbaby, Loris

New World Monkeys
or *Platyrrhini.*
Marmoset, Spider monkey, Tamarin, Capuchin monkey, Squirrel monkey Howler monkey

Old World Monkeys
or *Cercopithecidae.*
Baboon, Macaque, Vervet Monkey, Mandrill, Colobus monkey, Proboscis monkey

Lesser Apes
or *Hylobatidae.*
Gibbon
4 Genera: Hylobates, Hoolock, Nomascus, Symphalangus

Ponginae
Sumatran Orangutan, Bornean Orangutan

Gorilla
Gorilla

Pan
Chimpanzee, Bonobo

Homo
Sapien

Present Day

10 Million Years Ago

20 Million Years Ago

30 Million Years Ago

40 Million Years Ago

50 Million Years Ago

Primates are on most continents. Old World and New World Monkeys had already become separate lines back around 50 million years ago. The Hominid line which will lead to apes and humans branched away from the Old World Monkey line at around 30 million years ago.

Pictured (not to scale), from left to right:
Bushbaby, Capuchin monkey, Mandrill, Lar Gibbon, Sumatran Orangutan, Gorilla, Bonobo, Homosapien

Whereas most mammals have large litters of offspring, primates usually have single births; probably because it is difficult to carry an infant through the high altitude maze of a forest. A large number on teats is no longer required and since every appendage has a biological cost, primates evolve to have just two nipples.

In the expansive lands of the continental interior, some of the browsing mammal species evolve much longer legs. They are beginning to look a bit like horses but because they are browsers and eat low calorie shrubbery, they have a larger gut and a lower metabolism.

As the African plate continues to subduct beneath Europe/Central Asia, sediment on the continental shelves and the sea floor between them will be scraped off and added to the continents. Most of the sediments will be added to Europe, forming the Alps, but some will be added to the Sahara.

Even though the Himalayas are still rising, they are already eroding. Debris sloughs off the peaks and fills in low spots of the plains below.

Whales living in the shallowing sea off the northern coast of Africa get trapped and marooned. Their skeletal remains are entombed into the fossil record of the Sahara.

A **super plume**, a hot spot, emerges underneath the horn of Africa. A triple junction of rifts opens and lava pours out.

Neogene
20
Million Years Ago

Ch11:7

The Yellowstone Hotspot erupts.

The Yellowstone Hotspot erupts repeatedly. The North American tectonic plate is moving slowly southwestward and it is sliding over the stationary hotspot. At about 16 mya the hotspot poured out lava on the border between Oregon and Nevada. Major eruptions followed at 15 and 11 mya, Old calderas are buried under subsequent flows and the trail of flows forms extends northeastwardly, forming what is called a hotspot track. The Castleford Crossing Eruption at 8.1 mya qualifies as a supereruption; it leaves a layer of basalt (solidified lava) 1.3 km thick.

As the tectonic plate moves along, the hotspot will eventually end up where it is today, under Yellowstone, Wyoming.

The **grey wolf** is a social carnivore that hunts in packs.

The ancestor of the **camel** evolves in the southern North America.

Flightless birds have increased in size and fill the large predator niche on the isolated continent of South America.

The sperm whale dives to great depths hunting giant squid. Their heads are packed with a strangely named oil that is notable not so much for its murky white color but its utility. The density of spermaceti oil changes greatly with temperature. The whale can take on seawater to cool the oil which becomes denser allowing the animal to sink for a dive.

Toothed whales evolve echolocation. They emit a pinging **sonar** like sound which bounces off objects and they listen for the return of the sound wave. Their brains measure the time it takes for the pings to return and paints a picture of their surroundings, in the deep murky depths where there is not enough light for eyes to see.

Other scientists think that the spermaceti oil also enhances the whale's ability to echo locate by allowing it to measure an additional internal echo, which helps it to keep track of its own position. When a roving whale emits a ping, it has moved a bit before the ping comes back. Because that signal also has to go through the oil inside the whale's head, which it does at a different speed than when it travels through water, the whale can precisely track its own dynamic position relative to its surroundings or its prey- quite a plus in close encounters with giant squid.

Mountains effect high altitude winds.

The recent rising of the Alps causes the jet stream to move northward which causes the climate at mid-latitudes to become drier.

A new kind of grass evolves.

The new kind of grass, called **C4 grass** because of the way it fixes carbon, uses the energy from bright sunlight more efficiently, when temperatures are high.

To review, all photosynthesizing plants take CO_2 from the air and break this molecule apart using the energy of sunlight. Plants utilize the carbon part of the CO_2 to make sugars for their own energy use and to build their leaves, roots and other structures. They release the oxygen atoms, which then latch onto each other, forming O_2, free oxygen, which animals can inhale.

Grasses and other **C4** system plants will soon out compete plants that still use the old **C3** method, but only at low to mid-latitudes, where the sunlight is intense and temperatures are high.

The **Hominin** line of primates branches away.

Hominins diverge from other **Hominids** around 6 million years ago. The word Hominid refers to all Great Apes, alive or extinct. This includes Orangutans, Chimpanzees, Gorillas, and Humans, as well as all of their ancestors. Hominin, however, refers only to humans and our immediate ancestors. Today there is only one extant species of Hominin which is, of course, us. Long before Homo sapiens will appear on the scene, however, many other hominins will have their day.

Miocene
10
Million Years Ago

A new kind of whale, a filter feeding, or baleen, whale evolves.

Baleen replaces the teeth that whales have always had with a mineral plated filter. These whales take in a mouthful of water and then close their mouths and push the water back out through the baleen plates. The tiny but numerous and nutritious plankton in the water remain inside the whale.

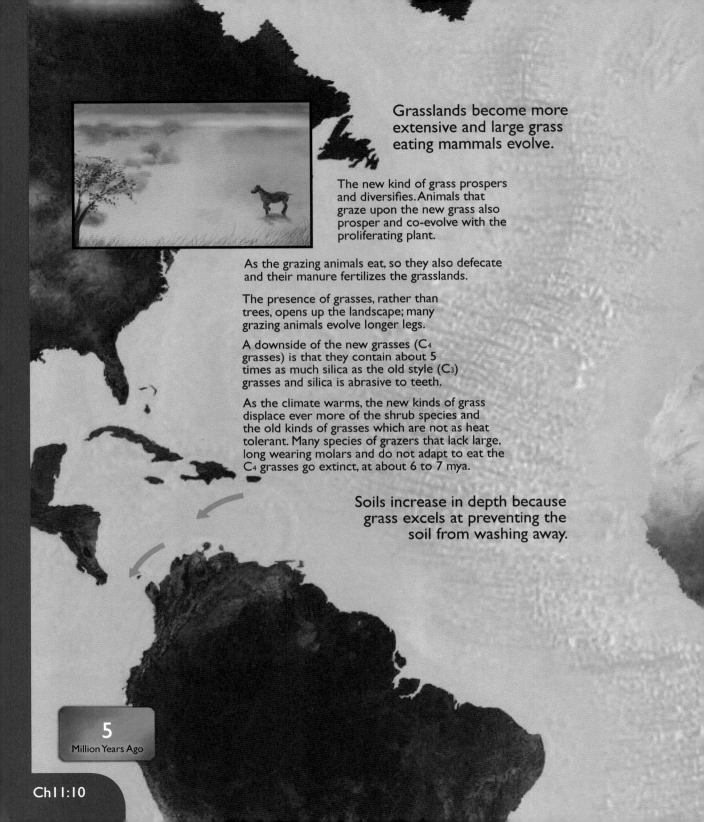

Grasslands become more extensive and large grass eating mammals evolve.

The new kind of grass prospers and diversifies. Animals that graze upon the new grass also prosper and co-evolve with the proliferating plant.

As the grazing animals eat, so they also defecate and their manure fertilizes the grasslands.

The presence of grasses, rather than trees, opens up the landscape; many grazing animals evolve longer legs.

A downside of the new grasses (C_4 grasses) is that they contain about 5 times as much silica as the old style (C_3) grasses and silica is abrasive to teeth.

As the climate warms, the new kinds of grass displace ever more of the shrub species and the old kinds of grasses which are not as heat tolerant. Many species of grazers that lack large, long wearing molars and do not adapt to eat the C_4 grasses go extinct, at about 6 to 7 mya.

Soils increase in depth because grass excels at preventing the soil from washing away.

5
Million Years Ago

The Mediterranean Sea had been cut off from the open ocean and subsequently dried out. Now, rivers have cut a new trench at Gibraltar and the waters of the Atlantic are rushing back in.

Tectonic uplift and changing wind patterns cause the jungles of Africa to become savannah, open grasslands with scattered trees.

Zebras were among the first grazers to adapt to the new (C_4) grasses, about 9.9 mya. Ancestors of elephants made the switch 7.4 mya. Giraffes never did switch; they are adapted to browse leaves in the tops of bushes and trees.

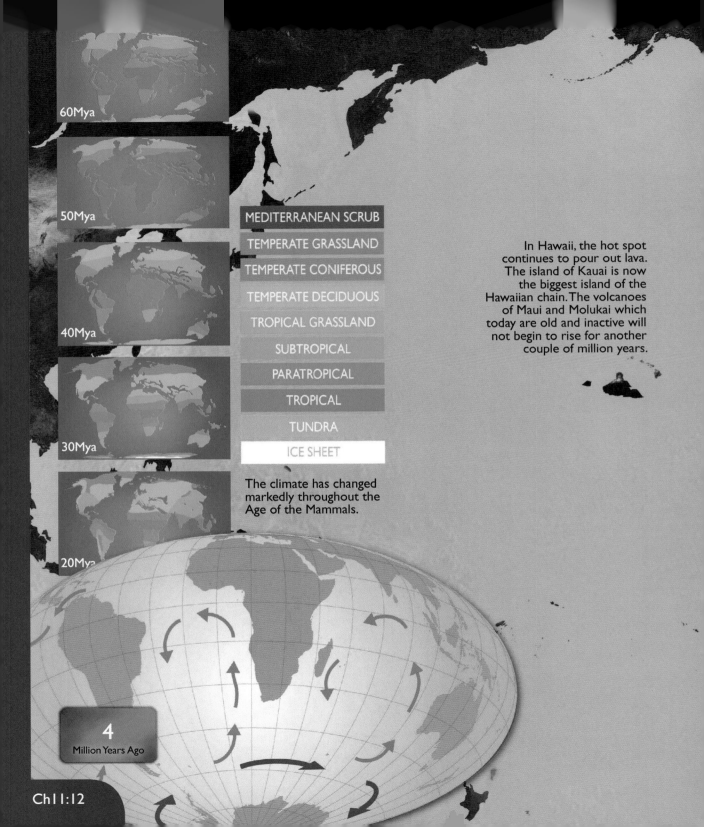

60Mya

50Mya

40Mya

30Mya

20Mya

MEDITERRANEAN SCRUB

TEMPERATE GRASSLAND

TEMPERATE CONIFEROUS

TEMPERATE DECIDUOUS

TROPICAL GRASSLAND

SUBTROPICAL

PARATROPICAL

TROPICAL

TUNDRA

ICE SHEET

The climate has changed markedly throughout the Age of the Mammals.

In Hawaii, the hot spot continues to pour out lava. The island of Kauai is now the biggest island of the Hawaiian chain. The volcanoes of Maui and Molukai which today are old and inactive will not begin to rise for another couple of million years.

4
Million Years Ago

The apex predators of North America are the Dire Wolf, the Short Faced Bear, and the Saber Tooth Cat.

The open seaway between North and South America still separates the continents.

Volcanoes between North and South America pour out lava and erupt clouds of ash that build into new islands. A strip of land is building that will soon bridge North and South America into one traversable landmass.

The apex predators of South America are the giant flightless birds that geologists call **Terror Birds**. They, like all birds, are descendents of dinosaurs. Far more massive than modern ostriches, they run down their prey and strike with their beak which is embedded in a massive skull. Forward momentum alone was probably enough force to kill the prey.

The new **land bridge** between the Americas disrupts the existing ocean currents which will soon profoundly change Earth's climate and usher in the Ice Ages.

There hadn't been an ice age in ages. At the warmest point during the age of the dinosaurs, there were no polar ice caps at all.

Throughout Earth's history, it has usually been pretty warm. The first Ice Age was associated with the Great Oxidation event (when photosynthesizing bacteria changed the composition of the atmosphere 2.4 billion years ago. Then there was Snowball Earth around 700 mya. A slight dip occurred in the Ordovician. When the coal that we burn today was being buried back in the Carboniferous, the climate was similar to the modern regimen of glacial and interglacial periods.

The time of the modern ice ages begins two and a half million years ago and continues today. Times when ice at the poles increases and grows to cover mid-latitude areas are called **glacial periods**. Warmer times, when the ice melts back to the polar regions are called **interglacial periods**.

There will be several pulses of glaciation. The last episode began about 110,000 years ago and reached its peak about 20,000 years ago. When it ended about 12,000 years ago, the current interglacial period began. We still have significant ice at both poles so we are still in an ice age.

Animals now move from one American continent to the other.

Volcanic activity creates new land, which bridges the previously separated North and South American Continents. The animals of each land had evolved differently but now they will meet and compete with one another.

Conversely, the connection between the oceans is severed when the connection between the continents is forged and the Atlantic and the Pacific become separate.

Among the animals on the move are the apex predators. Saber toothed cats, cougars, wolves and bears move south and the terror birds of South America migrate the other way.

The terror birds could not travel north through the dense vegetation of Central America until the volcanos had belched out enough ash, some hundreds of feet of it, that smothered the jungle and paved a path for the them. Some of these giant predators make it as far north as Texas and Florida.

3

Million Years Ago

Primates are continuing to adapt to life in the African savannah. Apes evolve and diverge into different species some of which stand and walk on two legs some of the time.

As forests give way to savanna, bipedal walking becomes a more efficient mode of transportation. Standing upright improves the view, frees the hands, and uses less energy for traveling on the ground. Many species of bipedal apes evolve, and the ones that walk on two legs all of the time are collectively referred to as Hominins.

A new hypothesis, "Scrambler Man" proposes that bipedalism is encouraged by agile movement through the steep, rocky outcrops and complex topography of the East African Rift zone. In this model, apes that adopt bipedalism exploit the niche that this tectonically new landscape presents. As hominins pursue prey up rocky slopes and down steep dales, the ability to move with agility and to jump, grasp and balance is rewarded. Scientists from the University of York presented this hypothesis in the archeological journal *Antiquity* in May 2013. Most scientists are still satisfied with the *Adaptation to the Savanna Theory*, even though a small minority of climatologists claim that forests did not give way to savanna until after bipedalism had been achieved.

There are many different species of hominins, some prosper and some go extinct.

Some hominins become specialists; they adapt to a limited range of resources. Some, like Paranthropus boisei (above), are specialized to eat grass almost exclusively.

Generalists, such as **Homo habilis**, are adapted to make use of a wider range of resources. They can eat meat, fruits, nuts insects and more.

Biologists classify organisms with two names. The first name is capitalized and states the genus and is followed by the lowercase species designation. *Homo habilis* is more closely related to us than is *Parathropis bosiei*.

The stone hand axe evolves. It is likely that wooden tools evolved first but were not preserved in the fossil record.

Tools are powered by the large muscles of the arm and controlled by the fine muscle movement of the hand. The earliest stone tools date to 3 million years ago.

Sticks and stones reduce the load placed on teeth. Teeth evolve by the slow process of biological evolution while tools evolve at a cultural pace.

Some Hominins develop bigger brains. Where does imagination come from?

Dreaming forges new connections.

Perhaps one of the functions of dreaming is to try out and juxtapose different causes and effects. Recent dream research suggests two different kinds of dreaming: REM dreaming and non-REM dreaming. REM dreaming seems random in its correlating of things and can be wild, surreal and seemingly nonsensical. The non-REM sleep seems to be a replay, almost like a movie, of the day's events, while the brain plays memories of somewhat similar previous events.

Chapter 12: Control of Fire and the Cooking of Food Shapes a New Hominin

Fire is tamed and the use of fire will transform hominins; the ancestors of humans begin to eat cooked food.

Fire, although a dangerous and frightening thing, provides warmth, cooked food, and safety from predators. Cooking renders food easier to eat and digest. This helps to make the large brains of the Hominins worth the calories required.

Undisputed evidence for the widespread use and control of fire dates only to 125,000 years ago, but most scientists consider the evidence for the control of fire by *Homo erectus* 400,000 years ago to be convincing. A new hypothesis, advocated by Richard Wrangham in his book *Catching Fire: How Cooking Made Us Human* places the date for the control of fire at almost 2 million years ago. Hopefully, more evidence will eventually be found to pinpoint this date.

The Panama land-bridge has now been passable for over a million years.

Species who traversed the bridge are changing the ecosystem of the land they enter. The changes to North America are minor but many South American species go extinct.

Wind patterns shift in response to changing ocean currents caused by the closing of the seaway between the Pacific and Atlantic oceans, contributing to climate change.

Many of South America's highly specialized species are hunted or out-competed by the species coming down from the north

Many species of Marsupials (mammals who nurse their young in a pouch), who had evolved to fit specific ecological niches of South America, go extinct. Only the opossum gains new territory and moves northward

The top South American predator had been the terror bird but these solitary hunters are now outmaneuvered by these new predators. Some of these predators had expansive ranges on the North American continent and are generalists. After the bridge opens they cross south for some easy pickings. Terror birds make it as far north as Texas and Florida but do not prosper long as the social carnivores there out-compete them

Social carnivores who live in packs and hunt as a team continue to evolve. The grey wolf coexists with the much larger dire wolf and they are not a threat to one another. The dire wolf has short legs and a big head and preys on large, slow moving game whereas the grey wolf is smarter and faster and preys on smaller game that the Dire wolf is unable to catch

Pleistocene
2
Million Years Ago

The Hominin known as **Homo erectus** evolves 1.8 million years ago. They have enough imagination to tame fire and journey out of Africa in a wave of migration and expansion.

Homo erectus is the first Hominin in the human lineage to expand past the boundaries of Africa. They will reach Western Asia by 1.7 million years ago, Indonesia by 1.6 mya, and Spain by 1.4 mya.

The use of fire transforms Hominin behavior and anatomy.

Primates usually sleep in trees and seldom on the ground. All other primates are better at climbing than hominins and sleep in high, safe places; cliff sides, tree branches or holes in tree trunks. Based on their physiology, Homo erectus probably did not climb trees any better than modern humans do. This suggests that H. erectus primarily slept on the ground, but the African woodlands (and the savannahs that are supplanting them) are dangerous places, with all manner of large predators. The control of fire allows H. erectus to come down out of the trees, by providing protection from predators overnight.

The emergence of Homo erectus is perhaps the biggest evolutionary leap in human ancestry. H. erectus is larger than its predecessors, and has smaller teeth, a narrower pelvis and a less flared rib cage, redesigned shoulders, and a much larger brain. With the shift to dwelling on the ground, climbing-specific adaptations of the arm, shoulder, and torso are lost. Arboreal life favors smaller body plans and the switch to the ground frees Homo erectus to grow in size.

Cooked food requires less chewing and digestion, and provides more usable energy than raw food. It also allows a wider variety of foods to be eaten. Cooked food provides the fuel for the increase in body size and especially brain size. The advent of cooked food also reshapes the species by favoring those individuals with smaller digestive systems and smaller teeth; larger guts and big teeth are no longer necessary and reducing their sizes saves calories and increases agility.

In the evenings, Hominins gather around campfires for warmth and safety. Together they listen to the spit and crackle of the fire, and to each other. In this leisure time, imagination grows. They could see each other's faces in the dancing flickering light and experiment with making sounds of their own.

The climate continues to change and the savannahs continue to dry out.

In Africa, Hominin generalists are able to adapt to the changing climate, but the specialists lose the staple food that they had become dependent upon and go extinct.

Tectonic uplift associated with the rift activity topographically elevates East Africa which causes more climate change.

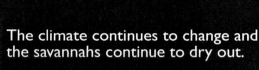

Hominins who have tamed fire and eat cooked foods prosper and develop bigger brains and better social skills. Team work further increases success.

I

Million Years Ago

Equivalent to

1,000

Thousand Years Ago

Some Hominins evolve bigger brains, but brain power is expensive.

In humans, the brain requires about 20 percent of our energy budget. Unless being smart can bring in that much more food, it isn't worth having a bigger brain.

Deductive reasoning evolves. Some Hominins are able to infer that there are food sources that they cannot see or smell directly. For example, from birds of prey circling in the sky, they deduce that there is an injured animal or carcasses on the ground below.

Hominins also deduce that the impressions made by the feet of animals are tracks which can be followed to their source.

Hominids are likely **scavengers** rather than primary hunters.

They have traits that allow them to out compete other scavengers. They can deduce the presence of a carcass from seeing vultures above and can travel swiftly to it in the heat of the day. By functioning as a group wielding sticks and stones, they can scare off the predator that brought down the prey or the other scavengers (like hyenas) that have already done so. If they do arrive after the meat is gone, they can still get the nutritious and calorie-rich bone marrow by using their stone tools to break the bones apart. Some scientists think that getting the marrow out of bones was the driving force for the development of stone tools.

Changes also occur in other primate families; chimps speciate into common chimps and bonobos. Because neither species swims, they seem to have become isolated from each other after the Congo River developed, about 1.5 mya. Bonobos are only found on the southern side.

Homo erectus is highly successful.

Some scientists have argued that *Homo erectus* evolved in Asia, not Africa, possibly because more fossilized specimens have been found in Asia than anywhere else or simply out of habit, because the first specimen ever found was found in Asia. In any case, a million years after their appearance, *Homo erectus* becomes widespread. The populations everywhere are similar enough to still be a single species. *Homo erectus* is highly successful.

Some Archeologists have argued that the African and European populations had already diverged from their Asian counterparts enough to be called a new species, *Homo ergaster*, by a million years ago, but those scientists had been comparing early African forms and late Asian forms and using those differences in generalizing about all African and Asian specimens.

When wood fires are routinely made in the same hearth, a siliceous layer of ash is left since wood contains silica which does not burn. This is the hard evidence for the use of fire that is indisputable. Other fuel sources such as dung leave less of this residue.

When the Hominin trail reaches the bamboo forests of Asia, remnants of the stone axe are no longer found along it. Perhaps, bamboo could be fashioned into tools with less effort. Bamboo tools have never been found but they would not easily be preserved.

The Stone Age is so named only because the artifacts that survive until the present day are the ones made of stone. Most tools were likely made of wood which is much easier to work.

500
Thousand Years Ago

At a cave in China, *Homo erectus* endures cold conditions and competes with giant hyenas.

When the first skull of a *Homo erectus* was found in Indonesia in 1912, many scientists were skeptical that it was really a new species and not just the skull of a diseased ape but a second skull was later found at the Zhoukou cave near Beijing; it was named Peking Man and confirmed the new species. Since that time, scores of fossilized bones and skulls and some complete skeletons of *Homo erectus* have been found in Africa and throughout Europe and Asia.

Inside
the cave
there are bones
and debris left by hyenas
and this debris includes skulls
from Peking man. Hyenas are scavengers
and might not have killed the hominins but simply
dragged parts of their already dead bodies into the cave
to eat. Scratches and cut marks on the skulls were originally
interpreted by western scientists to be evidence of cannibalism,
much to the dismay of their Chinese counterparts. Years later, after
forensic techniques were improved, the marks were proven to be from
the teeth of hyenas.

There is much debate as to how Peking Man lived. Evidence of fire and stone tool use in the cave abounds but the ash layers are somewhat scattered and a debate rages as to whether Peking man cooked over permanent hearths in the cave or only used fire in the cave occasionally.

Anatomically modern humans arrive on the scene in Africa. This new breed of bipedal primate will soon out compete all others. Some of these humans will soon journey out of Africa in a new wave of expansion.

Many different species or subspecies of hominins had evolved. They had sometimes evolved in isolation (either by geography or by inhabiting a specific niche) and at other times interbred with other sub species. Some had prospered and some had gone extinct. Only neanderthals, denisovans, florensis and perhaps a few other hominin species or sub species still exist at this time.

Homo sapiens likely evolve from Homo heidelbergensis who evolved from the African branch of Homo erectus. The European branch of heidelbergensis likely evolved into Homo neanderthalensis and the Asian branch into the Denisovans. The Denisovans might also have interbred to a small extent with Asian Homo erectus. Many other branch lines of Homo erectus went extinct.

There is wide consensus among scientists that **Homo sapiens** evolve somewhere in sub-Saharan Africa.

Time estimates vary; some say 200,000 years ago, but others estimate closer to 125,000 years ago.

Most scientists subscribe to the 'Out of Africa' hypothesis that humans migrating out of Africa replace earlier hominin groups with little to no interbreeding. The competing 'multiregional' model has the migrating humans interbreeding extensively with local populations they encounter.

200
Thousand Years Ago

The climate in Africa was in a state of flux, frequently alternating between wet and dry, and Homo sapiens adapted well to change.

The Earth, like a spinning top, wobbles on its axis and completes one cycle in 20,000 years. It is just a minor wobble, but if it coincides with other factors, it can trigger rhythmic climactic changes. The climate of the whole planet had gone through profound changes during the rise of the mammals. The creation of the Himalayas and then the Alps changed global wind patterns. The forming of the Panama land bridge fundamentally changed ocean currents and initiated the deep water conveyer system. The 20,000 year wobble cycle sometimes coincides with other factors causing the Sahara to become green and lush.

Humans develop a new hunting technique.

Since humans have very little hair, they can keep themselves from overheating more easily than other animals can. Humans also have sweat glands and sweating cools more efficient than panting and also frees up the mouth for sound. Improved cooling enables humans to run down furry game like antelope by outlasting them in the heat of the midday sun while other hunters, like lions, are finding respite in the shade.

Evolution is a complicated web -not a simple tree.

While it is possible that a new species diverges only once, and then continues to evolve in isolation; divergence can also be followed by new cross breeding. And this process can occur repeatedly. New sub-species can evolve which then interbreed, to varying degrees, creating new hybrids. The difficulty of defining *species* is called **The Species Problem**. Many textbooks still use Ernst Mayr's definition of a species as "Groups of actually or potentially interbreeding natural populations, which are reproductively isolated from other such groups".

This definition of species lacks definitiveness when describing separate species that do interbreed under unusual circumstances. This can happen when species court and mate at different times. For example, if a mallard is blown off course on a windy day and falls in with another tribe of fairly closely related birds say pintails or black ducks, it will probably take part in their mating rituals when the time comes around and produce fertile hybrid offspring (at least some of the time). There are many other examples that also show the difficulty in defining species.

Humans have a voice box, which is to say that their larynxes are lower in the throat, allowing sound to resonate. This made the development of language more likely- or perhaps auditory communication was so useful that the lowered larynx evolved because those with greater auditory range were more likely to survive or to attract a mate. The lower larynx comes at a cost as it makes choking on food more likely.

When Hominins walk or run together, the one-two cadence produced by their bipedal gait allows them to synchronize, if they are listening.

What color were the eyes of earlier Hominids? The whites of our eyes make it easier for humans to know where another human is looking which in itself is a limited form of communication.

Homo sapiens spread along the coasts of the lands they inhabit and learn to utilize the resources of the sea.

That these early humans are beachcombers and eat shellfish is evidenced by the shell middens they left. Middens -heaps of emptied shells- have been found in Eritrea that are 125,000 years old.

An alternative hypothesis about early human evolution is the **Aquatic Ape Hypothesis** which proposes that proto-humans, perhaps as long ago as *Homo erectus*, adapted to aquatic environments.

There are several supporting points for this not widely held hypothesis. Humans have a higher fat content than other primates such as chimps. Baby humans are buoyant in water and instinctively hold their breath when submerged. Bipedalism would be fostered and rewarded by wading in water as some of the weight of the body would be supported and standing upright allows the head to be held high for breathing. Humans, according to this view lost their covering of hair to facilitate swimming. They retained hair on the top of the head to shield from sunburn.

Human breathing patterns could have evolved in a semi-aquatic environment. There are three kinds of breathing behaviors in mammals; voluntary, involuntary and both. Marine mammals such as dolphins are voluntary breathers which means they must think about every breath they take and therefore they cannot allow their entire brain to sleep and do not engage in REM sleep, where some dreaming functions important to humans occur. Humans are both unconscious and conscious breathers which means that they can breath even while fully asleep and can also voluntarily hold their breath to dive. Other mammals with both breathing modes are amphibious such as otters and seals. The control of breath might have helped facilitate language development in humans.

Perhaps hominins adapted to shoreline environments to exploit richer food sources or because there was less competition in this habitat or because they could escape predators. The large human brain needs fatty acids like omega-3 which is common in fish and shell fish.

The Sahara Desert, a barrier harder to cross than a mountain range, has not always been so formidable.

It periodically becomes wet and green. One of these Green Sahara epochs was likely under way when our ancestors were roaming in Africa.

This pictoglyph, found in Southwest Egypt, depicts people swimming. This cave painting was made during a recent Green Sahara episode just 10,0000 years ago. Fish bones are also found in nearby garbage heaps.

DNA can now sometimes be extracted from fossils. This new science is yielding a wealth of data even though only a small fraction of older fossils retain DNA. Scientist using the **molecular clock** can estimate when various lines of people became isolated from one another. The molecular clock is based on the idea that every new generation carries some random mutations in their DNA and by comparing these markers in different populations, the time of their divergence can be calculated. The first molecular clock estimates on human fossils used not the DNA within the cell nucleus but the shorter strands of DNA that are in the mitochondria. Nuclear DNA studies have been performed recently. Mitochondrial DNA mutates more rapidly than nuclear DNA but the first estimates of this rate seem to have been too fast. The molecular clock is still a relatively new method and not necessarily accurate. The date of fossils of artifacts can be made using all available methods. When all sources of evidence yield the same result, our confidence in the date is strong.

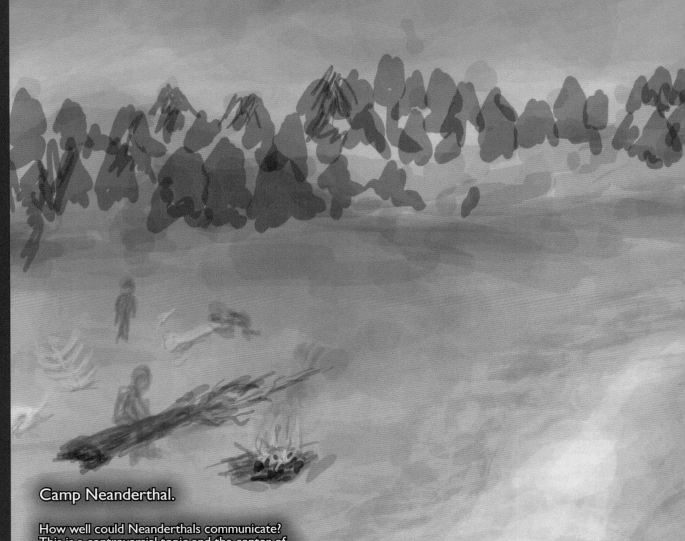

Camp Neanderthal.

How well could Neanderthals communicate?
This is a controversial topic and the center of
much research. One of the indications of speech
is the position of the larynx in the throat. No
fossils have yet been found that show how
Neanderthal throats were configured because
tissue and cartilage is rarely preserved.

80
Thousand Years Ago

As they migrate and spread forth from Africa, Homo sapiens encounter some of the descendants of the first wave of Hominin migrants, such as **Neanderthals**.

Humans almost certainly have evolved some rudimentary language before they journey out of Africa. It is likely that language is part of the genetic makeup of our species because language is common to all the human groups and cultures ever known. Many people, and some scientists, find this idea unpalatable and would prefer the idea that language is a purely cultural institution. However, almost all human children acquire language skills fairly easily- even people who are not considered to be very smart conjugate verbs and mark the plural properly. Language is so important to the survival and prospering of our species that it would have been a criteria in natural selection.

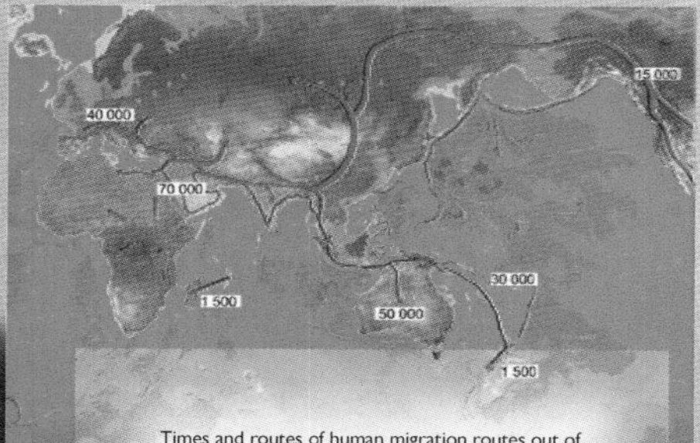

Times and routes of human migration routes out of Africa.

Mount Toba, a **super volcano**, erupts in Sumatra, causing a global volcanic winter lasting about a decade. According to the Toba Catastrophe Theory, environmental disruption causes human population to drop to its lowest level. Because of this genetic bottleneck, where the number of humans is thought to have dropped into the thousands, all humans today are closely related.

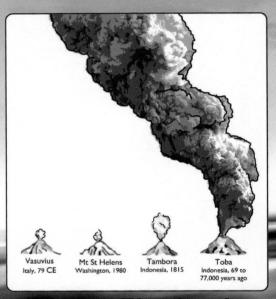

Vasuvius
Italy, 79 CE

Mt St Helens
Washington, 1980

Tambora
Indonesia, 1815

Toba
Indonesia, 69 to
77,000 years ago

The explosion of Toba was huge; orders of magnitude larger than Krakatoa and other recent volcanic events.

75
Thousand Years Ago

About 3,500 generations ago

Human migration out of Africa is proceeding along the coast of the Indian ocean and has perhaps reached as far as the Indian subcontinent. Humans have not yet arrived in East Asia but the effects of the super volcano are felt world wide.

Human populations recover and migration proceeds along the Indian coast, past the site of the eruption of Mt. Toba.

People cross the stretch of ocean to Australia, a land that they cannot even see, presumably by building rafts.

Pleistocene
50
Thousand Years Ago

Australia is lush and populated
by giant animals known as
Megafauna.

 Australia is settled by humans when
sea level is lower than it is today but
Australia would still not have been visible,
even after a few days of rafting. Did the
intrepid humans guess that a land lay
beyond because of migrating sea life or
were they accidently swept out to sea?

Australia experiences a wet period
between 60,000 and 40,000 years
ago. Thus it is a lush, green land
when humans arrive.

The mega-fauna eat grass or
animals who feed on grass and
they fertilize the vegetation
with their droppings of
manure. Much of Australia
will become desert with the
demise of the giant animals.

The giant animals have had
no experience with humans
or bipedal apes of any kind;
Homo erectus had not
voyaged across the watery
expanse to isolated Australia.
The giant animals are easy
prey and soon go extinct.

Humans journey into Europe and encounter the Neanderthals whose reign of some hundreds of thousands of years is coming to an end.

Neanderthals have been portrayed as clumsy, hairy, slouching brutes, but new evidence suggests otherwise. The Neanderthal skeleton that had been used as the basis for depicting Neanderthals as big and dumb was from an individual suffering from arthritis. Neanderthal stone tools are sophisticated and assembled with handles fastened with a gluey pitch that they manufactured by heating birch bark without allowing it to burn. Reanalysis of old artifacts shows that they contain pigments which might have been used for ornamentation.

The Neanderthals are better adapted for cold temperatures; they have more body mass and shorter limbs.

Hands were stenciled by blowing or spitting pigment on a cave wall in Spain, probably by Neanderthals. The lower painting- made 10,000 years later- is probably painted by *Homo sapiens sapiens*.

Pleistocene
30
Thousand Years Ago

The climate is still cooling and the ice age has not yet reached its peak, but the intrepid humans are already encroaching deep into the range of the Neanderthals. The Neanderthals are not so different from the humans, and new genetic evidence suggests that we interbred with them to a limited degree. Homo neanderthalensis and Homo sapiens are likely both descended from *Homo heidelbergensis* and are related closely enough to both be species of humans. There is much debate as scientists attempt to tease out the fine points of the evolution of Hominins.

Many scientists use the nomenclature of *Homo sapiens sapiens* for current humans and Homo sapiens neanderthalensis for Neanderthals. The DNA of all peoples, not recently from sub Saharan Afric, contains roughly 1 to 4% Neanderthal DNA. These genes probably conferred some helpful immunity. Further to the east, other migrating humans are encountering the **Denisovans**. Some genetic transfer happens and the group migrating on to Taiwan and Melanesia have about 6% Denisovan DNA in their genome. Those who go on to other parts of Asia have about 3%.

Human population expands by journeying from Asia across the **Bering Land Bridge** into Alaska and eventually into all of the Americas.

Bison also journey from Asia. Horses, which had evolved in North America, journey the other way, westward across the bridge into Asia, as do the gray wolf and the camel.

Exactly when did humans cross? Evidence, by way of ancient human feces found in a cave in Oregon and genetically analyzed, show humans here by at least 14,000 years ago. At this time the open land corridor between the vast continental, **Laurentide Ice Sheet** and smaller Cordilleran Sheet is overgrown with ice and therefore people probably followed the coast and used boats. Some scientists have recently claimed that two separate migrations occur, one through the land corridor and one by sea.

Sea level is low and the land bridge is exposed because of the formation of glaciers of snow and ice at polar latitudes. There is only so much water on the planet. When more is locked up in ice then there is less water in the oceans.

The beginning of the end for the dire wolf is brought about by the demise of the mega-fauna that was the specialization of the species.

Pleistocene
20,000
Years Ago

It is the **Last Glacial Maximum**.
The ice age reaches its peak sometime
between 26,000 and 19,000 years ago.
Since this time, the glaciers of Earth
have been melting and receding.

As the climate changes and the glaciers retreat,
large mammals around the globe go extinct.
In some cases, the timing of the die-off is
suspiciously close to the arrival of the humans.

When humans entered this new continent, they had already adapted
to cold while living in Asia (recent genome studies estimate that they
came from the Lake Baikal area). Relatively few people migrate over as
evidenced by the fact that there are only 5 genetic haplo groups among
all Native Americans today. It is truly a New World, a frontier where no
previous hominins have ever before hunted. No early hominins such as
Homo erectus have ever been found in the Americas. The mega fauna
are naive and plentiful and spear technology known as **Clovis points**
are soon developed. As the size of the migrating group is small, they
likely lose most parasitic disease, and as they travel southward into a
relatively disease free, ever warming world, their populations expand
quickly. Some of them reach Chile about 14,000 years ago.

The Sahara Desert becomes green again as the **African Humid Period** begins. Long dried up lake beds fill with water and existing lakes in the rift zone grow larger and interconnect.

The "African Humid Period" is an interval from 16,000 to 6,000 years ago when Africa was much wetter. This is due to changes in climate caused the by the wobbling of Earth on its axis. Ironically it is when the axial tilt exposes the Southern Hemisphere to more solar radiation that the prevailing winds shift northward which brings more rain to Africa.

The 20,000 year wobble cycle is a minor enough factor that it only has serious effects when it happens to coincide with other factors else the Sahara would green up every 20,000 years.

As humans hunt and gather and interact with plants and animals they create selection pressures that cause the plants and animals to adapt themselves to the human presence.

Hunter gatherers do not wander around on ever changing routes but rather they 'tend the wild'. They know from experience when nuts and berries ripen in certain places and when animals migrate and where they congregate.

Holocene
12,000
Years Ago

Equivalent to

10,000
Before Common Era

People living in the temperate latitudes of Southwest Asia find themselves surrounded by bountiful resources. They inadvertently cultivate fruits, nuts and other plant foods just by picking them and dropping the seeds along trails and in garbage heaps.

Gourds are used as containers before the advent of pottery and are one of the first plants to be domesticated.

Sheep and goats abound and people soon learn not just to hunt them but to protect the herd from other predators. They herd these still wild animals to lush pastures and to blind valleys where they can be confined and then hunted and harvested when convenient.

Although humans prey on these animals, it is still a mutually beneficial relationship. Humans learn not to take too many goats at once since taxing the herd too heavily will result in a less productive herd.

People harvest wild wheat and rye which grow on dry hillsides.

From the Nile River Valley to the Tigris and Euphrates is the bountiful swath of land known as the **Fertile Crescent**.

Wheat and other cereal crops are deliberately cultivated in the Fertile Crescent, around 10,000 years ago.

Humans who had long hunted grazing animals become grass eaters themselves with the onset of agriculture; wheat, rice, rye and so many other crops are all grasses.

The dry-summer climate of the Middle East is conducive to the evolution of annual plants with large seeds or fruits. The hilly topography creates a variety of micro climates and a large variety of species. Grains such as wheat and legumes such as peas nourish the human inhabitants who begin to settle into agricultural societies.

The domestication process begins with a wild species and progresses in predictable ways, called the domestication syndrome. Traits that tend to get selected include: higher rates of germination and predictable simultaneous germination, increased sizes of edible parts which are often the reproductive organs of the plants, a tendency for the ripe seeds to stay on the plant, fewer chemical defenses or mechanical defenses such as thorns.

The seeds of a wild plant often ripen at different times over a long interval. If the seeds grow in clusters, the clusters tend to break up when they fall off the plant. These traits help the wild plant to disperse its seeds over a larger area over throughout a varied set of weather conditions, whereas having the ripe seeds remain together on or near the plant helps the humans harvesting them.

Although the African Humid Period lasts a long time, there is a thousand year period within it of cooler dry weather called the **Younger Dryas** which occurs between 12,800 and 11,700 years ago. It might have been caused by the collapsing ice sheets in North America changing ocean currents but there are other theories as well. Some scientists hypothesize that it reduced the carrying capacity of the land so severely that pastoral hunter gatherers who had become semi-sedentary were at first forced to become more mobile in order to gather enough food but later, as the climate worsened further, they were forced to adopt cereal growing.

8000
BCE

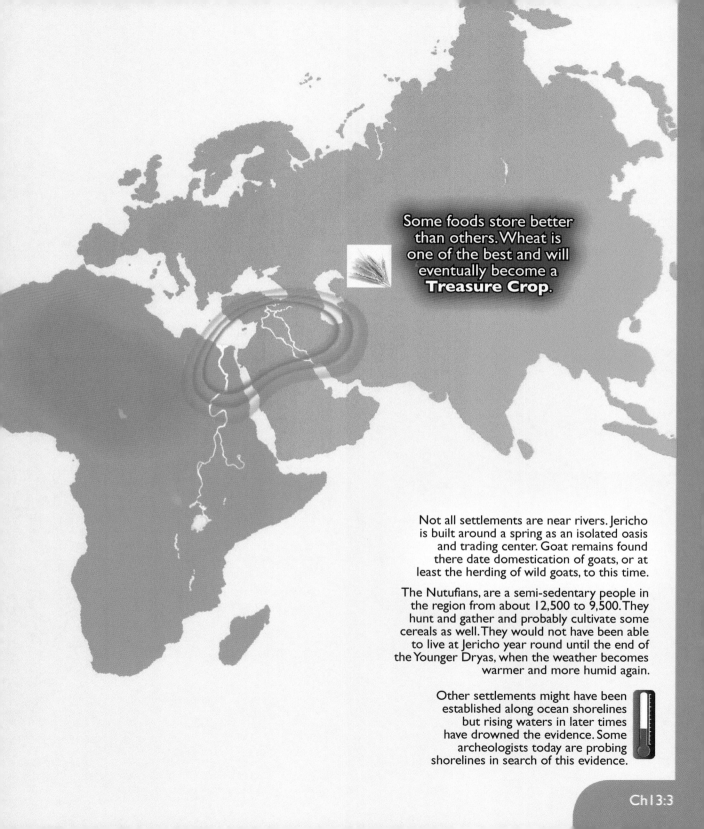

Some foods store better than others. Wheat is one of the best and will eventually become a **Treasure Crop**.

Not all settlements are near rivers. Jericho is built around a spring as an isolated oasis and trading center. Goat remains found there date domestication of goats, or at least the herding of wild goats, to this time.

The Nutufians, are a semi-sedentary people in the region from about 12,500 to 9,500. They hunt and gather and probably cultivate some cereals as well. They would not have been able to live at Jericho year round until the end of the Younger Dryas, when the weather becomes warmer and more humid again.

Other settlements might have been established along ocean shorelines but rising waters in later times have drowned the evidence. Some archeologists today are probing shorelines in search of this evidence.

The climate warms as the
Holocene Climatic Optimum begins.

The Holocene Climatic
Optimum is a warm period
between approximately 9,000
to 5,000 years ago.

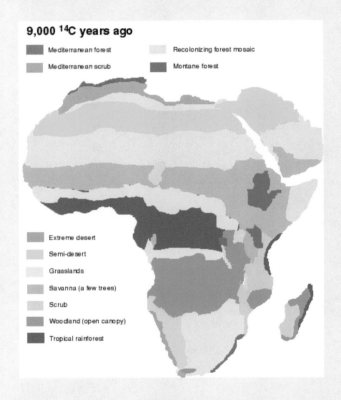

9,000 ^{14}C years ago

- Mediterranean forest
- Mediterranean scrub
- Recolonizing forest mosaic
- Montane forest

- Extreme desert
- Semi-desert
- Grasslands
- Savanna (a few trees)
- Scrub
- Woodland (open canopy)
- Tropical rainforest

7000
BCE

Millet and then rice are domesticated in China.

Millet is domesticated in China, around 7500 BCE. Some paleo-anthropologists think that rice cultivation also begins at the same time. Other scientists put the date for the domestication of rice a bit later.

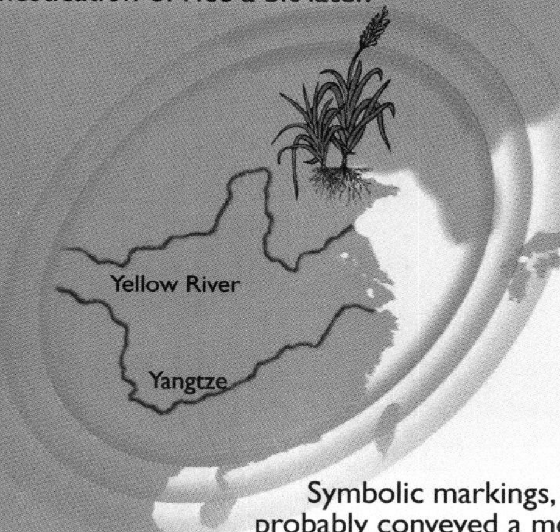

Yellow River

Yangtze

Symbolic markings, which probably conveyed a message but did not yet encode language, are carved into tortoise shells between 8,000 and 9,000 years ago in China. These may or may not be forerunners of oracle bone script.

People also play a rather modern looking flute.

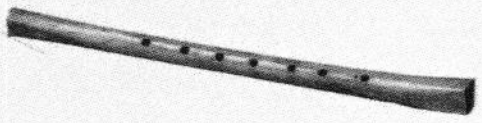

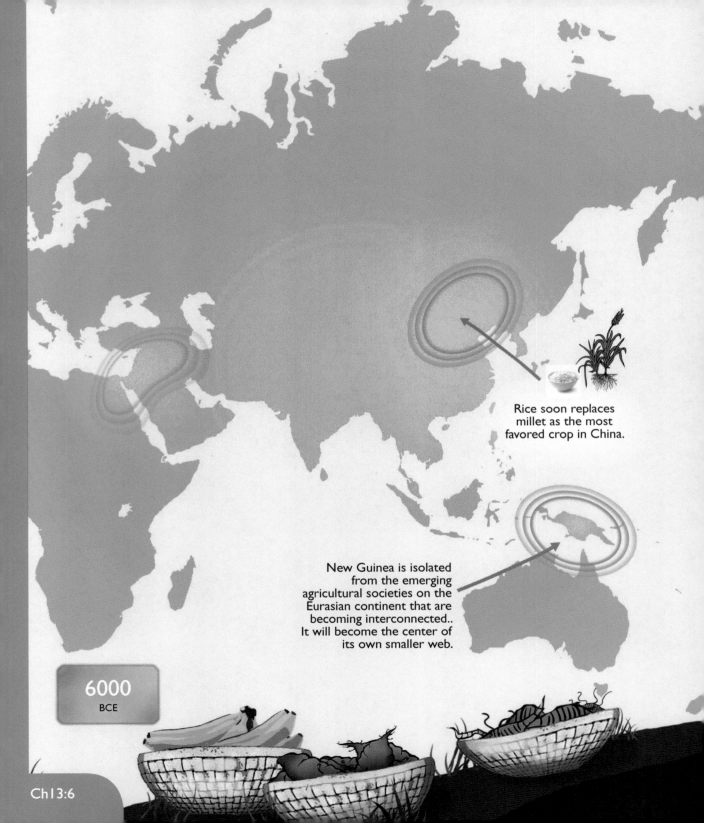

Rice soon replaces
millet as the most
favored crop in China.

New Guinea is isolated
from the emerging
agricultural societies on the
Eurasian continent that are
becoming interconnected..
It will become the center of
its own smaller web.

6000
BCE

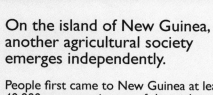

On the island of New Guinea, another agricultural society emerges independently.

People first came to New Guinea at least 40,000 years ago in one of the early waves of expansion out of Africa and they spoke a proto-Papuan language. Sea level had been low and New Guinea had been connected to Australia in a landmass that geologists call Sahul. As the ice age came to an end, and sea levels rose, New Guinea became an island. Not only was it separated from other landmasses, but regions within New Guinea were separated from each other by its mountainous terrain. Each separate region developed its own dialect that became increasingly distinct over time. With the passage of tens of thousands of years, the people of this isolated and fractured land, develop an unusually high number of dialects that are virtually separate languages.

The oldest known site for agriculture in New Guinea is the Kuk Swamp area. It is a wetland margin and is occupied by about 10,000 years ago although it is not clear if agriculture starts that early. There is unequivocal evidence for agriculture; the digging and staking of plants, mounding of soil and maybe drainage for the cultivation of taro, banana, yams and sago by 6,500 years ago.

On this island in the Pacific, people learn to gather sugar cane, bananas and some root crops which they begin to cultivate. These crops grow well but do not store well. People leave the fruits on the trees and the root crops in the ground until needed for consumption.

Taro

Yam

Banana

The geometry and orientation of continents
make some more amenable to the spread of
agriculture than others.

All across Eurasia seeds from the crops developed in one area can be planted
in the next region, and skills or methods to cultivate those crops can also
be easily transmitted. As humans journey across Eurasia they can stay at the
same latitude because the continent extends from east to west. The seeds
they carry with them will be exposed to the same amount of daylight in the
new land, which increases the likelihood of germination and growth.

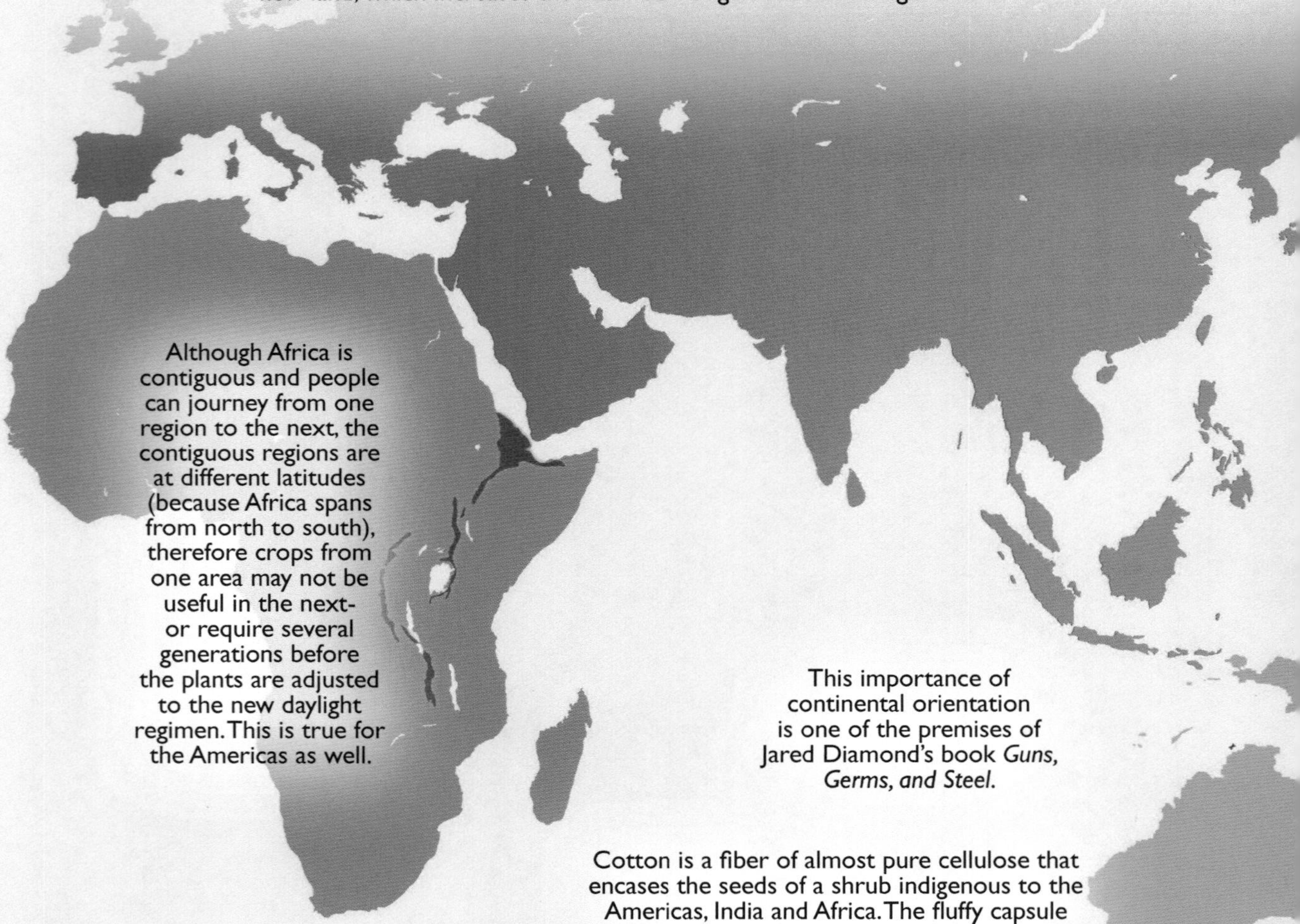

Although Africa is
contiguous and people
can journey from one
region to the next, the
contiguous regions are
at different latitudes
(because Africa spans
from north to south),
therefore crops from
one area may not be
useful in the next-
or require several
generations before
the plants are adjusted
to the new daylight
regimen. This is true for
the Americas as well.

This importance of
continental orientation
is one of the premises of
Jared Diamond's book *Guns,
Germs, and Steel*.

Cotton is a fiber of almost pure cellulose that
encases the seeds of a shrub indigenous to the
Americas, India and Africa. The fluffy capsule
gets caught in the wind helping the seeds
disperse. Fragments of cotton cloth from
5000 BCE have been found in Mexico and in
Indus Valley in what is now Pakistan.

5000
BCE

Agriculture originates independently in a few locations.

From these independent sites of origin, agriculture will be copied and adopted.

In California, oil seeping out of the ground forms hazardous pools which trap and preserve the remains of unsuspecting animals. Asphalt trails give way underneath large herbivores in the summertime heat and as they become mired in the thick, sticky oil, predators are attracted. These traps, known as The La Brea Tar Pits, preserve the skeletons and even some of the organic matter of these animals as exquisite fossils. The lower levels of the pits contain skeletons of mammoths, saber-toothed cats, dire wolves and other animals who lived in California during the ice age.

Although humans and wolves competed when hunting the same animals, hunting at the same time likely made the hunts more successful to the benefit of both species (presumably with the wolves finishing up after the humans had taken most of the carcass).

 Dogs are domesticated from the gray wolf in the Middle East, Asia and possibly in North America. Early theories of their domestication centered around the human adoption of orphaned pups. A more recent hypothesis is that dogs domesticated themselves; wolves with less fear of humans came closer to human encampments and ate from our garbage dumps.

Lightning is fascinating and scary. We notice that dogs are afraid too. We wonder about lightning but the dogs do not.

The grey wolf has completely supplanted the dire wolf which went extinct shortly after the ice age ended.

People in the Andes cultivate wild potatoes 5,000 to 8,000 years ago. The narrow strip of land between the sea and the Andes extends from north to south along the edge of the South American continent and is very productive. Although this strip is narrow, it contains many micro climates. Tomatoes (a cousin of the potato) are still in the wild, as of yet uncultivated.

Camps become villages as crops are cultivated. People make ever improved huts and tools which leads to the specialization of jobs. Hunting and gathering continues alongside agricultural development.

This is likely a time of relative peace, prosperity and egalitarianism. People who do not get along can move to the outskirts of the village, It is likely that people are still accustomed to sharing since they still do some hunting. Hunting societies usually share because cooperation is required to bring down large kills and the meat must be eaten soon or it will spoil. There is yet no ruling class to exact tribute. People eat a varied diet.

People have been keeping track of amounts using tokens which are kept in clay jars. Now they are starting to use tally marks drawn in wet clay which will lead to cuneiform.

The Sahara is still a green region. Ample evidence of this includes the archeological remains of numerous human encampments around (now dried up) lakes that include fish bones in their garbage dumps. But now the Sahara is again slowly becoming arid as the 'African Humid Period' ends. This time period is still within the Holocene Climatic Optimum when the climate was most favorable.

More animals are domesticated as people settle in villages.

Animals are no longer used just for meat, milk, wool, sinew and other by products. They are beginning to be harnessed up and used for their muscle power. Cattle are proving to significantly enhance village life by proving a large quantity of milk- and their strength is almost unbelievable, although they are first used only to drag the occasional heavy load.

Most domesticated animals are naturally social and their wild counterparts lived in social groups. In a social group, some animals lead and some follow. When humans capture and control a lead animal, other in the flock will follow. Humans effectively become the leader but the herd must already have the natural tendency to respond this way.

Domestication of animals works by what Darwin called "Artificial Selection." In the wild where nature is the selector, well adapted animals are more likely to live long enough to reproduce while the less fit animals die young. People select for qualities like tameness and help animals with those traits to survive and bear young. Domesticated animals have less choice in picking their mates as humans try to get 'desirable' animals to mate with other animals of the humans choosing.

Domesticated animals begin to change in unexpected ways as well. For example, dogs that were selected for tameness also have floppier ears and shorter snouts. This is because genes often influence more than one aspect of behavior or anatomy.

People may be imagining riding some of the wild animals they see but if so, they ride them only in their dreams.

Livestock complement agriculture. They can feed on leftover stubble in already harvested fields and fertilize these fields as they graze.

The Fertile Crescent has a large number of animals that can potentially be domesticated including dogs, sheep, goats, cattle, donkeys and pigs. Asia also has pigs, cattle and horses. There are no large domestics in New Guinea and few in Africa or the Americas.

Dogs are put to use in North America, and llamas are domesticated in South America. Africans attempt to domesticate zebras, but because large socially organized mammals in Africa contend with lions, they are too flighty, nervous and defensive to be domesticated. Elephants take too long to mature (about 15 years) to be practical.

4000
BCE

An abrupt change in the climate forces people to migrate into river valleys as previously lush areas become desert.

The Sahara rapidly becomes a desert in just two hundred years.

The causes of this event, named for its start date and called the 5.9 Kiloyear Event, are debated. There is a possibility that it had to do with a quasi periodic cooling event of the North Atlantic failing to make a normal recovery and its effect on the weather. There is also a chance that it actually had to do with human agricultural activities.

The fertile valleys of the Tigris and the Euphrates, the Nile, the Indus, the Yellow and the Yangtze are all corridors of civilization, linear layouts of crops, humans and their associated livestock. Each corridor functions as an entity, like a super organism with its own ecosystem, its own microbes and diseases.

Writing becomes ever more sophisticated as rulers learn to keep better track of goods, debts and taxes.

Cuneiform script evolves.

Some of the earliest writing is cuneiform, a tally mark script. It is developed by the Sumerians who use symbols to record business transactions such as the acquisition of grain or livestock. Writing in the form of business transactions establishes civilization. These symbols evolve over time into a somewhat phonetic alphabet. Stories and other cultural concepts, which were already being expressed in paintings, on rock walls and other venues, are also expressed.

History has been defined by academics as the record of events after the advent of writing. However in pre-historic times, people have a sense of what came before from oral traditions and the presence of monuments or debris left by their ancestors. The old formal definition is no longer always adhered to; for instance scientists even use the term 'geologic history' when discussing previous tectonic events.

Agricultural societies become agricultural civilizations as large numbers of migrants are absorbed into burgeoning cities.

Grain must be stored and guarded against mice, insects, heat, moisture and theft.

Spring floods brings fresh nutrients to the soil. People rely on the river and try to predict its behavior. A priest class emerges whose learned members study calendars to predict the flood. They also collect shares or offerings from their constituents and hoard this grain to dispense it for seed for the spring planting or extra food in times of hardship and for their own luxury.

The first granaries are simple stone cellars that provide safe storage from pests and weather. But they become more elaborate and an added floor gives them a pyramidal shape. They are fortified, enlarged, and guarded by a new warrior class. Scribes and bureaucrats are employed to keep track of the goods and the people, the majority of whom work in agriculture.

3700
BCE

The invention of the wheel is probably by potters who use it like a lazy-susan.

The invention of the wheel comes late to humanity's tool chest. First, we invent boats, baskets, the sewing needle, woven cloth, rope and even the flute before figuring out the wheel. The wheel represents a leap in imagination as there are few analogs in nature for humans to draw upon.

A potters wheel dating back to 3,500 BCE is depicted on clay tablets in the ancient Mesopotamian city of Ur.

The Bronze Age begins.

Metal tools soon supplant stone as humans learn to smelt copper and alloy it with tin. The earliest working of bronze was around 3300 BCE in Sumer, in modern day Iraq.

Wheeled carts evolve from a series of improvements to sledges placed on rollers.

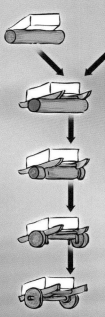

The invention of the wheel could have proceeded in a step wise fashion. Loads are carried by putting them on runners (this is called a sledge) or by putting a roller underneath. In the next step both are combined as a sledge is placed on a roller. With use the sledge cuts a groove in the roller. The groove helps keep the sledge from slipping off. People notice that the deeper the grooves the easier it is to push the load, like shifting down a gear. Soon the inner part of the roller is hewn away at the start. Finally, the wheels and axel are made as a separate pieces and assembled with bushings or pins Four wheeled carts follow soon after.

Complex agricultural societies evolve along rivers. These are sometimes referred to as **Hydraulic Civilizations.**

Due to irrigation, a wide bank along the river is a green zone in a now arid land. The river can be fished in and used as a highway with boats. The Nile is especially good as the current flows northward while the wind blows to the south allowing easy movement in either direction.

Horses are domesticated and harnessed.

Wild horses had long been hunted; they are depicted in 30,000 year old cave paintings along with other animals of the chase, and piles of their bones have been found near ancient encampments.

It is likely that horses are domesticated at a several different times and locations in Eurasia based on their genetic diversity. In contrast, there is less genetic diversity in sheep or in goats which suggests that these were domesticated from a much smaller number of animals.

Horses may have been ridden by people of the Botai culture of Kazakhstan as early as 3,500 BCE. The Botai had neither cattle nor sheep and might have ridden horses in order to hunt. According to A.K. Outram's 2009 report in the journal Science, three separate lines of evidence support early domestication by the Botai. Marks on horse teeth show sign of wear presumably from bits or harnesses. Clay pots contain residues of fats that likely came from mare's milk. Horse bones found in Botai sites were more slender and less robust than their wild counterparts, although these horses were still much stockier than modern horses.

This image is actually from 2500 BCE but wheeled vehicles were in existence by 3200.

Buffalo are domesticated in near-tropical regions of Asia. They are highly valued in the Indus River (or Harappan) Civilization, 3300-1300 BCE, which is still in its early phase. The Indus River will soon become the seat of one of the greatest of the hydraulic civilizations with an emphasis on accessibility, clean water and hygiene. Buffalo will decorate its official seals.

The Nile River Valley Civilization is prosperous.

Bureaucracy is created to extend the power of rulers, who cannot be everywhere at once. Bureaucrats must be recognizable as genuine agents of the state in order to wield power in remote locations. Egyptian couriers who carry the messages and decrees of the Pharaoh wear elaborate or recognizable dress and carry state seals.

The power and wealth of Egypt's early pharaohs is demonstrated by the elaborate *mastaba* tombs they build for themselves. They justify their rule by claiming a connection to the divine, and exploit the fruits of society's labor to secure their power- and to glorify themselves and bid at immortality with the Gods.

Egypt was built on the banks of the annually flooding Nile River (each Spring's flood brought a fresh, nutrient rich layer of soil). Every year the government would resurvey and reestablish property lines. Teams used three ropes whose lengths were in the ratio 3 /4 /5 and measured off right triangles to aid the survey, which sufficed to do the job- although they did not understand the Pythagorean Theorem.

Egypt is one of the most prosperous and most stable of the new **Hydraulic Civilizations**. The Tigris and Euphrates corridors are the earliest but only last for several hundreds of years, due to salt build up in the soil from irrigation. Irrigation of the Nile was different. The Nile flooded annually and the flood brought fresh sediment and plenty of water. The water was held back by dikes for later release. The Nile could be navigated in either direction; boats could drift downstream and then be sailed upstream, since the prevailing wind is from the North.

With writing, bureaucracy and the increased division of labor, administration of large-scale projects becomes possible, which leads to more class distinctions and inequalities.

Cities merge into larger empires as populations continue to expand and administration becomes ever more sophisticated.

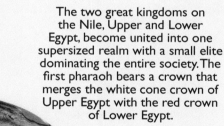

The two great kingdoms on the Nile, Upper and Lower Egypt, become united into one supersized realm with a small elite dominating the entire society. The first pharaoh bears a crown that merges the white cone crown of Upper Egypt with the red crown of Lower Egypt.

Egyptian hieroglyphics

Although Egyptians did not fully understand geometry, they created simple 'rules of thumb', crude approximations of geometric relations to construct their great buildings. If it didn't come out perfectly, they just added or removed a few stones to make it fit.

#

 The pharaohs will keep their hold on power and build ever more elaborate tombs and statues such as the Great Sphinx and the Great Pyramids of Giza which are built around 2550 BCE

2000
BCE

The pyramid is an apt symbol for social stratification.

An elite form the utmost tier of society and are supported by a more numerous but still privilege echelon of priests, managers, bureaucrats, generals and accountants. Most of society fills the much larger bottom tier. Wealth is funneled up from the expansive bottom tier by the administrative middle tier.

People try to psychologically adapt to life under civilization and create new myths and stories.

Earlier religions had been chiefly concerned with food safety and fertility. The change in focus might be due to the increasing inequality between people and urbanization. Since the transition from early agricultural societies into agricultural empires with their tribute taking elites, inequality and injustice are realities that most people must adjust to. Life in cities brings new psychological challenges; there are always some people who are sick or dying and the reality of the human condition cannot be ignored. In cities people do not know and recognize everyone they pass which might also cause stress and bring a sense of anonymity. The idea of humanity as an entity becomes more evident and causes humans to speculate.

The story of Gilgamesh addresses the tensions between farmers and pastoralists, between urban and rural people and issues of identity. By around 2150 BCE, snippets of some poems about civilized Gilgamesh and his wild brother, Enkidu, are written down in cuneiform and end up preserved in the historical record.

The story of Gilgamesh is still popular and the whole epic is transcribed in cuneiform. Many of these clay tablets survive in the historical record.

The Indus River Civilization migrates.

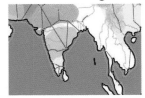

In India and what is now Pakistan, the civilizations that had sprung up along the Indus River are abandoned and people move to the valley of the Ganges River, between 1,800 and 1,700 BCE. Overuse, salinization or climate change are all probable causes.

Codes and philosophies about proper human behavior become formalized.

Hammurabi's Code engraved on a stile, a standing rock.

1750 BCE

An eye for an eye and a tooth for a tooth seems draconian today but it was an improvement over unbridled vengeance. It demanded proportionality as retribution could not be greater than the original crime.

Laws and punishment for crimes were not uniform across the classes. The wealthy and upper classes received less harsh punishments and had to adhere to a different set of laws than the poor and lower classes. However, the weak were provided some protection against the tyranny of the strong.

For example: "anyone caught stealing livestock that belongs to the court or God is required to repay thirty times the amount stolen. If the property stolen belonged to a freed man of the king, the penalty is ten times the amount. If the thief has nothing with which to pay, death is the punishment."

Hammurabi's code is perhaps the most well known code. The slightly older code of Ur-Nammu is the oldest surviving law document and relies more on fines than physical punishment.

A positional numbering system allows for multiplication.

The Babylonians invent a number system that uses 60 as the base. The modern system that we use today is also positional but uses a base of 10. Our base 10 system has a one's place, a ten's place, a hundred's place etc. and units in each place or column have a value 10 times greater than those in the previous column. In the Babylonian system, the first column has room for 60 items (not our usual 10) and the next column also has room for 60 units so it has a one's place, a sixty's place and a 3600's place and units in each column are worth 60 times more than those in the previous. Relics of this system survive; we have 60 seconds in minute and 60 minutes in an hour and we calculate degrees of latitude and longitude by dividing up the sphere of the earth into 360 degrees. The Babylonians also make astronomical observations and a calendar.

The Austronesians sail forth.

 On the island of Taiwan, the fishing and farming Austronesian people feel the pressure of population growth. They begin a string of migrations- to the Philippines, the islands of the Celebes, Borneo and Indonesia. On some islands they are the first inhabitants; in other places they mix with local populations. Distinct dialects of Austronesian develop.

In China, a new idea, *The Mandate of Heaven*, emerges and proclaims that rulers cannot rule on might alone, but must rule justly.

 The Mandate of Heaven is used by the Zhou Dynasty to justify their overthrow of the Shang Dynasty, 1046 BCE. The Shang had claimed to be direct descendents of deities and used their self-proclaimed divine status to justify their rule. The Duke of Zhou explains that because of the unjust actions of the Shang king, heaven has withdrawn his right to rule.

The idea of The Mandate of Heaven will endure in Chinese political philosophy. It will grant the right to rebel against injustice - providing a rebellion is actually successful.

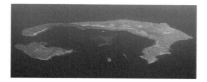

The Santorini Volcano explodes.

Around 1550 BCE, a volcano off the Greek Peninsula explodes in an eruption about 4 times larger than Krakatoa. It sets off a giant tsunami that destroys the Minoan Empire and inspires the legend of Atlantis. Today the remnants of the volcano form a circular island atoll.

The *Rigveda* sings praise to deities and describes early Vedic Hindu cosmology.

The *Rigveda* is one of earliest intact texts of any Indo-European language, written in Sanskrit. Organized into ten books (or Mandalas), it contains 1,028 hymns (or *sukta*) made of 10,600 verses. Its continued use in Hindu religious ceremonies and rites of passages makes the *Rigveda* perhaps the world's oldest religious text in continual use.

By around 1300 BCE, Chinese Oracles are using characters that are still recognizable today, making Chinese the oldest continuously used system of writing in the world.

The Spring and Autumn Annals are transcribed.

The official chronicle of events from 722 to 481 BCE in the State of Lu, the annals are a concise year by year record of events without the inclusion of explanations or speeches. They include the births and deaths of prominent individuals, natural disasters and astronomical phenomena. They will later be attributed to Confucius and be included as one of the Five Classics of China. Shown here is a portion of a replica.

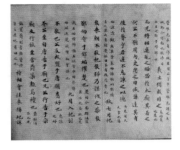

Life might have emerged from nature and not by some supernatural power.

An early Greek, Thales of Miletus, philosophizes that water is an essential substance and that life emerged by spontaneous generation from natural materials, not from a supernatural source.

Distances can be calculated from shadows.

The well-traveled polymath, Thales, (625-547 BCE); calculates distances, including the height of the Pyramids of Giza by using trigonometry and measuring the length of shadows. He also uses a similar technique to calculate the distance from the shore to ships at sea.

Cyrus unites Persia and rules with tolerance and compassion.

The codes of Cyrus the Great are transcribed in cuneiform on a cylinder that can be rolled over wet clay leaving new copies of his edicts which are the world's first 'Bill of Rights'.

Cyrus allows the peoples he conquers to worship the gods they choose. He outlaws slavery, and helps the Jews, enslaved in Babylon to return to Jerusalem.

The Hebrews write about Cyrus in the Torah, the Old Testament. They refer to him as a Messiah (Isaiah 45:1).

Although Cyrus is a conqueror, he stands up for peacefulness in a region that had grown accustomed to wanton violence. He is not just a shrewd tactician but a manager as well and his policies benefit his subjects.

Cyrus The Great
Reigns 560-530 BCE

Sun Tzu writes a classic Chinese text on military strategy and tactics during the chaotic warring states period. It is also an early codification of game theory. He takes into account human psychology. One of his tactics is to recommend never completely encircling an enemy but instead to leave them 'golden bridges' to retreat on because if soldiers can see a route to retreat on they are more likely to lack valor and cut and run.

Buddhism gets its start in Nepal and India.

Buddhism is the only major religion that will not be spread through military force.

The Buddha renounces his kingdom and searches for enlightenment. He finds it through peace, moderation, gratitude and fulfillment, not in the hard asceticism that is common among other seekers. Buddhism answers the troubling problem of caste and reincarnation. The caste system had already been in existence for centuries. People are born into their caste status and cannot advance out, not even by marriage. Belief in reincarnation mitigates this problem by promising that acceptance of one's status and other good conduct will result in being reborn into a higher caste in the next life. The Buddha undermines this system by claiming that a person of any caste can become 'enlightened' in this life and thus put a stop to the endless cycle of reincarnation.

The Buddha, Siddhartha Gautama, is born in Nepal about 563 BCE and lives until about 485 BCE. He is born as a prince, at least according to legend, and to a life of privilege. His father sees to it that he is completely sheltered; he sees no poverty, disease or other suffering. Siddhartha already has what most people yearn to acquire when he leaves his wife, young son and all the pleasures of the palace to see what the world is really about. On his path to enlightenment, he turns away from the severe asceticism that predominates religious seekers of the time. He finds a 'middle way'; a path stressing peace, moderation and the freeing of oneself from attachment (the grabbing and grasping for money, food, prestige or even holding on too tightly to the memories of those we love).

550 BCE

In China, two new and very different religions emerge.

Taoism is a philosophy embracing the fluidity and chaos of the natural world.

The way to harmony, as described by Lao Tse, is through wu-wei, which is explained as action through non-action; meaning, 'go with the flow.' Naturalness, simplicity, and spontaneity are virtues and the Three Treasures are compassion, moderation, and humility.

Confucius espouses the principle, "What you do not wish for yourself, do not do to others".

This principal of reciprocity, is also known as the 'Silver Rule'.

Confucius proclaims that knowledge, virtue, and keeping one's place in the human hierarchy are the keys to harmony.

Society is a web of unequal human relationships -not a collection of autonomous individuals, according to Confucius; the key to harmony is for everyone to accept their place within the hierarchy and act accordingly. Beginning with the family unit, with the relationships of parent/child, husband/wife, order must be established. Government can then be similarly modeled by extension. Although power must be respected, the powerful are not without obligation and leaders should lead by good example and not rule just by threat of punishment.

The concept of 'lin' is that there should be a two way flow of responsibility, a requirement of reciprocity; those who faithfully submit to the 'natural order' must be respected and treated appropriately.

Democracy is instituted in the Greek city state of Athens.

Democracy makes Athens strong.

Democracy begins in 501 BCE when Cleisthenes, an aristocrat, makes the unusual move of enlisting the help of poor people to overthrow the other aristocratic rulers. He promises to give them a voice in government.

A decade later, when the Persians invade, Athens and the other Greek city states resist and their success is largely due to the leadership role that Athens plays. Athens becomes the head of the defensive alliance that the Greek city states form to repel any future invasion attempts.

The democracy evolving in Athens values more than freedom- it fosters intellectual curiosity and mechanisms such as moderation and oratory to facilitate the transmission of ideas. In the Battle of Marathon of 490 BCE, Athens plays a leadership role in keeping Greece independent against the Persian king Darius. Athens does it again in 480 when his son, Xerxes returns with an even larger force.

Perhaps it is because Athens is democratic that her men, who had a stake in their society, fight so bravely. Perhaps it is because of democracy that a brilliant battle plan is devised; Athens is to be evacuated and the Persian fleet with its large ships is to be lured into the narrow Straits of Salamis. Together the Athenians abandon their city and from a distant encampment watch the blaze of their houses and temples burning. They will later rebuild after destroying the Persian fleet.

The Athenians appreciate mathematics for its beauty. They explore beautiful patterns and proportions occurring in nature.

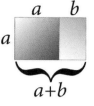

$$\frac{a+b}{a} = \frac{a}{b} = \varphi$$

The Golden Ratio is discovered. This proportion of height to width is pleasing and resonates in the human mind. It becomes the standard proportion used in architecture, for instance in choosing the shapes and placement of windows and doors in designing the facades of buildings. The ratio is commonly found in nature- like by the ratio of the size of a tree limb to its sub branches.

Ideas about science, philosophy and culture flourish.

Philosophers continue to wrestle with the nature of matter and the origin of life.

Empedocles defines the essential substances to be earth, fire, air, and water. The later scholar, He looks for mechanistic causes and principles to define and describe natural phenomena and posits that life arose spontaneously from atoms of earth under the influence of fire.

Atoms are very small particles.

Democritus writes about the existence of atoms - very small particles that join together in different combinations to make different materials. Born around 470 BCE in the northern part of the Greek world in the city state of Abdera in Thrace, he inherits his father's fortune and uses the money to travel to Egypt and parts of Asia. He is one of the most well traveled people of his day. He is able to afford books and to meet other scholars. His cheerful disposition and ability to laugh at the foibles of humans earns him the moniker of the 'Laughing Philosopher'.

Atoms have different characteristics according to Democritus. Iron atoms are hard and have some kind of mechanical attachment points like hooks and eyes that allow them to form solid blocks while water atoms are smooth and slippery. Salt atoms are sharp, which accounts for their prickly taste. Empty space within and between atoms allow them to flow as liquids.

Although hampered by their non-positional numbering system, the Greeks excel in math, especially geometry. The limitation of the number system (more like Roman numerals than the Arabic numerals we use today) pushes them to explore the logic behind the relationships of shapes and to discover such things as the Pythagorean Theorem $a^2+b^2=c^2$ which describes the ratios of the lengths of the sides of a right triangle. Pythagoras (570-495BCE) is from the Greek city state Ionia and he also contributes to philosophy.

In China, **legalism** arises and flourishes in the Warring States Period as a method of governing.

Rules are devised and applied even-handedly, without exception, even in exceptional situations. Legalism is an iron fisted method, but it promises to provide some stability, even during times when the hereditary ruler is a weak leader.

The Warring States Period is a 225 year-long period of chaotic military competition between several small kingdoms in China.

Arrogance and greed lead Athens into folly.

As the head of the defensive coalition formed to protect the Greek city states from Persia, Athens takes possession of the war chest and organizes the building of a great navy. Each of the city states contributes to the fund.

As Athens prospers, the Parthenon and other great buildings are built and adorned with statues and sculptures.

Scholars from all the other city states study in Athenian schools.

The arts of drama, music, philosophy, mathematics, and science flourish. Ships ply the azure blue waters of the Aegean Sea with goods bound for the busy port of Athens. The whole of the Aegean becomes one great Athenian empire.

The Athenians are building their monuments with some of the monies levied on their allies for common defense against Persia. Although some Athenians are uneasy about this re-appropriation, others point out that it was Athens that had been razed in the war, and none can deny the magnificence of the buildings. Any cities that refuse to pay are forced to. Some of the prosperity of Athens comes from another source; silver in the nearby hills is mined by slaves under the watchful eye of Athenian guards.

Athens prepares to make war on those city states who have tired of paying tribute to Athens. The Peloponnesian War begins.

Although many citizens object to fighting a non-defensive war, Pericles, the leader who had pushed for and administrated the building of the Parthenon and many other monuments and who is a great patron of the arts, beats the drums of war and appeals to Athenian vanity until successful.

The Athenian war plan is to rely on the navy to bring in food and supplies and not to try to defend the farmlands surrounding Athens. A new fortification wall is built that extends all the way to the harbor. The people living in the adjacent farm lands move behind the city walls.

400 BCE

The war takes an unexpected turn as disease strikes.

This Peloponnesian war, 431-404 BCE is against Sparta, Corinth, Thebes and some smaller city states such as Stagira. The war goes well enough for Athens, until an Athenian supply ships unloads some germs along with its regular cargo. The citizens of Athens, packed in behind the fortified walls, quickly fall victim to disease. The war grinds on a bit longer as the bodies of the dead accumulate in the streets of Athens, until eventually, there is nothing to do but surrender.

Surrender marks the end of the Classical Period for Athens.

Both of the legitimate sons of Pericles, Paralus and Xanthippus, die in the epidemic which kills a third of the Athenian population. A change in the laws of citizenship is then made to allow Pericles the younger, the son he fathered with his beloved mistress, to be declared a citizen and heir, although Pericles himself had proposed the original law which had restricted citizenship to those with two Athenian parents.

After Athens surrenders, Sparta dominates the Greek city states.

Other Greek city states soon band together and cut Sparta's hegemony short and Athens is able to once again be democratic and independent. Although Athens no longer enjoys great wealth, new generations of Athenian scholars continue the heritage of cultivating science and art.

Herodotus gives history an investigative style.

Often called 'the father of history', Herodotus (484-425 BCE), breaks from the Homeric tradition by treating historical subjects critically and systematically.

Science and technology suffer from snobbishness.

Wealthy, educated Athenians look down on those who must work, and therefore have little incentive to create useful, labor saving machines. For example, a steam engine is created where a piston moves in a cylinder driven by expanding steam- but this is just a parlor trick, it is powered by a candle and the moving piston cracks a walnut for the party guests.

Homing pigeons are used for communications.

Homing pigeons are used to announce the winner of the Olympics.

Scholars succeed each other.

Socrates espoused that humans have a soul separate from our body. He leaves no written work himself but his student Plato later writes about him. Plato founds his own school of philosophy called the Academy. Aristotle, 384-322 BCE, will become a pupil of The Academy.

Socrates had engaged in discussions about morality and ethics that annoyed many Athenians and he is brought to trail and executed in 399 BCE.

Aristotle contests previous ideas about atoms, preferring the notion that there are four fundamental substances: earth, air, fire and water. Aristotle does embrace the idea that life arose from natural processes, but he adds the idea of vitalism - that there is some vital essence of life, a life force that is not a property of matter.

Aristotle considers Earth to be the center of the Universe.

He explains why objects tend to fall to the ground by declaring that rest is the natural state of things. Projectiles always slow down and fall to Earth because they only flew due to the violent action imparted by the thrower and when this fades, they naturally come to rest.. They fall to Earth because Earth is the center of the Universe and everything moves naturally to this center. This erroneous paradigm will reign until it is overturned by the physics postulated by Isaac Newton. Aristotle makes so many achievements in astronomy, history, biology, philosophy and methods of science that his endorsement of this error will make it hard to overturn. Another error of Aristotle's concerns comets which he considers to be atmospheric disturbances. Aristotle divides the universe into two realms; the earthly and the celestial. Since comets are erratic, he concludes that they cannot belong to the heavenly realm.

King Phillip of Macedonia conquers Athens and makes a deal with Aristotle to tutor his son, Alexander, a reluctant pupil more interested in riding horses.

Phillip offers to rebuild Aristotle's hometown of Stagira which he had destroyed and to free its now enslaved inhabitants, if Aristotle will tutor his son.

After inheriting the throne in 336 BCE, Alexander takes the army to Persia where he defeats Darius III. He rides on to Egypt and is crowned pharaoh, then back through Persia and on to India.

Alexander The Great does not follow Aristotle's advice to be "a leader to the Greeks and a despot to the barbarians, to look after the former as after friends and relatives, and to deal with the latter as with beasts or plants". Instead, Alexander tries to unite the cultures by encouraging his men to take foreign wives and incorporating the officers of defeated armies into his own.

Erastothenes proves that the world is round.

In 240 BCE, Erastothenes who studies in Alexandria Egypt, uses logic and observation by applying the laws of geometry to measurements of shadows cast by the sun in different places at the same time to show that the Earth is a sphere and he estimates its circumference.

300
BCE

In India, Ashoka Maurya seeks to expand his empire. Presiding over an army of many tens of thousands, he successfully invades the lands of Kalinga to the south.

So great is his bravery and skill, he is said to have once hunted and killed a lion with only a wooden rod.

Ashoka's conquest of Kalinga results in the deaths of 100,000 people and the deportations of an even greater number of civilians.

After his decisive victory, Ashoka joyfully tours the battle grounds but when he sees the corpses, piled high and scattered all around the burned out houses, he is overwhelmed with sorrow and remorse.

"If this is victory," he famously asks, "what then is defeat?"

Ashoka becomes a devout Buddhist and uses his position to preach and nurture the still relatively new religion.

Ashoka seems not to be quite able to completely live up to his newly adopted beliefs and is said by some to have executed members of a Jainist sect for denigrating the Buddha.

Ashoka replaces the notion of divine kingship with the model of 'Buddhist kingship' in which kings are to earn the approval of Buddhist priests, establish monasteries and help to resolve disputes peacefully.

China is unified.

The establishment of the Qin Dynasty in 221 BCE finally brings The Warring States period to an end and unifies the multi-ethnic region into a single empire. The king of Qin renames himself Shi-Huang Di, meaning the first emperor. He standardizes weights and measures and the system of writing.

A comet is recorded.

Comets are dirty snowballs of rock and ice that are dislodged from their orbits far out in the solar system and fall toward the sun. Some comets fall into the sun but many establish a new, highly eccentric orbit and will periodically travel by. Halley's comet, has a 75 year periodicity and is recorded by a Chinese historian in 240 BCE.

The Terracota Army is interred.

This collection of life-size figures and horses is buried with the first Emperor of China to protect his soul in the afterlife. It is not mentioned in any texts or records of the time, so the discovery of the Army, unearthed by farmers in 1974, will take the world by surprise.

Networks of roads and shipping routes are built as power is consolidated and long distance trade is established.

The Romans unite all the shores of the Mediterranean into one empire.

The Romans excel in administration and allow people to worship their own gods as long as they pay their taxes. But there is no satisfying Roman religion, code of behavior or uniting philosophy. Many religious ideas, old and new, compete to fill this void.

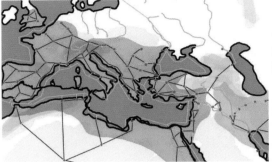

The Roman navy could be brought to bear on any rebellious province near the coast.

The regions around the Mediterranean share a similar climate, which means that agricultural methods that work in one area of the Roman Empire work in another area.

In Rome, a postal service is established as is a newsletter that records legal proceedings, significant births or deaths and other events. News is also carved on stone or metal and presented in public places.

An eruption rocks the island of Sicily.

Mt. Etna on the Mediterranean island of Sicily is the legendary prison of Typhon, the most formidable monster in Greek mythology. It discharges a plinian eruption in 122 BCE. To mitigate the extensive damages to the town of Catania and the surrounding area southeast of the volcano, the Roman government exempts the affected population from paying taxes for a decade.

The manufacture of glass is refined by the Romans who experiment with shaping it and discover that if a piece of glass is thicker in the center and tapers to the edges it makes and object viewed through it appear larger.

Not only trade goods and soldiers move along Roman roads; new ideas are also afoot. Christianity emerges.

Judaism, like many religions, foretells of the coming of a messiah to rescue them from their enemies. Some Jews believe that following the multitude of rules outlined in the Torah will his arrival. But for other Jews, the belief that God will send a prophet to smite their enemies, if they will only become more obedient, has worn thin as the Roman Empire has continued its interminable reign. Christianity changes the problem and offers a new solution; believing in Christ will save a person, not from the Romans but from death. The new messiah will not be a mighty military leader, instead the 'lamb of God' will show the way to an afterlife in heaven, far removed from the injustices of this mundane world.

Judaism is admired by many non-Jews who refer to them as the *People of the Book* but Judaism offers no conversion path and proclaims that the Jews are the chosen people of God based on heredity. Christianity opens a door by declaring that a person must believe and by this act they will be admitted into the new church.

Jesus and the money changers.

The numerous rules set out in the Torah or proscribed by Rabbis govern everything- from what to eat and when to eat it, which dishes to use and how to wash etc. Some say rules increase spirituality by turning the most trivial tasks into acts of religious significance but Jews like Jesus think that an emphasis on rules reduces religion to a formulaic, legalistic method lacking in spirituality. Many rules also proscribe ritual offerings that are payments to the religious establishment. Many Jewish leaders also personally benefit from their role as intermediaries to the Romans (Judea had been conquered by the Romans and made a Roman Province). These factors lead Jesus to accuse the Jewish leadership of coveting money and power and being too caught up in worldly affairs.

United under the Han dynasty, China flourishes.

The Han come to power 206 BCE. They base their government on Confucian principles and rule for a period of 426 years. Great advances in technology are made, and the Silk road is established as a trade route. Although the Silk Road is not yet the thoroughfare that it will become in later centuries and is only passable by intrepid travelers, goods and ideas do move across it.

Paper quality is improved by adding materials like hemp, bark and silk to the paper making process. The world's first seismograph is invented by the polymath, Zhang Heng. It allows the approximate direction to and magnitude of earthquakes to be estimated. Zhang also writes epic poems that record terrains and resources of cities within the realm. He is also known for his prowess in mathematics and is made the imperial astronomer.

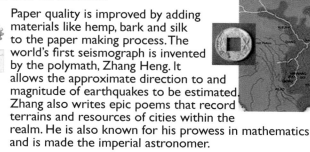

Pliny the Elder authors the model for the encyclopedia.

Naturalis Historia, is one of the single most expansive written works that has survived from the Roman Empire. Gaius Plinius Secundus -popularly known as Pliny the Elder- organized the work into ten volumes expounding on subjects from astronomy and anthropology to sculpture and pharmacology. Particularly due to the manner in which Pliny indexed its content and referenced works' initial authors, *Naturalis Historia* will provide an archetype for encyclopedias and reference materials hereforth. Pliny the Elder suffered from asthma and died on the beach fleeing the 79 CE eruption of **Mount Vesuvius**.

Vietnam reestablishes independence.

Vietnam has been a vassal state, paying tribute to China since the expansion of the Han Empire in 111 BCE. Two women, the Trung sisters, lead an uprising, consisting mostly of women. They are overwhelmingly successful but their rule is short-lived, only three years, until Vietnam is recolonized by the Han in 43 CE. Some scholars wonder if this suggests that Vietnam was matriarchal before being subdued by the Han. Although their rule is brief, they continue to inspire.

Pliny the Younger describes his uncle's death.

A polymath of public and civil offices, Pliny the Younger was the nephew of his older namesake, who was present for his upbringing and education. Pliny the Younger is perhaps most famous for the collections of his letters or *Epistulae*, many of which survive today. In two letters to his friend, the historian Tacitus, Pliny describes the eruption of Mount Vesuvius, and his uncle's resulting death. Pliny the Younger described the events surrounding the eruption in such careful portrayal that his is perhaps the oldest and most detailed account of a volcanic eruption. As a result, vulcanologists refer to similar eruptions as **Plinian**.

Around 200 CE, sky lanterns are made in China. They are small hot air balloons which are made of paper, open at the bottom with a small candle or fire suspended are used as military signaling devices. Today they are used in festivals.

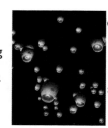

Christianity challenges class structures of the reigning social hierarchy.

That Jesus is a carpenter and not a member of the elite further drives home the message that salvation is for anyone and the idea that all people are equal in the eyes of God is a welcome respite from the rigid social class system of the Romans.

Christianity emphasizes compassion and a non-violent method of conflict resolution; turn the other cheek and think of your own sins before you judge others.

The Jewish holy book, The Torah is called 'The Old Testament' by Christians who will, over the next several decades, add an additional volume called 'The New Testament' which packaged together they call 'The Bible'.

Austronesians sail across the Bay of Bengal to Sri Lanka.

Equivalent to

0 BCE

2,000 Years Ago

Christianity becomes the dominant religion of Rome during the rule of Emperor Constantine.

The adoption of Christianity, in 313 CE, is sometimes called The Triumph of the Church, the Peace of the Church, or the Constantinian shift.

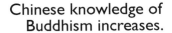

The invention of stirrups improves the utility of horseback riding. Among the oldest evidence for this invention are a pair of primitive stirrups from a Jin Dynasty tomb, dated 322 CE.

Constantine orders the Church of the Holy Sepulchre be built on the spot where Jesus had been crucified.

Chinese knowledge of Buddhism increases.

Disobeying the Emperor, a monk named Faxian slips out of China in 396 CE and travels along the Silk Road to India. There he studies original texts and brings back around 600 Buddhist scrolls and statues to enrich the libraries of China. When he returns 16 years later, the Emperor pardons and rewards him.

The Roman Empire is disintegrating and splits into Eastern and Western Empires.

Rome is sacked.

The Gauls briefly invade Rome after the Battle of Allia in 390. Rome is sacked by the Visigoths in 410 and the Second Sack of Rome is by the Vandals in 455.

The Western Roman Empire eventually completely collapses. Eastern Roman Empire endures. It remains Christian, with a headquarters in Constantinople, and is also known as the Byzantine Empire.

The Byzantine empire will last until 1457.

400
Common Era

With the collapse of the Western Roman Empire, Europe becomes isolated while the areas to the south are still connected with each other and the rest of Asia.

The Gupta empire ushers in a golden age for India and Buddhism spreads further.

Great advances in science, technology, art, law, literature and architecture are made.

Nalanda University is built in Bihar, India. In its heyday, scholars come from as far away as Tibet, China, Persia and Greece. One can imagine, from the ruins shown here, its grandeur sprawling across an extensive campus.

Buddhism is introduced into Japan by 522 although some sources claim that it happened a bit earlier. This relief of the Buddha is a Gupta creation.

Decimal notation and the concept of zero enhance our mathematical abilities. #

Gupta chemists learn to crystallize sugar around 350 AD. This allows sugar to be stored in containers whereas previously the bulky raw cane had to be kept until it was sucked and chewed.

Like other empires, the Gupta will eventually succumb to the forces that bring down empires; raids by competitors and pastoralists, food shortages, political instability and disease.

The Polynesians reach Hawaii.

Sometime between 300 and 800 CE people of Polynesian descent settle Hawaii and then Easter Island a few centuries later. They carry the suite of plants used in their agricultural system as well as semi-domesticated pigs.

Muhammad founds the religion of Islam.

Muhammad is born in Mecca in 570. Orphaned young, he is adopted by his uncle and brought up in a merchant family, but he remains illiterate.

As an adult, Muhammad works as a merchant in Mecca and prays alone in a cave on nearby Mount Hira for several weeks each year. Islamic tradition holds that during one of these visits, when Muhammad is 40 years old, the angel Gabriel appears and commands him to recite verses that will become the Suras of the Quran. His first revelation is followed by a span of three years where he is not visited during his trips to the cave. When Gabriel appears to him again, he is told to begin preaching the Suras publicly.

Muhammad's wife Khadija, is said to have been the first to believe his revelations. Soon, family members, friends, and disenfranchised members of the tribes and merchant-class of Mecca join him as followers. Intense opposition forms as Muhammad begins to preach against the worship of idols and polytheism and those who engage in it. In 622, when an assassination plot against Muhammad is discovered, he and his growing number of followers are forced to flee Mecca and head northward.

In a journey known as the Hijra, they relocate to Yathrib (now called Medina). The toll on the fleeing Muslims is heavy. Having left behind most of what they own, the Muslims are forced to raid caravans heading to and from Mecca in order to survive. Codes of conduct for communal and tribal living under such conditions are drafted and enforced; blood kinship is very important.

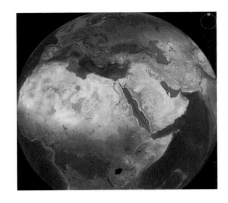

Islam acknowledges a long line of prophets,

including Abraham, Moses, and Jesus with Mohammed as the last. Recognizing the forgetfulness of humanity, the Islamic ritual of prayer five times a day seeks to remind people to pause in their activities and reconnect with higher principles. Islam has similarities to Judaism in its reliance on ritual, and similarities with Christianity in its emphasis on individual belief.

Islam recognizes Muhammad as a prophet of God, as it does Moses. However Islam's own ten commandments are not exactly the same. In the Islamic tradition, as in the Jewish counterpart, idolatry is prohibited. For Muslims, this means that decorations are often geometrical designs or calligraphy but never depictions of Mohammed to assure that he is never recast as a god. Jesus is also recognized as a prophet but he is not considered to be divine (the son of God) as he is in the Christian religion. Mohammed is not considered to be divine either. There is no God but God. God is greatest- Allah Akbar.

According to Islam, the Quran (or Koran) is not to be translated from the original Arabic because that is the language in which God spoke to Muhammad, through the angel Gabriel. Its themes, however, can be discussed by people in their native tongue. There are 114 chapters of the Quran, called suras, and to protect them from editorial manipulation, they are not arranged in chronological order, but by their approximate length in Arabic. The first sura revealed to Muhammad is short and appears as the 96th.

'Islam' roughly translates to "voluntary submission to God," and one who calls themselves 'Muslim' is an active adherent to this submission.

600
CE

Church of the Holy Sepulchre

In 637 the Muslims conquer Jerusalem.

They do not burn the city nor force the vanquished to convert. Although they do impose a significant tax on all infidels, they allow Christians to continue to practice their own religion and reinstitute the rights of the Jews to do so as well. As Jerusalem surrenders, the priests of the Jerusalem's largest Christian church, the Church of the Holy Sepulchre, invite the victors to come inside to pray to Allah but they refuse to do so and instead pray outside, in the street, so that later generations of Muslims will not turn the church into a mosque to commemorate the site of the first Muslim prayers in Jerusalem.

China experiences a golden age during the Tang Dynasty.

The Tang Dynasty is established in 619 and presides until 907. The capital city, Chang An, is the largest city in the world. Chinese culture flourishes and further matures during this cosmopolitan period. The Silk Road is reopened and trading resumes between China and Europe, although conflict with Tibet will see it closed occasionally. Buddhism becomes a major influence in Chinese culture. Gun powder is invented, wood block printing is refined, and national building standards are codified.

The Tang continue the system of organizing officials and bureaucrats under a civil service system that relies on recommendations and standardized tests. According to their census, they preside over a population of 50 million. Women enjoy greater rights than they will in later centuries; for example foot binding is not yet practiced.

The only woman ever to rule China, Wu Zetian, becomes empress after seizing the throne in 690. She had long had some influence: first as a consort of Emperor Gaozong and later when one of her sons becomes emperor. Wu's reputation will later be maligned; having a woman as ruler goes against Confucian teachings and she will be the last. After seizing the throne, she elevates the foreign religion of Buddhism above Taoism and Confucianism by building temples and creating political positions for monks. She makes the civil service more meritocratic by relying principally on entrance examination scores for positions within the imperial bureaucracy and allowing any man, even commoners, to take the tests.

Although still unknown in the West, stirrups are in widespread use as shown by this Chinese statue of a female polo player.

The population is estimated to have grown to about 80 million people by the end of the Tang Dynasty.

In 711, Muslims conquer Spain.

The first Muslims speak Arabic but as their empire expands into North Africa and Central Asia, they encounter Berber and Turkic speaking peoples. Turkic is a language group. It is thought that the first Turkic people lived in Central Asia including Siberia and China back in the 6th century. The oldest written records of Old Turkic are 8th century inscriptions found near the Orhon River in Mongolia. Modern Turkish is the most widely spoken Turkic language derivative found today.

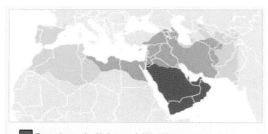

Expansion under Muhammad, 622-632
Expansion under the Rashidun Caliphate, 632-661
Expansion under the Umayyad Caliphate, 661-750

In Northern Europe, population growth has been slow and the standard of living low because the growing season is short and the heavy soil hard to plow. Agricultural technology that had been developed by the Romans is not applicable in most of Europe.

The first soils to be farmed in Europe are the lightest ones that are most similar to Mediterranean soils. As the heavy plow is developed, more land can be brought under cultivation. Once the heavy plow is developed and the heavy clay rich soils of Northern Europe can be utilized, they prove to be fertile.

The Romans had used a two field system of crop rotation; every year only half the fields were planted with crops and the other half lay fallow in order to recover. The Europeans develop a three field system which allows fields to be left fallow only one third of the time. Because fallow fields must actually be plowed twice a year for weed control, the new system reduces the required amount of plowing as well as keeping a higher percentage of the land productive.

In order to maintain the fertility of the soil under the intense use of the three field system, crops had to be rotated, planted in a specific, alternating, sequences. For example, springtime, peas could be followed by a crop of wheat and then that field left fallow.

The simple scratch plow that the Romans had used worked well enough in the light, gravelly soils of Mediterranean lands. This plow has a pointed stick, sometimes reinforced with iron mounted on a handle that tears into the land a little. It can be pulled with a single ox or even a human.

The heavier European plow evolves by the addition of a coulter which cuts a deep vertical slice into the soil and this is mounted to a heavy wheeled carriage with handles the farmer can use to lean in to steer it. It requires draught animals to pull it. The next step is the addition of a plowshare which follows the coulter and makes a horizontal cut several centimeters below the surface.

Finally, the plow is fitted with a horizontal board, called a mould board, which flips the cut sod over. This plow requires 4 to 8 oxen to pull it.

The peasants of a village plow its lands cooperatively because no single family can afford a plow and the draft animals to pull it. Large teams of oxen are hard to turn, making long fields the more efficient shape. Peasant families have separate small plots for vegetable gardens and sections of the long plowed field where grain or legumes are grown.

The heavy plow has many advantages. It turns the soil over which buries and disrupts weeds and buries weed seed to a level where those seeds will rot. It mixes in the remains of the previous crop and any manure or mulch at the surface and brings nutrients from below to the surface. It leaves deep furrows which helps the clay laden soil both to drain. In wet seasons, some plants will still prosper on the top of the furrow and in dry seasons some plants will survive in the low areas.

Agricultural improvements and widespread adoption of the horse allow Europeans to move out of The Dark Ages.

 Horses make the best draft animals to pull the plow; they move faster and have more endurance. A team of just two horses can replace an ox team of six but they replace ox teams only slowly. A horse costs more than a couple of oxen restricting their acquisition. Horses also must be fed grain in winter and this is grain that in lean years hungry peasants could be eating. Horses also require shoes to protect their hooves when working in the damp soils of cold clay. The horse collar which allows a horse to be harnessed without partially choking it is a technology that diffuses out from Asia and reaches Europe around 900.

The mould board plow was actually first invented in China. Small one piece iron mould board plows had been used there in around 300 BCE. In Europe, evolution of the plow seems to proceed only after the adoption of the three field system. The three field system itself developed after or along with the development of a sustainable crop rotation sequence. Europe is isolated from the rest of the world by the time during the development of these systems. Therefore the European heavy plow probably develops independently from its lighter Asian cousin.

In Europe, the decentralized power structure of competing kingdoms, requires leaders to buy the military services of nobles with land grants. The manors built on these lands become local power centers and define the feudal system of the middle ages. Serfs are bound to the land and pay rent with their labor, creating the foundation of the medieval European economy. In times of war, armies are assembled as nobles draft their serfs and arrive with armed men at the king's bidding.

 The widespread adoption of the horse in Europe changes economic patterns. Horses increase overall prosperity but increase economic inequality. Horses allow more grain to be grown and also allow it to be brought to markets quickly. The horse allows nobles and armies more mobility.

900

Islamic Empires expand rapidly in the centuries after the reign of Muhammad in the 7th century. Universities in Islamic cities become perhaps the greatest centers of learning in the world.

Scholars write poems and literature and add words like algebra and algorithm to the vocabulary of math and science. They also translate many books and documents from Ancient Greece and preserve these texts.

Islamic lands are divided between rival caliphates.

In Andulasia (now Spain), another rebel, a descendent of the earlier Umayyad caliphs, sets up an independent kingdom but does not declare himself caliph. Universities, libraries and scholarship flourish and are visited by Europeans.

A Shiite caliphate based in North Africa, the Fatimid, becomes a rival to the Sunni Abbasid Caliphate based in Bagdad. The Fatimids claim to descend from Muhammad's relatives. They gain favor with the Berbers who still speak their native languages and feel little allegiance to the far off Abbasid overlords. When the Fatimids have gained enough power, they move eastwards and take over the fertile lands of Egypt.

With control of the Egyptian breadbasket, Fatimid power increases. They take control of both shores of the Red Sea and the holy cities of Mecca and Medina, which adds to their prestige and 'soft power'. The first 3 of their hereditary caliphs govern with tolerance and efficiency but the 4th heir is a despot whose policies bring resentment and incompetence.

The brightest supernova ever seen in human history is visible in 1006. People from all around the world watch and wonder.

The Egyptian astronomer, Ali ibn Ridwan records the location of the 'guest star' and describes its size as two and a half to three times the size of Venus and its brightness as a quarter as bright as a full moon. Ridwan is also a physician who reads ancient Greek medical texts, particularly Galen and he also writes his own works.

Another star explodes as a supernova in 1054, and is noted by Ibn Butlan. It is visible in the daytime for 23 days and leaves a remnant that slowly fades from view. Today, with telescopes, we can see the remnant which we call the Crab Nebula.

In China printing techniques are improved and paper money is issued.

In the 1040s, printing techniques are improved with the development of movable type.

During the Song Dynasty (960-1279), China creates paper money to be used in lieu of silver or gold which are scarce in China. The notes work well for a while but during times of crisis, the government prints too much money which undermines its value- causing people to lose confidence in the currency. Without some form of currency, commerce is restricted to barter.

In the name of Islam, Mahmud of Ghazni leads his army down the Indus valley to plunder the Indian temple of Somnath.

The temple is famous for its gold but the official reason for the raiding expedition of 1025 is to punish infidels and destroy their idols. Somnath is dedicated to the god Shiva and is one of the twelve holiest Hindu temples. In addition to regular worship, hundreds of thousands gather at the temple during lunar eclipses. Mahmud's soldiers pack up all the gold they can find but some of it was moved just before their arrival. Mahmud destroys the temple and slays hundreds of the worshipers.

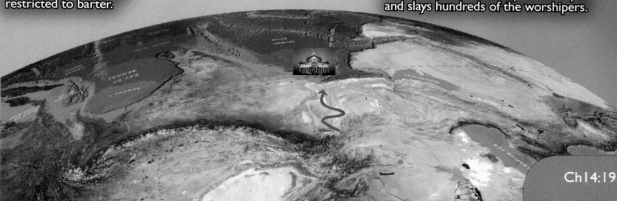

A rising tide of prosperity washes over Europe, spurring trade within and with the outside world. Ideas in science and philosophy from Ancient Greece are introduced into Europe through contacts with Islamic scholars.

Churches and cathedrals are the tallest buildings in European towns, reflecting the power and importance of religion and the power of the church in organizing the affairs of society.

The Crusades begin in 1095 under the instruction of Pope Urban II. European soldiers are recruited from all echelons of society; some monarchs pledge their servants to accompany embarking nobles and prisons are emptied of convicts who are promised that their sins will be forgiven if they participate in this holy war. Some simply seek adventure, the chance to escape their defined role in feudal society, economic or political gain while others sincerely believe that they can show the utmost devotion to God as a soldier of Christ. The stated goal of the First Crusade is to restore Christian access to holy sites in and near Jerusalem. Jerusalem had been conquered by Islamic forces in 637. The crusaders take back the city in 1099 and the streets of Jerusalem run with blood with the wholesale massacre of the Muslim and Jewish inhabitants by the Christian soldiers.

Classical Greek texts were discounted by Byzantine Christian scholars because their authors had been Pagan. Although some Byzantine scholars would have access to some of these texts, they did not translate, copy or distribute them.

In Germany, old Pagan symbols of fertility are incorporated into the Christian holiday of Easter. Eggs are an ancient symbol of life and rabbits are known for their rapid proliferation. Biologists now know that rabbits reproduce quickly because they are 'induced ovulators,' meaning that the actual act of copulation causes a female to release eggs and become pregnant. Domesticated chickens remarkably ovulate and lay an egg every day!

Trade routes to the Mediterranean were active and some towns and cities flourished, notably Genoa and Venice. Although armies often pillaged, they would also trade for provisions along their route and Byzantine officials would sometimes organize markets for crusaders passing through their  territories. Crusading consolidated the identities of European Christians and gave rise to medieval literature and philosophies but also strengthened ties between feudalism, militarism and Christianity and did not fulfill the stated aim of promoting peace.

Buddhist scholarship is besieged.

Nalanda University, near Patna in India, is set afire in 1197 by Muslim warriors led by Bakhtiyar Khilji. The great library burns for three months. Monasteries are also destroyed and many Buddhist monks are slain.

Leonardo Fibonacci brings Arabic numerals and the modern decimal number system to Europe.

As a young boy, Leonardo travels to a port near Algiers in North Africa with his merchant father and observes that the merchants there can make calculations very quickly. He recognizes that the Hindu-Arabic numbers they use are simpler and can be manipulated more efficiently than Roman numerals. He travels throughout the Mediterranean world, studying with many leading mathematicians and returns to Italy at about the age of 30. He publishes his book "Liber Abaci" (Book of abacus or calculation) two years later in 1202. In his book, he demonstrates how to use the modus Indorum (method of the Indians) and explains the workings of a positional number system. He advocates that Europeans adopt this place value system and its digits 0-9.

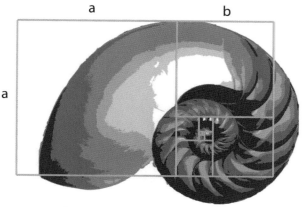

$$\frac{a+b}{a} = \frac{a}{b} = \varphi \approx 1.61803$$

1200
CE

Leonardo Fibonacci also popularizes the sequence of numbers that now bear his name.

The Fibonacci sequence is a series of numbers where each subsequent number is the sum of the two previous numbers.

1, 1, 2, 3, 5, 8, 13, 21, 34, 55, 89, 144, 233, 377, 610, 987....

The Fibonacci sequence is commonly found in the ordering of parts in biological systems; such as the branching of trees, the organization of petals, spirals in seashells, or the size relationships of limb segments in animals. If two consecutive numbers of the sequence are divided into each other the result will approach the Golden Mean, the ratio of aesthetic proportion, also called the Golden Ratio, that was treasured by the ancient Greeks. This sequence of numbers had been discovered in ancient India and concerned metering in Sanskrit verse. In their oral tradition, 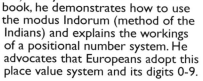 the patterning of long and short syllables and the number of syllables in a unit of verse are important devices.

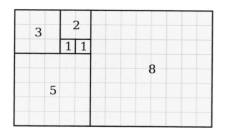

The horses of Genghis Khan thunder across 'the Land of the Eternal Sky.'

From their home base on the steppe, the Mongols forge an empire that stretches from China to the Middle East. Ironically, despite all their mayhem, they create the stability needed for the Silk Road to become a highway of inter-continental trade.

The steppes are semi-arid grasslands suitable for grazing livestock but too barren for intensive agriculture. The Mongols are pastoralists and their populations are thinly dispersed across the great expanses of the steppe. Horses allow them to negotiate the vast distances and are central to their lives. On their southern borders, the Mongols are in contact with agricultural civilizations.

The Mongols herd the 'five snouts'; horses, yak, camels, sheep and goats and manage them carefully. The right proportions of the different types and an appropriate mix of ages is essential. Animals past reproductive age are harvested for food. 15 to 20 animals per person and 5 horses per soldier are required. From these animals they get meat and milk, wool, leather and transportation. They need some goods that are manufactured by their sedentary neighbors to the south; they especially need iron to make bits, bridals and stirrups. They get these goods either by trading or by raiding.

1258
CE

The Mongols sack Baghdad in 1258, ending the Golden Age of Islamic civilization.

The House of Wisdom, the world's largest library is completely destroyed.

Genghis Khan astutely manages his empire with a ruthless Machiavellian style. He promotes based on merit only. He unites warring tribes and then names the amalgamated group with a new name, 'People of the Felt Walls', rather than using the name of any preexisting tribe. He retains the loyalty of families who have lost men in his service by allowing them to continue to share in the spoils of new conquests. He encourages the telling of stories about what happens to people who do not surrender to his forces in order to create legends which reinforce his power. He slaughters the aristocracy of peoples he conquers to reduce the chances of them organizing any future rebellions against him. According to the legends, in towns that do rebel against his rule, every living soul is slaughtered, including all dogs and livestock and every last chicken.

After uniting the Mongols in about 1205CE, Genghis Khan, conquers the largest city in China, Kaifeng and then subdues the peoples known as the Tanguts (Tibetans), the Uigars and Khitans. After the Persians offend him and he vanquishes them, he notices the importance of the Silk Road and takes control of it.. He conquers lands south of the Caspian and Aral seas as far as central Pakistan.

Traders and goods move safely and swiftly upon the Silk Road. Officially sanctioned travelers are identified by medallions which function like passports. They are provisioned and accommodated at stations located every forty kilometers or so along the many thousand mile long route. The Mongols do not tolerate banditry-they alone have the monopoly on violence. Tribute is paid to the Mongols by every village and town in the realm and petty wars between any of these entities are not tolerated.

Some intrepid European travelers also journey along the Silk Road and visit India and China. Accounts, by such authors as Marco Polo, become best sellers in Europe and motivate future European explorations. Marco Polo writes of the riches of China and of the many barges that ply the yellow river with their loads of lumber, rice, paper, porcelain and other resources. The economic output of China is much greater than the output of Europe at this time.

While Genghis Khan still follows the traditional Mongol religion of Shamanism, he is aware of other religions, like Buddhism, Christianity, Gnosticism and Islam. There are already converts to many of these religions among his countrymen. About religious freedom, he is more than just tolerant; he exempts religious leaders from taxation and public service. His successors will expand the practice of tolerance by building temples, shrines and mosques.

In Europe, cathedral building is at its height, with amateur scientists and engineers competing to have their town build the tallest cathedral. Many people are literate and are reading about the new ideas in physics, history and philosophy coming through contacts with the Byzantine Empire and the Muslim world. The Muslims had developed many ideas and also relay ideas from India, China and ancient Greece.

The Pope feels his authority dwindling and issues crippling new decrees including forbidding anyone to read the bible for themselves, or to partake in bathing in the recently built bath houses, as well as many more rules.

The Chinese invent **gunpowder** and this technology moves out on the silk road. The Arabs improve the technology which eventually reaches Europe and Europeans will later develop more sophisticated guns.

The Arab slave trade in Africa continues.

Muslim slavers have been taking African people captive and transporting them across the Sahara Desert, the Red Sea or the Indian Ocean for centuries. Many African chiefs are willing to sell people from rival tribes to the traders for several reasons; to reduce the probability that members of their own tribe will be captured as slaves, to reduce competition for resources, to profit monetary from the sale, and to take women from the defeated rival tribes as extra wives, which is a source of prestige. Many Africans convert to Islam because Islam forbids free-born believers to be enslaved. A large portion of those taken as slaves are women who will serve as concubines or domestic servants. Male slaves are sometimes castrated before being sold off to be laborers, servants, or soldiers.

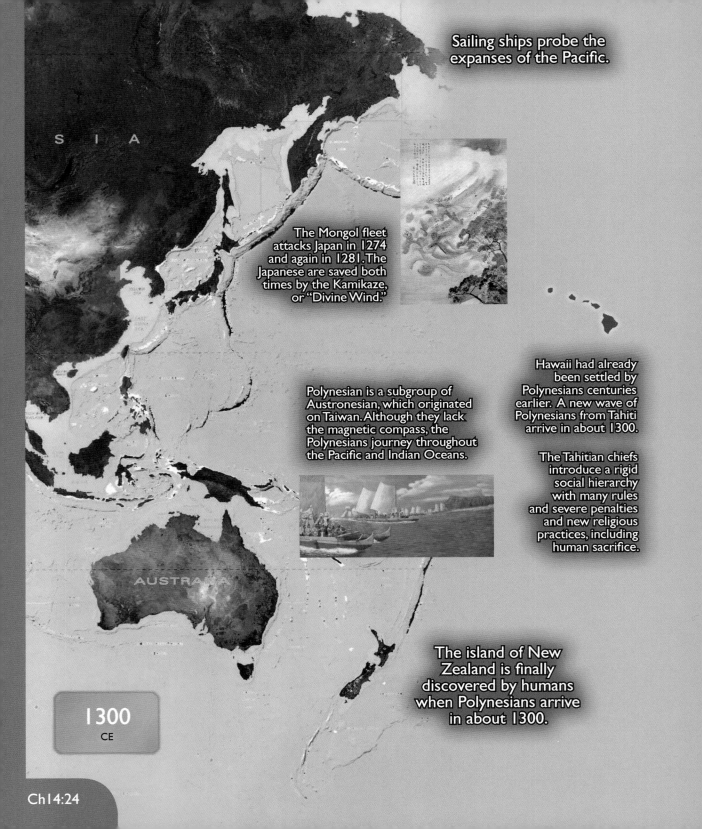

Sailing ships probe the expanses of the Pacific.

The Mongol fleet attacks Japan in 1274 and again in 1281. The Japanese are saved both times by the Kamikaze, or "Divine Wind."

Hawaii had already been settled by Polynesians centuries earlier. A new wave of Polynesians from Tahiti arrive in about 1300.

The Tahitian chiefs introduce a rigid social hierarchy with many rules and severe penalties and new religious practices, including human sacrifice.

Polynesian is a subgroup of Austronesian, which originated on Taiwan. Although they lack the magnetic compass, the Polynesians journey throughout the Pacific and Indian Oceans.

The island of New Zealand is finally discovered by humans when Polynesians arrive in about 1300.

1300
CE

Democracy makes its first appearance in North America.

The Iroquois, known as the *Haudenosaunee* in their own language, live in the Great Lakes regions of North America. The Keepers of their oral histories say that the Mohawk, Oneida, Onondaga, Cayuga, and Seneca nations were in a period of war when a man known as the Peacemaker came to the Mohawk nation. Canoeing from Lake Ontario, the Peacemaker met with a woman named Jigonsaseh. Because she was the first to believe his message of unity and peace, women now hold esteemed roles in the Iroquois Confederacy, and she is remembered as the 'Mother of Nations'.

The Peacemaker traveled to the Mohawk Nation where he met Ayonwatha (or Hiyonwantha), who would travel with him to the other four Iroquois Nations to help spread his message of peace. After many years of work, the five nations all accepted The Great Law, the constitution that the Peacemaker put in place. On the site of the place where the five nations had agreed to this Great Law, a village was built called Ganondagan, or the village of peace.

Iroquois tradition holds that the day that the the Great Law was agreed upon and the Five Nations united, a Solar Eclipse entirely (or very close to entirely) darkened the sky. Using this information, the location of the site of unification, and contextual anthropological evidence, many researchers put the date of the unification somewhere between 1400 CE and 1600 CE.

New research, however, points to placing the date of the Haudenosaunee unification to much earlier than originally thought. Researchers have used information from Iroquois keepers of oral history, more accurate information of historical lunar movements and archeological evidence, combined with knowing the time of year, time of day, and exact location of the ceremony. These researchers believe that the only solar eclipse capable of blotting out the sun entirely - or almost so - occurred four centuries earlier than before believed. NASA's eclipse database places the date of the eclipse at the 22nd of August, 1142 CE.

NORTH

AMERICA

SOUTH

AMERICA

The isolated continents of the Americas, separated from the great Afro-Eurasian network, contain their own ecosystems, micro-biomes and societies.

The Aztec capital of Tenochtitlan is founded in 1325 on an island in Lake Texcoco in the Valley of Mexico.

In Mexico, the Aztecs are consolidating their power. Their religion incorporates fear that the sun will not rise again and attempting to avert this, they make blood sacrifice of their neighbors to appease the gods.

The Silk Road unites Europe, China, the Middle East and India into not just a global economy, but a single ecosystem.

Trade routes that had brought prosperity now carry something ominous - **The Black Death**.

It hasn't been just trade goods or even ideas that have been moving across the route, bacteria and viruses have been moving between previously isolated populations of humans. Traders have been interacting with other traders and the proprietors of supply stations. Those who fall sick en route can stay at the outposts until they recover. In the earlier centuries, traffic on the Silk Road was infrequent and because there had been no way stations, anyone who fell sick along the route died along the way and so germs were not so easily transmitted from one area of the continent to another.

Black plague strikes England in 1347 after coming by ship from Genoa.

Fleas are large enough to see but too small for much detail to be discerned without magnification. A few centuries after the plague pandemic, this drawing of a flea is made by Robert Hooke and published in his book Micrographia in 1665.

Many people figure out that the plague follows the trade routes, although they do not understand the specific transmission mechanism of the disease. Plague is caused by a bacteria that is transmitted by fleas living on infected rats. In Europe, some Christians incorrectly blame for the spread of the plague on their Jewish neighbors; many of whom engage in commerce and some of whom had come from the east, as had the plague.

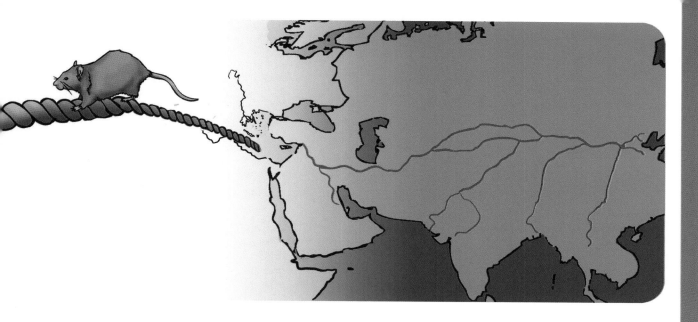

Bubonic Plague strikes first in China, and then makes its way along the Silk Road. In the ensuing chaos, the Mongol Empire collapses and the Silk Road shuts down.

Plague first breaks out in a northern Chinese province and weeks later it strikes the royal Mongol family at their compound near the Gobi Desert. Within two decades the population of China is reduced by 30-50 percent.

Plague is caused by a bacteria that is transmitted by fleas living on infected rats. In Europe.

Fleas are large enough to see but too small for much detail to be discerned without magnification. A few centuries after the plague pandemic, this drawing of a flea will be made by Robert Hooke and published in his book Micrographia in 1665.

The grandson of Genghis Khan, Kublai, had built a new capital on the site now called Beijing in about 1290. Kublai adjusted somewhat to Chinese ways but he had his Muslim architect design a miniature version of the steppe, like a small theme park and there he rides his horse, relaxes and escapes the scoffing eyes of his resentful subjects who consider themselves more refined than their Mongol masters. The compound will later be redesigned as the Forbidden City.

The growth of the Mongol Empire in the 1200s had been dramatic. Many Turkic tribes had fled their lands east of the Caspian Sea (now Turkmenistan). Some tribes were pastoralists and some were farmers. They migrated away from the Mongols but into lands that were already occupied by the Seljuk Turks, who had migrated even earlier. The Seljuks allowed them to pass through the Seljuk heartland and settle on the border with the Byzantine Empire. As the power of the Mongols waxes, the power of the Seljuks wanes. In 1299, Osman, leader of one of the tribes along the Byzantine border, announces his independence from the Seljuks and founds what will become the Ottoman Empire.

1

0.36 Billion

Having survived the plague pandemic, the people of Eurasia have substantial immunity to disease. Population levels are rebounding, except in Central Asia, where the tempest of Tamerlane further decimates the population.

World population stands at 360 million.

In Central Asia, the warlord, Emir Timur, known to the West as Tamerlane, attempts to reestablish the Silk Road in order to collect its tributes and tariffs for himself.

Tamerlane brings together a diverse army of Mongols, Turks and other tribesmen be they nomads, pastoralists or settled farmers. Tensions are high because pastoralists are grazing their herds on lands that in previous years had been planted with crops., perhaps because irrigation works are in disarray following the chaos of the plague or because of drought. A skillful opportunist, Tamerlane, alternately adorns himself with religious symbols or asserts his Mongol kinship ties; not a direct descendent of Genghis Khan himself, he marries a woman who is. Born in what is now Uzbekistan, he defeats his rivals there and then in a series of campaigns, rides across the Euphrates and subdues Baghdad and most of Persia. When the Persian city of Isfahan surrenders to him, in 1387, he is fairly merciful, as he tends to be with surrendering cities but later, after some of his tax collectors are killed, he orders his troops to massacre the inhabitants-more than 100,000 people. He spares the artistic and technical elites. His troops make dozens of horrifying towers, each one a pile of some thousand severed heads, in a strategic show of terror designed to dissuade other cities from rebelling.

The Crimean Khanate is established on the Crimean Peninsula by the Tatars.

Many Turkic peoples migrate across the vast treeless grasslands of the steppe and establish small, new khanates as the Golden Hoard, and other remnants of the once mighty Mongol Empire, continue to weaken.

The Crimean Khanate is founded in 1441 and is its credibility strengthened by the nomination of a direct descendent of Genghis Khan to be its khan. However, independence will be short lived and the Khanate annexed by the Ottoman Empire in 1475. The Khanate will still have some autonomy as a 'protectorate' in the Ottoman Empire.

Although devastation and horror follow in his wake, he does also patronize the art and architecture of the Islamic elite and in doing so gains some legitimacy. His troops must then turn toward the Black Sea and the Volga river and fight his former Mongol allies, The Golden Horde, headed by Tokhtamysh who has rebelled against him. The territory of the Golden Horde includes much of what is now Eastern Europe and Siberia. After Tamerlane's attacks in 1396, the Horde breaks into several smaller khanates known as the Tartars. Then he turns his forces south toward India. He rides down the valley of the Ganges where other Muslim warlords had ventured centuries before and destroys the Delhi Sultanate.

China, freed from paying tribute to the Mongols, is independent once again.

The Ming Dynasty begins in 1368 after the Yuan dynasty of the Mongols is finally overthrown.

The Ming reinforce and add additional sections to China's Great Wall. New construction techniques use stone and bricks, not just rammed earth.

Smoke signals communicate over long distances. Wolf droppings are preferred because they are thought to create smoke that rises straight up and is less susceptible to dispersal in the wind.

The Ottoman Empire has been growing at the expense of the declining Byzantine Empire.

The Byzantines get a temporary reprieve in 1402 when Timur attacks the Ottomans from the east at Anakara.

Coffee beans are enjoyed in Ethiopia.

The Chinese emperor authorizes the building of a fleet of sailing ships to explore the adjacent coastlines and the world beyond.

The great expeditions begin in 1405 and Chinese sailors reach India, the middle East and North Africa. Then the expeditions cease abruptly in 1433. Subsequent voyages are forbidden and China turns inward.

Under Emperor Yongle, Admiral Zeng He administers the building of the fleet. These large sailing ships, some over 400 feet long, remain the largest wooden ships ever to be built.

Most of the ships and their logbooks are destroyed. A new law is passed making it a capital offense to build a ship with more than two masts.

Why did the Chinese curtail their explorations? Could some have feared that plague would again follow trade routes? Or had the emperor thought that foreign influences would be corrupting or that China already had everything it needed and was better off just keeping to itself?

1400
CE

The European trade route with the Far East is blocked by the conquest of Constantinople by the Ottoman Turks.

1453

Constantinople had been in Christian hands since Emperor Constantine had made Christianity the official religion of the Roman Empire. Turkish Ottomans call the city Istanbul but it won't be officially renamed until much later.

This spurs European efforts to find a sea route to the Indian Ocean.

In Northern and Western Europe, people are living in relative freedom and prosperity. In the preceding century, at least a third and probably half of the population had died in the plague which had opened up many skilled occupations to people of low social rank and increased the amount of land and resources per person. Population has been recovering and markets for goods have been expanding.

Constantinople is located on the narrow corridor of land, a bottle neck, that connects Europe to the Middle East and the Far East.

On the Atlantic coast of Europe, oceangoing ships are built and navigation is studied.

To reach the trading ports of India, European ships will have to sail around the continent of Africa.

This ushers in the European *Age of Exploration.*

Coffee is enjoyed by Sufis.

Coffee drinking spreads to Yemen on the Arabian Peninsula, where Sufis, a mystical sect of Islam, drink coffee in their monasteries to enhance their devotions and to stay awake during all night rituals.

Johannes Gutenberg improves the printing press.

Wooden movable type had been invented in China in 1040 CE and metal movable type in Korea in 1234 but these systems did not lead to widespread popular use, possibly because Chinese script has many characters or because powerful scribes were able to limit its use but in any case, literacy continued to be confined to the elite. In about 1450, Gutenberg adapts the screw press that had been used to compress grapes for making wine, to push the ink coated movable type against a sheet of paper or parchment. He also manufactures type with more efficient methods and makes inks that are more durable.

Christopher Columbus seeks to lead an expedition to reach India by sailing west, across the open ocean.

Columbus, in his eagerness, makes an impression on Queen Isabella, who gives him a small stipend that allows him to continue to hang around. Columbus had been sailing since his early teens. He had previously been shipwrecked after a pirate attack off the coast of Portugal. While in Portugal, he had put forth his idea of finding a new sea route by sailing west to the Portuguese monarchs but they had declined.

Columbus makes his first appeal to the royal couple in 1486 but their court astronomer points out that Columbus has vastly underestimated the size of the ocean. For centuries it had been known to astronomers and navigators that the Earth is round. An estimate of its size that was made by Eratosthenes in the 3rd century BCE. The curvature of the Earth can be seen, on very clear days, as the hulls of ships disappear behind the sea while the upper hull and mast can still clearly be seen.

The Janissaries, the formerly Christian warrior slave class of the Ottoman Empire, distinguish themselves.

Since the 1360's, when Sultan Murad I founded this military unit of kidnapped Christian boys, the Janissaries have made themselves indispensable. They have garnered prestige for themselves by serving as the elite personal guard of the Sultan. Most of the boys were kidnapped from Balkan lands, Poland, and sometimes Russia, are trained in Spartan conditions and are indoctrinated into Islam.

The Iberian peninsula is populated by separate Christian feudal kingdoms and a Muslim caliphate.

The marriage of King Ferdinand of Aragon with Queen Isabella of Castile united the Christian kingdoms of Spain and they intensify the war against the Muslim population to the south. Muslims had been living on the Iberian Peninsula since the Arab/Berber conquest/migration in the 8th century.

The Islamic Emirate of Granada surrenders to the Catholic Monarchs, in 1491.

The terms of the surrender, expressed in the Treaty of Granada, explicitly allow Spain's Muslim inhabitants to continue to practice their faith and customs.

The Jewish population, unlike the Muslim, is forced to convert to Christianity immediately or to emigrate, as stated in the Alhambra Decree.

After the war against the Muslims is concluded, Christopher Columbus is finally able to get Ferdinand and Isabella to sponsor his expedition.

He sails westwards and when he reaches the Caribbean, he calls the people he meets Indians since he assumes that he has reached India but he has actually reached the shores of the Americas.

Portuguese and Spanish explorers finally do sail around Africa. Bartolomeu Dias and his crew make it around Africa's Cape of Good Hope in 1488 but turn back before reaching India. In 1498 Vasco da Gama becomes the first to sail around Africa and across the Indian Ocean to India.

1492

From Columbus' logbook :

"The natives ... brought us parrots and balls of cotton and spears and many other things, which they exchanged for the glass beads and hawks' bells. They willingly traded everything they owned... They were well-built, with good bodies and handsome features....They do not bear arms, and do not know them, for I showed them a sword, they took it by the edge and cut themselves out of ignorance. They have no iron. Their spears are made of cane....They would make fine servants....With fifty men we could subjugate them all and make them do whatever we want."

Columbus sets up Spain's first colony in the New World on the island of Hispaniola, now called Haiti and the Dominican Republic. He leaves some of his men there and returns to Spain. He doesn't have much gold to present but suggests that the natives, and he has brought several to show, would make good slaves and could be imported cheaply. Isabella is offended and declares that the peaceful natives should be converted to Christianity and not enslaved.

The Ottoman Empire reaches its zenith.

Control of the direct overland route between Europe and the remnants of the Silk Road is one of the sources of the Ottoman Empire's wealth.

Although their religious rights had been guaranteed in the Treaty of Granada, Muslims remaining in Spain lose those rights in the following decade. Revolts by Muslims against pressure to convert to Christianity are used as a pretext to break the terms of the treaty. Muslims are now formally forced to convert to Christianity or go into exile.

Many of the Jews fleeing the Spanish Inquisition seek safe Harbor in the Ottoman Empire. Constantinople, still recovering from siege and war, has a population of only 70,000 and welcomes the Jews with open arms. Sultan Bayezid II remarks "Ye call Ferdinand a wise king, he who makes his land poor and ours rich".

The Shiite Safavid Empire unites Persia.

The Safavid Empire is founded in 1501 and will have largely the same borders as modern day Iran. This Shia empire is considered a threat by the Ottomans to their Sunni empire.

The Spanish soon colonize all of Hispaniola and then conquer Cuba. Hernan Cortes is appointed to lead an expedition to establish a trading post on the Yucatan Peninsula.

Bursting with ambition and having just heard new rumors of gold, Cortes, defies his orders and sets out to be the conqueror of Mexico.

Soon after his fleet departs, the superiors of Cortes suspect his intentions and order him to return to the colony. He disobeys their rescinding order and so he must succeed or face punishment as a mutineer. He has thus deprived himself of what Sun Tzu had called 'a golden bridge of retreat'. Similarly, when he deliberately scuttles his ships on the coast of Veracruz to deprive his army of any option to sail back home, he encourages them to fight on to victory. He spared one small ship for sending treasure back to the king of Spain, twenty percent, or a royal fifth, is required of conquistador.

Conquistadors fund their own expeditions and if successful, are allowed to keep the rest of the plunder. Most of those men who filled the higher ranks of the expedition were the younger sons of noble families because the oldest son inherited the family's entire estate; this system prevented the landholdings of the elite from being subdivided and provided men, in the form of younger brothers to fight in wars or other enterprises to gain honor and status.

Horses return to the Americas.

The Spanish bring back horses which had originated in North America but had gone extinct there thousands of years ago. Meanwhile back in Europe, Leonardo Da Vinci draws accurate depictions of both living horses and extinct organisms from the fossil record.

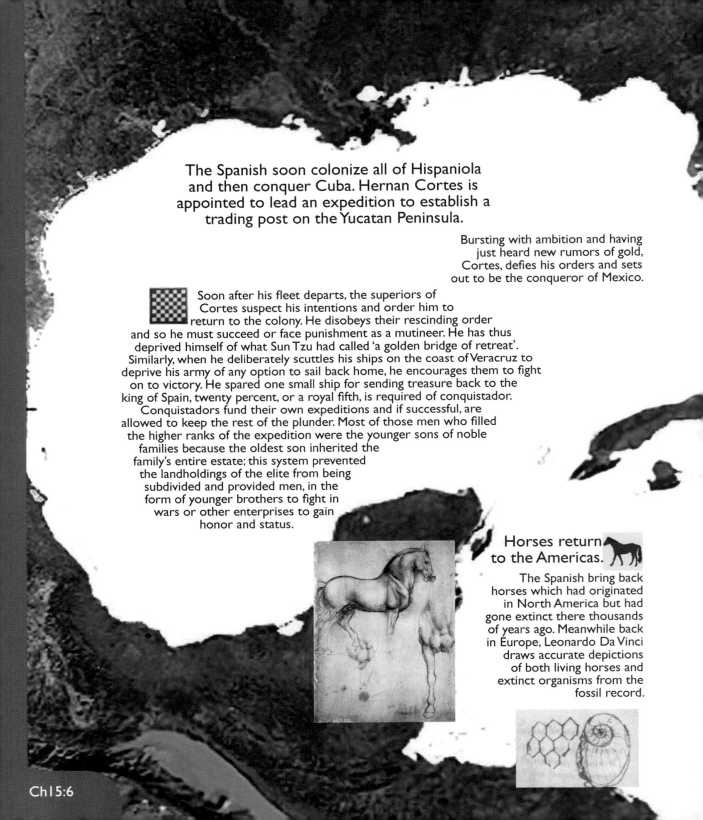

While Conquistadores seek their fortunes in the Americas, back in Europe, in 1513, Machiavelli writes *The Prince*. This handbook for acquiring and exercising power is a terribly realistic manual. Machiavelli hopes to advance himself but his blunt portrayal of ruthless tactics offends the pretenses of the nobles whom he wishes to serve. His book recommends, for example, that a new ruler immediately murder all competitors. This is to be done in one fell swoop because people will adjust to a single cataclysm but if the murder of political foes goes on incrementally, resentment will build and security become unmanageable.

In Germany in 1517, Martin Luther, the father of the Protestant reformation challenges the Catholic church with his 95 Theses. He targets the sale of 'indulgences', an exchange that trades a donation to the church for partial excuse from sin.

The first Spaniards to arrive on Hispaniola and Cuba were given Indian slaves and land to farm. Later arrivals however, find little land left and native populations depleted by disease and abuse. These latecomers are willing to risk sailing with Cortes.

1519

Hernan Cortes is as brave as he is ruthless.

Even as Cortes makes alliances with indigenous peoples who have been resisting dominion by the Aztecs, he never lets go of his sword. The army of Cortes begins with 508 men and some horses. The Tlaxcala and other peoples add soldiers to its ranks as this is probably their only chance to counter the ever increasing power of the growing Aztec empire.

The arrival of Cortes in the year of the prophesied return of Quetzalcoatl made the Aztecs gullible to the Spanish. Aztecs had a sophisticated calendar with a 365 day year and 52 year sub cycles and their religion was intricately tied to cycles of time. Quetzalcoatl was said to be a feathered serpent who sometimes took human form, with light skin and beard. He had been exiled to the east and would one day return, in a first reed year (year one of a 52 year cycle). 1519 was such a year.

He leads his army from the coast at Veracruz to the Aztec city of Tenochtitlan. Montezuma invites him in.

Tenochtitlan is located on an island in a lake accessible by a limited number of well guarded roads.

Alternatively, some modern scholars argue that this was a story fabricated by the Spanish and that Montezuma only invited Cortes and his army into the city because he expected it to be easier to subdue them once inside.

Martin Luther is excommunicated in 1520.

The printing press proliferates with presses now in more than 200 different European towns.

1521

Cortes goes with Montezuma into the most sacred temple of the Aztecs, where the smell of human blood is ripe and full.

The Aztecs had come to believe that the sun would not continue to rise without the blood of human sacrifice. Many other cultures, for example the Minoans and the Tahitians sacrificed human beings to appease Gods or to show loyalty to a king. What caused people to do this is debated. Perhaps, the real effect was to instill fear in the general population making them more submissive and easier to govern.

Although historical accounts of the behavior of the Aztecs are probably distorted toward making the Aztecs seem as bad as possible so as to justify the subsequent actions of the Spanish, the Aztecs brought the taking of human life as a ritual to an unprecedented level. The Aztecs endeavor capture their enemies alive in battle. Then they kept them in prisons, sometimes for weeks, so as to regulate the supply of offerings. The Aztecs empire has been growing and absorbing ever more tribes under its dominion.

Cortes manages to capture Montezuma and demands a ransom of gold be paid for his release.

While the gold is still being delivered, Cortes hears news that another Spanish expedition has landed and has orders to arrest him; to arrest Cortes! He leaves some of his army in the Aztec capital and sets out with the rest to meet Pánfilo de Narváez who has been sent to take over his command. With the help of his native spies and the power of surprise, he easily overwhelms his would be jailer and he jails Narváez instead. The enlisted men of the Narváez expedition readily join in with Cortes after their defeat.

Pánfilo de Narváez, who had been sent to arrest Cortes is instead imprisoned by him and held for 3 years before being released.

Narváez feels that he must regain his honor and eventually persuades the king to give him a charter to subdue 'La Florida', by which is meant Florida and all lands north of it.. He dreams that he might yet outshine Cortes.

During his imprisonment, the wife of Narváez, had efficiently forced the slaves on their encomienda to pan for gold and accumulated a small trove of treasure. Narváez returns to Spain with this money. He had hoped to see Cortes recharged as a traitor but Cortes has become wealthy and influential at court. The king has become dependent on the flow of gold from the Americas and does not want to draw attention to his lack of control over Cortes. Narváez also privately gathers financing from friends and borrows money from banks to outfit his expedition. He buys an assortment of old ships, guns and supplies. Small guns, personal armor and many other basics will be provided by the individual men who will join the expedition.

The king of Spain continues his wars in Europe.

The grandson of Ferdinand and Isabella becomes King Charles of Spain as well as of Naples, Sicily, Sardinia and Spanish America when Ferdinand died, even though he spoke no Spanish. In 1516, Charles inherited the Hapsburg lands in Germany and Austria from his other grandfather, Maximilian I. The Hapsburg dynasty had already been around for hundreds of years before reaching its apex under Charles. Its success is largely due to strategic marriages among the European nobility.

Although the gold pours into the port of Seville, it will be of little help to most of the people of Spain.

Cortes returns to Tenochtitlan and although Montezuma has had gold collected from Aztec temples to pay the ransom, he is not released. Some say that Cortes killed him and some say that his own people stoned him to death when he addressed them from a balcony; they knew that he had become a puppet of the conquistadors who were hidden with their guns and swords just out of view. The Aztecs reorganize under a new leader and drive the Spaniards out of the city. Cortes and his supporters are harried as they retreat and many are killed as they flee. The survivors take refuge in distant villages that are hostile to the Aztecs and Cortes concocts yet another bold plan; they will build lightweight boats and carry them back to the watery city for a surprise attack. With Native help, they builds boats and return the following year and finally conquer the city in the lake and destroys its temples.

Conquistadors compete among themselves for the king's favor in the hope of being awarded a charter to conquer a specific region.

That same year Charles also inherits the Netherlands, Luxembourg and parts of France upon the death of his father. Charles bribes archbishops and secular electors to insure that he will be elected Holy Roman Emperor. He will use the gold from the New World to finance wars to keep these lands and above all to try to stop the Protestant reformation. The pope declares, in a papal bull, that all territories discovered in the New World will be divided between only Spain and Portugal.

Narváez leads the Spanish expedition to conquer 'La Florida'.

The Spaniards do not bring large supplies of food on their expedition because they expect to find a wealthy agricultural civilization and to demand food with their guns. The adventure for gold and glory is soon reduced to a struggle for survival.

After unloading the ships in Florida, Narváez sends them on to look for a better port without specifying a rendezvous point at which the landing party can rejoin them at later. They find little gold in Florida, only a small golden whistle that had been washed into a native's fishing net. It had probably been taken by Conquistadores in Mexico and loaded along with other treasure onto a Spanish ship that had then been shipwrecked on its way back to Spain.

The hungry would be conquistadores come across empty, recently abandoned villages with little food and although they are well armed, the conquistadores, lack the skills to hunt their own food.

Although it is officially illegal under Spanish law to enslave natives, many slavers had been making raids along the Florida coast to supply labor for sugar cane plantations at colonies on Hispaniola and Cuba and so natives have adopted a strategy of elusiveness. Narvaez treats the few people they do find badly, bringing them along in chains hoping they will act as guides.

Narváez continues to make mistakes as his forces head inland into Florida.

The conquistadores don their heavy armor, head inland and attempt to walk through the swamps of Florida in search of gold and food. Native American archers pick off some of them when they are waist or neck deep in the swamps and unable to fire their weapons.

The Spaniards abandon their march into the continental interior and retreat back to the coast where they hope they might find the ships that had dropped them off. Just North of Tampa, they build a camp and subsist by eating the last of their horses. They build a primitive forge and melt down their guns and armor into tools, nails and hardware in order to construct large rafts. The rafts are more like flat bottomed boats, each one holds about 50 men. They attempt to row and sail along the coast to the Spanish outposts in Mexico.

Cabeza de Vaca is one of the survivors of the shipwrecking of the rafts after they are pushed away from the coast and far out into the Gulf of Mexico by the out flowing current at the mouth of the Mississippi River. He is one of only one of five who complete the long walk from Texas and he is transformed by the eight year journey.

Cabeza de Vaca returns to Spain and writes a memoir arguing that Native Americans not be treated so badly. ⚖️

Cabeza de Vaca's account is almost anthropological in its attempt to describe the tribes he encounters, their diets and marriage customs and other details. Many of these tribes will fall victim to disease and displacement in the decades that follow and no other account of them exists.

Food is in short supply in most places he travels through, according to his account. This has led some scientists to suspect that this was a time of severe drought. Usually, hunter gathering societies are expected to have low population density but relatively high standards of living.

Gold keeps pouring out of Mexico.

The gold is laden onto Spanish ships that sail for Seville where the gold is melted down.

All treasure must pass through the Casa de Contratacion; the only contract for one was issued to Seville, which makes this inland port very busy. Here the art work of the Aztecs is melted into bars, ingots and coins.

$

1530

Copernicus publishes a book hypothesizing that the Earth and other planets might be orbiting the sun in 1543.

A storm blows a Portuguese ship off course and to the isle of Japan. This ushers in a period of trade and the spread of Christianity in Japan.

Species of plants and animals that had evolved in different ecosystems on separate continents are now being interchanged.

1550

Potatoes are brought from the Americas to Europe, sugarcane arrives in the Caribbean, and horses return to the Americas.

This interchange of species, known as the **Columbian Exchange**, is still going on today. It is a wholesale mixing of ecosystems that extends far beyond deliberately intended imports- diseases and species such as mice and rats tag along. The exchanged crops greatly expand humanities inventory of crops on all continents. For example, the potato allows parts of Europe that were too cool or damp for any European domestic crops to grow to be utilized. Domesticated animals are also exchanged, which has a greater affect in the Americas as almost all domesticated animals are of Eurasian origin. Horses, the most cherished of the domestic animals, originally evolved in the Americas but had gone extinct about 10,000 years ago there, were brought back- influencing Native American culture.

Spanish and Portuguese colonies in The Caribbean, Brazil, Mexico and elsewhere cultivate sugarcane, coffee and other crops. Disease devastates Native populations and African slaves are imported to labor under European immigrant masters. Malaria accompanies the Africans, who have partial immunity to it, which will prevent the potential use of European indentured labor and encourage Europeans to try to govern their colonies in absentia as much as possible. The increased taking of slaves in Africa encourages competition between tribes and the militarization of those societies.

The Spanish colonial method is called the *encomienda* system. It allows land grants to be made by the king or his bureaucrats. The land itself is not given outright and its title is still held by the king of Spain but use of the land and all resources upon it, including human beings is controlled and owned by the grantee. Bartolomé de las Casas criticizes the *encomienda* system for encouraging abuse of the natives that is tantamount to slavery.

Born in Seville on the cusp of the age of exploration, de las Casas had joined a group of 2,500 settlers sailing to the island of Hispaniola in the Caribbean. Finding favor with the governor there, he was granted his own *encomienda* of prime land and one hundred native laborers. A few years later he returned to Spain and then went to Italy where he was ordained as a Priest. He set out as chaplain on an expedition to Cuba. There he witnessed a massacre of the Natives and criticizes this cruelty and devotes himself to the peaceful spread of Christianity. He persuades the king to strengthen the existing laws against enslaving Native Americans. The new laws pass in 1542 and they do make some difference as the colonists wait to see whether the new laws will be enforced or if their old business practices will actually still be tolerated. In 1550, a formal debate is held in Spain and de las Casas again makes his case.

The number of Spaniards in the Americas is so small compared to the Native population that Spanish policy recognizes any offspring of the Spanish and gives them more rights and privileges than other natives. This policy enhances the power of the Spanish beyond their original numbers.

A person's political station and rights depend on the percentage of Spanish blood they have. For example, half Spanish half native children have more rights than those who can only claim one Spanish grandparent. Over a few generations, it becomes confusing as to who is what and what rights they have. Illustrations are made that depict these different social castes, such as this one at right.

The Spanish have some immunity to the diseases they bring from Eurasia. Eurasia contains a large interconnected population that had suffered a devastating round of plague in 1350. These diseases decimate the Native American populations which have no immunity. Current estimates of native deaths vary from 50-90%. Although the Spanish are often aware of sickness among the natives, they do not comprehend the phenomenon.

Many native populations are decimated before their first encounter with the Spaniards, as diseases are brought to them by other infected natives along their own trade routes. Many of the European diseases evolved with animal hosts and close contact of people and domestic animals. The Native Americans have domesticated dogs but no horses or draft animals.

Silver is mined, refined, and shipped to China.

Mines are opened after the artistic treasures of the Aztecs and the Incas have already been shipped to Seville. Larger ships are built to haul the silver from Mexico and Peru across the Pacific to China. China's economy is booming and expanding.

Spain is producing about 85% of the worlds silver from mines in Mexico, Bolivia, and Peru. China is poor in precious metals, which is why it had experimented in paper money long ago, but that had only worked until they overprinted it, resulting in inflation and a failure to trust it. China trades silk, porcelain, and tea for Europe's silver.

China needs currency to facilitate its thriving economy and remove the burden of the barter system. China had restructured its tax system and requires taxes to be paid in currency rather than in goods, which encourages people to participate in the wage earning economy as well to participate in markets to sell their agricultural products.

Spain, superpower of the century, suffers from a variety of circumstances.

Spain has long since spent all the tons of gold looted in the initial conquest of the Americas to finance European wars against Protestants and to maintain its European empire. When the wars show no sign of ending, Spain takes on debt from foreign banks. With the blessing of the pope, Spain sends out its mighty fleet, the largest in the world, to conquer England in order to bring England back into the Catholic fold and to revenge attacks by pirates. In a dramatic upset, the English Navy which has learned to optimize ship cannon, and not just use ships for troop transport, defeats the Spanish Armada in battle. Only half of Spain's ships are able to limp home.

Defeat of the Spanish Armada 1588

Other European powers begin to compete with Spain for colonies in the New World.

1590

England had sponsored Giovanni Cabato to explore the New World in 1497. He had landed in New England and Newfoundland and discovered the rich fishing grounds of George's Bank which led to subsequent large scale fishing trips where Cod was caught, cleaned and salted down and carried back to Europe where it supplied soldiers and sailors and supplemented the diets of peasants in the north. Elizabeth I grants a charter to Walter Raleigh to found an English colony in North America, in 1584. He chooses Roanoke, Virginia but this colony is unsuccessful and comes to be known as 'the lost colony'.

Later, English colonies will grant individual colonists small land grants of their own which will give those colonists their own stake in commercial enterprises. This will ultimately prove more successful than the Spanish *encomienda* system.

France, in 1608 founds a colony on the St. Lawrence river in Canada which is the staging base for of an empire of furs. Trappers head upriver by canoe into the Great Lakes and onward to Hudson Bay and into the interior. Hoping to keep New France Catholic, Protestants are not invited. They trade firearms, tools, textiles and alcohol for the furs of fox, ermine, sable and others which will then be sold in Europe and China.

Akbar reforms the Islamic provinces along the Ganges Plain.

In India, Islamic forces had long ago journeyed down the Ganges plain and conquered towns as far away as Delhi and Agra. In 1556, 13 year old Akbar inherits the throne of this Moghul Empire, and is at first intolerant of non-Islamic religions.

However, as Akbar observes the diversity of people and ideas, he quests to understand other points of view. Eventually, Akbar rolls back some of the strict Islamic laws in place and abolishes the tax on people of other faiths.

Elizabeth I of England, when communicating in a letter with Akbar the Great, conveys that she has heard of his great humanitarian and cultural works.

Akbar brings scholars together to debate the merits and faults of different religions in a meeting of minds. He grants lands and funds for Hindu temples and a Christian church as well as for mosques. Akbar manages to fuse the cultures, and creates a zenith in arts, culture, architecture, and learning.

As a boy prince, Akbar had spent his time riding his horse. He managed to dodge the influence of the authorities and advisors that ruled in his name until he came of age. He never even learned to read and write. All are surprised that he proves such a capable ruler.

Europeans and many other peoples have been practicing whaling but only drift whaling, where they harvest the resource of dead beached whales.

Cannon and other firearms are developed by Muslim engineers. The Moghul, Ottoman and Safavid Empires come to be known as **Gunpowder Empires**.

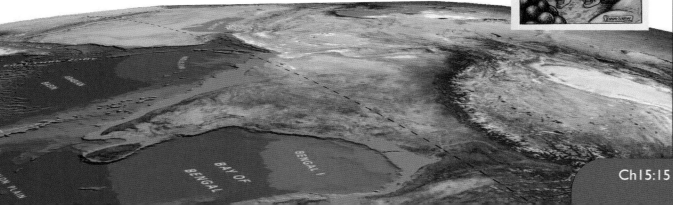

$ The world's first multinational corporations, The British East India Company and The Dutch East India Company are set up.

Banking is demanded by methods of warfare which have grown ever more dependent on the expensive technologies of navies of well outfitted ships and guns and cannons. Standing armies of well drilled soldiers are also expensive. Drills and marching maneuvers are not primarily for parades but to habituate soldiers to stand in their places and follow orders even in the chaos of battle. Some liken this drill to a form of software, an essential complement to fit with the hardware of the military.

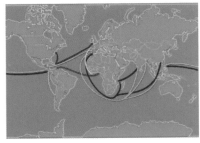

The first stock exchange is created in 1602.

The Dutch government sells stock shares in the company and the company pays yearly dividends commensurate with its profits to the shareholders. The government makes it clear that it will not ever buy back shares and that any buyer who later wants to sell must sell their shares to another individual; this creates a marketplace or stock exchange.

Both the British and the Dutch corporations are privately owned and managed but their governments, in order to promote them, guarantee them monopolies by promising not to grant charters to any new companies. The corporations are given almost state like powers: they are allowed to raise armies, negotiate treaties or conduct wars with foreign powers.

Galileo turns a spyglass upward, and observes the moon in greater detail.

Galileo observes the topography of the moon; the lunar highlands, craters and wide basins. The presence of topography shows that the moon is a place not some ethereal orb or perfect sphere. Galileo also sees that Venus goes through phases, waxes and wanes, like the moon does. The phases only make sense if Venus is orbiting the sun.

A Dutchman named Lippershey applies for a patent for the spyglass in 1608 but is denied and informed that other spectacle makers have simultaneously made similar devices. The government rewards him anyway and pays him for his designs. Galileo makes some improvements to this device that is used for viewing far away ships and then turns it upward in 1609.

Galileo proclaims the value of making careful, reproducible measurements in order to rigorously subject observations to mathematical and physical laws, in order to test the laws and make new inferences.

Several bright comets had been visible over Europe in the decades before Halley's comet returns in 1609.

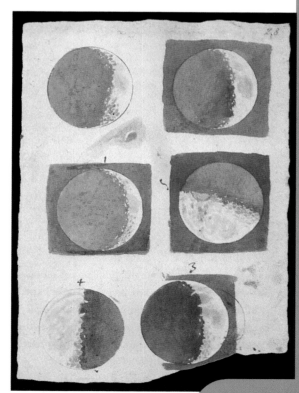

Comets had been considered by Aristotle to be atmospheric disturbances not heavenly bodies. In 1577, a bright comet is observed by Tycho Brahe in Denmark. Although Brahe worked before the invention of the telescope, he is able to take careful measurements of the comet against the background of faraway stars to show that the comet is much farther away than the moon. This is an observational blow to the Aristotelean theory.

Johannes Kepler determines, in 1609 that the planets move about the Sun in elliptical orbits. Copernicus had postulated that the planets orbit the sun and not the earth in 1543 but he had postulated perfectly circular orbits which subsequent observations later showed not to quite work out.

Some comets, like Halley's come from the asteroid belt between Mars and Jupiter and have a short periodicity; Halley's is 75 years. Others come from the farther off **Kuiper belt** and have much longer orbiting cycles. People are not sure yet if the same comets return or not.

In England, William Shakespeare, 1564-1616, writes plays about contemporary issues and dilemmas. Audiences already know most of the plot and most of the characters featured in any given play. A playwright makes their mark by adding new twists and nuance. There is no attempt to be original; on the contrary, a playwright conveys a point of view by adapting and combining dramas that the audience has recently seen. By building on the audience's existing knowledge, the playwright can efficiently present an opposing view and make great changes in meaning or emphasis by slight but clever changes.

Galileo makes several important scientific discoveries.

Galileo had considered going into the priesthood but his father convinces him to study medicine instead.

While at University, in 1581, he notices the motion of a swinging chandelier and uses his heartbeat to time it. Later, he sets up two pendulums with strings of identical lengths and sets one swinging in a large arc and the other in a small and notices that they stay in sync with each other even though one travels more distance than the other. Any two pendulums will have the same period (complete one back and forth cycle) if they have the same length string although they travel at different speeds. This discovery won't be useful until later inventors utilize it to improve clocks. He invents a primitive thermometer. He invents a hydrostatic balance and with the publication of a small book about it in 1586, he comes to be known on the scientific scene. He teaches perspective drawing at the Accademia delle Arti del Diegno in Florence.

In 1616 he writes about the tides, trying to show that they were caused by Earth's rotation on its axis and the pull of the sun which is not true; the tides are caused by the pull of the moon.

Printing presses exist by the hundreds throughout Europe but the ones in Holland get a real workout as books that are controversial in their home countries are welcomed here. Books, pamphlets and newspapers become cheaper and more common and circulate widely. Korea which has had moveable metal type since the 1300s still produces only a limited number of works for a small elite. Authorities of Islam prohibit the printing of the Koran, claiming that printing desecrates the sacred text which must be scribed by hand, an endeavor that brings blessings to the scribe and his family.

In 1611, the King James version of the Christian Bible is printed in English. One of the controversies between the Catholics and the upstart Protestants has been the reading of the bible by everyday people. The Catholic position is that only priests and clergy should have direct access and that the unlearned populace should not interpret scripture for themselves. The Bible had previously been printed only in Hebrew, Greek, and, most commonly, Latin. Mass is still conducted in Latin which the parishioners don't actually understand.

Dutch publishing houses thrive.

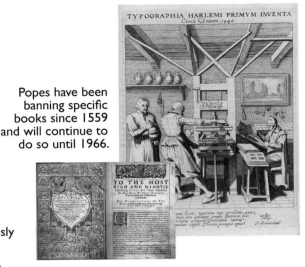

Popes have been banning specific books since 1559 and will continue to do so until 1966.

Dutch industry, especially shipbuilding, thrives. The lowlands of the Netherlands have an abundant and unusual fuel supply, peat.

Peat is ancient, non-decomposed swamp material which when gathered and dried out becomes can be burned as a fuel. Canals in the swampy landscape act as highways for transport. Winds blowing across the flat terrain power windmills.

The Netherlands are swampy, boggy, unstable watery low lands. Efforts to drain areas in order to grow crops began centuries ago.

A problem of subsidence occurs when the land is dried out or peat is removed. The peat is compressed, non-decomposed organic matter (but peat was never lithified and metamorphosed into coal) but peat shrinks much further in volume when it is dried out. Fields that are dried out function well for years but then start to subside and then become flooded. Any fields that subside below sea level must be protected by earthen dikes in order to maintain agricultural productivity. The organization and maintenance of the vast and intricate water works that evolve, leads to cooperation and political unification of the people.

Peat is harvested by scooping it up in nets.

Holland is a coastal region of the Netherlands but is sometimes used to refer to the whole country, not always to the liking to other Dutch citizens. The Dutch are the people of the great region known as The Netherlands.

Dutch ships continue to sail throughout the world and reap huge profits.

Spain claims had claimed most of the Netherlands as part of its Holy Roman Empire but Dutch resistance against Spain has been going on for decades. The Dutch Republic is established in the northern Netherlands, but Spain still controls southern regions. The Dutch Republic's Independence from Spain is finally achieved.

The port of Amsterdam becomes the busiest port in the world and the port of Antwerp just to the south which had been supported by Spain declines in vitality. Many Protestants had immigrated to Amsterdam such as French Huguenots and Puritans along with Jews who had fled Spain. Some Catholics move south and out of the northern Netherlands but others stay. The religious climate of the Netherlands is unusually tolerant.

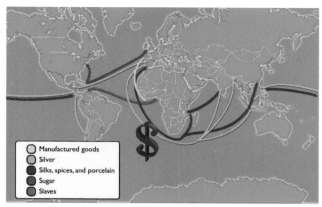

- Manufactured goods
- Silver
- Silks, spices, and porcelain
- Sugar
- Slaves

World wide trade interconnects far flung places by ship. Coastal communities flourish but land locked cities languish as trade on the high seas proceeds with haste.

The Janissaries of the Ottoman Empire depose the Sultan.

After being defeated at war with Poland in 1622, Sultan Osman II blames the Janissaries. The Janissaries, who have realized their own power and have won many rights for themselves, on hearing rumors that they will be disbanded, take the teenage sultan captive.

Waterwheels are few in Holland because most areas don't have enough difference in elevation to drive them. Wind power is used, especially for pumping water out of low areas.

Islamic pirates launch raids from the Barbary Coast.

The Barbary Coast stretches across North Africa. These pirates control the Southern Mediterranean, and make occasional forays to distant shores. In 1627, they raid Iceland and take hundreds of captives. One of the captives, a minister named Ólafur Egilsson, is released from enslavement in Algiers to return to plead for ransom of his fellow captives. Ten years later, 27 of the captives are ransomed by the King and make their way back to Iceland.

Galileo is forced to journey to Rome and face the Inquisition. He is threatened with torture but eventually sentenced to lifetime house arrest.

1633

All of Galileo's books are banned by the church but are printed in the thriving publishing houses of the Netherlands.

Galileo could have made a good living just from his developments to the spyglass; the spy glass could be used to see inbound ships while still out at sea. Such knowledge could be sold to merchants who would then quickly sell their last stores at high prices before the new supplies arrived. Instead, Galileo publicly challenged Aristotle's idea that the Earth is at the center of the Universe.

Galileo was needlessly contentious when he took on the Church. Perhaps, he thought he could get away with it because the man who became Pope Urban VIII had previously been an admirer and friend.

The pope gives Galileo permission to write a book showing the arguments on both sides of the debate on **heliocentrism**. He uses three characters to set out the two views of how the Solar System might be but he calls the character who represents the Church, *Simplicio*, a nickname for a simpleton or stupid person and presents his arguments clumsily.

One of the most devastating and longest continuing wars, The 30 Years War, continues.

It is a religious conflict between Protestants and Catholics- a power struggle between changing military alliances as the Holy Roman Empire attempts to maintain its far flung collection of European city states and regions.

Marauding military parties during the 30 Years War, 1616-1648, raid barns for harvested grain, or if it is still growing in the field- burn it. The potato, imported from the Americas, becomes the beloved crop of peasants, especially in Germany, the hard hit land of Martin Luther. The potato plant is not easily burned and the tubers are safe underground.

Serfdom is an old institution in Russia and many peasants are owned by landlords. Centuries earlier many peasants had fled northward from the Tartars and had arrived penniless on Russian estates where they stayed as serfs. Other peasants became serfs because of criminal activity or, more commonly, by indebtedness.

Serfs are sold by one landlord to another as individuals or by the family. Many of the children of serfs in the past were free peasants but around this time the law is changed to make serfdom hereditary.

The trafficking of human beings, continues in South Central Asia as the Tatars kidnap and transport Poles, Russians, Ukrainians and others, into the Ottoman Empire's conduits.

The Crimean Tatars launch kidnapping expeditions into Ukraine, Russia, Poland and throughout the Balkans from their bases on the Crimean Peninsula. *The Harvest of the Steppe* is vital to the Crimean Tatar economy.

Accomplished horsemen, The Crimean Tatars, a move easily throughout the grasslands and carry out recurrent raids in the steppes of Central Asia. Poles, Ukrainians and Russians are routinely kidnapped and then transported to Caffa, a city on the coast of Crimea that is the epicenter of the Crimean slave market. Most of the slaves are traded to the Ottoman empire and are transported on to various places in the Middle East, but some are added to the growing ranks of Crimea's slave caste.

The slaves are subjected to harsh conditions. Slaves are used as farm laborers, rowers on galley ships, and for sex. People captured but unfit for work because of age or illness are killed and disposed of. Sometimes older slaves were used by Crimean boys for military practice.

The Taj Mahal in India is built between 1632 and 1653.

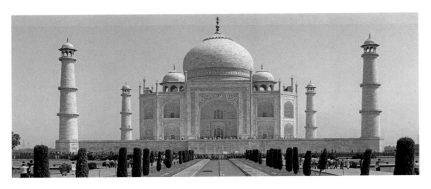

Growing tulips is a favorite pastime for Holland's wealthy merchant class.

They admire each others gardens and trade different varieties of tulip bulbs amongst themselves but soon they trade the bulbs for gold and money. As money changes hands and more people participate, the price of tulips rises and people make fortunes. Soon many more people enter the market and the price of tulips soars higher.

As the market climbs to a frenzy, the price of tulips skyrockets, with some bulbs trading for the price of a house. It had seemed foolish to many people at first, but as they watch their neighbors get rich and see that the price of tulips seems to do nothing but rise, they too enter the market. Everyone is making money until one day when no one at the auction house bids on the most expensive bulbs. Tulips will be a despised flower for a long time afterward.

$ The market tumbles quickly in the world's first well-documented market crash.

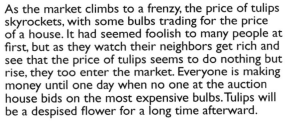

1637

Japan had been open to Portuguese traders and missionaries but they are expelled from Japan in 1620 as Japan closes its doors to the Western world. In 1640, very limited trade is resumed but only with the Dutch.

The Portuguese had been trading with Japan since 1549 and their Catholic Jesuit missionaries had converted approximately 150,000 Japanese, at least nominally, and these included many *daimyo* (warlords). By 1587 the ruling warlord or Shogun of Japan had begun to fear that the Christian converts were disrupting the hierarchical order of society and might also be used by the foreigners to destabilize Japan.

In 1620, all foreigners are expelled and converts are forced to renounce Christianity (or be killed or go into hiding). Any Japanese who are out of the country at this time, are not allowed to return. In 1640, some Dutch traders, whom the Japanese might not realize are Christians because they are not Catholic and are enemies of the Portuguese, persuade Japan to trade with them. They are allowed only to trade a limited variety of goods and are not permitted into Japan proper but must stay in a tiny port on a small island in Nagasaki Bay. They trade goods from China and other countries to Japan and pay a tribute to the Japanese shogun who keeps them under close supervision.

China succumbs to a foreign invader, in 1644.

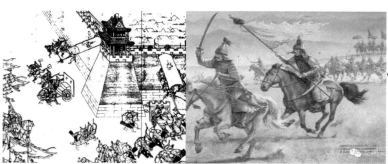

Manchurian warriors defeat the Ming armies and establish the Qing Dynasty. This is only the second time in history that the Chinese Empire is ruled by foreigners. The first time was when the Mongols took over the Song Dynasty in 1271 CE. China will be ruled by the Manchus until 1911. But the Manchus will also adopt many Chinese cultural practices; in effect, the conquerors will become Chinese (or so says the commonly held, modern interpretation).

The first coffee house opens in Europe in Venice in 1645. Soon thereafter, coffee houses gain popularity in Europe.

New York is founded.
The Dutch had set up a fur trading colony in the New world, at the mouth of the Hudson River called New Amsterdam but in 1664, the English, with superior cannon, take it from them and rename it New York.

American colonists are hunting whales by 1644. When a whale is spotted off shore, boats are launched and the whale is harpooned and towed in. On the beach, the whale is butchered and its blubber boiled into oil.

Isaac Newton discovers the rules of gravity.

Newton knows no explanation of how gravity works. He only knows that it follows the equations he discovers. No one else seems bothered by this. The new rules of thumb that he describes allow almost all known motion to be predicted accurately, such as why the moon stays in orbit or how far a cannonball will fly.

People are so impressed with this new tool that it almost does seem like an explanation to them. The only case where Newton's equations do not work perfectly is in describing the orbit of Mercury. Predictions as to where in its orbit around the sun Mercury will be found are always off by a small factor. An actual explanation does not come along until Einstein's new theory more than 200 years in the future.

Mass affects gravity.

The more massive an object is the more gravity it has. Two objects are attracted to their common center of mass.

Distance affects gravity.

This asteroid, for example, is not close enough to the Earth to be pulled all the way in, but its trajectory is diverted slightly.

Gravity between two objects is proportional to the mass of the objects, and inversely proportional to the square of the distance between them. This means that if the objects are bigger, the gravitational attraction between them will be greater; and if the objects are closer together, the attraction between them will be much greater.

$$F_G = k\,\frac{m_1 m_2}{d^2}$$

force of gravity = a constant × (mass of first object × mass of second object) / (distance between objects, squared)

Newton is a brilliant scientist and can be arrogant but sometimes shows humility. In his letter to Robert Hooke, Newton writes: "If I have seen further it is by standing on the shoulders of Giants."

This asteroid, although of a similar size, is closer to Earth and will collide with it.

An outbreak of the plague in an English city causes the young Isaac Newton to move to his aunt's farm.

The Great Plague of London in the 17th century kills approximately 100,000 people, 15% of London's population. The Great Plague outbreak of 1374 had killed 30 to 50% of the Eurasian population. Although the Plague had never gone away, later outbreaks of Bubonic Plague kill a declining proportion of the infected individuals.

The Great Plague of Seville, 1647-1652, did kill about a quarter of the population of that Spanish city. Seville had grown rapidly in size after it had been made the only port of entry for trade goods arriving from the Americas, and was a great center for trade. By 1647, Seville had become less prosperous and its city government less capable; quarantine measures were not implemented when the plague broke out.

While away from his formal studies in London, Newton has plenty of time to think for himself.

As descendants of the survivors of the Great Pandemic that ravaged the continent in the 14th century, Eurasian populations have acquired some immunity against the bacteria that causes bubonic plague. In the arms race that occurs between disease organisms and their hosts, the typical pattern that evolves is a host with more resistance and a less virulent bacteria. Less virulent pathogens are less likely to kill their host, who can then spread them further. This combination benefits both parties. Since less virulent pathogens and more resistant hosts are both more likely to reproduce; they are the forms favored by natural selection.

Scientists discover the cellular structure of living things.

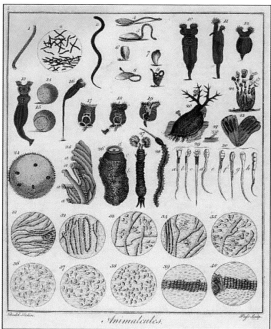

In 1676, Van Leeuwenhoek reports the discovery of micro-organisms, which he calls *animalcules*.

Dutchman Anthony Leeuwenhoek , with his interest in lens making, is one of the first scientists to discover cells, along with Robert Hooke.

This early microscope is a small, handheld contraption.

The armies of the Ottoman Empire attempt to take Vienna.

1683

The Ottoman Empire has been growing since the capture of Constantinople. They control not only the European land route to the East but Greece, Serbia and most of the Mediterranean sea as well as North Africa, South Central Asia, India, parts of Indonesia.

The Ottomans exact tribute from subjugated peoples but do not force religious conversions. Poor peasants in the Balkans actually have more freedom and prosperity under Ottoman rule than they had under their own aristocratic feudal masters.

A European alliance of The Holy Roman Empire, Venice and the Pope successfully defends Vienna. A Polish king also brings his troops in exchange for a promise of aid should the Ottomans try to march on Krakow.

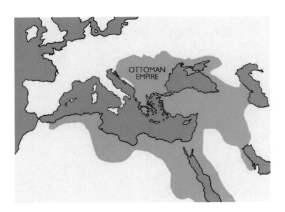

Because of the Koran's strict prohibition of graven images, calligraphy as an art form flourishes. Paintings are commonly limited to small sizes and these 'miniatures' are collected in books similar to photo albums.

The trans Atlantic slave trade grinds on.

Sugar plantations are the major users of slave labor but coffee, cotton and other crops are also grown in the colonies of the New World and worked by African slaves.

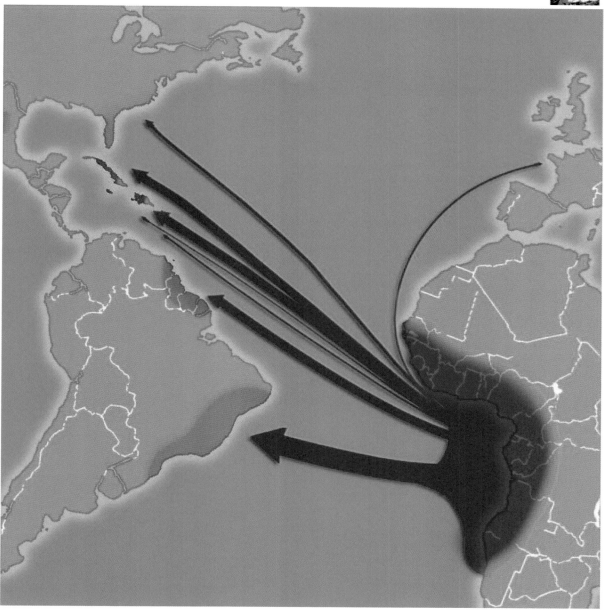

The width of the arrows in this graphic are relatively proportional to the numbers of slaves shipped. The Portuguese plantations in the vast regions of Brazil use more slaves than any other individual destination.

Newton postulates that the Universe is infinite in extent and has always existed.

The way Newton defines the Universe sidesteps the issue of God. Without a definite beginning, the Universe does not require or preclude a creator.

Later, this view of the Universe comes to be called the **Steady State** view. Perhaps Newton actually believes the Universe is infinite or perhaps it is a convenient way to keep the Church at bay and continue his work in peace.

Newton is troubled by a problem. Since gravity pulls objects together, they should all wind up in one big clump at the center of the universe. As we can see, stars are scattered throughout the heavens, and not clumped together. Newton continues to ponder this paradox his whole life but never comes across an answer.

Newton explains how objects like the moon stay in orbit.

The moon is moving away from Earth at the same speed that it is falling toward the Earth. When an object, is moving tangentially away from another body at the same speed that it is falling towards that body, these factors cancel and the object stays in orbit.

Newton uses a hypothetical analogy with a cannon ball to imagine how an object might stay in orbit. If a large cannon shoots a canon ball at high speed, the cannon ball will travel a long distance before contacting the ground. Then if that cannon is replaced with an even larger one that is loaded with even more gunpowder, the launched cannon ball will travel an even greater distance.

Then, if a still larger cannon is placed on the top of an imaginary mountain that is so high that it is far enough away from the center of the Earth that the force of gravity is lower at that altitude, it could, theoretically launch a cannon ball that moves out at the same rate that the Earth's gravity pulls it downward and so that cannon ball would stay in orbit.

1687

Newton makes discoveries in many topics, most notably optics and calculus. He successfully builds a reflecting telescope. Although, his primary reason for building the telescope with mirrors rather than lenses is to remove color aberrations in order to prove that white light is a composite of many colors, the telescope is so small and powerful that some of his contemporaries show it to the King and Newton is made a fellow of the Royal Society of London. He discover **Calculus** (his contemporary Gottfried Leibniz also independently discovers calculus at about the same time in Germany). Calculus is dynamic; and rates that depend on other rates that are in flux can be related. Very complex situations can be analyzed with the equations of calculus, and a simple snapshot of the results of many interacting factors can be generated.

Newton's book, *Mathematical Principles of Natural Philosophy* (aka The Principia) is published. He was born in 1642 and dies in 1727.

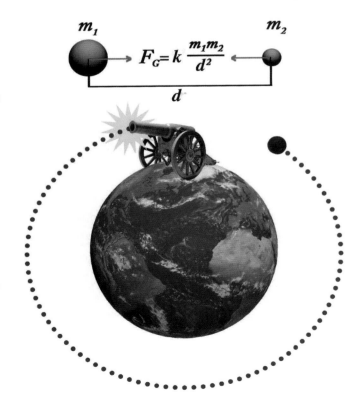

$$F_G = k\,\frac{m_1 m_2}{d^2}$$

Shipping continues to connect far flung peoples and goods into one world wide web.

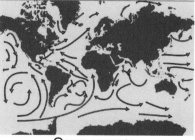

Ocean currents

Surface winds

Ships do not travel on just any route but sail with prevailing winds and ocean currents.

Mariners have been describing these winds and currents for centuries. A systematic study is presented by Edmund Halley in 1686 and he identifies solar heating as the engine that drives these atmospheric motions.

Halley also begins to understand the effects of pressure in air masses; he establishes that barometric pressure decreases at higher elevations and is greatest at sea level.

Earth's winds and currents flow in directions determined from a few simple rules.

The sun's heat is greater near the equator, winds and waters flow from warm areas to cooler ones but the spinning of Earth on its axis adds complication. On a planet that rotates little, warm air near the equator would rise up into the atmosphere and then head to the closer pole. In the case of the northern hemisphere, air near the equator would rise up and then head northward at altitude.

Upon reaching the north pole the air would descend and head back to the equator, completing the circuit. A person on the ground would always feel the wind blowing from the north. Thus there would be a single giant convection cell in each hemisphere, if the Earth did not spin.

The rules would be much simpler if the Earth did not spin on its axis. Because the Earth does spin we have tree convective cells in each hemisphere and different winds at different latitudes.

A *New Theory of the Earth* is published by William Whiston in 1696.

It is well received by his contemporaries such as Newton and Locke. This geology book makes a valiant attempt to be logically organized. The first section introduces the premises on which arguments will be based. In the next section he presents his hypothesis and explains his model.

The other sections discuss how evidence relates to his model. These valiant attempts at reason and scientific method are juxtaposed with analysis of biblical passages and the contemporary obsession with comets (a bright comet had appeared in the sky in 1682).

Whiston argues for the existence of the soul based on Newton's new laws of motion.

He postulates that since objects of mere matter do not move about spontaneously, living things especially humans but even including other animals and plants, must contain some other essence.

He argues that Earth predates Genesis because the waters exist before God's first act of creation on the first day. He further asserts that the Earth was originally a comet which God had formed out of the 'Chaos and the void' into a habitable planet. The Great Flood was caused when the Earth passed through the tail of another comet. Comets were known by this time to contain water.

Chapter 17: Persuasive New Ways of Thinking

1700

World population

0.64 billion

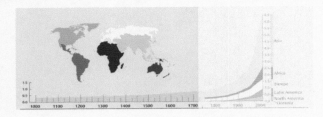

 Edmund Halley makes a scientific prediction in 1705.

He analyzes the historical records of comet sightings and postulates that three of the sightings describe the same comet and that this comet orbits the sun with a periodicity of 75 years. He predicts that it will come again in 1758. This is a scientific prediction, which if it later proves true, will be a good test of the theory that comets orbit the sun. The comet that now bears his name had most recently appeared in 1531, 1607 and 1682.

Ships sail between ports on the Atlantic coasts in a clockwise pattern in order to follow the winds and currents. A terrible, triangular trading pattern develops

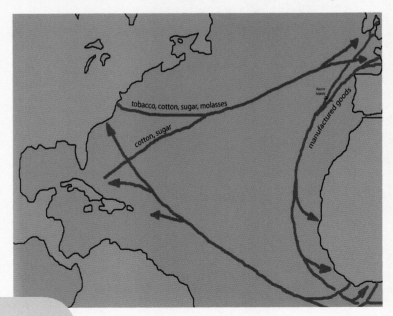

Even today, ships powered by modern engines try to go *with* rather than against ocean currents for greater speed and save economy.

Sugarcane is one of the most valuable crops.

The Triangle Trade transports slaves from Africa to The Americas, carries cargo from North America to Europe and then moves manufactured goods from Europe to Africa to trade for more slaves.

Knowledge of the pattern of winds and ocean currents on our spinning planet continuous to be developed.

On a rotating planet, air and water masses are deflected at a slight angle as they move along and the atmosphere has three vertical convective cells in each hemisphere.

The basic rules are the same. Heat flows from hot areas to cold ones (and not the other way around in accordance with the second law of thermodynamics). The hot area is where the sun beats in near the equator and the cool regions are the polar regions and up high in the atmosphere (warm Earth radiates heat into cold space). Also, air masses on the day side of Earth warm in the sun and migrate toward the night side.

A moving wind or current on a spinning planet is deflected in a way similar to trying to draw a straight line on a spinning turntable- the line drawn ends up being curved. This is difficult to conceptualize but you can read more about this by looking up **Coriolis Force**. In the northern hemisphere the moving current is deflected to the right and in the southern to the left. Yes, the water in a draining sink north of the equator swirls to the right and in the Southern Hemisphere, it swirls to the left.

Prevailing winds blow from different directions at different latitudes.

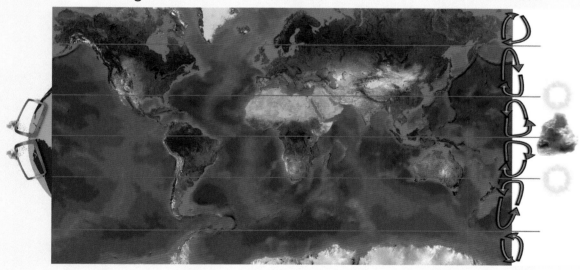

Warm moisture laden air rises at the equator and as it rises it cools and the moisture condenses out as rain. When this air later descends again, at about 30 north or south of the equator, most of the moisture has already been wrung out of it. Furthermore, descending air warms up as it descends and whatever moisture is still in it stays suspended even more easily.

Sometimes clouds are visible in the desert but disappear as they approach the ground without ever raining. Most of Earth's deserts are located at about 30 degrees of either side of the equator.

Firewood grows ever more scarce in England.

 The growing population clears forests to plant crops and needs wood for fuel and lumber. Wood is also turned into charcoal, a cleaner higher quality fuel and used in iron smelting. Coal is available as an energy substitute but it burns with a smoky haze and it can't be used in iron making because it contains so many impurities which get into the iron and make it brittle.

Wood from the great forests of North America is processed into charcoal and shipped across the Atlantic. The tallest trees are scouted out in the forests and reserved for building masts for the ships for the British Navy. In 1709, a new way to process coal into a cleaner derivative product called coke, is invented by Darby in Shropshire, England.

Europeans finally discover the recipe for porcelain in 1710 after importing it from China for centuries.

 Although this could have revolutionized the industry, the new wares are only marketed to the elite. Fussy, detailed, expensive figurines and dinnerware are made by hand for the dining tables of royal courts.

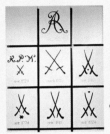 In 1720, a signature logo of two crossed swords is used to mark each piece of porcelain; one of the world's earliest trademarks.

Nantucket whalers discover a new kind of whale.

Around 1712, Nantucket whalers, hunting just off shore when a storm comes up are blown far out to sea where they spy a whale unlike any they have seen before. Whalers had been hunting baleen whales but the new whale has teeth. It doesn't filter feed but hunts big game by diving and navigating at great depths to hunt giant squid. The sperm whale, like the giant squid is one of the top predators of the sea.

There are two kinds of whales; baleen and toothed. Toothed whales hunt fish and other prey while baleen whales filter feed on millions of microorganisms called plankton or krill. Baleen whales are generally much larger than toothed whales and it is these that the whalers in the Atlantic had been hunting. Baleen whales swim with an open mouth taking in water rich in krill, then they close their mouth and filter the water as they push it out through their plates of baleen.

Whale blubber is boiled into oil and the plates of baleen are also harvested and used as a formable material almost like plastic. Sperm whales are by far the largest of the toothed whales and since they also contain oil that is a finer grade, they become the most sought after whales.

Whale oil is used to light lamps and lubricate machinery. The new spermaceti oil is of a much higher quality and burns cleanly. The sperm whale is so called because its oil is milky white. It has a vast store of this oil in its head.

The Tuscarora become the Sixth Nation of the Iroquois Confederacy

The Tuscarora people are indigenous peoples who had left the Great Lakes region to settle in the American Carolinas centuries before European contact. By 1701 the Iroquois people had driven warring tribes out of the Ohio River Basin and made their way far enough south that they had come into contact with the Tuscarora. Recognizing their distant kin by their shared language family, the nations were on friendly terms.

Between 1711 and 1713 the Tuscarora War is waged upon them, forcing the Tuscarora away from the coast and into the Appalachians. Over then next century or so, many of the Tuscarora people migrate northward to the Iroquois Nations, who welcome them back to their ancestral homelands. In 1722, the Tuscarora are accepted as the Sixth Nation of the Iroquois Confederacy.

A new invention, *The Flying Shuttle* allows wider fabrics to be woven quickly.

An English invention in 1732 in textile production, the Flying Shuttle, allows for wider fabrics to be woven quickly. Textiles are produced in several stages. Sheep are raised for their wool which is then cleaned and carded into rovings which are then spun into thread which is woven into cloth. A weaver in the village buys thread from several households and sells finished cloth in the weekly market.

Cotton and cotton cloth are rare in England because protectionist laws prohibit or tax their importation to protect the indigenous wool economy. The flying shuttle so speeds up the process of weaving that spinners can't create enough thread to keep up with demand.

 New technologies and the removal of protectionist policies poise England for an industrial revolution in textiles.

The spinning jenny is invented which creates thread on multiple bobbins at the same time. Protectionist legislation which had prohibited the widespread importation of cotton into England are lifted in 1736.

The textile industry is reorganized around 1740 with fustian masters handing out raw cotton to weavers who organize its carding, spinning and weaving to given specifications. The master then pays the weaver, collects the cloth, has it dyed and then sells it.

 A recipe for making candles from spermaceti oil is devised. They are a favorite of Ben Franklin who uses the bright light to write his manuscripts by. Spermaceti oil rapidly becomes one of Colonial America's largest exports.

Carl Linnaeus publishes a book in 1735 that outlines the basics of taxonomy, as scientific system of naming and classifying species that is still being used and refined today.

 The Nantucket Whalers are a close knit community of Quakers.

They organize all aspects of the business; outfitting ships, hunting, processing the oil, and selling the oil. Their children are trained in all of these jobs from accounting, to sailing and manufacturing harpoons. While the men are at sea, the women keep the community organized.

These thoughtful, organized people who believe in non-violence and will not fight in wars, do their chores responsibly and go to meeting on Sunday are the intrepid individuals who sail the high seas and hunt large, dangerous pray.

Killing a whale is a particularly bloody business as the whale's heart and brain are encased in fat and so the hunters must slash the whale repeatedly in the lungs until it bleeds out or drowns in its own blood.

Lightning is finally explained when Benjamin Franklin describes it as a **static-electric** phenomenon.

It had previously been described in a variety of ways, often as the action of an angry god. Contemporary church leaders attribute it to God's anger at people for their sinfulness.

Churches are often the targets of lightning strikes because they are situated on hills and have high steeples. When a thunderstorm was impending, bell-ringers would call the congregation to the church where they would pray and repent. Many bell ringers are killed as the churches were struck by lightning. Ironically, taverns and lower class dwellings are seldom hit.

1750

Benjamin Franklin had already been installing lightning rods on buildings when in 1752, he flies his kite outfitted with a metal tail and a wire during an impending storm just to show others that lightning is a discharging of electricity, in the hopes of de-mystifying it.

Franklin insulates himself and uses an electrical ground. Unfortunately, later experimenters who did not take such precautions were electrocuted. For example, Jorge Wilhelm on August 6, 1753.

 Lightning rods were used long before Franklin's time by Sinhalese kings in Sri Lanka thousands of years ago, but it was a new thing in Boston.

Benjamin Franklin invents the lightning rod which reduces the chance of a building being struck and minimizes the damage if it does get hit.

Lightning is the will of God. Those who are struck by lightning are being punished for their sins!

VS

Lightning is about static electricity. The sky can build up a positive electric charge and Earth has the opposite charge. When a bolt of lightning joins them, they are brought into equilibrium again.

A lightning rod system is a rod on the roof of the building attached to a wire that runs down the outside of the building and connects to a metal stake in the ground. If lightning strikes, the system will minimize the damage done by channeling the electric current down the outside of the building, rather than the charge traveling through the inside of the building.

The system also reduces the chance of a lightning bolt occurring at all because it allows the charge of the atmosphere and the charge of the building to equalize in a slow, steady way. If the electric charge is equalized, then lightning will not strike the building.

In 1755, an earthquake rocks Boston and the East Coast of North America.

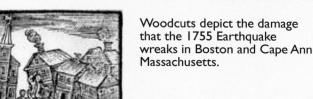

Woodcuts depict the damage that the 1755 Earthquake wreaks in Boston and Cape Ann Massachusetts.

Opposition to the lightning rod increases after the earthquake and it takes courage for people to choose science over superstition.

It is only a few years after lightning rods had been installed on many of Boston's buildings when the earthquake occurs. The earthquake causes destruction in several cities, but none is struck harder than Boston.

Religious leaders accuse Franklin and his invention to be the cause of the quake because Boston was struck the hardest and had the most lightning rods.

Jean-Jacques Rousseau publishes his famous *Discourse on Inequality*.

Directly across the Atlantic, a far more devastating earthquake strikes Lisbon, Portugal.

The Great Lisbon Earthquake occurs on November first which is *All Saints Day*, one of the holiest days of the year. The faithful are gathered in churches which crumble in the quake. Approximately 100,000 people die in the earthquake or the Tsunami that follows.

The prime minister of Portugal systematically collects data on the quake. He orders a query sent to all parishes asking for the time the quake struck, how long it lasted, if it seemed to come from a certain direction and in which direction buildings collapsed. The quake is discussed and studied by Enlightenment philosophers and scientists leading to the birth of seismology and developments in the philosophy of the sublime.

This quake occurs before Boston's but news of the event doesn't arrive until after Boston's November 18th quake.

Immanuel Kant in trying to grasp the enormity of the damage, further develops the philosophy of the sublime. He collects information from news pamphlets and formulates a theory for the causes of the quake. Kant attributes the causes to the shifting of subterranean caverns which, although wrong, is one of the first systematic attempts to find a natural, not supernatural cause.

The Great Lisbon Earthquake causes Portugal's colonial expansion to be curtailed.

The Lisbon Earthquake is estimated to have been almost a magnitude 9 on the Richter Scale. They are the largest earthquakes to have struck Boston or Portugal in recorded history.

The prime minister of Portugal is disliked by the aristocracy who consider him an upstart due to his humble origins. He in turn dislikes them for their corruption, and stifling inability to adapt to change. His capable management leads to a decline in the power of the aristocracy.

Church opposition to the lightning rod continues for another few decades during which time many more bell ringers are killed by lightning.

Andrew White, first president of Cornell University, will later document this debate and the sluggish adoption of the lightning rod in his classic work, *A History of the Warfare of Science with Theology in Christendom*. Eventually, all of Europe's cathedrals are fitted with lightning rods and the debate evaporates

One of Benjamin Franklin's many jobs is postmaster between England and her American colonies. He makes the first of several transatlantic voyages in 1757. He ponders the nature of the ocean currents. He brings a thermometer and dips it over the side at carefully recorded points along the way and by recording the difference in temperature of the different waters, identifies the Gulf Stream current.

Halley's comet shows up in 1758 as predicted. It is a big victory for science and popularizes the notion that scientific theories make testable predictions.

Apples grow well in America and are easily made into an intoxicating alcoholic beverage. 'Apple Jack' is made by simply placing a barrel of old cider outside in freezing temperatures. The water portion can later be removed as ice, leaving a concentrated liquor. Drunkenness is a popular pastime in early America.

Native American peoples readily adopted the horse into their cultures and continue to breed them.

The Nez Perce become particularly good at selective breeding and develop the Appaloosa- the first American breed of horse. Many other tribes, such as the Shoshone and the Comanche, practice selective breeding to remove disliked traits.

Native Americans have not only learned to ride the horse but have become the most adept at it. Horses, which had gone extinct in the new world, came over with the Spanish but have reradiated into their native home on their native continent with lightning speed.

Wild herds by 1800

Wild herds by 1625

Wild herds by 1550

| 1751-1800 | 1651-1700 | 1551-1600 |
| 1701-1750 | 1601-1650 | 1494-1550 |

Coffee houses in London are popular places to discuss ideas.

In 1765, Joseph Priestly, who is trying to fuse Enlightenment rationalism with Christian ideals, enters a London coffee house looking for the likes of Benjamin Franklin and other scientists who are experimenting with electricity. He hopes to assemble accounts of their experiments into a book to make the ideas more accessible.

Coffee houses create an informal venue for the exchange of ideas without the hierarchy that is imposed on discussions held in established institutions. The environment was so conducive to these conversations that Charles II tried to shut down all coffee houses for fear of losing his power.

Priestly appreciates rationalism and the idea of personal experienciality- which means to believe in things that you yourself have known or can see for yourself, and not in ideas that lack evidence and are presented by figures of authority or in venerable old books. He had been ill and possibly near death as a youth and the duress had caused him to question and ultimately reject the idea of the 'elect' that he had been taught in the Calvinist Church in favor of the idea of universal salvation. Priestly was forced to leave the Calvinist Church and will eventually go on to help found the Unitarian Church.

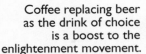

Coffee replacing beer as the drink of choice is a boost to the enlightenment movement.

He publishes a book on English grammar and is able to get a job as a schoolteacher. His book on grammar is not controversial but is innovative because up to that point, the rules of English grammar had not been analyzed as had been the old languages of Greek and Latin.

While in London, Benjamin Franklin hangs out with the Honest Whigs in London coffee shops and is invited to the court of Louis XV to meet French philosophers, artists and scientists. In the salons of France, he is at appalled by the excessive extravagances of the French elite but soon buys himself an expensive wardrobe and enjoys the conversation. The affluence of the nobility stands in sharp contrast to the excluded,exceedingly poor peasants of France.

The size of whaling ships increases as they make ever longer journeys in pursuit of declining numbers of whales.

As numbers of sperm whales near shore decline, the hunters are forced to sail far out into the Atlantic. They build bigger ships and outfit them with on board processing equipment and boil down the blubber in caldrons installed on deck. These factory ships stay at sea for weeks until the hold is filled with oil before making the long journey home.

Agricultural developments in Britain increase productivity and more food is produced to feed the growing population.

A change to the social system soon follows. Wealthy farmers claim that their good utilization of the land justifies them having more control over it and more of it. They petition for 'enclosure'. The old system of crop rotation and field use allowed commoners to use some fields as pasture. The old social contract is broken and new deeds are written to grant lands to already wealthy landlords. Sometimes the process involves force and bloodshed as fences are built and a new class of landless peasants become paupers and supply a labor pool of wage earners for the growing factories in towns.

A new four course crop rotation system of wheat, turnips, barley, clover allows all fields to be planted every year without requiring any to lay fallow. Turnips are the winter crop and are fed to cows  which allows for more cows to be kept over the winter whereas previously many cows had to be slaughtered in the fall. Milk and cheese become plentiful year round.

Growing crops can deplete the nutrients of the soil which is why earlier agricultural systems called for periodically leaving fields fallow. A field was planted two years in a row and then was left fallow to recover. Fallow fields still had to be plowed to control weeds. In the new system, weeds are easily removed from between the broad leaves of the turnip crop. The clover crop adds the necessary nutrient, nitrogen to the soil. Clover is a legume and this family of plants somehow does something to enrich the soil although scientists at this time do not know why.

The new seed drill allows seeds to be mechanically planted which is more efficient than sowing.

Through selective breeding, sheep double in size.

James Watt improves the steam engine.

The steam engine is already in existence but James Watt dramatically improves its efficiency.

In a steam engine, expanding steam pushes a piston and then the steam is cooled which causes it to contract which produces a vacuum which pulls the piston back. In this system, the cylinder is alternately heated then cooled. Watt's great insight is realizing that much energy is wasted by cooling the cylinder with cold water in order to condense the steam. He employs a separate condenser chamber in which to spray cold water on the steam and although the cylinder and the chamber are connected, with the steam circulating through both, the temperature of the cylinder does not drop substantially and so it is still pretty hot for the next stroke when steam will be heated in it.

Watt experiments on a model of a Newcomen engine and gains his insight in 1765 but it is not until several years later that the engine is commercially successful.

The Industrial Revolution in England ramps up.
The factory system is born.

A new cotton mill is built in 1771 by the inventor Richard Arkwright specifically to house the latest technology, the water frame, an improved spinning machine that runs with water power instead of human muscle. People are employed not sub contracted. Time is measured and the workday defined by the clock. The entire process, from raw material to finished product takes place under one roof in a continuous series of processes.

China and India still produce most of the world's wealth at this time. The combined output of the American colonies and Great Britain is less than 5% of the world total.

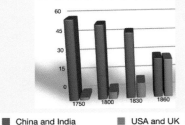

■ China and India   ■ USA and UK

The Colonial American war of independence from Britain begins.

Americans assemble in Philadelphia and debate what to include in their Declaration of Independence.

1775

Thomas Jefferson, although a rather quiet member of Congress, is "so prompt, frank, explicit, and decisive upon committees and in conversation" that he is nominated to write drafts of a Declaration of Independence.

In one of Jefferson's drafts *We hold these truths to be sacred* was changed to *We hold these truths to be self evident*, reflecting enlightenment sentiments about avoiding superstition and valuing independent experience.

John Locke's phrase 'the pursuit of property' is changed to 'the pursuit of happiness' to signify that voting rights will not be so dependent on wealth.

Ben Franklin espouses that "Those who would give up Essential Liberty to purchase a little temporary safety, deserve neither liberty nor safety".

$ Economics, the study of mechanisms in commerce, debuts as a philosophy and a science with the publishing of Adam Smith's *The Wealth of Nations* in 1776.

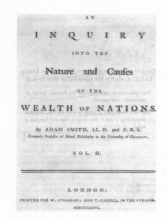

This pioneering work in the new "science of economics" extols the virtues of the free market in regulating itself and bringing the greatest good. Smith claims that supply and demand, if allowed to float and ride the currents of the market place, will motivate entrepreneurs to step in to fill the places of greatest need where shortages are worst and prices high. He also believes that free supply and demand will dissuade entrepreneurs from bringing goods or labor to places where the market is already flooded and prices are low, so a free market will naturally regulate itself.

Smith warns that a market tends not to remain a free and level playing field. He remarks on the proper role of government and the dangers of monopolies. He says, "A monopoly granted either to an individual or to a trading company has the same effect as a secret in trade or manufactures. The monopolists, by keeping the market constantly under stocked, by never fully supplying the effectual demand, sell their commodities much above the natural price, and raise their emoluments, whether they consist in wages or profit, greatly above their natural rate."

Smith also surmises that the division of labor brings efficiency. A factory, such as a pin factory, where several people each do one specific task such as cut lengths of wire, or form the head of the pin or sharpen its point or pack into boxes is able to create more pins per unit labor time than single workers who do each of the tasks can.

The new emphasis on competition between individuals and economies for greatest efficiency has ramifications for the biological sciences.

In biology, the emphasis will be of competition between individuals and species-' red in tooth and claw'. Ideas about cooperation between individuals to form more successful groups and the symbiosis of species to form functional ecosystems will be not be conceived or will fall on deaf ears for many decades to come.

France comes to the aid of the Americans.

The situation for the rebellious Americans worsens after the first year of the war. The tide turns after the young French aristocrat, Lafayette who had joined this cause of freedom at the onset is persuaded to return to France to convince his king to send the fleet.

An anatomy text is imported into isolated Japan.

The island of Japan, distrustful of foreign influences, had expelled foreigners and restricted trade with Westerners to the Dutch who were closely supervised and allowed only on a small island in Nagasaki Harbor. Anatomy texts which had astonished Japanese intellectuals had been smuggled past the supervisors but in the 1770s restrictions banning science books are lifted and these texts are translated into Japanese.

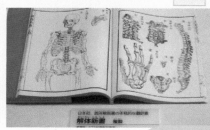

Laki, an Icelandic volcano, erupts and brings acidic weather followed by 'the little ice age.' French peasants suffer more than people of other European nations because they had not adopted the potato.

The volcano erupts in 1783 with such force that lava spews forth for eight months contributing to dramatic effects on the climate in every region of the entire northern hemisphere followed by an unusually strong El Nino from 1789 to 1793. Following the eruption, a fog of noxious gases spread over all of Europe and North America turning the sun blood red and killing livestock and people in Europe directly and indirectly from the resulting famine.

The hottest summer on record for some was followed by the coldest winter in 250 years. In France, it was known as the "volcano of the Revolution". In Iceland the far reaching, long-term effects were so detrimental the Icelanders stopped dancing. All told, over 6 million people died as a result of the eruption.

A recently proposed, alternative cause for 'The Little Ice Age' is that the decimation of the Native American population by disease after contact with Eurasians, causes environmental changes, like the regrowth of forests, that result in the lowering of carbon dioxide levels in the atmosphere. This hypothesis is so new that most scientists have not yet heard of it. Expect to hear the scientific community's response in the next months or years.

The potato grows well in cool, damp regions and had come from the Americas in the Columbian Exchange. The world wide exchange of crops increased the number of possible crops any region could grow. In each region, marginal lands, such as mountain slopes, damp or dry areas that had previously not been cultivated could now be planted with a crop that could grow in those conditions. All around the world more land is cultivated and populations world wide will steadily grow.

The great French chemist Lavoisier discovers the element oxygen.

Josiah Wedgewood, uncle to Charles Darwin, designs and mass produces the medallion at left. It becomes a symbol of the abolitionist movement. The medallions are fashioned into pins and brooches used to decorate clothing. Abolitionists wear them to get out their message, using fashion as a vehicle to spread the word. In 1792 one is sent to Ben Franklin and his anti-slavery association.

The tragedy of slavery continues on a massive scale and the abolitionist movement in Europe and in America intensifies. America wins the fight for independence from England and for democracy but the American republic begins with the stain of slavery upon its character.

It is not only political hopes that are soaring in France, a hot air balloon is launched in 1783.

The success of the American colonists in overthrowing monarchy emboldens others and fuels the dreams of oppressed peoples everywhere.

The balloon is designed by the Montgolfier brothers whose family is in the business of manufacturing paper. Joseph first got the idea after noticing that when pockets of hot air are caught by pieces of laundry drying above a fire, the fabric billows upward. He experiments with the concept by building a large, open bottomed box out of thin pieces of wood and lightweight taffeta cloth. He mounts the box on a stand and lights a fire underneath it. Soon the box rises upward ascending rapidly until it collides with the ceiling where it remains for a while. He notifies his brother Etienne who is the more sociable and business savvy of the siblings.

The brothers then build a larger contraption, a round balloon out of fabric lined with paper. This device has so much more lift than they expect that they can't hold on to it and it sails off for a few minutes of free flight over the town. Anxious for an officially recognized flight, they then build, with the backing of another paper manufacturer, a balloon large enough to carry passengers and decorated with the seal and face of the king. The demonstration is held at the Palace of Versailles before Louis XIV and Queen Marie Antoinette.

A duck, a sheep and a rooster go for the world's first hot air balloon ride.

The flight hints at the potential of a whole new mode of transport and the reality of air as a substance.

The balloon soars to an altitude of at least 450 meters and travels 3 kilometers during the 8 minute flight before landing safely. Within months, the first manned flight takes places and Ben Franklin, The U.S. ambassador to France is among those witnessing the flight.

To address the possible dangerous consequences of flight on Earthly beings the passengers are carefully selected. A sheep is chosen to approximate the affect on human health. A duck, a creature accustomed to flying is included to asses if some ill affects are created by the balloon rather than the altitude. A rooster which is a ground-dwelling bird is added as a further control.

World population has been increasing and is approaching 1 billion souls.

A deviation from this linear trend had occurred in the mid 1300s when population levels dropped as the plague swept across all Eurasia. Stricken cities lost 30 to 60 % of their inhabitants. The survivors had plentiful resources and the population grew at a steep linear rate for a brief time while stored up resources like an abundance of livestock and housing were available. Well fed and well housed people usually live longer, reproduce more and their children are more likely to survive into adulthood.

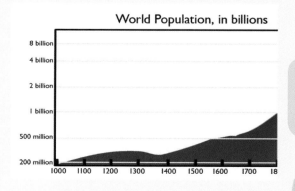

1 billion

The new ideas in the wind, Liberty, Equality and Fraternity erupt into the French Revolution.

Monarchy, the right of kings to rule over their subjects by a supposed divine and hereditary right is replaced by the people attempting to form a republic and the aristocracy is deposed.

Storming of the Bastille, 14 July 1789

1789

The prevailing paradigm was *The Divine Right of Kings* which was the ideology constructed to preserve the power of the feudal ruling class. This view held that Kings were holier than everyday people and to oppose or defy a king was an act against the church.

The new National Constituent Assembly adopts part of the 'Declaration of the Rights of Man and of the Citizen' as its first step to writing a constitution. The rights of man are considered to be human rights that belong to all, are universal, and stem from human nature itself.

The French Revolution is unable to consolidate its success and degenerates into a chaotic reign of terror.

Lavoisier, chemist but aristocrat, is guillotined during the reign of terror on May 8, 1794. The French aristocracy comes to regret their decision to help America in their revolutionary war.

In 1799, Napoleon conquers Egypt and orders a feasibility analysis for building a canal from the Red Sea to the Mediterranean (where the Suez canal is now). His engineers wrongly report that the two bodies of water are not at the same elevation which will necessitate the building of locks and pumping systems. Because of the extra expense predicted, Napoleon does not start the project.

THE WHALE FISHERY.

In 1790 the whaling ship, Amelia, rounds the Cape of Good Hope and ventures into the Pacific, establishing new fishing grounds for whalers.

In 1793, Eli Whitney invents the cotton gin which allows cotton to be cleaned and processed much more efficiently.

This will make cotton a more profitable crop. Although it is a labor saving device, it will heighten the demand for slaves to work in American cotton fields.

It had taken one slave a day to clean a pound of cotton whereas with a cotton gin, two or three slaves can process fifty pounds in the same amount of time.

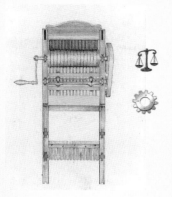

The industrial technology of England is copied in America.

Samuel Slater after working in a cotton mill in England since the age of ten becomes, upon the death of his father, indentured as an apprentice millwright. He learns that Americans hope to build similar mills but that there are laws against exporting the designs. He learns the craft well, memorizes the plans and embarks for America as soon as he is released form his apprenticeship. He partners with American businessmen to build the Slater Mill in Pawtucket, Rhode Island.

Johnny Appleseed becomes a legend in his own time.

In the 1790's John Chapman heads to the frontier which is only as far west as Pennsylvania, Ohio, Indiana and Illinois to plant apple trees. The agricultural technique of grafting was common knowledge, but he didn't use it, possibly for religious reasons. To make productive orchards, trees with strong roots are grafted to trees that bear good fruit. When trees are spliced together by grafting, the seeds produced by them will not grow into similarly productive trees.

The trees Johnny Appleseed plants by seed will produce only crab apples but people don't mind because it makes for some good, hard cider, an alcoholic beverage called applejack.

He was well liked and known for his kindness to children and animals. He was a zealous missionary who lived a spartan life, often sleeping on the floor of people he preached to. He once remarked that "I have traveled more than 4,000 miles about this country, and I have never met with one single insolent Native American."

Heat can be caused by friction.

In 1797, Rumford notices that when canon barrels are bored out to make them smooth inside, they heat up. He asserts that there is some equivalence between heat and work. He challenges the existing theory that heat is a substance. This will lead to the modern **Theory of Thermodynamics**.

In 1798 Thomas Malthus says that a population, if fed, will increase exponentially, therefore increases in agricultural yield, which are usually incremental, won't be able to keep up with the exponential growth and cycles of famine will recur.

1800 World population reaches 1.6 billion.

Napoleon manages to inherit the reigns of the French Revolution after it becomes mired in chaos.

Napoleon feigns an interest in the new egalitarian values of the revolution; he claims to support the abolition of slavery and mandates free public schools. But he is simply being pragmatic.

On the Caribbean island of Saint-Domingue, also known as Haiti, huge plantations produce sugarcane and lesser amounts of coffee and the proceeds from these exports directly fund the government of France.

Slavery on the island is among the most brutal of any colony; whippings, burnings and castration are used as punishments. Life expectancy is so low that new slaves need to be constantly imported from Africa. Slave rebellions are common and bands of liberated slaves live in the hills of the interior.

A series of wars ensue because France must be defended from other states who fear that revolution will spread and also because Napoleon seeks to hold onto foreign lands already under French control, in Europe and elsewhere. When Napoleon marches his army into Vienna, it is assumed that he is there as a liberator but soon it is apparent that he intends to take over.

In 1802, Napoleon officially reverses the French Revolution's ban on the institution of slavery in order to keep this source of revenue as well as to keep Haiti as a base from which to expand the French Empire in North America.

He sends his best troops to break the slave rebellion but they die from disease in the tropical heat and by the well coordinated guerilla attacks of escaped slaves. Sometimes the slaves attack and sometimes they just wait for disease to further weaken the French troops. The French are shocked by their defeat at the hands of slaves, whom they consider inferior beings.

The slaves on the island of Haiti have a revolution of their own and it leads to the foundation of a state.

The revolution begins with a rebellion of some of the African slaves in August 1791 and ends in November 1803 with the defeat of the French at the battle of Vertieres. Haiti becomes an independent country in January 1804.

Toussaint L'ouverture, a self-liberated slave, emerges as Haiti's first democratic leader.

England becomes the naval superpower.

In the battle of Trafalgar, in 1805, England's fleet destroys the combined forces of France and Spain.

England employs new tactics under the command of Admiral Nelson. 27 British warships defeat the 33 French and Spanish ships of the line.

European powers form ever changing alliances.

For example, France and Spain gang up on Portugal but then France turns on her ally and Napoleon attacks and occupies Spain.

Napoleon's greatest legacy will be the concept of transparency in law.

Before the Napoleonic Code, laws of France had been numerous, complex and sometimes contradictory. The existing laws made many exceptions for nobles and included much superstition with laws against witchcraft and blasphemy. An expert in the language of law was often required when a dispute arose and no one really knew what the law was.

Napoleon demanded that whatever the law of the land, it be concisely written in common speech. The lawyers and politicians objected saying it was impossible, but Napoleon stood fast and all the laws of France were compiled into a single three volume set.

The U.S. purchases the Louisiana Territory from France in 1803. Napoleon was hoping to create an Empire there, but the Haitian slave revolt and impending war with Britain forces France to sell it to the United States. Technically, Spain owns the Louisiana Territory because France had traded it to Spain in 1762.

Spain only used the territory as a buffer zone to protect its more profitable lands in Mexico. Because Spain is now in a militarily weak position, she doesn't bother to put up a fight and the United States is not really sure who owns the territory and is unconcerned with the technicality.

Mexico - which includes parts of what will be called California, Nevada and Texas - declares its independence from Spain.

Spain had long since passed its heyday as the superpower of the world and now it is losing control of its colonial territories. Mexico fights a war for independence from Spain (1810-1821).

Revolutionary ideas continue to spread throughout the Atlantic trading region.

Revolutionary ideas continue to spread throughout the Atlantic trading region. Back in Europe, Napoleon leads his once revolutionary armies in the quest for empire. Some of his forces attack and actually occupy Spain, rendering that once mighty superpower unable to devote resources to defend her American possessions, except for Cuba and Puerto Rico.

The United States will develop a policy called The Monroe Doctrine in 1823 to actively discourage the influence of European colonial powers anywhere in the Americas (with the exception of Spain's control over Cuba).

Napoleon leads France's half million strong Grande Armée deep into the Russian steppes where they die from exposure when winter arrives

In Russia, serfs gain some rights.

Prior to 1812, Russian serfs were not allowed to marry serfs owned by a noble other than their own. After 1812, a family can marry their daughter to a husband in another estate if they apply and present information to their landowner ahead of time. This minor change improves the lives of many because most people in Russia are serfs.

The eruption of Tambora is the most powerful in recorded history.

In a series of escalating explosions that lasted for more than five days, Tambora's eruption not only wiped entire local villages off its home island on Sumbawa, Indonesia, but significantly affected climate change (leading to extreme weather), crop failures, disease patterns, and even art trends. After several days of rumbling and ash clouds heard and felt as far away as more than 870 miles (1,400 km), Tambora detonated in a super Plinian eruption. Pyroclastic flows covered the entire island and the mountain's height was reduced by more than 4,000 feet (1,200 m). Neighboring islands were struck by tsunami waves with heights up to 13 feet (4 m).

The dramatic effects of Tambora led to 1916 being called *The Year Without a Summer*, *The Year of the Beggar*, and other monickers.

Arguably the world's first science fiction story, *Frankenstein* is written.

Mary Shelley, while in the company of other young artists on a summer holiday in Switzerland is forced to retreat indoors due to the inclement weather caused by the eruption of Tamboura. The artists compete in the telling of ghost stories and other Gothic-styled tales and she conceives a story of a man/creature built of human parts and energized in a laboratory. The popular appeal of the story attests to its building upon the current knowledge and laboratory techniques of the day and projecting them hypothetically into the future as well as its plot-line rooted in analysis of contemporary political and social realities.

A geologic map is made by William 'Strata' Smith in 1815.

While working as a surveyor, Smith notices that the distinctive layering patterns of rock strata, in mines, quarries, canals and other places where rock is exposed, are similar throughout the region; the different layers always seem to occur in the same relative positions.

Additionally, he realizes that each layer contains distinctive fossils that can be used to identify it. Although exposures of rock can be few and far between and not all layers are present at any particular site, Smith sets out to make a composite map of the whole country by analyzing the layers anywhere they are exposed using both the relative positioning of the layers and the distinctive fossils they contain.

He seeks to determine if the patterns that he sees in his local region are consistent over a larger area.

An engraving from William Smith's monograph for identifying strata by fossils.

Despite insight and diligence in the pursuit of science, William Smith is not welcomed by the academic community.

Gentleman, who can easily afford to dabble in science, do not appreciate competition. While not poor, William Smith is no aristocrat. His map is plagiarized, marketed and sold by the London Geological Society while he slides into debt, lands in debtors prison and loses his home of 14 years.

Upon release, he works as an itinerant surveyor and will later be recognized for his achievements, even given an honorary degree by Trinity College in 1838.

The realization that the oldest rock layers are at the bottom of sedimentary sequences was discovered by James Hutton some years earlier and is formalized as *The Law of Superposition*. Smith hypothesizes that similar fossils are from the same era and he tests this by seeing if the different fossil types always occur in the same sequence; an idea that he calls The Principle of Faunal Succession.

Even as industrial production reaches high levels and breakthroughs in science continue to be made, working people suffer.

A boy named Charles Dickens is sent to work packing shoe shine supplies at the age of 12, in about 1824. He works ten hour days in a rotting, rundown, rat infested house that is being used as a make shift factory for six shillings a week.

Charles' earlier boyhood had been pretty good. He had gone to school and had played outside but his father is now in debtors prison. Charles will later wonder "how I could have been so easily cast away at such an age."

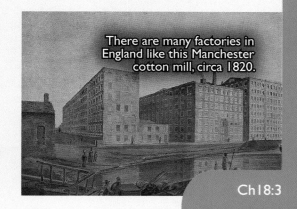

There are many factories in England like this Manchester cotton mill, circa 1820.

At university, Charles Darwin studies the works of Lamarck, Cuvier, Sedgewick, and others.

Today, Charles Darwin is often championed as the originator of the theory of evolutionary biology, but he built on the work of others. Scientists had long been classifying organisms and studying which features they had in common and it had become clear that all life forms share some common characteristics and some organisms are more closely related than others.

While at university, Darwin jumps from one field of study to another, seeking peers and tutors in fields such as medicine, biology, geology, botany, taxidermy and natural history. Darwin had been raised in a religious household and his historical understanding of the cosmos was hinged upon Creationism. This led him to stay critical and skeptical of the evolutionist theories of his contemporaries during his studies.

During the course of his education, at several schools, Darwin would study with Adam Sedgewick, the Reverend William Whewell (a mineralogist), Robert Edmond Grant (an anatomist who came up with the idea of homology), Thomas Charles Hope (a Plutonian geologist), and James Stephen, the author of Darwin's favorite book on entomology (the study of bugs), among others.

Despite his grandfather's (Erasmus Darwin) staunch beliefs in and research toward evolutionary theory, Charles was slow to abandon the Creationist beliefs he learned from his devout father. These contradictory philosophies will only be resolved in him gradually over the course of his travels. Years later, in his autobiography, he will write that he "had gradually come, by this time, to see ... the Old Testament [as a] manifestly false history of the world..."

Darwin's distinguishing contribution is not just advocating evolution but proposing a viable mechanism for it, Natural Selection. Without this mechanism, the theory of evolution might only have remained a hypothesis.

Coal represents the solar energy that those ferns converted into hydrocarbons which laid buried for all those eons- almost 300 million years.

Coal is mined by men but sorted by 'Breaker Boys'.

The great natural coal reserves of England continue to fuel the industrial revolution.

The coal was formed back in the Carboniferous times, when ferns had evolved the molecule lignin which allowed them to grow as tall as trees but before microbes had evolved that could digest this tough molecule that gave the plants their new found structural strength.

This watercolor, painted in 1830 by the geologist Henry De la Beche based on fossils found by Mary Anning, and is the first pictorial representation of a scene from deep time based on fossil evidence. The painting is made and sold to raise money for Mary who is now old, sick and poor. She had collected so many fossils including the best ichthyosaur finds that she is known to the geologic community although she had always been excluded from scientific circles, despite her knowledge and expertise, because of her gender and class. She is still known today by the tongue twister "She sells sea shells by the sea shore."

Charles Lyell publishes *Principles of Geology* in 1830 challenging the idea that all sedimentary rocks were laid down in Noah's flood.

Adam Sedgewick continues to correlate fossils with strata, creating a classification system for rocks formed in the Cambrian. He, along with some help from other geologists, identifies much later sequences of rock, the Devonian and Carboniferous layers. He distinguishes between types of cracks or fracture surfaces; he distinguishes between joints (which are large systematic cracks resulting from rocks no longer being subjected to great pressures) and cleavage planes (which are due to the mineralogy of the layers.) He is a 'natural Theologist' and does not believe in evolution but thinks that the world was created in 6 days by God.

Charles Lyell supports the paradigms of Gradualism and Uniformitarianism which state that sediments build up gradually with every rainstorm, over long periods of time, challenging the existing paradigm of **Catastrophism**, the idea that all the sediments were deposited in Noah's Flood. Geologists were expecting to find evidence of the Great Flood as they examined the layered bedrock of England and they, at first, interpret it all to have been deposited during a single flood. 'Seek and ye shall find' can be a problem in science.

Only later, do they realize that the layers of rock had been deposited in succession with some layers having been partially eroded before being buried by the next layer. Some layers had even been tilted before the next layer had been deposited horizontally over them. They revise their interpretation to be that there were numerous local inundations.

Georges Cuvier introduces the idea of the **extinction** of a species.

Georges Cuvier introduced the idea of extinction to the world in 1796, when he published a paper that concisely dispelled the previously-held concept that all fossils are examples of animals that had migrated to other areas of the planet earlier in time (and were still living there now). Because of his work on extinction, Cuvier became a staunch supporter of Catastrophism. Catastrophism was originally a school of thought that recognized only a single event, Noah's Flood, but is redefined by Cuvier to include multiple catastrophic events.

Cuvier believed that there were not only a series of catastrophes that have marked the history of the Earth, but that they are intrinsically linked with the biota of the planet. It was his understanding that all creatures were created by God in the beginning but with each new cataclysm some of the plants and animals go extinct and some of the remaining creatures become dominant.

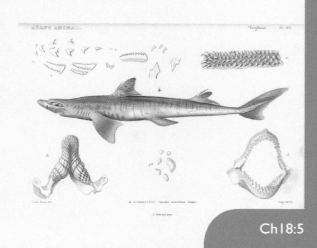

Young Charles Darwin sails off and away as the naturalist aboard the ship HMS Beagle.

22 year old Charles Darwin packs the latest texts scientific texts along with his bible for the voyage. On the voyage he pays attention to the flora and fauna along the route. He has his eye out to describe what lives in each locale and how similar or different it is from that in other places. He realizes that species are related to each other, and that some are more closely related than others.

Darwin also observes the native peoples, their cultures and the impact of the Europeans.

As the ship sails onward and goes about its mission to map the coast of South America for the British navy, Darwin is welcomed as a guest at plantations in South America. His dislike for the institution of slavery becomes acute as he sees its horrors firsthand.

British ships, including Darwin's never cease to be surprised to find whaling ships already sailing the seas and ports they are exploring.

On the isolated cluster of islands called the Galapagos, Darwin notices that the species of birds on each particular island are each a bit different and suited to their individual island.

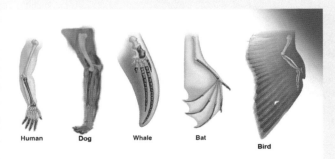

Human   Dog   Whale   Bat   Bird

Darwin notices that all land animals, except insects, have four limbs and a similar pattern of bones comprising those limbs.

Even when the front limbs are used for flight, as in bats and birds or used for grasping rather than locomotion as in apes and humans, the shapes of the bones are modified but the number and arrangement of the bones that make up the limbs is similar across all these species.

Darwin deduces that this similarity, now called **homology**, is due to the common ancestry of these species. These animals are all tetra pods, descendents of fishes that came out of the water and adapted to land.

The similarities of species is sometimes due to adapting to the same environment and sometimes due to common ancestry.

 Darwin notes that whales also have this same arrangement of bones. The bones of their front flippers clearly exhibit the pattern as do the bones of the hind legs which are still present, in most species although drastically reduced in size. He concludes that whales are tetra pods that returned to the sea. Whales share some similarities to fish because both types of animals adapt to the same aquatic environment. This type of relationship is called convergent evolution. Likewise, the wings of insects share some similarities to the wings of birds because both adapt to flying in air by developing lightweight wings. Unravelling the relationships takes a bit of detective work.

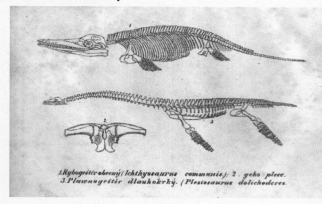

1.Rybogeiter obecný (Ichthyosaurus communis); 2. geko plece. 3.Plawnogeitr dlauhokrký. (Plesiosaurus dolichoderes.

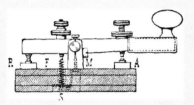

The Morse Telegraph is invented in 1837 by Samuel Morse, allowing messages to be transmitted quickly over wire.

Herman Melville goes to sea on a merchant ship in 1839 and later embarks on the whaling ship, Acushnet.

He has a variety of misadventures- including being shipwrecked and taken captive by Polynesians, that will inspire his novels. Melville also draws on well known events for his masterpiece, Moby Dick,: an albino sperm whale of unusual size and ferocity called Mocha Dick and a gigantic sperm whale that stove in (rammed from below) the Whaling ship, Essex after a seemingly contemplative calculation to sink it.

$ Friedrich Engels writes *The Condition of the Working Class in England.*

His father, a wealthy cotton manufacturer in Germany sends him, in 1842, to help manage a factory in Manchester, in the heart of England's Industrial Revolution. He had already learned of some of other new revolutionary ideas before he sees for himself the horrid conditions of the workers and the extent of the use of child labor.

Europeans attempt to venture into the African interior.

Dr. Livingstone, with an empathy for all who labor and an abhorrence of the slave trade, ventures into Africa. Christianity, Commerce and Civilization is his motto. Europeans had been sailing the coast of Africa since the 1400s but had not been able to reach the interior due to geography and disease; the Sahara Desert in the north is a more formidable barrier than a mountain range, waterfalls prevent large boats from sailing upriver from the coast and tropical diseases abound which Europeans have little immunity to.

His plans were derailed with the outbreak of the first Opium War in 1839 but the following year, he met a missionary who had ministered in South Africa. Armed with the idea put forth by T.F. Buxton that the African slave trade could be destroyed and replaced by the cultivation of legitimate trading and the spread of Christianity.

Livingstone's father was a door to door tea salesmen, a Sunday School teacher who read many travel and theology books. As a child of ten years, Livingstone worked 14 hour days in a cotton mill and studied afterwards. He heard of an appeal for medical missionaries in China in 1834, saved some money and in 1836 attended Andrew's College which endeavored to teach science, technology and medicine to ordinary people.

Livingstone sets out. He travels lightly and offers but does not force the Christian message. He barters with local chiefs and negotiates passage through their lands. He is able to venture where other expeditions, accompanied by soldiers and scores of porters and can not.

Charles Dickens writes a novella to immediate acclaim.

A Christmas Carol is published in 1843. Christmas Carol conveys Dicken's humanitarian vision in an intimate story where greed, poverty and sadness are followed by redemption and joy. Dickens hopes that reviving and refashioning English Christmas traditions might restore some social harmony that is missing in the modern world. Most of Dicken's novels are also published as a series of monthly installments.

Readers who can't afford an entire volume can buy an installment which includes 32 pages of text, 2 illustrations and 16 pages of advertising for the cost of just one shilling. Readership is further increased by readers who read aloud to groups of people for a fee. It is not just the illiterate who wish to be read to, it is also the habit of cultured people to read aloud to each other in their homes. The installment method also allows Charles to get feedback and alter his works to resonate with his readers.

The Opium Was begin as Great Britain forcibly imports the drug to China.

Britain has tired of trading silver to China and is eager to find something else to trade but the Chinese government makes it difficult for Britain to export anything else.

The number of drug addicts in China grows. The Chinese government shows no innovation in treating or managing drug addiction, but stubbornly holds to its no tolerance policy and it becomes ever more ineffectual.

Opium is grown on British plantations in India and many Chinese citizens imbibe its narcotic effects, although it is illegal in China. Britain's mighty navy destroys China's navy, and then the British openly smuggle the opium into Chinese ports.

Disease strikes the potato fields of Ireland.

In the Irish Potato Famine of 1845-1849, more than a million people die of starvation. This famine pushes many poverty stricken families to emigrate out of Ireland. Towns become deserted and shops close as their owners emigrate. Over just a few years, the population of Ireland drops by half.

The fertile fields of Ireland are ideal for raising cattle and beef is a valuable export, so Irish peasants are relegated to farming marginal soils that are only suitable for potatoes. Although many varieties of potato exist in South America, only one variety had been imported into Ireland, making the entire crop susceptible to the fungus-like pathogen.

The physics of work and heat are discovered.

James Joule publishes a paper in 1845 called "The Mechanical Equivalent of Heat." In his experiment, Joule, repeatedly drops a weight that turns a paddle wheel which is immersed in water. The temperature of the water increases every time the weight is dropped. The temperature increases more if the weight is dropped from a greater height.

 ## Karl Marx and Friedrich Engels write *The Communist Manifesto* in 1848.

As the Industrial Revolution has progressed, much wealth has been generated but in early decades of the process, the misery of the poor has actually increased while a relative few have grown wealthy and powerful. Many people wonder if industrialization with its factories, wage laborers and growing pollution is in fact progress.

Some intellectuals assume that industrialization is good and necessary but speculate that the socioeconomic system should be changed. The philosophy of Hegel, that an idea or paradigm exists for a while and then as its shortcomings become apparent an opposite idea emerges, is widely discussed by the intellectuals especially in Germany.

$ Gold is found in California.

Word of the discovery of gold in California in 1848 travels quickly. A newspaper publisher in San Francisco who also owns a hardware store, prints 2,000 copies of a special edition and sends the papers Eastward on the backs of mules. The 'mule train express' reaches St. Louis four months later.

Many are skeptical of the news but when President Polk displays gold nuggets and confirms the rumors, 'Gold Fever' spreads swelling hopes and ambitions. California had only just become part of the United States and the almost immediate discovery of huge quantities of gold adds fuel to the idea of 'The Manifest Destiny' of America.

Thousands scurry to reach California. Most pack wagons and head west. Those who can afford it take the faster route and book passage on ships that sail around the tip of South America and then northward to California. Some take the intermediate route and sail to Central America, hike across the isthmus and (unless they succumb to Malaria or Yellow Fever), board ships on the Pacific side for the last leg of the voyage.

California becomes the 31st state but has almost no state institutions. With the easy to find gold already panned, miners turn to more invasive methods like stream diversion and the use of high pressure water guns. Many of these ventures are owned by corporations and the adventures who went to seek their fortune become wage laborers.

With careful measurements that correlate the rise in temperature with the height the weight is dropped from, he shows there is an equivalence. This will lead to the First Law of Thermodynamics which states that energy can be converted from one form to another but that it cannot be created or destroyed. In physics, work is defined as "weight lifted through a height"

Marx applies this idea to politics and challenges the doctrine of Adam Smith by putting forth the idea that workers should (somehow) run the state and that it should not be run by the small, wealthy elite. The Communist Manifesto ends with the famous phrase "Let the ruling classes tremble at a Communistic revolution. The proletariat have nothing to lose but their chains. They have a world to win ... Working Men of All Countries, Unite!"

Many revolutions break out in 1848 but they are led by ad hoc groups of middle class merchants, disgruntled workers and nobles irritated by the absolute power of their monarchs. Pamphlets are written demanding democratic reforms (the right to vote by all adult males), the unification of city states into nations (especially for Germany and Italy) and only limited labor reforms.

Early arrivals strike it rich by finding large surface deposits in streams and smaller caches of gold continue to be found for a while. The freedom, adventure and optimism of 'The Rush of 1849' degenerates into a brutal competition between people as thousands of more seekers arrive. Soon, the Kalifornians, local people of Mexican heritage are expelled from mining claims as are all foreigners and non Caucasian citizens.

Miners seeking new deposits of gold move into Native American enclaves and disrupt fishing resources. Laws are soon enacted making the situation much worse and thousands of Native Americans are subsequently 'legally' murdered and some of the costs for this are reimbursed to the perpetrators by the state.

The Ottoman Empire has been in decline and the Crimean War breaks out as Russia and an alliance of European powers compete for influence and control of Ottoman Territories.

Britain, France and Austria prop up the ailing Ottoman Empire in order to thwart Russian expansion in Central Asia.

Detail of Franz Roubaud's *The Siege of Sevastopol*

The Russian Black Sea fleet destroys a Turkish Squadron.

France hopes for war against Russia to regain its self esteem after the terrible defeat of Napoleon in Russia. Austria secretly prefers to have a weak but existent Ottoman Empire on her border than a strong Russia.

Russia hopes to get control of the Turkish Straits in order to have a warm water port and access to the Mediterranean.

The Turkish Straits is a collective term for the two narrow channels, the Bosporus and the Dardanelles that separate the Black Sea from the Mediterranean.

Reports of the war are transmitted quickly enough to influence public opinion.

The Crimean War, 1853-1856, is the first war to be extensively documented by photographers and war correspondents. Reports arrive within days and later, after the laying of an underwater telegraph cable to the Crimean Peninsula, within hours The blunders of aristocratic officers and the bravery of ordinary soldiers excites and outrages the British public; The most notorious blunder, results in light cavalry being sent against entrenched positions. Tennyson's poem 'the charge of the light brigade', is penned within weeks of the incident and immediately becomes popular.

War photographer Roger Fenton's wagon

"Forward, the Light Brigade!"
Was there a man dismay'd?
Not tho' the soldier knew
Someone had blunder'd:
Theirs not to make reply,
Theirs not to reason why,
Theirs but to do and die:
Into the valley of Death
Rode the six hundred.

Florence Nightingale pioneers modern nursing techniques as she tends the wounded and also becomes a celebrated hero.

The Ottoman Empire controls the Holy Land of Palestine.

The Ottomans have been allowing Christian pilgrims to visit holy sites in Jerusalem since 1830. Most of the pilgrims are from Russia and are followers of the Eastern Orthodox Church and every Easter some 15,000 of them journey to Palestine, many of them on foot. The different churches determine the date of Easter with different methods but in 1846, Easter fell on the same Sunday for them all.

On good Friday, at the Church of the Holy Sepulchre, one of the holiest and most popular places, the Eastern Orthodox priests and the Roman Catholic priests fought at the altar and the fight grew as monks and pilgrims from both sides joined in, wielding crucifixes and candlesticks and weapons that had been smuggled in.

All of the Christian nations have some interest in protecting their pilgrims and in preserving the trade routes made possible by the Ottomans allowing them access to Palestine. Russia also hopes to use the eastern Orthodox Christians within the Ottoman Empire to help weaken the Ottomans, at some point in the future when their support might be decisive.

In France, Napoleon's nephew, Louis Napoleon III, usurps power in a coup d'état in 1851 and seeks to gather political support from both the left wing and from the Roman Catholic Church in France in order to consolidate his power. The Catholic Church seeks to out do their Orthodox rivals by being named the "sovereign authority" over the Christian population in Ottoman lands. Napoleon III appoints Marquis Charles de La Valette, a zealous member of the clerical party as his ambassador to the Ottoman Empire. This is one of the immediate causes for the outbreak of the war.

Whaling is no longer a glorious adventure.

Herman Melville publishes Moby Dick in 1851 at the peak of the whaling boom to lukewarm reviews and few sales. The romance of sailing ships, exploration and the dangerous gamble of the hunt are now but legend; contemporary ships run on steam and are staffed by hired hands with no stake in the venture- sometimes even impressed against their will, and are operated by corporations or governments.

Whaling voyages last for years and many of the men who are signed on are little more than prisoners aboard these factory ships. Many lament those long years spent 'before the mast', a reference to the living quarters of the sailors.

1856

Japan ends its self imposed isolation and opens its ports to trade.

Many Japanese, especially the merchant class, have tired of Japan's seclusion from the world. When Perry returns in 1854, the Japanese agree to engage in trading.

Japan had closed its ports and lived in deliberate isolation from the rest of the world for over two hundred years when United States naval officer, Commodore Matthew Perry steams into Edo harbor with four gunboats and asks that Japan open its doors to trade. He negotiates tirelessly and threatens to shell Japanese cities then announces that he will leave and let them think it over before returning the following year with a larger fleet.

One objective of opening trade with Japan is to purchase coal to secure a Pacific source of coal for steam ships to refuel.

During the time of the Indian rebellion of 1857, the Taj Mahal is defaced by British soldiers and government officials who chisel out precious stones.

Darwin finally publishes *The Origin of Species* in 1859. Just as he feared, this thrusts him into the limelight and he is the object of anger. It is only that another biologist, Wallace, is about to publish his similar theory of evolution that Darwin finds the fortitude.

 A giant **sunspot** produces a solar flare that causes a solar storm on Earth, disrupting telegraph communications and causing brilliant auroras.

The 'Northern lights' are seen as far south as Hawaii and the Caribbean.

An astronomer observes the first solar flare ever seen by humans in 1859. This first flare ever seen happens to still be the largest ever recorded. When the packet of charged particles that were released as a coronal mass ejection reach the Earth the next day, they overwhelm our protective magnetic field and auroras are visible around the world.

Slavery in the United States has been a divisive issue since the founding of the country. In 1861, one in seven Americans in the United States is enslaved- a total of four million men, women and children.

John Jay Chapman, an American essayist said it well: "There was never any moment in our history when slavery was not a sleeping serpent. It lay coiled up under the table during the deliberations of the Constitutional Convention. Owing to the cotton gin it was more than half awake. Thereafter, it was on everyone's mind though not always on his tongue."

The seeds of freedom and equality sprout naturally from the human heart. Injustice and economic inequality require an ideology of justification that must be enforced in order to keep a short changed population docile. All the propaganda and religion that was created to justify tribute taking and taxation to give special status to a king or social elite had been refuted in the simple words 'All men are created equal' espoused in the American Declaration of Independence.

Image on a Confederate Bank note 1862

Thomas Jefferson once said that slavery was "like holding a wolf by the ear, and we can neither hold him, nor safely let him go. Justice is in one scale, and self-preservation in the other."

While many advocated the abolition of slavery at the time of the writing of the declaration, others opposed it for several reasons. Some thought that Southern states, with their large agricultural plantations, would not join the cause of independence if slavery was outlawed. Some thought slavery was actually necessary for the economic well being of the would be young nation. Greed of individual slave holders, like Thomas Jefferson himself, played a roll. Others feared what uneducated and badly treated former slaves might do if they are freed.

The more brutal the conditions of slavery, the more extreme the ideology needed to rationalize the practice. The more people of color are purported to be inferior, sub-human, stupid and dirty, the more reasonable it seems to treat them harshly. It is a self perpetuating cycle.

While northern towns move at a hectic pace and everyone seems to be busy with their endeavors, south of the Mason-Dixon line, work lacks prestige and people lack ambition or perhaps this is just due to the heat.

Russia's defeat in the Crimean War motivates the Tsar to modernize his country and to deal with the problem of serfdom.

The serfs did not fight with the organized prowess and dedication shown by European troops. The shadow of serfdom hangs over Russia stagnating growth and threatening to erupt into revolution at any time. Agricultural production is poor and neither the serfs nor the landowners have real incentives to improve efficiency. Growth in manufacturing is impeded by a shortage of wage labor (although some factories are staffed by government owned serfs).

Serfs are not allowed to travel off the estates of their masters. Serf families are sometimes broken up and serfs toil endless hours and can be flogged by their masters. Escaped serfs can sometimes travel and then pass themselves off as free. Many serfs live less like slaves and more like poor peasants but some work on chain gangs.

The dissolution of this institution, like any political institution that has become entrenched in a society, is potentially dangerous; if the serfs are liberated, the aristocracy will be angry and maybe even impoverished and might rebel against the Tsar. If the serfs are freed, they may leave the farmlands to which they have been bound and could become roving bands of paupers fomenting chaos and revolution.

There are some 50 million serfs in Russia out of a total population of about 60 million.

Slaves usually toil from dawn until dark with a whip wielding overseer not far off. Escape is made much more difficult because the color of their skin makes them recognizable as slaves even at a distance. Slave families are regularly broken up not just because of the changing economic needs or fortunes of the master, but as deliberate ways to control the slaves.

The most widely read abolitionist newspaper is *The Liberator*.

The escaped slave, Frederick Douglas is an eloquent orator on the abolitionist circuit.

Harriet Tubman, left, with escaped slaves.

The escaped slave Harriet Tubman makes more than 19 forays back into the South to help more than 300 slaves escape using the network of the Underground Railroad. She also works as a Union spy. She suffers seizures and headaches due to a head injury sustained when struck by a metal weight during a beating as a young slave.

Jules Verne publishes *Cinq Semaines en Ballon*.

This engraving appears in Harper's Magazine in 1863. It claims to show the condition of an escaped slave who crossed to Union lines during the war. The engraving might be using the composition and details of an earlier photo.

In 1861, the American Civil War breaks out and Russia begins to emancipate its 50 million serfs.

Even as Civil War is breaking out in America the idea of 'Manifest Destiny' is ascendent.

This painting made by Emanuel Leutze in 1861 symbolizes the idea that the United States with her constitution, capitalistic economy and enterprising work ethic is divinely destined for expansion; from the original colonies on the Atlantic seaboard westward to the Pacific Ocean. Like Moses, who is actually represented in the ornate border, the pilgrim points to the Pacific.

"From whence shall we expect the approach of danger? Shall some trans-Atlantic military giant step the earth and crush us at a blow? Never. All the armies of Europe and Asia...could not by force take a drink from the Ohio River or make a track on the Blue Ridge in the trial of a thousand years. No, if destruction be our lot we must ourselves be its author and finisher. As a nation of free men we will live forever or die by suicide."

- Abraham Lincoln

The North had industrialized while The South had expanded its agricultural economy. The energy of industry is driven by oil and coal while agriculture is still relying on human muscle power. A well developed railroad and telegraph network and the capacity to make arms and other necessary manufactured goods on an industrial scale give The North a military advantage.

Many Southerners do not support ceding from the Union and going to war over the issue of slavery. Most people do not own slaves. Once war starts and Northern troops march south, more people feel like fighting.

Whether or not the institution of slavery will be allowed in the Western Territories is one of the causes of the war.

The rights of Native Americans don't get much consideration.

The draft is unpopular in the North; the sons of wealthy northern families can legally buy their way out of service.

African Americans (then politely called *Negro* or *Colored*) beg to enter the fight but are not allowed to join in until late in the war.

The bloody Civil War ends in 1865 and slavery is finally abolished in America.

The failure to find a compromise and avoid war costs the lives of 600,000 dead and many more injured. The South's infrastructure is destroyed and the once rich area becomes poor for a century.

James Clerk Maxwell unites electricity and magnetism, showing that they are different expressions of the same thing.

Maxwell's equations are simple, symmetrical and elegant. Their beauty resonates in the minds of mathematicians.

Maxwell shows how the motion of a magnet can induce an electric current in a wire and conversely how an electric current passing through a wire can make an electromagnet.

A generator produces an electrical current by using some fuel source to rotate a magnet around a coil of wire or to spin a coil of wire around a magnet.

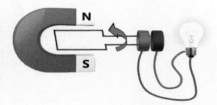

Japan decides to industrialize.

Japan had learned from its recent encounter with the west and now embarks on a deliberate road of modernization and industrialization.

The Meiji Restoration begins in 1867 after the Shogun is persuaded to retire and the Emperor, who had been but a figure head is made the official ruler along with a body of advisers in a quasi-parliamentary system. The army is modernized under the direction of French advisers and the navy is modernized according to the British model.

Additional schools are built and all children are taught to read and write. Foreign teachers are recruited to teach science, medicine, math, engineering and languages. Steam ships are purchased and plans are made to build a railroad between Nagasaki and Edo, a telegraph line and a steel mill.

Informational graphics are created that artistically convey statistical information.

The size of Napoleon's army is depicted by the width of the line. The line starts out wide at the left as the large army leaves France and gets narrower as troops die on the march eastward. When they retreat from the Russian winter, the line moves back from Paris narrowing further as troop numbers continue to decrease. Napoleon loses such a high percentage of men, France's population growth rate is low for some time afterwards.

The Pennsylvania oil rush brings a new source of energy to American markets.

Petroleum had been known in Pennsylvania because it breaks out at the surface in seeps. It was marked on maps but mostly just as places for farmers to avoid as there were not many known uses for it. Native Americans had used it at least for insect repellent and ceremonial purposes. In the 1850s, Samuel Kier begins experimenting with ways to refine the crude oil into a clean burning fuel that he calls 'carbon oil'. Then he begins to drill for it.

Others soon get in on the action. In 1859 a well strikes oil at 69 feet below ground and soon others dig wells nearby. In that first year an estimated 2,000 to 4,500 barrels are produced. By 1869 the output will rise to 4 million barrels. Boom towns spring up similar to those of the gold rush.

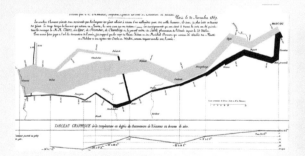

The new Suez Canal links the Mediterranean Sea to the Indian Ocean by ship.

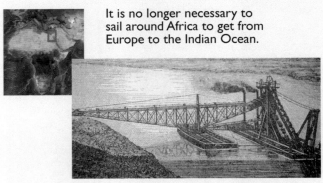

It is no longer necessary to sail around Africa to get from Europe to the Indian Ocean.

The construction of the Suez Canal is organized by the French diplomat turned developer Ferdinand de Lesseps. While delayed in Alexandria, he reads the report and memoirs of Napoleon's civil engineer who had tried to design a canal across the African isthmus. Using some of the connections he made as a diplomat, he gets a 99 year lease/concession from Egypt to build the canal. Construction of the canal is begun with forced (slave) labor and finished after ten years, opening in 1869.

Oil has been trickling out of the Baku Khanate in Azerbaijan since the early 1800's from shallow, hand-dug wells. It is shipped off primarily to Persia for lighting fuel and for use in ointments.

The American transcontinental railroad is completed.

The world's web of transportation corridors ramps up and the time required to move people or goods drops markedly in the single year of 1869. At Promontory Point in Utah, the Golden Spike unites America's transcontinental railroad in the same year that the Suez Canal opens.

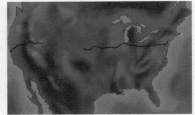

Whaling ships use steam engines in addition to sails.

As whalers depleted nearby whale populations, they had to voyage ever further out to sea to find more whales. The size of the whaling ships increased with the length of the voyage (in order to: handle the seas and weather, be able to carry more supplies for the men and hold more whale oil to make the long trip worthwhile).

The length of whaling ships can be said to have increased proportionately as the length of the voyage increased and inversely proportionately to the size of worldwide whale populations. Whaling ships evolved as the whaling industry evolved.

The North American Buffalo is deliberately exterminated to deprive Native Americans of their food and way of life.

When the fresh corpses of buffalo litter the landscape entrepreneurs will realize the value of buffalo skulls in fertilizer and some of them will be gathered up and shipped out by rail.

A pattern is discovered between the seemingly random multitude of different kinds of atoms and their chemical properties.

Chemists had been trying to discover all of the fundamental units of matter - which they call atoms - and have by now discovered most of them. Atoms are the smallest known units of matter (at this time). Substances like wood or water are known to be composed of smaller substances; wood is composed mostly of carbon atoms and water of hydrogen and oxygen atoms. There are dozens of different kinds of atoms. Chemists seek to organize the different kinds of atoms into groups with similar properties and endeavor to find some kind of explanation for or relationship between all the different types of atoms.

Dmitri Mendeleev has the intuition to organize them by weight and publishes his **Periodic Table of the Elements** in 1869. The smallest atoms are listed in the first row, larger elements in the next row and so on. Mendeleev tries many different arrangements of row length and notices that in some arrangements, atoms with similar properties line up in columns; for example the first column contains reactive elements and the precious metals copper, silver and gold are all in one column in the middle of the chart, and the last column contains inert, non reactive atoms.

Mendeleev doesn't know why the rows should be of these particular lengths, he only knows by observation that this arrangement of rows does create pleasing patterns in the columns and he surmises that there must be intrinsic properties in the nature of the atoms that are somehow reflected in this arrangement.

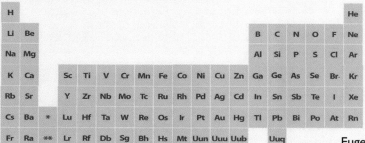

Eugenics is launched by Francis Galton who publishes *Hereditary Genius*. Inspired his cousin, Charles Darwin's work, he explores the idea of heredity and extrapolates the evolution of humans into the future. Charles had observed the breeding of dogs and pigeons and this helped him to develop his theory. If dogs can be bred by careful selection of the parents for specific traits, why not humans?

By 1873 oil production in Pennsylvania reaches 10 million barrels a year.

Petroleum oil is distilled into kerosene and used for illumination displacing the more expensive whale oil.

1875

Japan begins to carve out its own 'sphere of influence'.

Japan observes that Western powers are competing for trading opportunities and sometimes commandeering resources. Japan threatens Korea with attack in 1876 and demands trading privileges, as Japan lacks extensive coal reserves- which Korea posses.

Japan will also need more rice to feed the growing population.

The interior of Africa has been difficult for Europeans to colonize or even to explore.

Because Africa has many interior highlands, its rivers tend to be obstructed by waterfalls. The mighty Congo River leads to the heart of Africa, but its many waterfalls prevent ships from navigating it.

Africa spans the equator and its climate allows for tropical diseases, to which Europe's would-be explorers have little to no immunity.

Henry Morton Stanley explores the region in three separate expeditions.

Henry Morton Stanley is as enigmatic as he is intrepid. Born a bastard, orphaned, and raised in a poor house in Britain, he makes his way to America and fights in the civil war, first on the side of the Confederacy, then as a Galvanized Yankee, and finally in the Union Navy.

His endurance, despite the privations of the journey and its high number of casualties increase his fame, as he is thought to embody the mythic Victorian hero. In the following decades, he will become reviled by some for his brutality and his associations with the imperial interests who will utilize the paths he blazed.

After the war, he becomes a journalist and then is sent to Africa to find Dr. Livingstone. Stanley's story, with the quote, "Dr. Livingstone, I presume?" makes him famous. He is later sent on another expedition across the African continent from Zanzibar to the mouth of the Congo.

Currently, Stanley's personality and deeds are being reanalyzed. Perhaps the brutal methods attributed to Stanley, while befitting to many others, were not characteristic of the expeditions he actually led. For example, a December 2011 article in the Smithsonian Magazine by Roy Baumeister and John Tierney suggests that Stanley does not commit the heinous acts that his fellow European explorers do.

Modern oil tankers are developed by Ludvig and Robert Nobel between 1877 and 1885.

In 1883, the hulls of oil transport tankers are further improved by dividing them into many, smaller oil holds that run the length of the ship. Previously, the hulls had been split into only one or two tanks, causing the ships to be prone to rolling over when the oil sloshes back and forth.

Late in the nineteenth century, colonial powers are able to penetrate into the African interior, and the Scramble for Africa ensues.

Belgian
British
French
German
Italian
Portuguese
Spanish
Independent

The King of Belgium is keen to catch up with other European powers in plundering world resources. A conference known as the Berlin Conference is held assembling various European powers. Together they decide which part of Africa each will lay claim to. King Leopold II, acting not for the country of Belgium, but as an independent person, takes the interior province of the Congo as his fiefdom. Rubber, garnered as a sap from rubber trees, is a scarce and valuable commodity in industrialized countries. Rubber trees are plentiful in the Congo.

Afghanistan is caught between Britain and Russia as they play out their 'Great Game'.

Entitled "Save Me From My Friends" a political cartoon by J. Tennial published in Punch Magazine in 1878 shows the Amir of Afghanistan caught between the Russian bear and British lion.

"SAVE ME FROM MY FRIENDS!"

In 1882, British captain Jack Fisher advocates the conversion of British war ships to run on oil.

Coal had ignited the Industrial Revolution and Britain still has plenty of it. The mighty ships of the British navy run on coal and although it is expected that oil-powered ships would be faster, more maneuverable, longer ranging and quickly refueled, the ideas of switching to oil is met with fierce resistance because Britain does not have any oil reserves, some doubt whether there is enough oil in the whole world to fuel the British fleet. Oil is found the following year in Sumatra by the Dutch.

Oil has not yet been found in Texas, or the Middle East.

An arms race has been going on in Europe.

England has the world's finest navy but Germany has been eagerly catching up. The industrial and economic power of Germany has grown quickly since unification in 1871. The German Kaiser's advisor, Bismark had kept a state of peace by carefully maintaining alliances with the other powers: he made sure to always have the support of at least three of the five major European powers and to avoid a war on two fronts, never with both Russia and France. When Wilhelm II becomes Kaiser in 1888, he forces Bismark to retire.

Construction begins on the Eiffel Tower, which will serve as the gate to the World's Fair in Paris.

Construction of the tower begins in 1887. This iron structure becomes the tallest building on the planet – surpassing the Washington Monument. It served as the entrance arch to the World's Fair in Paris, 1889.

England invades Egypt, and with the assistance of the French and takes control of the Suez canal in 1882.

Krakatoa, near Java and Sumatra, erupts in 1883.

Buffalo Bill's show is the highlight of the World's Fair.

The legendary days of the wild west are showcased in their twilight hour.

 The *Murex* is the first tanker to pass through the Suez Canal, in 1892.

Development of the electric telephone has been going on for decades as the telegraph is successively improved. In 1892 Alexander Graham Bell places the first New York to Chicago telephone call.

Few of the attendees at the World's Fair understand what is really happening on the other side of the world in Africa.

King Leopold's agents and henchmen in the Congo are ruthless in ensuring that rubber trees are tapped and the sap processed and exported. The children of men who fall short of making their tax quotas have their limbs amputated. Soldiers of Leopold's militias must submit one hand for every bullet used to prove they are not wasting bullets In skirmishes with resistors. If not enough enemy combatants are killed, the soldiers sometimes make their quota by maiming civilians.

News of this policy, accompanied by photographs, will eventually bring international criticism. The Belgium parliament will demand that the private fiefdom be removed from the king and place the colony under state control, which is at least an improvement but this won't happen until 1908.

1893

Investigative journalism debuts.

In the last decade of the nineteenth century, the mass-circulation of magazines brings their publishers enough revenue to pay journalists to conduct investigations. Investigative journalists explore modern problems arising from the industrial economy and the rapid growth of cities, such as unsafe and unsanitary living and working conditions, child labor, political corruption, false advertising, and monopolistic business practices.

Japan flexes its new found industrial muscle.

1894

The First Sino-Japanese War, August 1894 – April 1895, is fought between Qing Dynasty China and Meiji Japan, primarily over control of Korea.

Science illustration attempts to become ever more realistic.

Charles Knight paints dinosaurs and other extinct animals as they might have been in real life.

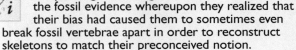

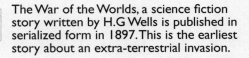

Leaping Laelops: Charles Knight paints this striking image of two competing dinosaurs in 1897. Dinosaurs had been imagined as lizard like beasts who dragged their tails as they shuffled along. Knight tried to paint dinosaurs with drooping tails but was unable to make a convincing illustration. His paintings encouraged scientists to reexamine the fossil evidence whereupon they realized that their bias had caused them to sometimes even break fossil vertebrae apart in order to reconstruct skeletons to match their preconceived notion.

The War of the Worlds, a science fiction story written by H.G Wells is published in serialized form in 1897. This is the earliest story about an extra-terrestrial invasion.

The Sinking of the Maine in 1898 is a pretext for war.
William Randolph Hearst's newspapers proclaim it!

The pace of information dissemination has quickened,
but the information itself is sometimes manipulated.

Spain's formerly vast empire
has dwindled to include
only Cuba, Puerto Rico, the
Philippines, Guam and some
nearby Pacific islands. Cuba
had been a province of Spain
for almost 400 years, and is
a trading base and source
of prestige. The Cuban
people had rebelled against
Spanish rule in 1888, but this
rebellion had been put down.

From exile, Jose Marti emerges
as the leader of The Cuba Libre
movement which through its offices
in Florida and New York attempts to
buy and smuggle out weapons and
launches a propaganda campaign to
gain support and to persuade the
U.S. government to put pressure
on Spain. The United States had
been dissuading European influence
in the Americas for decades and
the cause against Catholic Spain
finds sympathy with the mostly
Protestant U.S. citizenry.

As the rebellion in Cuba continues, U.S.
corporations with interests in sugar and shipping
lose money and desire resolution of the conflict.
Their interest is for stability, not justice. Some
hope that Spain will put down the rebellion and
restore order while others pressure President
McKinley to find a diplomatic solution.

McKinley, by threatening to recognize and
then arm the rebels, persuades Spain to cede
the territory. Eleven days before Cuba is to
become independent, the U.S. naval ship Maine
explodes in Havana harbor, killing 262 sailors.

Hearst, who has a monopoly
on American newspapers,
hijacks the information
system and portrays the
incident as a deliberate
act in order to sell more
newspapers and to start
a war. This sensationalist
portrayal of the incident,
later dubbed *yellow journalism*,
does cause the United States
to declare war.

By the time the American public
becomes aware of what has happened,
the war with Spain is well under way
and can't easily be stopped. It is still
a mystery as to whether The Maine,
which was loaded with munitions, had
an accidental fire, hit a Spanish mine, or
was sabotaged- and if so, by whom?

Heart of Darkness, an account
of the Belgian Congo by Joseph
Conrad, appears in Blackwood's
Magazine in three parts, in 1899.

George Washington Carver is allowed
to continue his research at a University.

The former slave
teaches new
methods of crop
rotation to deal
with the soils of the
American South
that are depleted in
nutrients from years
of growing nothing
but cotton.

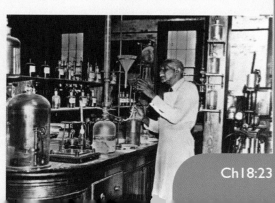

Chapter 19: A Cosmic Outlook Develops

 1900

 1.6 billion

World population is now over a billion. Humanity's numbers, which had been increasing at a linear rate, now really ratchet up the exponential curve.

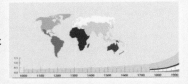

A desperate uprising, The Boxer Rebellion, erupts in China.

This nationalist movement of impoverished peasants and disenfranchised people wants to drive foreigners and foreign influences out of China.

Mighty China, now lumbers like a marooned whale; its economy disrupted by industrialized powers picking away within their 'spheres of influence'. It is riddled with opium addicts and nominally ruled by the entrenched Qing dynasty.

Missionaries accompany the foreign soldiers, sailors and merchants of the opium trade. Christianity spreads, especially among the poorest Chinese. Converts flout traditional ceremonious and sometimes the Confucian ideals of respect for family, elders and social hierarchy. Missionaries pressure local officials to side with converts in legal disputes. Many Chinese fear that the spread of Christianity will allow foreigners to take control of the country.

Rebellions against the Qing had been going on for decades. Conservative forces in the country redirect the rebels to drop their claims against the Qing and to focus only on foreign imperialists and the spread of Christianity. The governor of Shandong province enrolls bands of rebels as local militia and renames them Yihetuan, which translates to 'Righteous and Harmonious Militia'. These bands practice Chinese martial arts and calisthenics which leads to the nickname 'Boxers'. They come to believe that these arts actually could protect them from the bullets and artillery of their industrialized foreign enemies.

The Chinese Rebellion is easily crushed by the Eight-Nation Alliance of industrialized powers, who then divide the spoils among themselves.

The Eight-Nation Alliance of imperial powers consists of 20,000 well armed troops from Austria-Hungary, France, Germany, Italy, Japan, Russia, the United Kingdom, and the United States.

Great Britain was the first nation to industrialize on a large scale with North America and other European nations quickly following suit. Russia and Japan become aware of the power of industrialization, and deliberately reorganize their societies through governmental policies to adopt an industrial package. This package contains both the hardware of iron, steel, and mass production, and the social software of a wage earning class and increased access to education.

The other industrialized nations also enter the arms race and military spending increases by 50% in the five years before the 'Great War' breaks out. The spark that lights the powder keg comes when Austria-Hungary punishes Serbia after a Serbian student assassinates a prince. Austria-Hungary had previously snatched Serbia from the crumbling Ottoman Empire which neither the Serbs nor the Russians were happy about.

The United States is also at war with Spain, a country whose superpower status had long since faded. America takes over her last possessions: Cuba, Puerto Rico and the Philippines.

Teddy Roosevelt leads the troops, known as the *rough riders*. He wishes that there were a canal in Panama, so that U.S. ships could move easily between the east and west coasts without having to go around South America.

Members of the Philippine resistance.

Rockefeller's monopolization of the oil industry is exposed.

 Ida Tarbell writes a piece of investigative journalism about John Rockefeller's monopolization of the oil industry for McClure's Magazine in 1902. Ida's father was a Pennsylvania oil man whose enterprise was ruined as Rockefeller was able to dominate the industry,

 The first gusher in Texas, known as Spindletop, pours forth oil in 1901.

America, promising freedom, democracy and the potential to profit by one's own hard work, beckons immigrants.

Immigrants are now coming from Eastern and Southern Europe whereas previous waves of immigrants had been of Protestants coming from Northern and Western Europe. French Canadians also immigrate by migrating south to work in the industrialized textile industry in the New England states.

The breeding of dogs is high fashion.

Albert Einstein publishes a new hypothesis that shows that matter and energy are different expressions of the same thing.

Einstein publishes papers on the equivalence of matter and energy and on the Special Theory of Relativity in 1905.

1905

$$E=mc^2$$

Like two sides of a coin, matter and energy are different forms of the same stuff. This will upset our existing models of the cosmos.

Energy and matter are two forms of the same stuff. Either one can be exchanged for the other; just as dollars can be exchanged for gold or yen, an object can be transformed into a specific amount of energy. This exchange does not happen in every day circumstances; it takes something more extreme like the crushing pressure at the center of a star or a nuclear bomb to convert matter into energy.

Likewise, energy can be transformed into a specific amount of matter. We do not observe light rays congealing into particles of matter but shortly after the big bang when the universe was still extremely hot, energy did congeal into particles of matter.

To calculate the exchange, the speed of light must be used as an exponential multiplier. Multiply the mass of the object you wish to convert by the speed of light and then multiply that by the speed of light again to get the equivalent amount of energy.

In atoms of matter, the subatomic particles orbit each other in micro whirlwinds and quantum patterns. Energy is thus contained within the atoms of matter. The mass of an object is the measure of how much energy it contains.

A little bit of matter is equivalent to a lot of energy because according to the relationship $E=mc^2$, the amount of energy is magnified by the speed of light squared and the speed of light is incredibly fast.

Iranians seek to protect their political integrity from colonial powers and to establish democracy.

The Iranian Constitutional Revolution, 1905-1906, limits the power of the monarchy and ushers in a time of unprecedented debate, participation and a free press.

The Anglo-Russian convention of 1907 crushes the dream of Persian sovereignty.

Iran is partitioned into three sections; one for the British, one for the Russians, and a weak, neutral Iranian sector between them. This ends the rivalry between Russia and Britain for control of Central Asia, known as The Great Game, which has been a threat to the stability of both nations. Britain had feared the potential of Russian interference with its control of India and Russia had feared British interference with its southern expansion. Both had also feared the outbreak of a direct war between.

But now they both share a new fear: the growing industrial power of Germany. German industrial power has reached a high level, possibly surpassing Britain's. Germany has few colonies and seeks to compete with the other industrialized powers on the world stage. Germany also needs markets for its products. By ending their rivalry they can become allies against the new German threat.

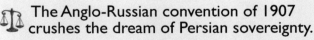

President Theodore Roosevelt wants a Panama Canal but Panama is in the sovereign country of Colombia.

 After their success with building the Suez Canal, the French have undertaken to build one across the Central American Isthmus. But after decades of struggling in the jungle, they are ready to give it up. The project is much more difficult than it had been in Egypt because of the difference in sea level between the Atlantic and the Pacific sides as well as tropical disease.

The Colombian government is prevented from moving more troops into the area by train because the guns of the USS Nashville, now just offshore, have the tracks within range. The 'rebels' declare independence and form a military junta. The U.S. pays 10 million dollars.

In 1903, the U.S. Senate ratifies a treaty to buy out French interests in the canal but Columbia won't take the deal. Instead of offering better terms, Roosevelt lets it be known to Colombian soldiers in the region and to some supposed Panamanian rebels that the U.S. will support them if they attempt to cede from Colombia. Rumors suggest that bribes are paid directly to these individuals but this is not confirmed.

The Panamanian ambassador, who is a french citizen and the chief engineer and a major stockholder of the French canal company, signs the treaty. This lack of protocol will cause some legal complications for the U.S. in later years.

An earthquake strikes San Francisco.

 The 1906 quake ruptures almost 300 miles of the San Andreas Fault. The epicenter is San Francisco, a city that had grown up haphazardly in the Gold Rush Era. Water mains and gas lines break. Most insurance policies cover fire but not earthquakes; many buildings undamaged by the quake subsequently burn.

Analysis of soil types and ground displacement measurements leads to the 'elastic rebound theory' and the concept that stored stress in the ground causes the earthquake and not that an 'earthquake' causes the ground to move. Scientists compile much data, however they lack of an understanding of plate tectonics and cannot identify the general cause for the stress build up.

Damage from the quake is photographed and studied. Seismographs from around the world record the quake. An earthquake emits 2 different kinds of waves; pressure waves or p waves arrive first, slower moving shear waves or s waves follow. The time difference between the arrival of the different types of wave, allows scientists to calculate the distance to the quake. In the actual seismogram of this quake shown above, the p waves are the small squiggles that begin about a centimeter from the left.

Rampant financial speculation leads to *The Panic of 1907*.

 The United States is already mired in recession when a stock scandal is perpetrated. United Copper is formed by the merger of several smaller mining companies and one of its owners attempts to corner its stock to manipulate its price. The plot fails and the price for United Copper shares collapses.

Money from around the nation and some from other nations pours in. This influx of cash and gold, reduces the liquidity of banks and causes interest rates to rise.

Depositors at banks affiliated with the company rush to remove their funds. On the New York Stock Exchange, investors lose their appetites and the value of the Exchange drops precipitously. Bank runs spread to other banks and trust companies. With major banks on the verge of declaring bankruptcy, the federal government earmarks 35 million dollars to quell the crisis.

J.P. Morgan, one of America's most powerful financiers, takes charge of this money and organizes with other bankers to redistribute money between banks, secure some international lines of credit and to buy ailing stocks of otherwise healthy corporations.

An asteroid strikes Siberia.

The biggest impact event in Earth's humanly recorded history occurs on June 30, 1908. A large meteorite or asteroid explodes in the atmosphere a few miles above ground level, flattening almost 900 square miles of forest.

Oil is found in Iran in 1908. After 5 years of searching, a geologist finally finds oil for the Anglo Persian Oil Company.

Exquisite fossils are discovered.

In 1909, the Burgess Shale is discovered. It contains exquisitely preserved fossils of early Cambrian life. A whole community of organisms was preserved in situ when the piece of shallow sea floor the plants and animals were living on, broke loose in an earthquake and tumbled down the continental shelf into deep anoxic waters. This chunk of fossil rich rock was later metamorphosed into a shale-y rock and pushed onshore in a mountain building event.

Japan annexes Korea.

An industrial fire galvanizes support for the American labor movement.

The deadly industrial disaster in the Triangle Shirtwaist Factory in NYC in 1911 kills 146 workers, mostly young immigrant women. In the previous year, there had been many strikes throughout the city by female workers protesting long hours, low pay and unsafe conditions. Many had been fired, harassed by being accused of prostitution and some had been beaten. Some shops were unionized as a result of those strikes but not so at the Triangle Shirtwaist Factory.

During the funeral procession, thousands of mourners line the streets as black cloaked horses transport the coffins of the young women.

The fire occurs during the regular Saturday workday in the late afternoon. The owners lock the exits as is common practice, to prevent workers from taking breaks or pilfering supplies. When the owners, who are at a luncheon nearby with their families, hear that flames have broken out and are engulfing the 9th floor, they rush to bring the keys. The fire department arrives promptly with their horse drawn wagons but their ladders are not tall enough to reach the windows. Many of the young women jump to escape the flames as witnessed by the helpless crowd gathered below.

England claims to be the **Cradle of Humanity**.

In 1912, a seemingly fossilized human skull and jawbone are found in a gravel pit in Piltdown, England. The bones purportedly show evidence for human evolution and point to Great Britain as the cradle of humanity! It all seems almost too good to be true for many in the scientific community who hail from English or at least have Western European roots. The skull and jawbone are enshrined in a case in the British Museum and are not examined very carefully.

Continental Drift, now the Theory of Plate Tectonics, is proposed by Alfred Wegener in 1912 to few supporters and much laughter.

$ **The Federal Reserve Bank is established.**

The Panic of 1907 led to pressure for the creation of a central bank that could step in to manage future crisis. With the urging of President Woodrow Wilson, the Federal Reserve System, with its public and private components, is established in 1913. The Federal Reserve System also makes it easier to raise money for the war effort.

China becomes a republic on January 1st, 1912.

The aristocracy in Europe is still entrenched.

The aristocrats of Europe are closely related. The emperor of Germany, Kaiser Wilhelm II and the reigning king of England, King George V, are first cousins. The Russian Tsar, Nicholas II is their second cousin. Kaiser Wilhelm II spent some of his childhood summers in Britain playing war games in the garden with his English cousins. He never outgrows these games or his love of parades and dreams of military glory.

Delusions of military grandeur, romantic aristocratic military traditions and the euphoric feelings of belonging that accompany the new sense of nationalism, are mixed together and become mired down in the interminable reality of trench warfare. On occasion, it occurs to individual soldiers that the men in the opposing trenches are people like themselves.

The British Royal Navy begins to convert its ships to run on oil.

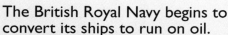

Some engineers and policy makers, namely Winston Churchill push to build some oil powered ships. When these ships, including the HMS Queen Elizabeth, are launched in 1913, all reservations are dispelled. The new class of battleships, the **superdreadnaughts**, would prove to be so reliable that they will serve in both World Wars.

British geologists search for oil reserves in order to spur on the conversion of the rest of the fleet and the British government brokers a deal between the Anglo-Persian Oil Company and the Shah of Persia, sourcing oil from fields in what is now modern-day Iran. The Anglo-Persian Oil Company is known today as The British Petroleum Company.

War breaks out in June 1914 after the Austrian Archduke Franz Ferdinand is assassinated in Sarajevo.

The Panama Canal opens in 1914.

Einstein continues to develop his theory of relativity and expands it to include gravity, publishing his **General Theory of Relativity** in 1915.

Gravity is no longer an unexplained, almost magical force like it is in Newtonian physics where objects with mass just pull together across vast distances as if with an invisible rubber band. In the new theory, objects move toward other objects because they are moving down unseen inclines in the topography of space. The inclines are due to depressions in the topography of the fabric of space that are caused by the presence of the objects of matter.

Gravity is redefined by the new physics, not as a force but as the consequence of objects moving naturally and freely through the contours of the topography of space.

Objects of matter distort the fabric of space/time as a bowling ball distorts the fabric of a trampoline.

In our solar system, the most massive object is the sun and it creates a deep gravitational well around itself.

Each of the planets create their own small well. The planets would roll down the gravitational hill into the sun but each planet is constrained by the lip of its own small gravitational similarly to a boulder on a mountainside which doesn't roll downhill because it is dug in slightly. The planets thus lean in toward the sun and orbit it.

In Einstein's new theory, space is redefined as a fabric woven from the threads of both distance and time. Spacetime is distorted and warped into topographical contours by objects of matter. Massive objects like stars create deep wells in the fabric; the more massive an object, the deeper the well. Any object that is moving through spacetime follows the contours of this topography. As the physicist John Wheeler will later say "matter tells space how to bend and space tells matter where to move."

Oil becomes a hot commodity during WWI. The UK and Germany fight over Iran for its oil supplies.

Einstein's new equations lead to the implication that the size of the Universe is changing.

The prevailing paradigm, hypothesized by Isaac Newton, is that the Universe is infinite in extent and relatively similar throughout. According to this view, the Universe has always existed and has no point of origin. It never had a beginning and it will never end. This new idea that the Universe might be growing or shrinking is a paradigm shift and many people prefer the stable, familiar, steady state model.

No one is more upset that the size of the Universe could be getting bigger or smaller than Albert Einstein himself, since the implication comes from his own theory. Einstein broods about this and looks back over his equations, hoping to find a mistake. He actually invents a new term to neutralize possible change. He himself knows that this is a retroactive, cheap fix, which irritates him further. Ironically, this fudge factor he attempted to add is the cosmological constant, which proves useful decades later.

A couple of problems that had always bothered Isaac Newton are solved by new physics. Newton had been troubled by the fact that he had no explanation for why or how gravity actually works and that he could only describe how objects are attracted to each other. Newton had also wondered why all of the objects in the universe, under the influence of their mutual gravitational attraction, didn't eventually wind up as one big clump in the center or the universe.

The quest to understand the Universe goes on even in the trenches.

Karl Schwarzschild is an artillery officer on the German side. He manages to write three scientific papers from the trenches; two on relativity and one on quantum theory. Using Einstein's field equations, he shows that matter, if compressed into a very small space can take a strange form. This work presages speculation that Black Holes might exist. Schwarzschild contracts a rare skin disease while in the trenches on the Russian Front and dies in 1916.

 The new theory of relativity needs a good test.

Einstein's new theory and Newton's old one are compared by scientists. Einstein's theory describes all phenomena as well as Newton's old equations had, and in the peculiar case of describing the orbit of Mercury, Einstein's equations are better. Mercury is the one planet whose motions were never adequately predicted with the use of Newton's equations; the planet was always found to be a little bit ahead or behind its predicted position.

Mercury's orbit is peculiar because it is so close to the sun's deep gravitational well. Newton's rules of thumb are only approximations of how gravity acts in more average circumstances. Newton's rules work in most of the circumstances we observe because we are far enough from the sun (or any other giant object) to be in a rather flat area of space/time.

Since predicting the orbit of Mercury was an existing problem, solving it would not be a great test of the new theory. The greatest test of a new hypothesis is making a prediction that does not solve an existing problem because of possible bias, circular reasoning or the possible 'look and you shall find' problem, where so much data is generated and picked through until convenient facts are found that substantiate the desired conclusion.

Japan, in order to expand its own sphere of influence, participates in the war and sides against Germany.

The Japanese navy secures sea lanes against the Germans in the South Pacific and Indian oceans.

There is unrest within the Russian state and the war has only added to the discord already threatening imperial rule.

Russian war casualties are staggering, much higher than those sustained by any other nation. Russia had somewhat modernized itself as the Czar had copied some western European technology such as building railroads and had changed its social organization to a more egalitarian model by having abolished serfdom and allowing some parliamentary participation.

The industrial revolution in Russia is still in its early stages. Rural poor flock to cities whose populations swell beyond the capacity of the infrastructure. Hours are long in the new factories because of war production quotas. Wages are low but the new city dwellers are exposed to merchandise, ideas and opportunity they had never imagined while in the countryside. The Tzar, proud head of the Romanov monarchy, believes in his divine right to be leader. His idealized vision blinds him to the true state of affairs in his country and is unable to take further reforms.

The Tzar had hoped a foreign war would bring him prestige and unite the ethnic groups within his empire. The Russian army is no match for fully industrialized Germany. By the end of 1916, five million Russian soldiers have been killed, wounded, taken prisoner or are missing in action. The Tsar had backpedaled and stripped the parliament or Duma of most of its already limited power and the peasants are crushed by heavy debt payments for the plots of land that accompanied their emancipation.

The dream of democratic participation in government, the dignity of the individual and other Enlightenment ideas have been cherished by Russian intellectuals, despite imperial repression for decades. A revolution ensues as moderates join the popular uprising along with socialist and well organized communist groups and set up a new provisional government.

The February Revolution deposes the Tsar, but the new provisional government is unable to consolidate itself and lead effectively. It is overthrown by the October Revolution led by Vladimir Lenin.

The Great War ends, but in its wake an outbreak of influenza kills many millions more.

Millions of people died in the war. There were more than 9 million deaths of soldiers with another 21 million wounded. Many of the civilians and soldiers who survived have been maimed. Many civilians died, mostly of disease, but this was chiefly due to vulnerability caused by malnutrition rather than to any particularly virulent disease.

The Flu usually kills only already weak, sick, elderly or young individuals. The pandemic of 1918 strangely kills mostly young adults in their prime. It is still uncertain why this virus reacted the way it did. Did the conditions during the war mold a more virulent strain or did the high levels of human stress cause an unusual reaction? Returning soldiers and worldwide transport carry the disease to every corner of the world.

The Great War won't be renamed World War I until the next world war begins. The American motto was, "The war to end all wars."

The long ailing and debt ridden Ottoman Empire collapses.

The Ottomans lose battles on many fronts during World War I. British forces defeat the Ottoman army and capture Bagdad in 1917.

Amid much squabbling, the Treaty of Versailles emerges at the end of the war and defines new borders, alliances and agreements.

 China had entered The Great War on the side of the Allies on condition that Chinese lands, which had been occupied by Germany, be restored to Chinese sovereignty when the war ended. However, the Versailles Treaty gives the Shandong province to Japan instead, setting off nationalistic protests called the May Fourth Movement, in 1919. Many students and Chinese intellectuals turn away from western ideals of liberal democracy and study Marxism.

Japan is denied a statement on racial equality.

Although Japan had also fought against Germany in WWI, its demand for a statement of racial equality in Versaille is rebuffed by Australia whose government fears Japan's growing influence in the South Pacific and a potential influx of Japanese immigrants.

Germany is saddled with reparations that are beyond its $ ability to ever repay.

President Wilson signs legislation prohibiting child labor but the statute is soon overturned by the Supreme Court.

 Woodrow Wilson, advocates that a *League of Nations* be founded to avoid future wars by diplomatic means.

Isolationists in America reject their president's bid. Some fear that America will be unable to act independently if such an international body is vested with authority or that America might paradoxically be forced into more foreign wars and, some business interests fear that future neocolonialist practices might be prohibited.

Prohibition, the ban on drinking alcoholic beverages in the USA, is ushered in with the passage of the eighteenth amendment, in 1919.

1919

Einstein's theory of relativity is put to a robust test in 1919.

Einstein had thought of a better test involving the bending of light rays traveling through space; the rays should travel straight until they happen to pass close to a star and then they should bend toward that star (because the star, being massive, should curve the fabric of space/time in its vicinity).

Exactly how to conduct such an experiment is a challenge. A plan is devised to measure light rays passing near our own sun. This can only be done during a total eclipse of the sun- so that the light from our sun, which would overwhelm our view, is blocked out by being covered up by the moon. Scientists plan to make the measurements during the next total eclipse and appoint Arthur Eddington, a prominent English astronomer, to lead the expedition to Africa where the eclipse will be visible.

Eddington is a Quaker and does not believe in war. His colleagues are relieved to get him out of England before he is thrown into prison as a draft dodger. The war, which had looked as if it might go on indefinitely, actually ends before the eclipse. When the results come in, they confirm Einstein's theory, which becomes front page news.

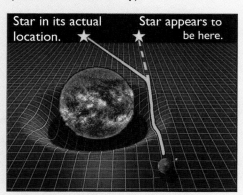

Star in its actual location.   Star appears to be here.

Following World War One, the lands of the defeated Ottoman Empire are partitioned up amongst the prevailing European powers.

The British take Palestine, including Jerusalem, from the Ottomans shortly after the Ottomans enter the war on Germany's side. Iraq becomes a League of Nations mandate under British control, but a 1921 revolt results in a British administered semi-independent Kingdom of Iraq. Egypt remains a British protectorate; it had been an autonomous vassal state in the Ottoman Empire until taken by Britain in 1914 after Britain became apprehensive of Egyptian support of the Young Turks, who advocated for an alliance with Germany.

France presides over Syria and Lebanon as mandates and retains its North African colonies of Algeria, Tunisia and Morocco that it had picked off of the ailing Ottoman Empire some decades before. Italy retains control of Libya. Iran had not been part of the Ottoman Empire and had already been partitioned in 1907 between Britain and Russia.

Women in America get the vote.

On August 18, 1920, all American women are granted the right to vote when the Nineteenth Amendment to the United States Constitution is ratified.

Oil keeps gushing out of the ground in Texas.

Eugenics attempts to legitimize racism.

The Eugenics movement in the United States sponsors popular contests; 'Better Baby' is followed by 'Fitter Families' which debuts in 1920 at the Kansas Free Fair. Participating families compete for medals (and receive free check ups). Size of the family, attractiveness of members (it is assumed that a 'Nordic' heritage is best) and desirable behaviors which are believed to be inherited such as intelligence and generosity are weighed against any alcoholism, paralysis or feeblemindedness in the family's lineage. The winners are presented their medals from the governor.

Approximately six million Russians die in the famine of 1921.

The instability and trauma of the Great War, the Revolution and subsequent policies, result in food shortages. The weakened, vulnerable population is further tormented and decimated by lice which carry typhus.

Throughout the 1920's, the U.S. continues to secure and build up Central American resources for its own use.

U.S. Naval ships, using the Panama Canal, easily move throughout the Caribbean, Central America, and access the Philippines. The plantations that raise bananas, coffee and other fruits and nuts are worked with the indigenous labor force under the control of the United Fruit Company and other corporate entities. Although they wield enormous power, these corporations are not directly controlled but act with the tacit approval of the U.S. government as part of an overall strategy of unofficial colonization.

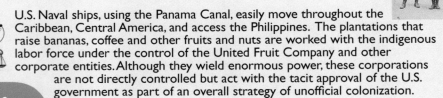

American businessman Charles Ponzi pays investors remarkably high returns.

A Ponzi scheme is a form of fraud where a pseudo-business is established and investors are promised an unusually high rates of return. The first round of investors is rewarded with dividends that they believe are coming from profits that the company is earning however, the money is actually coming from the second round of investors that has been attracted.

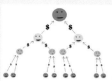

If any of the money coming from new investors is being invested in the production of goods or services, it is only to keep up the illusion of legitimacy. The schemer must attract an exponentially increasing number of investors to keep paying out dividends. Eventually, the schemer takes off with the rest of the money or fails to attract more investors and the pyramid scheme collapses. Ponzi was also involved in other fraudulent business schemes in the 1920s.

Parallax is a tool that allows us to determine which stars are closer than other.

The positions of stars in the sky relative to each other is drawn out and charted. Then, the astronomer waits half a year until the earth is on the other side of its orbit and a new chart is drawn. The charts are compared and the stars that have moved a bit are the closer stars.

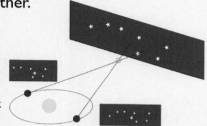

It is similar to looking out the window of a moving car: trees and telephone poles and other nearby objects move but far away objects like mountains move very little. However, this technique only works for stars that are only moderately far away and doesn't work for the more distant stars.

To determine if the wispy patches of light are far enough away to be separate galaxies, astronomers need a new technique to measure vast distances.

Astronomers keenly follow the ongoing great debate about whether or not there might be other galaxies besides our own.

Astronomers had found many wispy clusters of stars and patches of bright dust and are not sure what these objects are. The idea that Andromeda, which appears as a smeared out star to the unaided eye, might be a separate galaxy like our own was introduced in 1755 by Immanuel Kant who referred to it as an 'Island Universe.'

As telescopes improved, many more wispy patches were found and were referred to as 'nebula', which means 'cloudy region'. William and Mary Parsons of Ireland made drawings of the nebula they observed through their Leviathan Telescope, which was completed in 1845 and remained the largest in the world until the Hooker Telescope was built on Mount Wilson in 1917. The Leviathan was able to resolve some of the nebula into disc shaped collections of stars whose spiral arrangement hinted at some kind of organization based on 'dynamical laws'.

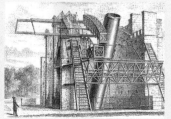

The Leviathan Telescope in Ireland

The Soviet physicist, Alexander Friedmann, follows Einstein's equations further and postulates, in 1924, that the Universe could be expanding.

1924

We now know that Andromeda, visible on the right side of this photo just above the trees, is our closest neighboring galaxy but in the 1920s, people wondered if it were an aberrant star or a closer grouping of a handful of stars or if it actually could be another galaxy.

In Iran in 1925, Reza Shah Pahlavi comes to power.

Iran attempts to modernize its army and founds the Persian Cossack Brigade which it models after the Russian Cossacks and staffs with Russian officers.

After the Russian Revolution of 1917, most of the officers quit, in order to join the White army in fighting the Bolsheviks. Following this, the British take control of the Cossacks, placing British and Persians in the officer roles. Reza Khan had joined the Persian Cossack Brigade at 16, and had quickly risen through the ranks. As the country's first Persian to reach the rank of Brigadier-General, he travels with the now thousands-strong Brigade to Tehran in 1921.

Tehran in is chaos following WWI with British and Russian forces both trying to manipulate the weak Qajar Dynasty for their own benefit. Finding Tehran in such a state, Reza Khan moves to take control himself. He dissolves the government and appoints himself minister of war. He signs a treaty 'of friendship' with the USSR in order to control and minimize their interest.

Khan and his Persian Cossacks then travel the country, quashing several uprisings and revolts. Upon his return to Tehran in 1923, Khan is appointed as the prime minister by the Majles, forcing the Qajar Shah to flee to Europe. Gathering a cabinet around him, and an ever-strengthening power base, Reza Khan is crowned Reza Shah in 1925 and takes the surname Pahlavi, marking the beginning of the Pahlavi Dynasty.

The whole American economy, especially the stock market, seems to be expanding without bound and soaring ever upward!

With the invention of the elevator, tall steel buildings become viable. The tallest buildings are no longer churches or state houses but financial centers.

The Chrysler Building is completed in 1930.

1929

WALL ST

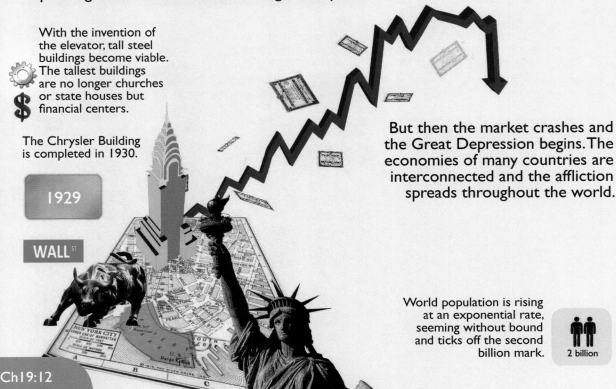

But then the market crashes and the Great Depression begins. The economies of many countries are interconnected and the affliction spreads throughout the world.

World population is rising at an exponential rate, seeming without bound and ticks off the second billion mark.

2 billion

Edwin Hubble uses a technique employing a certain kind of star that is thought to have a specific brightness as a standard unit of measurement.

Just as the headlights of an automobile appear bright if the car is near and dim if the car is far away, a star with a particular brightness should appear bright if it is in our own galaxy and dimmer if it is farther away.

Henrietta Leavitt had discovered that a certain kind of star, a **Cepheid Variable**, always has the same brightness. As a female astronomer at Harvard, she had been relegated to tedious jobs at the observatory but fortunately, Leavitt made the most of it. While measuring and cataloguing the brightness of stars on hundreds of photographic plates, she discovered that Cepheid Variable stars emitted periodic pulsing beams of light which correlated with their rotation dynamics.

Further, all Cepheids have approximately the same brightness and can be used as standard candles, a term she coined. Hubble, using the Hooker Telescope, looks for Cepheids and shows that the some are within our own Milky Way Galaxy but Cephids in the nebulas are much dimmer and much further away.

Other galaxies *do* exist!

Andromeda, Triangulum, and a handful of other densely packed, distant wispy specks are actually separate galaxies with discrete shapes. The Andromeda nebula and some of the other strange wisps are shown to be much more distant than any of the stars. They are faraway separate galaxies, whole separate other worlds like our own Milky Way.

Discovering just a handful of other galaxies makes us realize that the Universe is much bigger than we had imagined but we will not realize that there are billions of other galaxies until the space telescope that bears Hubble's name is launched decades later.

Widespread violations of 'Prohibition' allow wealth and glamour for gangsters, higher rates of alcohol consumption among the general public and a general climate of disrespect for law.

The Big Bang Theory

Not long after we finally figure out that there are other galaxies besides the Milky Way, we realize that the other galaxies are all moving away from us and away from each other. This is indicative of the whole universe expanding.

A Catholic Priest from Belgium espouses a theory of the expansion of the Universe.

Lemaître independently repeats some of the same work that had been done by Alexander Friedmann and published in Europe in 1924. Alexander Friedmann, who was an aviator in the Great War and had scientific interests in hydrodynamics and meteorology as well as general relativity, died in 1925; just months after participating in a record setting balloon flight. Friedmann was only 37 when he died from typhoid fever which he contracted during a vacation in Crimea.

Red Shift

Blue Shift

No Shift

Hubble's Law

Speed

Distance

There are a few exceptions to the rule that all galaxies are moving away from us; the galaxies very close to us are orbiting around with us in a little cluster of galaxies that we call 'The Local Group', and because of this local rotational motion, a few of these galaxies are approaching us and the light from stars within them appears blue shifted to us.

In 1927, Georges Lemaître publishes a paper titled "Un Univers homogène de masse constante et de rayon croissant rendant compte de la vitesse radiale des nébuleuses extragalactiques" ("A homogeneous Universe of constant mass and growing radius accounting for the radial velocity of extragalactic nebulae"). In his paper, he presents his measurements of Doppler shift of Galaxies and shows that the spectra of far off galaxies are redshifted more than nearby ones. He presents the idea that the Universe is expanding and makes a rough calculation of the pace of expansion.

Unfortunately, the journal in which he publishes is not widely read. Two years later, Edwin Hubble will derive the same result and popularize the idea.

Most scientists still do not accept the idea that the Universe is expanding.

The old idea of a steady state Universe is still solidly entrenched. Although there is consensus in the scientific community, and with the general public to the extent that they understand, that Einstein's ideas about the interchangeability of matter and energy and the notion of relativity are true; many scientists are still unaware or opposed to the concept that the size of the universe could be changing, even though the equations of relativity imply that a Universe of finite size that is evenly dispersed cannot be in a steady state.

The evidence of expansion is both theoretical and observational.

 The observational evidence that the galaxies are moving away from us is that the spectra of the light coming from each of them is shifted toward the red end of the spectrum.

 Doppler shift is a theory based on the idea that a 'redshifted' spectrum is indicative of motion away from the viewer. Telescopes of Doppler's day were not yet refined enough to discern the effect that Doppler sought but he hypothesized that the effect could also be demonstrated with sound waves. In 1845 an experiment was devised where musicians played from a moving train while observers listened at the station. You can hear the effect for yourself as an ambulance siren's pitch increases as it approaches and then gets lower as it travels away.

 The observational evidence that the whole Universe is expanding is that the starlight coming from the galaxies farthest away from us is redshifted more than the light from closer galaxies.

Not only are the galaxies all moving away from us, but the galaxies farthest away are moving away fastest. The speed at which a galaxy is moving away from us is directly proportional to its distance away from us (a galaxy twice as far away is moving twice as fast; and a galaxy three times further away is moving away three times faster). Lemaître and Hubble noticed this relationship and realized that it is indicative of general overall expansion. It is well described by an analogy of raisins in a rising loaf of raisin bread. The raisins all move away from each other as the whole loaf expands.

The point of view from any galaxy (like any raisin in the dough) is that everything is expanding away from it. Far away raisins move much farther away from each other because there is more dough between them to expand. It all happens over one interval of time (the time that the universe has been expanding or the dough rising) so the raisins that move farthest also move at the fastest rates. While it might at first seem that there is an alternative explanation for why it appears that all the other galaxies are moving away from us- that we are the center of a giant explosion-, but this is not the case and neither is a loaf of bread exploding.

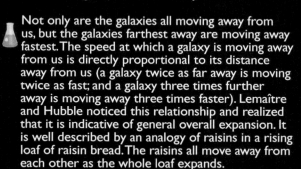

Galaxies get further apart as the universe expands. They move away from each other in much the same way as raisins in a loaf of bread become further apart as the dough rises and the loaf expands. From the vantage point of any raisin, such as this one, raisins farthest away from it are the most redshifted.

The Great Plow Up of the High Plains continues.

With modern tractors the hard sod of the prairie had been broken and the almost limitless landscape of hardy native grassland replanted in wheat. Luckily, rains brought adequate moisture for several years and the price of wheat rose during the first world war. More and more acres are planted.

Even as the lines at soup kitchens in eastern cities lengthen and despite the fairly dry summer of 1930, optimism still runs high on America's Great Plains, where the wheat crop continues to deliver. In 1931, there is a bumper crop- so much wheat is harvested that it won't fit in the silos! But then with the oversupply and the reduction of the average American's buying power, the price of wheat suddenly drops dramatically.

Mahatma Gandhi leads a march protesting the British Salt Tax in India in March 1930.

1930

Einstein journeys to Mt. Wilson in 1931 to look at the evidence for expansion of the Universe first hand. After his visit, he stops arguing against the hypothesis and there is some unity in the scientific community.

Einstein's dislike for the implications of his own equations is further intensified by the fact that it is a priest who proposes the new hypothesis of an expanding Universe. If the Universe is expanding, then it must be expanding from some point, a point of origin.

Every creation story has a point of origin for the world and every human culture has always had a creation story, and a corresponding religion to match.

The Church, which had tortured many people for considering contemporary science in centuries past, tacitly admitted wrongdoing when they conceded to the fundamental idea that the earth is round and orbits the sun. Isaac Newton had proposed the paradigm that the Universe is infinite and eternal, conditions which don't require or preclude a creator. This allowed a kind of truce between science and the Church, since the Church at that time was willing to keep a low profile.

Lemaître, who is a dedicated physicist but also a priest, calls his idea 'the Primeval Atom' hypothesis which further agitates scientists who fear that the church is attempting to reassert itself into the affairs of science.

The Iranian Shah shocks the Western world by canceling the country's oil concession with Anglo-Persian Oil Company.

The share of the profits that Iran received from the British-controlled company came only from the money made off of the crude oil, excluding Iran from any of the proceeds from the highly profitable oil refining and its products. Less than a year later, the Shah renegotiates with APOC, asking for a higher percentage of the crude oil profits based on the market price of oil, instead of a previously set price.

The APOC refuses to budge on the main issue. The Shah's only small victory is that Persia's approximately 17% share will now be 21%, but it will be a share of a fixed price, regardless of the market value of the oil at the time of its production. The ghost of what is lost in this concession will follow him throughout his time as Shah.

The first dust bowl erupts on the American prairie in 1932.

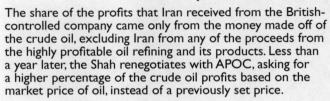

Top soil is carried away by the wind in Oklahoma and other western states when lands recently brought under the plow and no longer covered in native grasses are exposed to drought.

The aftermath of World War One leaves Germany under stress.

Frustration with the ineffective democracy known as the Weimar Republic and the economic stress caused by worldwide depression and unsustainable payments for war reparations causes a minority of the German people to come under the spell of Adolph Hitler, who promises a return to pride and prosperity.

Joseph Goebbels, who will become the Nazi Minister of Propaganda makes effective use of technology; even his earliest speeches are broadcast on radio.

Adolph Hitler takes control of the state; Germany descends into fascism.

Hitler is appointed chancellor without ever winning a majority vote of the people. Four weeks later and only six days before elections are to be held, in February 1933, a fire breaks out in the parliament building and burns it to the ground.

Hitler, uses the fire as a pretext and moves quickly to consolidate his power. His propaganda machine portrays the fire as the opening salvo of a communist plot that seeks to subject prominent people to acts of terrorism and to banish private property.

The Reichstag Fire Decree establishes a legal basis for Hitler to imprison political opponents and to suppress newspapers and publications without due process. The swiftness of the imprisonment of large numbers of people causes fear in the population. The German people, Jews as well as Gentiles, are already culturally inured to respect authority and exercise patience and discipline, are gripped by fear but adopt a wait and see attitude that seals their fate as Hitler and his Nazi followers quickly establish the machinery of a totalitarian state.

The Nazis unite proletarian frustration with nationalist fervor.

The Nazi platform attempts to tap into working class economic resentment at the elite and thus attract members who might otherwise join the Communist or Socialist Parties. The procedural organizational conventions of German society like planning, punctuality, and a respect for the boundaries of individual jobs in the division of labor are hijacked by the National Socialist party.

The Nazis build their first concentration camp at Dachau in 1933.

Political prisoners are rounded up and arrested. Religious leaders compete with the Nazis for the spiritual allegiance of the German people, so priests are among the thousands interred at Dachau.

The Hoover Dam nears completion.

At large scales, every patch of the universe seems to be similar to every other.

Any model of the Universe that we make depends upon the premise that our sector of the Universe, the part of it that we can see, is representative of the whole.

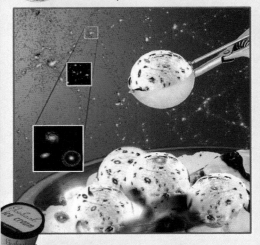

The Universe does indeed seem to be isotropic, but we should never forget that our models depend on this premise being true.

We don't find any trends with direction; for example, galaxies are not bigger in one area or further apart in another. This means that the Universe is isotropic. Some substances, like vanilla ice cream, are homogenous. Others, like Rocky Road ice cream, are heterogeneous but isotropic. If the ice cream is sampled with a small spoon, every spoonful of the vanilla is the same as every other but a spoonful of the rocky road can be quite different than another- one spoonful can contain a walnut while another spoonful has a piece of chocolate. However, if you use a large enough scoop to dish it out, every scoop will contain roughly the same hodgepodge of stuff as every other.

There is much evidence to support the premise that the Universe is isotropic. Because isotropy is a fundamental premise of any model that we make of the Universe, astronomers are always testing it with the latest technology. For example, the Sloan Digital Sky Survey, conducted from 2000 to 2008 was able to observe and analyze the distribution of galaxies up to a distance of 3.5 billion light years, and found no trends in any direction. The more recent WiggleZ Dark Energy Survey, conducted between 2006 and 2011, was able to analyze a patch of the Universe 7 billion light years wide, and again could find no directional trends.

The German propaganda machine disseminates distorted information. The official ideology is of the genetic superiority of one race. Books that were written by Jews or communists or deemed controversial are burned. Jews are targeted as scapegoats.

In 1935, Reza Shah publicly announces that the name "Persia" is to be replaced by "Iran," the historic title of the country, for official and diplomatic purposes. Iran will soon replace Persia in common use as well.

Following the Shah's decision to officially refer to Persia as Iran, the British-based Anglo-Persian Oil Company, renames itself to the 'Anglo-Iranian Oil Company.'

The Soviet Union industrializes at an astonishing pace. A sequence of 5 year plans reorganize the recently feudal, agrarian society into an industrialized country under the ruthless dictatorship of Joseph Stalin.

Stalin continues to consolidate his hold of absolute power. He launches the Great Purges in which he has political rivals and ideological opponents tried for sedition or sabotage. Hundreds of thousands are executed or exiled to Gulag work camps.

1936

Somoza becomes dictator of Nicaragua. The Somoza family will control the country for decades to come.

Anatasio Somoza García is the son of a wealthy coffee planter. While the U.S. Marines occupy the country, he is appointed the head of the National Guard. In 1937, he is able to win the presidential election. He uses his political and military power to amass a huge personal fortune and to control the outcome of elections. He will eventually be assassinated by a poet, and then be succeeded by his eldest, and then by his younger son. The Somoza Dynasty will remain in power until deposed by the Sandinista Revolution in 1979.

Hitler annexes lands that contain large populations of German speaking peoples, as the first step in creating a Greater German Reich.

Austria is annexed in March 1938 . Large numbers of German speaking people live in peripheral regions of Czechoslovakia; these areas, known as the Sudentenland, are also soon annexed.

In 1938 Nazi storm troopers along with civilian sympathizers rampage through Germany and Austria destroying Jewish businesses and synagogues in an orchestrated campaign called Kristallnacht, the night of breaking glass.

More than 30,000 Jews are arrested. This is but the opening salvo of the Nazi campaign of genocide that is soon to be unleashed.

News is transmitted, almost mystically, on invisible radio waves.

So important is the medium that many American households acquire radios despite the scarcities of the Great Depression. Most broadcasts are of the gathering storm of war in Europe or of strikes and breadlines, dust storms and accidents. So powerful is this new medium that most people readily accept what is broadcast as fact. On the night before Halloween in 1938, Orson Wells broadcasts a science fiction story called *The War of the Worlds* in a seemingly realistic fashion. Many people panic and evacuate their homes fearing an actual invasion from mars. In the following days, Wells and the CBS network are threatened with lawsuits and a public debate ensues about critical thinking and the power of the media.

Japanese nationalism unleashes an ideology of Japanese genetic superiority.

The Japanese military had moved into China in 1931 and declares all out war in 1937. Japan controls the coast and major cities and sets up puppet regimes throughout China.

In a surprise move, Hitler and Stalin, dictators from opposing ideological camps, make a pact.

They agree not to go to war with each other and to simultaneously invade Poland and divide it between themselves. Hitler views the pact, made in August 1939, as a temporary convenience that will prevent Germany from having to fight the Soviet Union in addition to Britain or any other country that might oppose Germany's eastward expansion. It had long been a Nazi goal to permanently eliminate communism, to seize prime Soviet lands and resettled them with Germans, and to eliminate Jews who the Nazis claimed were the intellectual advocates of communism.

Stalin's sign off on the pact stuns supporters of communism worldwide; that the leader of International Socialism should enter into a pact with a fascist right wing dictator is enough to shake some of them out of their romantic delusions about the character of Stalin, if not on the concept of communism itself. Hitler's armies march victoriously through France and the Low Countries of Holland and Belgium in July of 1940 and only weeks later Hitler will sign the order to plan Operation Barbarossa, the invasion of Soviet Union.

1940

In June of 1941, Germany breaks the pact and invades the Soviet Union.

Stalin is caught off guard as German tanks, troops and airplanes rapidly advance across a front spanning over a thousand kilometers. The blitz works; hundreds of thousands of Soviet soldiers are killed or captured, thousands of Soviet tanks are destroyed and much of the Soviet airforce is destroyed on the ground. But the Soviets are not completely wiped out in a single decisive campaign, as Hitler had planned.

Oil and gas are coveted as strategic military resources.

The pipelines of Ukraine make its oil and the oil of its neighbors accessible.

The Shah of Iran is forced to abdicate.

The Shah of Iran is deposed by Britain in 1941, who force him to abdicate in favor of his son, Mohammad Reza Shah, who they believe will be a weak and easily-controlled leader.

America enters the war in December 1941 following attack on Pearl Harbor.

Almost the entire American fleet is anchored in Hawaii making an easy target for the Japanese. Most Americans had been unwilling to enter the war. Now American industry, already robust, is ramped up.

In 1942, the Soviet defenders reorganize and new tanks roll off Soviet assembly lines.

The battle of Stalingrad claims more lives than any other battle in history.

Stalin will later portray the German advance into Russia as a strategic trap set by the Soviets; analogy will be made with Napoleon whose army was devastated by the Russian winter, but new records, released since the dissolution of the USSR in 1991, show that Stalin ordered his troops to stand and fight, to try to hold the line against the Germans. Stalin's advisors pleaded for organized retreat against the initial onslaught but Stalin stubbornly refused. The following year, Stalin attempted to enforce his no retreat order by installing special squadrons just behind his front lines with orders to shoot fleeing soldiers. Both Hitler and Stalin will incur monumental troop casualties by stubbornly refusing to engage in strategic retreats.

Late in the summer of 1942, Germany begins the attack on Stalin's namesake city. The Battle of Stalingrad incurs more casualties than any other military engagement in history, with more than a million soldiers killed and an even greater number of civilians. After German troops run out of supplies and surrender back the city, Germany will no longer seem an unstoppable force,

The Germans sweep across the Crimea in the opening offensive but the Soviet Port of Sevastopol, home to the Black Sea Fleet, holds out for months.

In 1944, the Russians drive the Germans back out of Crimea. As soon as the area is liberated from the Germans, Stalin commands the Soviet army to swiftly round up and deport much of the ethnic Tatar population. He accuses them of having had collaborated with the Nazis during their occupation but there is no evidence that there was more collaboration by the Tartars than other residents. It is simply part of Stalin's larger plan to break up any pre-existing ethnic groups and destroy their ethnic identities. Over 180,000 Tatars will be deported immediately for Siberia; almost half will die in transit or within the first year.

American industrial might is brought to bear.

On June 6, 1944, the Allies operate the largest seaborne invasion in history, known as D-Day. This operation begins the liberation of German-occupied Northwestern Europe from Nazi control and contributes to the decisive Allied victory on the Western Front.

Human industrial processes continue to create a handful of new minerals. The total number of minerals on the planet has by now grown to exceed 4500.

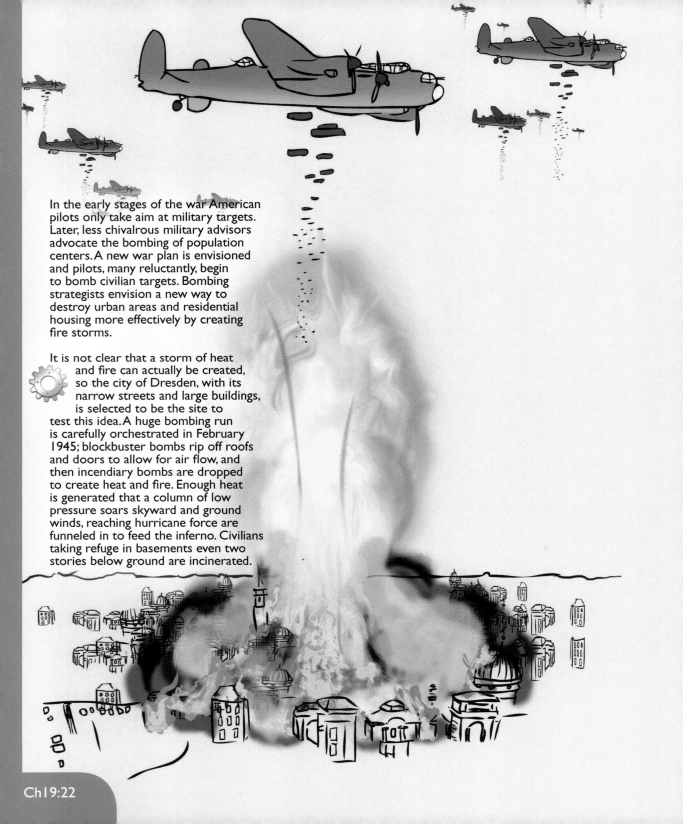

In the early stages of the war American pilots only take aim at military targets. Later, less chivalrous military advisors advocate the bombing of population centers. A new war plan is envisioned and pilots, many reluctantly, begin to bomb civilian targets. Bombing strategists envision a new way to destroy urban areas and residential housing more effectively by creating fire storms.

It is not clear that a storm of heat and fire can actually be created, so the city of Dresden, with its narrow streets and large buildings, is selected to be the site to test this idea. A huge bombing run is carefully orchestrated in February 1945; blockbuster bombs rip off roofs and doors to allow for air flow, and then incendiary bombs are dropped to create heat and fire. Enough heat is generated that a column of low pressure soars skyward and ground winds, reaching hurricane force are funneled in to feed the inferno. Civilians taking refuge in basements even two stories below ground are incinerated.

Americans win the race to develop the atomic bomb and unleash it on citizens of Japan to prove their power and hasten the war's end.

The theoretical physics behind $E=mc^2$ is realized in this terrible display. Only about a gram of matter is converted into energy in each of these explosions.

The bomb leveling Hiroshima on August 6, 1945 contains 64 kg of uranium of which less than a kg undergoes fission and about half a gram of that is converted into energy. It kills about 100,000 people, mostly civilians.

Three days later, Nagasaki is levelled by a softball-sized 6 kilograms of plutonium. Just over a gram of this is actually converted into energy.

1945

At the end of the war, the full extent of German war crimes becomes evident, even to those who were previously in denial.

Germany is still largely in ruins, Britain is reeling from the loss of its Empire, Japan is watched by occupying forces. America, while stung, actually experienced low casualty rates in the war and has a robust workforce, compared to other nations and American industry is booming.

The United States of America emerges as a Superpower and a new international monetary system based on the U.S. dollar is established.

The United States pledges to back the dollar with gold that it holds in reserve. The U.S. commits to correlate the value of its dollars to an exchange price of $35 per ounce of gold. The allied currencies will be correlated to the dollar; allied nations promise not to inflate their currencies but to keep them commensurate with the dollar.

The new monetary system, which goes into effect in 1945, was decided upon at the Bretton Woods Conference held in New Hampshire in 1944, before the conclusion of the war. Representatives from all 44 allied nations attend. The new system is intended to prevent 'beggar thy neighbor' policies of domestic protections and import tariffs that were thought to have been some of the triggers of the Great Depression and international strive. The International Monetary Fund is established.

India's long non-violent struggle for independence finally brings sovereignty in 1947, but the victory is bittersweet.

India is partitioned in order to separate Muslims and Hindus against the wishes of Mahatma Gandhi who believes the two groups can live in peace. The Dominion of Pakistan and the Republic of India are created. Citizens are forced to move based on their religious identity. This is the largest forced migration of humans in history with more than 10 million made to migrate. Hundreds of thousands of casualties occur.

The State of Israel is established in 1948.

The original text of the British Mandate of Palestine from 1922 had included a preamble which declared what would become known as the State of Israel a 'national home for the Jewish people'. In the aftermath of World War II, survivors of the Holocaust sought to start a new life in Israel, far from war-torn Europe. The Jewish communities living under the rule of the Mandate chafed at the British rule, and many groups militarized and actively fought back. With the massive influx of Jews from Europe and surrounding Muslim countries, Britain attempted to broker a solution that would sufficiently provide for the existing Arab community and the massive emigrating populations. In 1947, unable to find any solutions, the British announces its intent to dissolve the Mandate of Palestine. On the day that the Mandate would officially dissolve, May 14, 1948, the Israeli declaration of independence is signed, bringing the British Mandate of Palestine to an official end.

Meals are industrialized.

A barbecue restaurant started by Maurice McDonald is reorganized into a hamburger stand using production line principles. The industrialization of food preparation and consumption will eventually lead to profound changes in the diet and health of Americans.

A civil war ensues in China and a communist party proclaims a new People's Republic.

The Chinese Civil War ends in 1949 with the victory of the Communist Party under the leadership of Mao Zedong.

The communists will not let business interests, foreign or domestic, exploit the country; they will make no attempt to use the balancing principles of a market economy at all; but instead, the leadership will try to implement the ideals of equality and prosperity through a classless society by decree. The party will do the planning and implement changes in order to quickly modernize and industrialize the country. The party will decide how farms will be organized, how much land will be farmed, and which people will work in factories and what those factories will produce. At the end of the year, Mao travels to the Soviet Union.

Nato, the North Atlantic Treaty Organization, is formed. This multi-state military alliance is committed to the mutual defense of its members.

The treaty is signed in 1949 by members including the United States, Britain, Germany and France. Its allied commander resides at its is headquartered in Brussels, Belgium

The theory that the Universe is expanding from a point of origin is nick named 'The Big Bang Theory' by its staunchest critic.

1950

Fred Hoyle, while acknowledging that the Universe does seem to be expanding, disagrees that this requires the Universe to have had a beginning. He claims that arguing for an origin point for the Universe is irrational and similar to arguing for a creator. He calls the theory that the Universe is expanding from a point of origin pseudoscience and refers to it as the 'Big Bang Theory in a BBC radio broadcast in 1949.

Hoyle proposes his own rival hypothesis of a 'Steady-State' Universe. In this hypothesis, new matter is constantly being created in the voids between galaxies so that the density of matter in the Universe stays constant even though it is expanding. This is somewhat analogous to how a river endures and stays essentially the same over time even though individual molecules of water move away.

Hoyle will make major contributions to astrophysics in the coming years as he works to find evidence for the creation of the new matter.

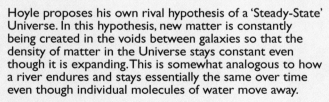

Fred Hoyle also points out that, if there had been a 'Big Bang,' it would have released high energy waves and there would still be some relic evidence of the event. This idea will inspire other physicists to look for this evidence. The physicists, George Gamow and Ralph Alpher, attempt to calculate how hot the Big Bang would have been in order for hydrogen atoms to have condensed out. When the atoms had condensed out, waves of radiation (hotter than x-rays) would have emanated from everywhere in the Universe and these waves, although now cooled off, should still be traveling about, equally distributed everywhere in the Universe.

Their calculations yield a temperature for this background radiation that is just a minuscule amount higher than the temperature of space and it will therefore be very hard, if not impossible, to ever detect. They also calculate that while the hydrogen atoms were forming, it would have been hot enough for about 20% of these to fuse together into helium atoms and that a very small amount of lithium, the next largest element will also be formed. These proportions of elements are what we actually find (by spectroscopy) in the oldest portions of the Universe.

A Cold War grips the planet from the west and in the east.

The Western Bloc is united under NATO, with the United States at the helm and the Eastern Bloc has the USSR heading the Warsaw Pact.

The superpowers do not battle directly but political tensions are high and proxy wars occur. Huge budgets are allocated for arms, armies and military engineers.

America is a flawed democracy with a two party system, elections, lots of individual liberty and a capitalist economic model.

Its citizens are united under the banner of the lofty goals espoused in the Declaration of Independence and the Constitution. American culture tends toward optimism and many Americans are unaware of their nation's shortcomings. For example, most believe that all adults have the vote but African Americans in southern states, are prohibited from actually voting. Many children are educated to believe that there is a level playing field and that any American can become wealthy and successful if they are smart and work hard.

America wants Germany to recover from the devastation of the second world war to become a trading partner.

American corporations view the environment as a resource to be exploited for their own profits.

The National Security Agency or NSA is a U.S. intelligence agency founded in 1952. It collects, monitors, and analyzes information in an effort to ensure the strength the U.S. and its allies.

The Korean War begins in 1950 as North Korean forces invade South Korea with support of the Soviet Union and China. A month later, U.S military units, under UN auspices intervene. Three long years later, an armistice is signed and the Korean Demilitarized Zone is created between the two countries.

1953

America orchestrates a coup d'état and reinstates the Shah in Iran.

The prime minister, within the Shah's constitutional monarchy, Mohammad Mosaddegh, introduces a wide range of social reforms, including workers' compensation and, with the backing of the parliament, nationalizes the Iranian oil industry. Britain retaliates by pulling out their employees and technicians and enforcing a worldwide embargo on all Iranian oil.

By 1952, Iran's exports have dwindled to virtually nothing, making Moseddegh's proposed reforms almost impossible. The Prime Minister and the Shah clash when the Shah insists on appointing the members of Moseddegh's cabinet and Moseddegh resigns. The next prime minister, a noted monarchist, announces plans to renegotiate with British oil industries. Mass demonstrations and strikes occur and the Shah is forced to reinstate his old prime minister. Mosaddegh returns and reforms the centuries-old feudal farming system, reigns in the monarchy's powers by limiting the Shah's personal budget and prevents him from communicating with foreign diplomats. Late in 1952, Mosaddegh declares that Britain is an enemy and cuts off all diplomacy.

Despite reigning in the monarchy and getting new benefits for citizens, Mosaddegh's public image suffers from the economic impact of the British embargo. Incensed by the loss of Iranian oil, Britain turns to the U.S. for help, in 1953. In a joint venture, the C.I.A. and MI6 work together to depose Mosaddegh in what is known as Operation Ajax. Ajax hires strongmen to intimidate religious leaders to withdraw their support of Mosaddegh; they also portray him as a paranoid, ready to exert deadly force against anyone who disagrees with his decisions. Ajax also pressures the Shah to depose the troublesome prime minister. A CIA-vetted referendum to dissolve the parliament is put to a vote. There are separate booths to vote yes or no, making it clear who is voting for what. It passes with 99% approval.

Capitalism and Communism are two very different socioeconomic paradigms that come to dominate human political thought.

Humans often seem to think in just two categories; black and white, good versus evil. During the cold war, the dichotomy of capitalism vs. communism will so dominate human thinking that other alternatives will rarely be considered.

The Soviet Union is a one party state with secret police.

Communist ideology allows for a vague 'dictatorship of the proletariat' which will supposedly, someday, no longer be necessary.

$ Russia does not want to see Germany recover but wishes for a weak Germany to be a buffer zone on their western flank. Russia wants to force Germany to pay large reparations.

Resources are valued for industrialization but wealth, according to the party, really only comes from human labor. The environment doesn't rate on a philosophical level.

Stalin makes a show of decentralization in decision making by encouraging worker participation and voting within the worker cooperatives. However, the information flowing upward is used by Stalin and his secret police to keep tabs on his underlings and to ferret out the intelligent, vocal dissidents. In Stalin's Soviet Union, information flowing upwards does not contribute to policy making; Stalin dictates from above.

The Shah flees the country to hide in Rome, but the CIA offers to restore him to power, handing him two royal decrees they have prepared for him to sign. The first deposes Mosaddegh, while the second replaces him with General Fazlollah Zahedi, a royalist who had served the Shah's father. Meanwhile in Iran, the CIA is fomenting chaos by funding opposing factions, monarchists and nationalists, to riot in the streets. Out of the chaos, the CIA-picked pro-monarchist forces emerge, backed by the old military, to quell the violence. They imprison Mosaddegh and his former supporters, blaming them for the riots and the hundreds of casualties.

Joseph Stalin dies.
Stalin dies of a stroke
March 5 1953.

Kruschev becomes head of the Soviet Union.

Nikita Khrushchev was born in a Russian village, married a Ukrainian woman and fought against the Germans on the Soviet front and then became a manager of reconstruction in Ukraine and was eventually appointed premier of the Ukrainian SSR. Ukraine had suffered terribly; 1 of 6 people had died in the war. Khrushchev sought to rebuild Ukraine and ease the burdens of its people but he did so by completing the imposition of the Soviet system upon it. He oversaw the force collectivization of farms and other Soviet projects. When Khrushchev becomes head of the Soviet Union, he gives the Crimean Peninsula, with its seaside resorts, to Ukraine as a good will gesture to solidify his support there, although Crimea had been a part of Russia since 1783.

 The Anglo-Iranian Oil Company is renamed to British Petroleum Company.

French Colonial power in Vietnam is resoundingly defeated.

Ho Chi Mihn had argued for Vietnam's independence at Versaille but had been excluded from the official treaty negotiations and the allies allowed the French to keep their Southeast Asian colonial possessions. At the battle of Dien Bien Phu in 1954, the French realize that they have underestimated the will of the Vietnamese. In an attempt to reassert control in the increasing difficult to manage colony, the French had adopted a new strategy of creating large military bases in remote locations. They had hoped that by locating the bases far from population centers, they would not be subject to guerrilla warfare and they assumed that they could keep the bases supplied by air.

The Vietnamese dismantle their artillery into pieces and carry them by foot through hundreds of miles of roadless jungle to challenge the flagship base of Dien Bien Phu. After they install their artillery around the base and set up anti-aircraft guns to keep the French from resupplying, the French surrender and end their involvement in IndoChina.

Crimea is transferred from Russia to Ukraine.

Crimea had the designation of 'autonomous republic' within the Soviet Union, but a year after the mass deportation of the Tatars in 1944, its status was changed to 'province.' In 1954, Khrushchev transfers it to Ukraine. This transfer seems of little consequence because all provinces are ultimately controlled by centralized Soviet authority, even though the port of Sevastopol, the Soviet Unions only warm water port, is on the Crimean Peninsula. Sevastopol is a key base for Soviet Nuclear Submarines.

DNA, the mechanism of heredity is discovered.

Living beings are made of cells that contain a double helix of the molecule DNA. Because DNA is a spiral made of two strands, it is able to replicate itself: the double strand separates into two single strands, each which then rebuilds itself into new double strand by picking up new matching molecules. Today we know that DNA codes for proteins.

Stellar nuclear fusion is described.

While searching for evidence of his Steady-State Universe Theory, Fred Hoyle figures out the mechanics of how stars work. In the cores of stars, many small atoms are fused into a lesser number of medium sized ones which also liberates energy, causing stars to shine. This information propels the sciences of astronomy, astrophysics and nuclear physics forward and seems, at first, to help the Steady State Model by showing that new matter can be created. But the new matter created by stars uses hydrogen for the starting fuel and it is only the Big Bang Model that has an explanation for the origin of the hydrogen atoms.

Rosa Parks, in 1955, refuses to move to the *Negro* section in the back of a public transit bus in Alabama and sets off the Montgomery Bus Boycott. She is shown here with Martin Luther King Jr., one of the thousands of other African Americans to protest segregation and Jim Crow laws.

Fast food grows in popularity and agri-business conglomerates grow to dominate food production at all levels.

The U.S. interstate highway system rolls out.

The National Interstate and Defense Highways Act is passed in 1956 to facilitate troop and tank movements, should they be required, as well as to foster economic development. More automobiles drive on America's burgeoning freeways.

The Soviets win the first round of the space race.

The Soviets beat the Americans into space with the launch of the Sputnik satellite in 1957. Its beeping radio signal can is detected by HAM radio operators in the U.S. It orbits the Earth every 90 minutes and the 90 minute repetition of its incessant beep builds a frenzied tempo and is a psychological spark for the cold war and the space race.

The topography of the ocean floor is revealed.

Sonar, developed in World War II, is turned to the task of mapping the ocean floor. When the first map of oceanic topography is published in 1957, a vibrant symmetrical pattern is revealed. It is evident that a volcanic ridge runs down the center of the Atlantic Ocean floor. Further studies of the ocean floor will soon provide the evidence to substantiate the fledgling theory of plate tectonics.

The alliance between the large communist states of China and the Soviet Union is already fracturing, but to the Americans they seem like a monolith.

Mao Tse-tung and Nikita Khrushchev during the Russian leader's visit to Peking in 1958.

Until 1956, all oil tankers were built to fit through the Suez Canal.

The Suez Crisis forces oil tankers to travel around the Cape of Good Hope. With size restriction no longer an issue, supertankers are created.

China announces the 'Great Leap Forward.'

The campaign begins in 1958 with the Chinese government forcing many peasants into large collective farms and mandating a policy of backyard iron production. The party has decided that these policies will improve economic output. Peasants tend the small furnaces, sometimes long into the night.

China, which had been following the advice of Soviet engineers and bureaucrats partially diverges from the Soviet model with the small scale production of iron.

The Soviet economy stresses heavy industry and organizes it in a centralized fashion; steel making and industrial production of machinery and weapons are given priority and huge factories are built.

1959

The Great Leap Forward was a disaster.

The Great Chinese famine between 1958 to 1961 resulted in somewhere between 15 and 45 million deaths.

In his farewell address, President Dwight Eisenhower warns the citizenry of the United States of the dangers of the Military Industrial Complex.

Nuclear war threatens to break out as the two superpowers face off during the **Cuban Missile Crisis.**

High quality photographs from high flying aircraft allow landscapes to be analyzed. This image, taken on October 14 1962 by the U2 spy plane shows missile transporters on the ground in Cuba. It sets off the 13 day crisis.

Another U2 spy plane, flown by Gary Powers, was shot down over the Soviet Union in 1960. The capture of Gary Powers motivates American Military and Intelligence agencies to develop better spy satellites as well as remotely piloted vehicles.

New agricultural techniques kick off 'The Green Revolution.'

The Green Revolution is begun by the work of American scientist, Norman Borlaug researching in Mexico. He produces new varieties of wheat that are less long and lanky. Because of their bushier shape, the new breeds can be grown to large size with the use of synthetic fertilizers without their getting so tall they fall over. The new shapes are also amenable to mechanized techniques. He uses traditional techniques of selecting the plants with the most desirable traits and breeding them to create new varieties. He also selects plants for disease resistance. Mexico goes from being an importer of wheat to being an exporter.

Agricultural technology is refined around a methodology based on evolved crops, the use of petroleum, synthetic fertilizers and pesticides.

After standing tall against the Soviets and risking the outbreak of nuclear war, Kennedy sets out a path of peaceful coexistence and reconciliation.

Kennedy makes a speech June 10, 1963. "*What kind of peace do I mean and what kind of a peace do we seek? Not a Pax Americana enforced on the world by American weapons of war. Not the peace of the grave or the security of the slave. I am talking about genuine peace, the kind of peace that makes life on earth worth living, and the kind that enables men and nations to grow, and to hope, and build a better life for their children- not merely peace for Americans, but peace for all men and women, not merely peace in our time, but peace in all time...*"

Kennedy's bid moves Americans and the Soviet leadership. The Nuclear Test Ban Treaty is signed.

 Somehow America gets dragged into a full fledged, if undeclared, war against Vietnam, a not-yet-industrialized state.

World population reaches 3 billion.

3 billion

 An awareness of the biosphere and effects of pollution are popularized with Rachel Carson's book 'Silent Spring' in 1962.

Folk music plays a part in organizing the peace and equal rights movements.

1963

Seeking to further modernize and westernize Iran, the Shah launches a program of reformations in 1963.

Collectively, these reforms will come to be known as the White Revolution due to their bloodless nature and will continue over the next 19 years. The reforms include the right to vote for women, abolishment of feudalism, nationalization of forests, pasturelands, and water sources, and literacy programs. While the revolution did much for the peasant class, the Shah received heavy criticism for much of the program. The wealthy elite were angered by being forced to cede land to the Shah (which would be deeded out to the peasant class), the lower urban classes saw little of the wealth funneled into the commercial sector from the oil industry that was intended to trickle down, and the secular nature of the reforms angered the religious communities.

Ruhollah Khomeini emerges as the Shah's leading critic and the public face of dissent, openly attacking him and denouncing him as unfit to rule. Khomeini is forced to flee the country in exile, but his influence is unflagged within Iran. Soon after, the Shah has Khomeini arrested. Riots ensue for three days, and when the Shah's secret police finally put the violence down, several thousand have died.

African Americans demand equal rights. Martin Luther King emerges as a powerful speaker, advocating the process of non-violent resistance.

King delivers his now famous "I Have a Dream" speech during the March on Washington in August 1963. King is not the only eloquent speaker of the movement, but he becomes idealized by the movement.

President Kennedy is assassinated in Texas in November 1963.

Lee Harvey Oswald is convicted of the crime, but John F. Kennedy's assassination remains the subject of widespread debate. Many American's theorize it was a larger conspiracy- in fact, as of 2013, a Gallup Poll indicated that 61% of Americans believed that Oswald did not act alone.

Unfortunately, Oswald's case never made it to trial because he was shot- live on television- by Jack Ruby, a Dallas nightclub owner. Oswald's motives remain clouded in mystery- lending to conspiracy theories.

Scientists have been trying to construct a detector that can resolve enough detail to ascertain whether the afterglow of the Big Bang, the cosmic background radiation, is there or not, are beaten by engineers who stumble across the signal.

In 1964, engineers who are simply trying to make satellite phone calls have less static but can't get rid of a last remnant of it, contact the scientists for help. When the scientists ask "what frequency is this static you can't get rid of?" The engineers report the frequency that corresponds to the signal the scientists have been looking for. It's fantastic- no matter which direction the engineers point their antenna, the signal is the same. The background signature exists!

Most scientists accept the Big Bang Theory after the cosmic background radiation is detected.

However, the prominent and skeptical astrophysicist from England is still not convinced and makes another challenge to the theory.

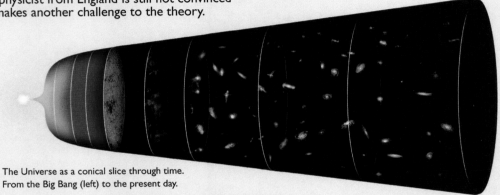

The Universe as a conical slice through time.
From the Big Bang (left) to the present day.

Even finding the correct level of Cosmic Background Radiation is not enough for the famous opponent of the Big Bang Theory! Fred Hoyle comes up with yet another challenge. He points out that this cosmic background signature, since it would have had to have come from a quantum event, should have a chaotic quantum signature and not be completely uniform.

Detecting the CBR, whose signal is so weak, only a few degrees above absolute zero was a technical triumph. Detecting a slight, random in-homogeneity in this weak signal seems an impossible task. Scientists and engineers get to work on creating, designing and building a detector to answer the question.

Such precision will be required that no land based instrument will suffice; the new detector, if one can be devised must be launched into orbit to make its observations without the complication of our atmosphere.

1965

In the United States, the Voting Rights Act of 1965 allows African Americans the actual ability to vote.

Although slavery had been outlawed for almost a hundred years and people of color could legally vote, they had not been able to in practice; when an African American would try to register to vote, the clerks office would suddenly close or worse, hooded vigilantes might visit that person's home at night.

In 1965 the first commercial scanning electron microscope is developed.

Mao introduces the Cultural Revolution in 1966.

Communism is a hard road to follow; many individuals stray from the true path and relapse into old habits, says Chairman Mao, as he tries to consolidate his grip on power. Those individuals who would relapse into the old habits and patterns of greedy, individualistic or capitalistic behavior must be rooted out of all walks of society. Not only are western goods, music and fashions signs of corruption but adhering to old traditional Chinese ways is also deemed corrupt.

 Mao creates the Red Guards, loosely organized students and young rabble rousers, and unleashes them with little to no supervision, to ferret out non believers. The police and army are forbidden to stop them. School teachers are a favorite target; former pupils hold teachers hostage, forcing them to confess their old ways.

Red Guards are allowed to travel- a rare privilege in China- to attend rallies and protests. They burn ancient manuscripts and vandalize venerated statues and altars. A few army commanders dare to interfere and save some of China's archeological heritage. Many high ranking politicians and bureaucrats are also denounced. Eventually, the chaos is too much even for Mao and he dissolves the Red Guards and has some of them relocated to the countryside.

"Destroy the old world; build a new world" proclaims this poster, which shows a member of the Red Guard crushing a crucifix, a Buddha and classical Chinese books.

中国人民解放军是毛泽东思想大学校

Portraits and murals of Mao are plastered up everywhere as the personality cult of Mao grows.

Martin Luther King is granted a meeting with the President in 1966.

The 1967 War breaks out between Israel and its neighbors.

The Six-Day War, also known as the Arab-Israeli War, was fought by Israel against Egypt (then called the Unite Arab Republic), Jordan and Syria.

The Iranian Shah crowns himself.

Oct 26, 1967. Mohammad Reza Shah takes the ancient title of "Shahanshah" (meaning "King of Kings" or Emperor), 26 years into his reign. Having always been in the shadow of his powerful father, he had been swept onto the stage in 1953. Although he was timid at the beginning of his reign, he has come to relish power and its trapping. He crowns himself Shah at the same age that his father had 41 years before.

He also crowned his wife, Shahbanou Farah, making this the first time that a woman has ever been crowned in Iran. The event had been highly publicized, so dignitaries, politicians, and news networks from all over the world were present. The Shah is touted in international media as the leader who "rescued Iran from darkness." The festivities last for an entire week.

The Viet Cong launch the Tet Offensive in 1968.

The Viet Cong, although fatigued by the ongoing war against a superpower, launch what comes to be known as the Tet Offensive. The Americans are shocked by the ferocity of the offensive and the determination shown by the Viet Cong. Smoke rises even over Saigon, the capital city.

Martin Luther King is assassinated on the balcony of his hotel in Memphis, April 4th 1968.

Martin Luther King was a persuasive orator but had become almost a supreme leader in the movement. It was ironic that a mass movement was so reliant on one individual. Many of America's dissidents turn to violent means or apathetic skepticism.

Robert Kennedy, brother to the assassinated president is assassinated in June 1968.

Huey Newton and Bobby Seale found the Black Panther Party on October 15, 1966. More people join after 1968.

In 1969, the US military draft is changed to a lottery system. This tends to fragment opposition to the war as families no longer worry for their sons unless they are among those randomly selected (by birthday).

Groundwork for the internet is laid.

Research about "packet switching" begins: one packet switched network, ARPANET, would lead to what we now know as the internet.

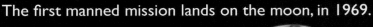

The first manned mission lands on the moon, in 1969.

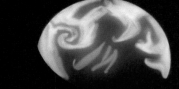

McDonalds unveils their new logo in 1968.

Rising above the lunar horizon, we see our planet as it appears from afar.

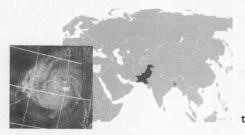

Fallout from the Partition of India continues to afflict Bangladesh.

East Bengal, which eventually becomes Bangladesh, battles for independence from West Pakistan Although it is separated by the Indian subcontinent, it is actually part of the country of Pakistan. The war and associated famine claim thousands of lives, as does a huge typhoon in 1970.

The Iranian dissident, Khomeini, condemns any government, except clerical rule.

Iran's most influential dissident, who will eventually become Ayatollah Khomeini, reverses his previous position supporting the Iranian Constitution of 1906-1907. In a series of lectures in Najaf on Islamic government and in his book, titled Islamic Government: Governance of the Jurist, he outlines the idea that all aspects of life should be in accordance with Islamic religious law, known as Sharia. He declares that all those holding government posts should be knowledgeable of Sharia and that the country should be ruled by a Supreme Leader who surpasses all others in knowledge of Sharia.

Khomeini asserts that "Those claiming to be representatives of the majority of the people" (i.e. elected legislatures) are 'wrong' in the eyes of Islam. Aware that he needs a large power base, he is careful not to publicize these ideas outside religious networks.

$ Nixon abandons the Gold Standard, the backing of paper dollars by gold.

Public debt in the United States had grown due to expenditures on the Vietnam War and the Great Society programs. The Federal Reserve had printed more money which fueled inflation and reduced the proportion of gold held in reserve to back the currency. After fearful investors redeemed several billions in paper currency for actual gold early in 1971, Nixon hurriedly closes 'the gold window'.

The Nixon Shock makes the U.S. dollar a 'Fiat Currency', a free floating currency based on nothing. Nixon unilaterally cancels the direct convertibility of dollars into gold ending the international monetary system based on the Bretton Woods system that had been in existence since 1944.

 President Nixon launches the War on Drugs in 1971.

Construction of America's Interstate Highway system continues. Interstate 55 in Mississippi in 1972.

 Dictators in third world nations come and go. François Duvalier, ruled Haiti with the backing of the United States. His 14 year reign of terror that resulted in 30,000 deaths ends in 1971.

1971

World oil consumption has been steadily increasing at a fast pace and the United States is the largest consumer by far.

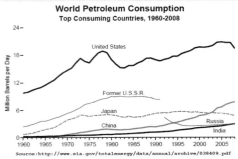

World Petroleum Consumption
Top Consuming Countries, 1960-2008

Source:http://www.eia.gov/totalenergy/data/annual/archive/038409.pdf

A computer model is made to simulate the potential effects of continuing exponential population growth, increasing resource use and pollution on the biosphere.

Produced by a think tank, called The Club of Rome, *The Limits to Growth*, is published in 1972.

1972 Polaroid SX-70 Camera debuts and is an instant hit.

- Nominal
- Real (2008 dollars)

1861–1944 US domestic first purchase price
1945–1985 Arabian Light posted at Ras Tanura
1986–2008 Brent Spot
Source: Energy Information Administration

Although demand for oil keeps rising, prices remain flat.

Oil producing countries are not realizing a fair share of the profit for this resource that has become so important in the world economy. Oil prices have always been low; originally set by the oil companies and treaties imposed on producing countries decades ago.

Oil producing countries have been trying to get a larger share and to raise prices for a long time, and the formation of the Organization of Petroleum Exporting Countries (OPEC) in 1961 is the latest attempt to gain sovereign control over the resources within their borders. After the United States abandoned the Gold Standard (the Nixon Shock), the real value of the dollar declined and so the real price of oil actually declined from the already low levels, as it was paid for in dollars.

Israel is invaded in the Yom Kippur War.

Egypt and Syria launch a surprise assault on Israel and seek to reclaim territories lost in the Six Day War. American military support of Israel during this war is the trigger for the OPEC states to not only increase oil prices but to also decrease oil production. Although triggered by American support of Israel, the seeds of the embargo had long ago been planted.

An oil embargo causes the Oil Shock of 1973.

The price of oil rises from $3 per barrel to almost $12.

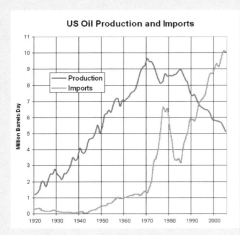

US Oil Production and Imports

- Production
- Imports

American dissidents are marginalized.

 Many of America's dissidents become disillusioned and retreat from political engagement or join fringe groups. In 1974, the Simonise Liberation Army kidnaps Patty Hearst, a sophomore at University of California, Berkeley, and heir to the publishing empire of William Randolph Hearst. One of the demands of the SLA is for free food to be distributed in poor neighborhoods. Violence erupts at one of the food distribution outlets when much larger crowds than expected arrive. Rattled workers throw boxes of food into the crowd.

The first cellular phone call is made.

  In 1973, Martin Cooper of Motorola places the first cellular call to Joel S. Engel of Bell Labs. Cooper informed Engel, who was also trying to build a mobile phone, to tell him that he had done it first.

The Gaia hypothesis is proposed; living organisms actively influence the temperature and composition of the biosphere.

 According to the Gaia hypothesis, which is proposed by J.E. Lovelock, life will respond and change conditions to suit itself. If the biosphere is disturbed by extraterrestrial events (like a meteor hit or a solar flare) biologic responses will tend to restore an environment favorable to life.

The woman of Iceland go on strike.

On October 24, 1975 an estimated 90% of women in Iceland participated in a one day strike. Women refused to work or perform household duties for one day to make evident the importance of women for Iceland's socioeconomic wellbeing and raise awareness for women's rights and gender equality. At this time, an employed woman in Iceland makes less than 60% of the wages of a working man. As a result of this strike Iceland's parliament passed a law that guaranteed gender equality. Five years after the strike Iceland elects Vigdís Finnbogadóttir, the world's first democratically elected female president.

World population reaches 4 billion by around 1974.

4 billion

1975

The Vietnam War ends with 'The Fall of Saigon' in 1975.

The last American combat troops are withdrawn from Vietnam in 1973. The South Vietnamese Regime left in place by the Americans lingers on but American financial support is reduced in the wake of the recession and although the South Vietnamese have more tanks than North Vietnam and over 1400 aircraft, rising oil prices hamper their use of this equipment.

Mao Zedong dies in 1976.

His body is embalmed for public viewing and placed into the Mausoleum of Mao Zedong, located in Beijing. A struggle for power ensues. Deng Xisoping, twice purged from the communist party, emerges as the new Chinese leader.

In 1977, the East Germany Politburo decides to withdraw most coffee, which is becoming increasingly more expensive, from markets. Luckily, in 1978 coffee prices drop slightly and East Germans are able to secure a coffee supply from Vietnam, which will become one of the world leaders in coffee production by the 1990's.

The Iranian Shah's firm grip on power is looking shaky. The population, terrorized by his secret police for years now, is rebelling despite large personal risk.

In 1977 the research submarine Alvin explores the depths of the world's oceans and discovers creatures living around the hydrothermal vents. Soon, a new hypothesis will be proposed that life itself originated in the deep sea vents.

The honeycombed fossil below, Paleodictyon, was thought to have gone extinct 50 million years ago but recently, the Alvin submarine discovered living specimens vat the bottom of the very deep sea. Most likely, this species was unable to compete with later evolving animals and migrated to an environment that although less desirable has less competition. This is an example of a once prolific organism moving into 'refugia.'

Fossils fuels keep on burning. Oil companies eclipse medium sized countries in wealth and power. The temperature continues to rise as it has since the 1850's.

Jimmy Carter promises straight talk, hard work, fair play and justice.

The son of a peanut farmer, Carter is the first in his family to pursue a professional career. He becomes a navy submarine officer and serves on a nuclear sub under Captain Rickover. He is placed in charge of U.S. personnel in the cleanup of the partial meltdown of the Chalk River Labs' experimental nuclear reactor. The extreme measures necessitated by the spill will influence his later decisions to avoid developing nuclear energy and the neutron bomb.

Americans, disillusioned by the Watergate scandal and their government's conduct in the Vietnam War, elect Jimmy Carter over Gerald Ford in 1976.

Carter declares the energy crisis a danger to the nation and a moral injustice on a scale equivalent to that of war. Carter fears that at the rate Americans have been burning oil, the world oil supply might soon be depleted. His push for austerity in the national budget and in energy use strikes most of the American public as too heavy-handed. Americans are already feeling stressed by high rates of inflation, a consequence of the previous administrations. He urges homeowners to insulate their roofs, keep daytime heat to 65°F and 55°F at night, and imposes, rather than recommends, a national maximum speed limit of 55 mph.

When it becomes apparent that some chemicals may be damaging the ozone layer, the environmentally conscious American public asks for a CFC ban.

The ban of CFCs is an incredible triumph, a documentable success of humanity's ability to make constructive changes. Inexpensive alternatives are found to replace these chemicals in air conditioners and foam production.

In 1978, Congress approves a budget to build a Large Space Telescope to explore deep space.

Protests against Nuclear power plants occur in America.

President Carter has solar panels installed on the White House roof, in 1979

China introduces the One Child Policy.

The policy is introduced in 1978 and enacted in 1980. Party leaders hope this policy will avert a population bomb that would outstrip gains in productivity rates.

The Iranian people rebel against the Shah; against monarchy and autocratic rule, and against Western influence and imperialism.

The Iranian Shah fights to hold onto his power. His troops shoot down demonstrators and yet people continue to pour into the streets in open rebellion.

The Shah flees and the demonstrators are suddenly standing in a power vacuum. With no practice in government, and fearing that any number of foreign powers might invade, a leader is hastily chosen. Ayatollah Khomeini is the most popular choice. Many non-religious people hope that Khomeini will not try to build a personal empire because of his advanced age. And being a scholar who had been forced live abroad, it is also hoped that his worldly viewpoint will help to keep him above local power politics. But the Ayatollah sees a re-institution of Shiite Islam, in a fundamentalist fashion, as the route to resisting foreign pressures. He believes that Iran must resist not only the power of Western interests but also those of Sunni Muslims Iran is the only country with a Shiia

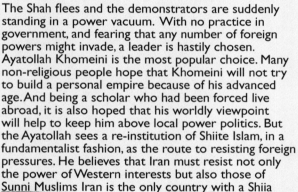

majority and Sunnis make up more than 85% of Muslims worldwide.

After decades of dictatorship, the Somoza regime is overthrown by the Sandinista revolution.

In July 1979, the dictator finally loses his hold on power. The Sandinista Party will endeavor to make Nicaragua an independent sovereign country that fulfills the ambitions of its populace.

In order to set the conditions for a sovereign state, the Sandinistas enact a plan to raise literacy and to provide basic healthcare.

They build hospitals and schools. The Nicaraguan Literacy Campaign is launched in 1980 and trains teachers to train peasants, about 50% of whom are completely illiterate. In just six months illiteracy is reduced by more than a third.

In 1979 the Soviet Union invades Afghanistan.

Soviet troops roll through the Hindu Kush into Afghanistan supported by Soviet air cover.

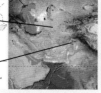

1979 Oil Shock occurs because of the Iranian Revolution.

Iraq invades Iran.

Iraq invades Iran in September, 1980 from the land and air, beginning the Iran-Iraq War. The United States and some western European countries support Iraq's leader Saddam Hussein. The U.S. provides military, monetary, and diplomatic support to the Iraqi strongman. Iran is a Shiite Muslim country while Iraq has a Shia majority but is run by its Sunni minority.

Mount St. Helens erupts.

The internet debuts.

The internet is not a point to point form of communication; instead information can move through a network of multiple relay stations. This network redundancy makes communication less vulnerable to single point failure. Much of the funding for its development came from the Department of Defense which sought to insure military communications. The Internet Protocol Suite is standardized in 1982. Using TCP/IP protocol, networks from anywhere in the world can transfer information.

Situated in the Cascade Range and almost equidistant from Seattle, Washington and Portland, Oregon, Mount St. Helens is classified as a stratovolcano (AKA composite volcano), with the characteristic steep slopes that reach over 2,500 m. The two months of earthquakes that preceded the May 18, 1980 eruption culminate in a massive quake that registers 5.1 on the Richter scale. The seismic blast triggers the largest landslide ever recorded, blowing out the side of the mountain and reducing its elevation by over 400m and leaving a mile wide crater. The explosion reaches 24 km into the atmosphere, dropping ash over 11 U.S. states and 5 Canadian Provinces.

Ronald Reagan becomes America's new president.

Reagan is a Hollywood trained actor and his oratory resonates with much of the American public. His vice president is George Bush, a former director of the CIA and a Texas oil man (who will later be known as George H.W. Bush or George Bush 1, to distinguish him from his son). Shortly after taking office in 1981, Reagan orders the solar panels to be removed from the White House roof, even though they are functioning well.

Reagan promises to restore American pride by cutting taxes, improving the armed forces, cutting government spending and reducing the deficit; a package that was called 'voodoo economics' (by Bush during the primary). He claims that cuts in the capital gains tax will help all citizens because of 'trickle down economics'.

China's share of the world economy begins to rise.

China had the largest proportion of the world economy before the Industrial Revolution, and its share is on the rise again. This chart, based on data from Angus Maddison, "The World Economy", shows those trends. Here, the combined output of China and India is compared to the combined output of the United States and Britain.

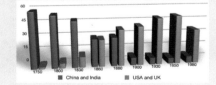

China creates Special Economic Zones.

In the late 1970s, the Chinese government decides to try out market balanced models of economic organization in several small but representative zones. As part of its economic reforms and policy of opening to the world, between 1980 and 1984 China establishes special economic zones. Sino-foreign joint ventures take place within the zone and products are primarily for export. The purpose is to function as zones of economic growth by using tax and business incentives to attract foreign investment and technology but be done at a small scale to test the feasibility of the idea in a controllable way.

The Sandinista reforms are successful but the new gains are soon in peril.

Seeking to discredit and bring down the Sandinista Regime, rightist elements organize a 'Contra War.' The Sandinistas have organized their political agenda, at least partially, on Communist ideological lines and if it were to prove a viable model, even in a state as small as Nicaragua, it might- according to the worst fears of State Department ideologues- inspire other poor nations to emulate them, causing a domino effect. The Contras immediately target the new hospitals and schools and soon move on to killing and torturing Sandanista supporters. The atrocities are well documented and exposed in the American media and the American electorate objects. The Boland amendment passes which limits funding for the Contras.

In order to continue financing their operations, the Contras ship and distribute large amounts of cocaine to the U.S. The Reagan administration turns a blind eye to any reports of a Contra-cocaine connection. Cocaine use in the U.S. surges and the price of the illegal drug plummets.

Crack cocaine hits the street.

To offset the low price, drug dealers use a newly contrived version of cocaine known as crack, a smokeable form of cocaine that is even more potent, and which can be sold in small quantities. This new drug is marketed in low income neighborhoods. Crack soon makes its way into most major American cities.

The coca plant is indigenous to the slopes of the Andes.

There are four closely related species of the plant and they were domesticated thousands of years ago. The leaves have been traditionally used as a chew, tea or tonics for medicinal and spiritual purposes. Coca leaves contain very small amounts of several psychoactive alkaloids including cocaine and their use is not considered to be addictive. Cocaine must be extracted from the leaves with solvents to make the modern recreational drug. Coca use remains a part of traditional culture.

"Just Say No!"

Nancy Reagan coined this slogan when giving a talk at a California elementary school in 1982. The "Just Say No" campaign was put into effect in an effort to educate children and teenagers on the subject of illicit drug use. The campaign asserted that the most effective way to reduce illegal drug use and abuse is to resist peer and societal pressure, to "Just Say No."

The slight nuance to the Cosmic Background Radiation is detected, further supporting The Big Bang Theory.

The Cosmic Background Radiation would not be completely uniform if the Big Bang had really happened since it would have been produced by a quantum event. Such a small fluctuation would be ridiculously difficult to detect but scientists had set forth. Engineers built a better detector which would have to be placed in orbit above the disturbance of the Earth's atmosphere, to have any chance at all of measuring the texture of the relic signal.

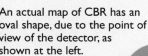

They build their detector and are given a slot on one of NASA's next rockets but space becomes scare and years pass before the detector is launched. In 1982, the results are in- the quantum signature is there! The prediction and detection of the CBR is a triumph.

An actual map of CBR has an oval shape, due to the point of view of the detector, as shown at the left.

The space shuttle Challenger explodes 73 seconds after launch.

Its a disaster for the space program. The crew of the shuttle includes a teacher and millions of American school children watch the launch; it's a public morale disaster.

After being approved in 1978, with the aim for a launch date in 1983, the building of the Hubble Space Telescope was beset by obstacles. NASA encountered problems with engineering, construction, and budget; the launch is rescheduled for October 1986. Unfortunately, the Challenger explosion causes much of the American space program to be put on hold, including the Hubble launch. The cost of keeping the Hubble Telescope in working condition, without launch, is about $6 million per month.

The Contras find yet another source of funds.

Between 1985 and 1986 the U.S. sells weapons to Iran despite an official trade embargo. Funds acquired from the clandestine sales are secretly sent to Nicaragua to fund the Contras, in violation of the Boland Amendment

1986

In Bhopal, India, a factory that produces pesticides leaks tons of poisonous gas into the environment. Many people in the slums that house workers for the plant awake with burning eyes and congested lungs. The gas is heavier than air and follows the contours of the ground. This poisonous fog leaks into houses and along the roads suffocating thousands of people.

The factory was built by Union Carbide, a sophisticated, Multi-National Company and Union Carbide profited from the plants production but it hired out the running and maintenance of the plant to local contractors that it had consigned with and took no responsibility for its safety. It drove a hard bargain and the refrigeration unit, which would have kept reactive substances cool had been turned off to reduce energy costs amid many other instances of safety violations.

In 1986 in the United States, in response to a grass roots outrage over The Bhopal disaster and fear of similar disasters at home, the Right To Know Act is passed which requires companies to disclose information about the storage and releases of toxic chemicals in the U.S.

World population reaches 5 billion.

5 billion

Motivated Muslims travel to Afghanistan, forming the Mujahideen, in order to help repel the Soviet invasion.

The Special Economic Zones in China have prospered.

China's economic planners have been experimenting with a market run economy but only in limited areas. People will now be allowed to open private businesses in more areas. Large industry will remain under state control and political dissent will continue to be illegal.

The recruits are soon tested. Casualties are high as they battle against a superpower's military machine but they are empowered by discovering each other.

Access to the internet increases.

In 1986, the National Science Foundation increases access to the internet by establishing the CSNET, Computer Science Network, which use its supercomputers at research and educational institutions.

There is no central station for the internet.

Sadam Hussein uses chemical weapons against the mostly Kurdish population of Northern Iraq.

Estimates from Human Rights Watch are between 50 and 100 thousand killed. Some Kurdish sources estimate the number at 182,000. Villages of other ethnic groups, such as the Shabaks and Assyrians, are also destroyed. While other nations protest these abuses and violations of the Geneva Accords, the United States does not; Sadam Hussein is considered an ally worth turning a blind eye for.

Forest fires burn freely at Yellowstone.

For decades, all forest fires in American national parks had been extinguished as soon as possible which eventually resulting in the build up of brush and dead wood throughout the forests. Furthermore, ecologists realized that fire is a natural part of the forest system. The fire suppression policy was changed in 1972 and naturally occurring fires caused by lightning strikes were no longer put out. Since that time there had been 235 fires in Yellowstone but, owing to wet weather, none were great in extent, and most of the brush had not yet been reduced to normal levels. When the park is ravaged by fire in the dry summer of 1988, some wonder if the policy should have been phased in gradually.

More American prisons are built.

Many new prisons are built to house America's growing prisoner population. Many prisons are privatized. Prisoners are often shipped out of state to serve their sentence in states that encourage commercialization of prisons.

A single company, DeBeers, controls the worldwide diamond industry. Some diamonds, known as 'blood diamonds,' are found in war-torn regions of Africa. These are sought by warlords and investors and become the currency of war.

A large solar flare causes a coronal mass ejection.

The CME is unleashed on March 13, 1989. The entire province of Quebec, Canada, suffers an electrical power blackout. Hydro-Québec's power grid uses very long transmission lines to carry electrical power from distant dams. Its exposed continental rock shield seems to have been harder for the current to enter than its 735 kV power lines. Auroras are seen as far south as Florida.

The Berlin Wall falls in 1989.

The old order of the Cold War in Europe collapses.

380.000 Soviet troops remain in East Germany. The Soviet Union has the legal right to occupy East Germany based on from armistace treaties signed at the end of WW2. Gorbachev proposes new institutions be created to replace Nato and the Warsaw Pact. but Washington seeks to hold onto a larger share and does not want NATO replaced.

In February of 1990, U.S. secretary of state James Baker and Chancellor Helmut Kohl of West Germany each journey separately to Moscow, but within a day of each, other to hash out an agreement.

To get the Soviets to withdraw their troops, without the disbanding of NATO, Baker promises "that NATO's jurisdiction would not shift one inch eastward from its present position?" Baker leaves a letter outlining the agreement and it is made public later, when Kohls official papers are released.

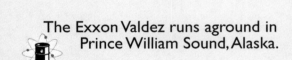

Reagan administration officials are brought to trial

U.S. Lieutenant Oliver North relished his role in the sale of arms to Iran and directing funds to the Contras. Prior to his trial in 1988, North destroys or hides important documents. He claims to be a patriot but admits that he participated in the scandal and in concealing it from the American people. Despite the fact that guns were sold to a foreign enemy to support an atrocity-ridden guerilla army, North is touted by right wing groups as a glamorous and heroic figure, as the 'fall guy' for the Reagan administration.

The Exxon Valdez runs aground in Prince William Sound, Alaska.

The oil tanker spills more than 10 million gallons of oil into the ocean.

The United States supplies the freedom fighters of Afghanistan with arms and intelligence.

The rebels learn to use Rocket Propelled Grenades with unexpected efficiency against the Soviet helicopter gunships.

The Mujahideen are victorious and the Soviets withdraw from Afghanistan.

The withdrawal begins in 1988 and finishes up in February 1989.

Afghanistan ranked as one of the world's poorest countries at the beginning of the war and by 1989 the country is in a ruinous state. Over 850,000 Afghan civilians were killed and another 5 to 10 million fled the country as a result of the war.

The Soviet War leaves Kabul in Ruins. Rival warlords and various factions compete to take control and fill the vacuum.

No serious attempts, by the Soviets, the Americans, or any of the other world powers, are made to help rebuild the country.

A civil war in Afghanistan follows the Soviet withdrawal and lasts from 1989 to 1992. Buildings, farms, irrigation equipment, and canals not completely destroyed during the Soviet War sustain more damage, resulting in widespread famine, death, and disease in Afghanistan.

Protest erupts in Tiananmen Square.

The '89 Democracy Movement takes place in the spring of 1989 in Beijing, and later nationwide. It is a student-led demonstration and receives broad support from city residents. The protests are suppressed by the government leaders who order military to enforce the martial law in Beijing. The crackdown is known as the Tiananmen Square Massacre.

Apartheid officially ends in South Africa, in 1990.

South Africa has elections in 1994 that all people can vote in and Nelson Mandela is elected.

Iraq invades Kuwait in 1990 and the First Gulf War begins.

In August 1990, the Gulf war begins as 100,000 Iraqi troops cross the border and occupy Kuwait. The Americans respond with Operation Desert Storm in 1991. It begins with an air campaign.

Iraq blows up Kuwaiti oil fields and invades part of Saudi Arabia.

USAF aircraft fly over burning Kuwaiti oil wells

Saddam Hussein, dictator of Iraq, claims that overproduction of oil by Kuwait and the United Arab Emirates is 'economic warfare' against Iraq because it is depleting underground stores of oil. Later he will also claim that Kuwait is using slant drilling techniques to take oil clearly in Iraq. Relations between Kuwait and Iraq had already been strained during the Iran- Iraq war, where Kuwait had at first tried to remain neutral but later supported Iraq in order to protect itself from Iran, which was trying to export the Iranian style revolution to Kuwait. When the Iraq- Iran war ends, Iraq does not have the money to repay its war loans but Kuwait refuses to forgive them.

In 1991, the USSR dissolves, ending the Cold War.

1991

9 4
3 8
10 14
11
5
1
2
6
13 15
7

The 'Storm of the Century' in 1993 is the largest known to date.

At its maximum, the storm stretched from Canada to Central America. Cuba was badly damaged by winds in excess of 100 miles per hour, a foot of snow was dropped on the state of Georgia, and a mighty storm surge battered coastlines.

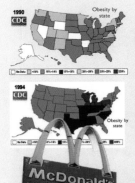

By 1990, at least 10 percent of American citizens in most states are obese. The health of the nation is strained. In 1993, McDonald's sells its 100 billionth hamburger. By 1994, all states have an obesity rate of more than 10% and many states have rates in excess of 15%. Many of the affected and overburdened individuals are children. Rates of Type II Diabetes and other diseases associated with obesity are increasing.

The industrialization of food continues and fast food is ubiquitous. In 1993, McDonald's sells its 100 billionth hamburger. Other fast food outlets are similarly productive and fast food items line grocery store shelves.

FDA approves the FlavrSavr tomato in 1994, making it the first Genetically Modified food product on the American market.

The internet takes off when it becomes fully commercialized.

 Commercial internet providers emerged in the 1980's and early 1990's, and commercialized internet had started to boom in Europe, Asia, and Australia.

In 1995, the internet in the United States is fully commercialized with the removal of the educational requirements that were on the National Science Foundation's Network.

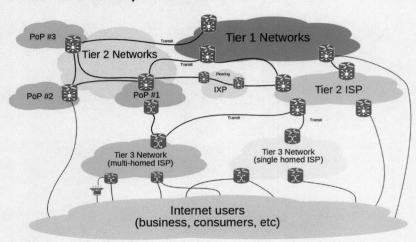

Genocide in Rwanda claims up to a million lives.

The majority of Rwandans are from the Hutu tribe and they attempt to eradicate the minority Tutsi population. In the course of approximately 100 days, between 500,000 and 1,000,000 Tutsi and moderate Hutu people are killed.

International pressure on the Hutu led government resulted in a cease-fire in 1993 and accords to allow Tutsi participation in the government. This displeased many conservative Hutus who stir up ethnic hatred and disseminate propaganda about Tutsi plans to reinstate a Tutsi monarchy.

The mass slaughter begins the day after an airplane carrying the presidents of Rwanda and neighboring Burundi, both Hutus, is shot down on April 5, 1994. An organized effort by soldiers and police executes influential Tutsis and moderate Hutu leaders and then constructs checkpoints, and using national identity cards to verify the ethnicity, executes Tutsis. Hutu civilians are invited and pressured to rape, maim and kill their Tutsi neighbors and to steal their property.

In 1935, the Belgians issued apartheid like identity cards formally labeling each individual Hutu or Tutsi. The distinction was a class distinction; the Belgians were unable to find racial differences with which to distinguish the two groups. Previously, particularly wealthy Hutu had been able to become honorary Tutsis but now class status was set by the designation on an identity card. The colonial period came to a close, the Hutu majority came to power and the country gained independence in 1962.

The genocide occurs during the Rwandan Civil War which began in 1990 when Tutsi refugees, who had fled to Uganda during previous waves of Hutu violence, returned as the Rwandan Patriotic Front.

Hutus and Tutsis share a common language but historically had different occupations; the Tutsi were cattle herders and the Hutu were farmers. Several kingdoms formed in the region by about 1700 but the Kingdom of Rwanda, ruled by one of the Tutsi clans, became dominant and Hutu people were forced to work for Tutsi chiefs. During the Scramble for Africa, Germany took control of the area and they thought that the Tutsis had originally migrated from Ethiopia and were thus partially Caucasian and therefore superior to the Hutu. The Germans supported the Tutsi monarchy and used it to control the territory. After World War 1, a League of Nations mandate passed control of the country to Belgium. The Belgians further concentrated resources and power in favor of Tutsis over Hutus.

1995

The Oklahoma City Federal Building is bombed by Timothy McVeigh and Terry Nichols on April 19, 1995.

Ethnic distribution in Bosnia and Herzegovina before and after the war

Sarajevo

1991

Sarajevo

1998

Boundary line between Bosniak-Croat Federation and the Bosnian Serb Republic

■ Predominantly Croat ■ Predominantly Serb
■ Predominantly Bosniak Bosniak-Croat mixed

A Bosnian - Serb organized program is orchestrated to force minorities out of majority Serb regions, which they call 'ethnic cleansing'.

The Taliban emerge from the chaos as the dominant force and enforce a violent new order that they claim is based on Sharia law.

The bedlam and struggle for power continues in Afghanistan after the end of the Civil War in 1992. The Taliban attempt to bring down the government after it is overthrown by the Mujahideen and in 1996 they have success and take reign over Afghanistan. The United Nations reports that the Taliban are responsible for numerous massacres, human trafficking, terrorism, and death to civilians.

Aside from occasional reports of Taliban atrocities - especially against woman and girls - the country of Afghanistan fades from world view.

$ Futures can help balance markets.

Futures originated as a way of smoothing out gluts and shortages in markets. For example, a bread baking company buys wheat but the price of wheat fluctuates making it difficult for the bakery to plan and to cover its costs when wheat prices are high. And farmers need to plant their wheat crops but they worry that the price for a bushel of wheat might drop too low before harvest time.

If the farmer and the baker agree on a price for the wheat to be bought on a future date, the price they agree on will not be as high or as low was the price the wheat might actually fetch on the open market, but they will both have security. Futures markets can provide not only security but can also stimulate farmers to grow the crops that will be most in demand, thus expanding and improving the market- almost giving a kind of intelligence to the market.

An energy company named Enron, moves far beyond its original role of piping gas.

Although Enron owns and operates extensive pipelines, it sets its sights on making money in 'Futures' markets.

As energy markets are deregulated, Enron begins to broker energy futures. Enron is deemed "America's Most Innovative Company" by Fortune magazine 1996.

 Enron fosters a climate of boldness; its extravagant offices mirror its self confident corporate culture.

Enron is created in 1985 by the merger of pre-existing companies that transmit and distribute natural gas and electricity, and to a lesser extent, also produce plastics and petrochemicals. The very large energy company, InterNorth of Omaha, Nebraska acquires the much smaller Houston Natural Gas company and a wag-the-dog situation ensues.

Although InterNorth was the larger entity, owning Northern Natural Gas Company among others and operating the nation's largest gas pipeline, after it acquires HNG the company is moved to Houston and put under the control of HNG's CEO, Ken Lay.

Dr. Lynn Margulis is given the Medal of Science for her theory of **symbiogenesis**.

This theory explains that organelles within cells, like mitochondria and chloroplasts, did not evolve incrementally within complex cells but were once free swimming individual organisms that were incorporated into the cell through merger.

NATO expands into formerly Soviet Territory.

1949
1952
1955
1982
1990
1999
2004
2009

Poland, Hungary, and the Czech Republic join the North Atlantic Treaty Organization in 1999. Although NATO is supposed to be an alliance for mutual defense and none of its members are under immediate threat and despite the concerns of some members and the virulent opposition of Russia, the new members are admitted.

Putin comes to power.

Vladimir Putin, a veteran KGB officer, becomes acting president of Russia in 1999, after the resignation of Boris Yeltsin. He then wins the subsequent election of 2000.

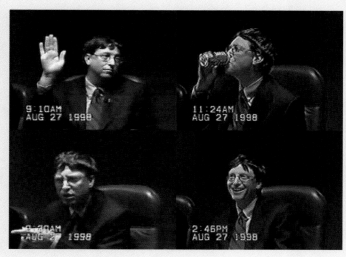

Anti Trust laws, enacted in the Progressive Era, are brought against Microsoft in 1999.

Microsoft is declared a Monopoly. A federal judge requires that Microsoft cease to require its operating system be installed in all new computers that use its other products.

The percentage of Americans gaining enough weight to impair health continues to increase.

World population reaches 6 billion.

6 billion

1999

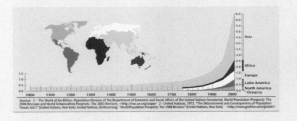

6 billion

2000

China, with nearly a quarter of the world's population, has been industrializing rapidly and is building an economic powerhouse, and adding to the Earth's pollution load.

The polar ice caps continue melting, ocean temperatures continue to rise and tropical storms keep getting bigger.

Ancient Buddhist statues are destroyed.

In March of 2001 the Taliban destroys two large Buddhist statues. Dating back to the 6th century the two statues were carved into a cliff in Central Afghanistan. The Taliban claims that the monuments are Buddhist idols and thus not in accordance with Sharia, the religious and moral code of Islam. The Taliban follow and impose their own strict interpretation of Sharia.

The smart phone debuts.

The year 2000 is the advent of the smart phone. The first smart phone program is the Symbian, which is the predecessor to the Blackberry and iPhone.

In order to get accurate enough figures to enable GPS location services on cell phones, Einstein's relativity equations must be used. Newton's cruder equations won't work well enough because the signals travel at almost the speed of light and travel a bit of distance, up to the satellite and back.

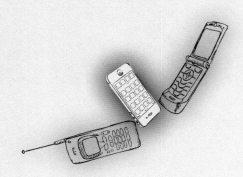

On September Eleventh 2001, the United States is attacked.

On what comes to be known as 9-11, four United Airlines flights are hijacked. One is aimed at the United States Capitol, but crashes into a field in Pennsylvania. Another crashes into the Pentagon and the other two crash into the World Trade Center in New York City. Nearly 3,000 people are killed in this attack against American political, military and financial targets.

America launches its *War on Terror*. American troops enter Afghanistan in October of 2001 and Iraq in 2003.

The United States launches the War on Terror invading Afghanistan in October 2001 and Iraq in 2003, on the basis that they are harboring terrorists. Laws protecting the rights and privacy of American citizens are suspended under emergency measures and the torture of prisoners becomes official policy.

Nouri al-Maliki returns to Iraq.

Nouri al-Maliki will eventually become Prime Minister of Iraq. He was forced into exile by Saddam Hussein in 1979. Hussein, a Sunni Muslim, had the backing of the United States at that time and used his military machine to root out members of the Dawa Party, a Shia group dedicated to combatting secularism and establishing a Shiite Islamic state in Iraq. Al-Maliki was able to flee to Damascus but many of his colleagues were rounded up by Hussein and imprisoned, tortured or killed.

Al-Maliki lived in Syria and spent much of his time over the more than 20 years of his exile in Iran, a Shiite majority Islamic State. During the Iran/Iraq war, the United States preferentially backed Iraq. The population of Iran is overwhelmingly Shia while the population of Iraq is majority Shia but is run by its Sunni minority. Dawa administrators and operatives worked to help Iran and to topple Hussein. They orchestrated an attack on the Iraqi embassy in Beirut in 1981 and attacks on the US and French embassies in Kuwait in 1983, although al-Maliki himself was never directly tied to those activities.

After the American invasion of 2003 topples the dictator it had once backed, Al-Maliki returns to his native land. He becomes the deputy leader of the De-baathification Commission for the interim government, purging prominent Sunnis from military and civilian institutions.

America's National security agency, the NSA, steps up its surveillance program.

The NSA is concerned with collecting and storing metadata, which is data about data. Telephone metadata includes the number of the originator of a given phone call, the number that receives the call, and the time and duration of a given call. By analyzing telephone metadata over a period time the NSA is able to recognize trends in calls and ultimately infer information about a caller or a receiver of calls. Internet metadata includes a user's website history, map searches, account information, e-mail activity, and passwords.

An executive order from President Bush pushes the agency to tap phone calls made by U.S. citizens to persons outside the US without even obtaining warrants from the Foreign Intelligence Surveillance Courts (FISA).

Cassini, a NASA spacecraft launched in 1997, enters Saturn's orbit.

2004

The health of the average American continues to decline as obesity rates rise. Several states move into the red zone.

The notorious Abu Graib prison is used, this time by Americans.

Iraqis are rounded up, sometimes almost randomly and brought the prison. When reports of abuse surface, the Bush administration claims that they are isolated incidents due to rogue soldiers, and the result of under-staffing and typical war-time chaos. However, documents that come to be known as the Torture Memos surface a few years later. These documents were prepared before the invasion of Iraq by the United States Department of Justice and authorize 'enhanced interrogation techniques' which are generally considered torture. The documents also put forth arguments that the Geneva Convention does not apply to American interrogators overseas.

Facebook is founded.

Mark Zuckerberg, along with some of his fellow students at Harvard in 2004 create the website. Its use is at first limited to Harvard students and then expanded to other colleges. By September 2006, it is available to anyone over 13 years old with an e-mail address.

Shortly after the start of the War on Terror, the company Halliburton is awarded a contract for work in Iraq and Kuwait. The CEO of this company had been Dick Cheney but he retired from this role in order to run on the presidential ticket with George W. Bush. Although still a major stockholder, Cheney claims that there is no conflict of interest. The company makes an estimated $39.5 billion from the war.

The flow of information continues to become more restricted by monied interests and by the passive gullibility of people. Competition between news corporations shrinks as they merge into large conglomerates; sometimes controlling all the newspapers and TV stations in a region. Politicians, who face expensive reelection campaigns, receive information from lobbyists who are hired by contributors to their campaigns.

Stability in a democracy relies on its members having hope for the future, and thus a stake in the common good. Investment in the future requires hope for a later return. The segments of the population that 'discount their future,' as game theorists and sociologists say, often engage in high risk behaviors if those behaviors have a chance of bringing short term gains. Junkies will commit risky robberies and share needles for their next high. Soldiers in dire wars will go back for an ambushed comrade for the respect and companionship of others regardless of the risk. Young men will chance violence and prison terms for a shot at establishing a name for themselves.

Neo-Darwinists claim this is an expression of a 'selfish gene.' According to Neo-Darwinist views, individual genes within our larger genome compete with other genes.

A magnitude 9.2 earthquake in the Indian Ocean creates a devastating tsunami.

In 2004, an earthquake in a subduction zone in the Indian Ocean causes a large tsunami that kills over 230,000 people in fourteen countries, including Indonesia, Sri Lanka, India, and Thailand.

Drones are deployed in large numbers.
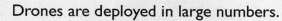

Drones are unmanned aerial vehicles, UAVs, and most are controlled from a remote location by pilots. As technology improves more drones will be controlled autonomously by an on board computer.

Wikileaks is founded.

Wikileaks, an organization that publishes previously secret and sometimes classified information on a public website, is founded in 2006. Wikileaks is committed to protecting the anonymity of their sources.

WikiLeaks

Noura al-Maliki becomes prime minister of Iraq in 2006.

With a year, Maliki began to undemocratically grab more power. When the secular group, Iraqiya gained more votes than Maliki's own Shiite State of Law party but still failed to win a majority in parliamentary elections, he pressured the courts to change the laws to grant his party the right to put together the new coalition government.

New Horizons is launched.

January 19, 2006- Carrying a payload of 7 different analysis instruments, the spacecraft is heading to the Kuiper Belt with a scheduled fly-by of the Pluto system.

Global energy use varies widely.

A picture of the Earth at night and graphics of daily patterns of airplane flights are snapshots that show where energy is used.

During daylight in the U.S. domestic flights are underway. As evening comes to the East Coast, planes bound for Europe head out.

Global population is not evenly distributed, and some people use more kilowatts than others. This composite satellite image is an informal census of economic wealth. Small compensation to populations unseen in this image is that they see a more vivid night sky, unspoiled by light pollution.

The Large Hadron Collider, built by CERN, opens.

Built by the European Organization for Nuclear Research, the collider begins launching particles at high speed into its huge circular tunnel in September, 2008. It will allow physicists to test theories of how particles might have interacted in the energetic conditions during the Big Bang.

 A new hypothesis about the evolution of mineral systems is published.

For centuries, the study of minerals had been chiefly concerned with distinguishing one mineral from another and describing the properties of each mineral. Most minerals (which are stable solids that have a specific chemical formula and whose atoms are arrayed in a repeating geometric pattern) were named without knowledge or regard of their chemical composition. With over 4,000 different varieties known, the science of mineralogy has always been burdened by complex nomenclature and a plethora of detail. Many geologists, during the course of their educations, memorized scores or even hundreds of mineral names and formulas, but only some dozens of minerals are important and commonly occurring.

Minerals can be classified into several groups according to their basic shape at the atomic level; there are minerals made of block-y chunks, of sheets (like mica) or of long single or double chains of atoms (pyroxenes). Another classification scheme was devised by Goldschmidt which grouped elements by their affinities for different environments; such as those with an affinity for iron which would form minerals in the core or those with a tendency to bond with sulphur that would make minerals found in ores, and those lithophile elements that were easily incorporated in silicate rocks. But for the most part, students of mineralogy wander about in an ocean of seemingly unrelated details.

In 2008, a new way of thinking about minerals is unveiled in a paper by Robert Hazen, D. Papineau, W. Bleeker and others which is published in American Mineralogist. The new approach is to view minerals in order of their appearance in the geologic record. There were not yet any minerals in the immediate aftermath of the Big Bang. Diamond was the first mineral to form- after the explosion of the first supernova. About 60 different mineral species existed in the early solar system. That number rose to about 250 by the time Earth began to cool. Once life evolved and photosynthesis was initiated, the presence of oxygen in the oceans and atmosphere allowed a whole host of new minerals to form.

Minerals arise from a sequence of physical, chemical and sometimes biological processes. Certain kinds of minerals might be required to exist before life can emerge. Life, once it does occur, has a tremendous impact on the further evolution of mineral types. Biology and geology are not separate subjects.

The housing bubble in America bursts and a hedge fund shell game enters its last round.

As the market tumbles in 2008, the American middle class is gutted and the economies of many other nations tumble.

The gulf between rich and poor has for been steadily widening, for a decade or two. The gutting of the retirement savings of the middle class in the Wall Street Collapse of 2008 widens the gap farther. New tax breaks for the wealthiest Americans allow less than 1% of the population to control half the wealth of the nation, the largest spread since the 1920's.

China hosts the 2008 Summer Olympics despite the poor environmental conditions that are the result of its rapid rise as an industrial power.

Outraged protesters become the Occupy Movement.

The Occupy Movement is an international protest movement. This large and loosely affiliated group of protesters strive to end extreme economic inequality. The Occupy Wall Street Movement in the U.S. adopts the slogan "We are the 99%" and asserts the financial collapse is a consequence of the wealthiest 1% having undue political influence.

A lack of defined demands becomes the major hurdle for the Occupy Movement.

By 2008 the website Facebook has 100 million active users. Facebook users have a profile in which they can include pictures and personal information. Users are able to search and view other user's profiles and can friend and message other members.

America elects its first African-American president. Barack Obama takes office in January of 2009.

Obesity endangers the health of more than a quarter of the citizens of the United States.

An oil rig, the Deepwater Horizon explodes in April 2010 in the Gulf of Mexico, creating an oil slick visible from space.

2010

A 7.0 magnitude earthquake rocks Haiti in 2010, killing over 300,000 people and making it the deadliest Earthquake in nearly 500 years.

The supply of natural gas flowing to Europe from Russia via pipelines in Ukraine is sharply reduced.

Russian sales of fossil fuels are a vital export for the country. Shutting off the supply of gas gives it leverage in a pricing disagreement with Ukraine. The dispute concerns payments on accumulating debts as well as raising prices for the gas and setting transit tariffs. The dispute allows Vladimir Putin to remind Europe of the might of Russia as a powerful country on the world stage.

Fossil fuel poor France continues down its nuclear path. Nuclear reactors in France produce almost 40% of its electricity.

2011

Energy supplies are bought and sold globally. Russia earns hard cash from its sales of natural gas to Germany and other European countries. Although Germany had enough coal to be among the first nations to industrialize, those supplies were small by modern standards and were long ago exhausted. The German government adopts a policy to foster alternative energy to gain some energy independence. Subsidies for solar power lead to the sprouting of solar panels on rooftops in every village in Germany.

A 9.0 Magnitude earthquake in March 2011, off the coast of Japan, on the 'ring of fire', wreaks havoc on the island nation.

World Population puts on another billion.

7 billion

NASA's Curiosity rover lands on Mars.

This is the first time that a video camera has ever landed on another planet. The rover has 4 goals: to determine if conditions able to support life ever existed on the planet, to study to climate and geology of Mars, and to prepare the way for future human exploration of the planet.

Al-Maliki grabs more power and further diminishes Sunni representation. Sectarian violence within Iraq escalates.

In 2011, Maliki pressures the courts again- this time to amend the law to allow him to take control of the agencies that investigate corruption, run the central bank and oversee elections. He has the chairman of the elections commission arrested. As Sunnis become more persecuted and more excluded from any part in the government, more of them join underground organizations like Al Qaeda and the emerging Islamic State of Iraq. He becomes even bolder as US troops withdraw and allows Iran to fly military supplies through Iraqi airspace to Syria to support the Assad government.

$ China's share of the world economy keeps growing.

China had the largest proportion of the world economy before the Industrial Revolution, and its share is on the rise again. This chart (based on data from Angus Maddison, "The World Economy") shows those trends. Here, the combined output of China and India is compared to the combined output of the United States and Britain.

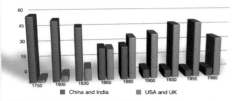

In 2013, the Chinese government announces the decision to relax the One Child Policy.

It is now estimated that this policy averted at least 200 million births between 1979 and 2009. Chinese authorities consider this policy a great success in having helped China achieve its current economic growth.

By 2012 Facebook has over 1 billion users.

The number of drones flying in the skies grows at a fast rate.

Drones become more efficient and are put to deadly use in Pakistan, Afghanistan and Iraq. In the 21st century drones are used for a number of civil applications including police work, fire fighting, border patrol, and surveillance of pipeline inspections. Drones are expected to be approved for commercial use in the U.S. in 2015.

In 2013 Edward Snowden discloses classified information to WikiLeaks regarding the extent of the spying by the NSA. It is revealed that the agency collected telephone and computer metadata on a massive scale, both domestically and abroad without warrants.

Various internet and telephone companies including Facebook have been collaborating with the NSA and have allowed the agency to run a mass electronic surveillance data mining program that gathered private information from users.

The strongest tropical cyclone ever to make land-fall, Super Typhoon Haiyan, wreaks havoc on the Philippines.

The ice at the poles of the earth is melting at a highly accelerated rate; within the last twenty years, more ice has melted than in the last ten thousand years.

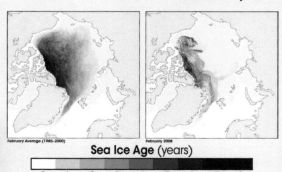

Sea Ice Age (years)
0 1 2 3 4 5 6 7 8

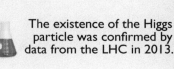

The existence of the Higgs particle was confirmed by data from the LHC in 2013.

Telescopes have evolved as our models of the Universe and our technological abilities have evolved.

The **Hubble Space Telescope** has shown us that there are billions of galaxies in the Universe and it also allows us to see far away galaxies as they were shortly after the birth of our Universe and thus allows us to continue to improve our models.

Science advances both as new observations bring us more data and as we logically distill that information into more cogent theories. Thus, science is a weave of data and logic. Larger telescopes led us to discover that ours is not the only galaxy.

We were able to distinguish much just with our naked eyes. This motivated us to construct our first simple telescopes which helped us to explore our solar system and opened up questions about the possibility of other galaxies.

In physics, the quest for a **Unified Theory** continues. Scientists seek to find one force to encompass and replace the four separate forces we now recognize.

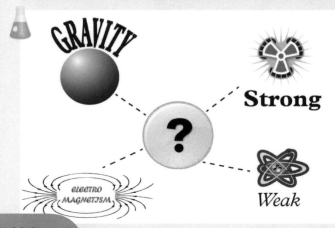

The four forces are: **gravity**, **electromagnetism**, **nuclear strong**, and **nuclear weak**.

Scientists seek one set of equations that can measure and calculate large and small things. Right now we have two types of equations; quantum mechanics for the micro level and relativity for the macro.

This next great hurdle in physics is to unify into one theory and one set of equations, an explanation of the cosmos.

Telescopes allow us to see objects
as they were in the past.

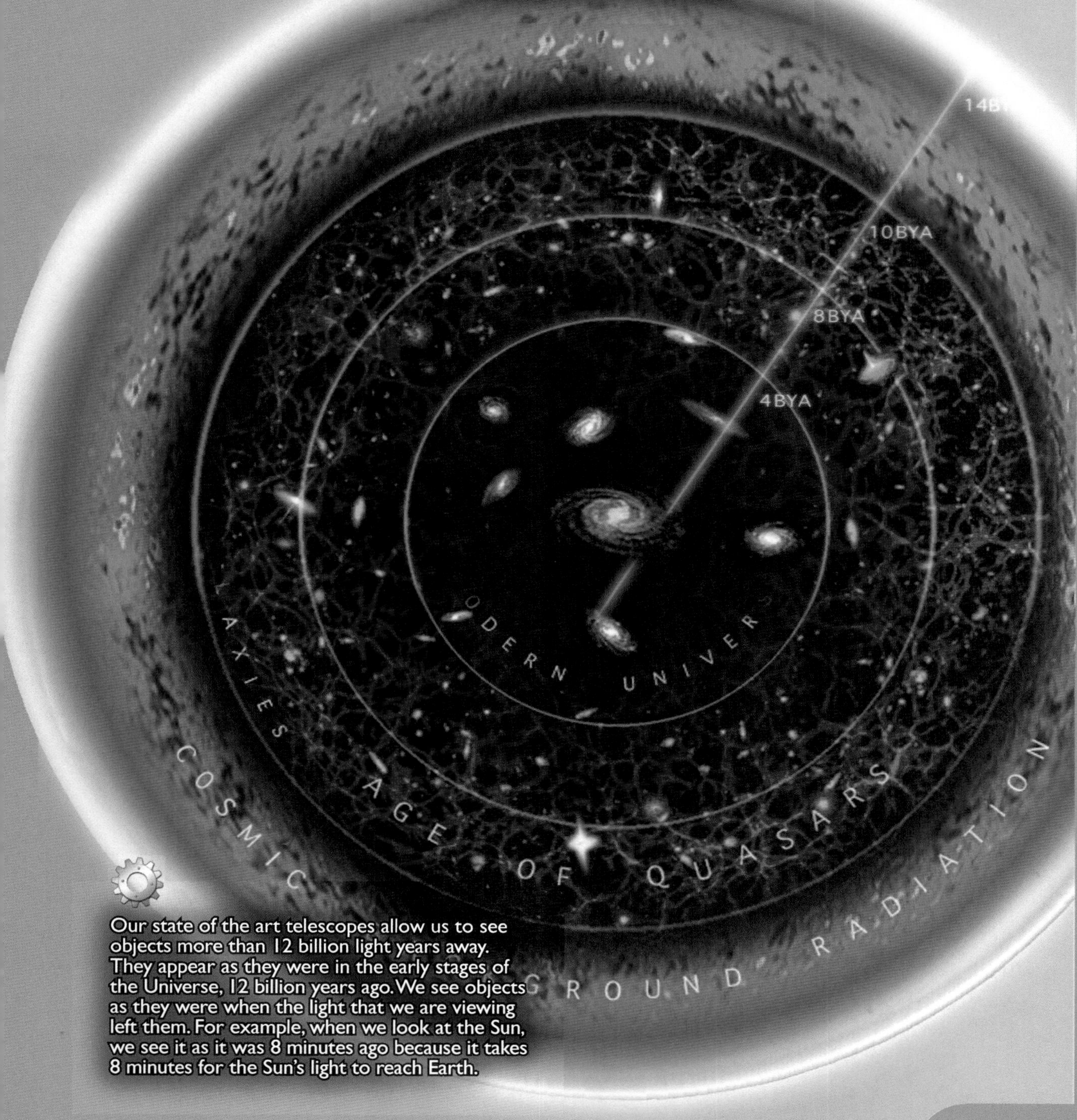

14BYA

10BYA

8BYA

4BYA

MODERN UNIVERSE

GALAXIES

AGE OF QUASARS

COSMIC BACKGROUND RADIATION

Our state of the art telescopes allow us to see
objects more than 12 billion light years away.
They appear as they were in the early stages of
the Universe, 12 billion years ago. We see objects
as they were when the light that we are viewing
left them. For example, when we look at the Sun,
we see it as it was 8 minutes ago because it takes
8 minutes for the Sun's light to reach Earth.

This model of the Universe evolving through time from a singularity has become the modern paradigm.

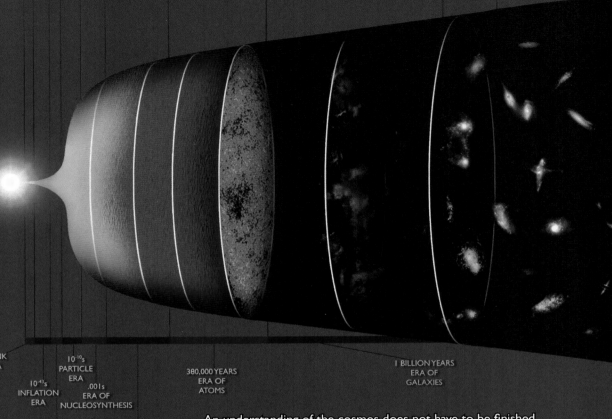

PLANK ERA

10^{-43}s INFLATION ERA

10^{-35}s ELECTRO-WEAK ERA

10^{-10}s PARTICLE ERA

.001s ERA OF NUCLEOSYNTHESIS

3 MINUTES ERA OF NUCLEI

380,000 YEARS ERA OF ATOMS

1 BILLION YEARS ERA OF GALAXIES

An understanding of the cosmos does not have to be finished or completely correct to still function as a paradigm, at least for a while. Even if the Big Bang Theory is eventually superseded, in part or in whole, it will still have functioned as a vehicle that helped us discuss models of the cosmos and think of new ideas.

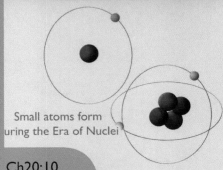

Small atoms form uring the Era of Nuclei

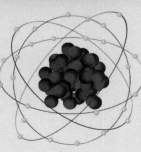

Atoms as large as iron formed with Stellar Nucleosynthesis and larger atoms formed by Supernova Nucleosynthesis

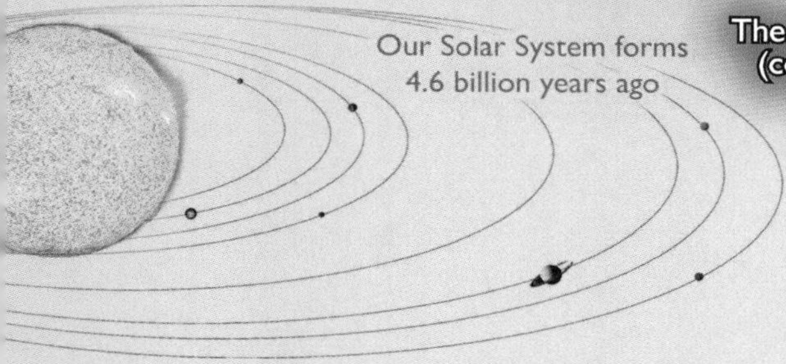

Our Solar System forms
4.6 billion years ago

The pillars of the Big Bang Theory :

The pattern of the CBR
(cosmic background
radiation)

The Universe is
expanding
(the redshift of
the galaxies)

The relative abundance
of the elements

The Big Bang Theory

The pillars of the theory rest on
the assumption that the Universe
is isotropic, that one sector of the
Universe is similar to any other.

The **internet** connects us in new ways.

The internet has evolved and changed drastically. What was once simply a way to send information and programs back and forth from one computer to another has become its own organic entity.

Information is no longer limited to a linear life, the rules of language are no longer as strict as grammar once was. Search engines are picking apart all of the nuances of our queries, omitting that which is unneeded, and anticipating what it is we really want. Our online activities are reduced to keywords and content is served to us based on predictive algorithms.

The worlds of our discrete information and social lives are growing closer and closer as well. Computers can monitor our heart rates and blood pressure by communicating with our wrist watches; instantly call up directions and make suggestions of where to eat lunch on our phones; take and post pictures immediately with appropriate time, date, angle, and interpersonal information tagged on. Our desktop computers can talk to our phones. Our phones can talk to our shoes, our cars, our houses, our televisions.

Not all of the advances in internet technologies are vanity based. When violent regimes oppress their peoples, cutting off internet, phone, and electric utilities to keep information of their atrocities from reaching the outside world, satellite technology enters. 3G and 4G networks allow cell phones to connect to the internet and digital phone lines without using local towers. The result: those very victims are able to instantly broadcast pictures, video, voice recordings, and text to the internet at large, even without the 'permission' of their dictators.

In the wake of 9/11 - the largest foreign attack on American soil in history - citizens of the U.S. felt vulnerable. The Bush administration moved quickly to give more power to military and intelligence organizations. Stunned Americans acquiesced or did little to protest as new powers were granted to the CIA and NSA to detain indefinitely without trial, wiretap without warrant, and create databases of otherwise private statistics on citizens. As soldiers went off to war in Iraq and then Afghanistan and civil rights at home were eroded, the phrase "freedom isn't free" was heard from all angles.

America's power stems not only from its strong military and economic machine but also from its 'soft power'. Soft power is the ability to persuade and influence without the use of force or intimidation. The American dream of democracy, equality for all, and the expectation to prosper from one's own ingenuity and hard work on a level playing field, not only brought hopeful immigrants to American shores but also made America a beacon of hope to many people around the world.

For many decades, the entertainment industry's TV shows, movies and music have been one of the largest exports of the United States. This may come as a surprise to most Americans but the sales of Hollywood's products dwarf most other industries, like auto production or computer software. Further, few Americans realize that these slices of quasi-reality are often viewed as authentic pictures of life in the U.S. and the values of U.S. citizens, by people all over the world and are another example of America's soft power. The actions of corporations based in the U.S. and actions of the U.S. government also affect American soft power.

In December of 2014, the senate intelligence oversight committee releases a 525 -page portion of its 6,000 -page report now commonly referred to as the 'Torture Report'. This report analyzes the CIA's interrogation techniques and its use of torture on detained individuals between 2001 and 2006. It also contains details about misleading and false information that the administration had given to the media.

U.S. government-sanctioned torture undermines more than just America's soft power. Potential informants, who might have voluntarily offered information or defected, do not come forward because of disillusionment or fear. Most people who are tortured and their relatives become mobilized against the U.S. Torture often produces false information, with dangerous consequences. Many of those who implemented the torture eventually return to civilian life, desensitized to violence, which causes new problems at home. Additionally, the safety of America's soldiers and citizens is jeopardized; if captured, they are more likely to be tortured in retaliation. Further, as the report surmises, torture does not yield much useful or actionable information.

Being that it is against the American Creed and outlawed by signed treaties, the condoning of torture contributes to an atmosphere of disregard for the law. Americans, at this same time, are also disillusioned by the disregard for the law shown by some prominent bankers and other high-level white collar criminals; it is much like the atmosphere during prohibition when America became a 'Nation of Scofflaws'. While the moral argument against torture is obvious and sufficient for most people, pragmatic reasoning shows that torture is not even an effective method, as the report also concludes.

Citizens of the U.S. have given up much of the power behind their founding creed and ideology, which had been the most influential 'soft' power on the planet. Americans have traded it in for a set of policies that undermines their own security by exposing them to the retributions of new-found foreign enemies they continue to create, and also makes them vulnerable to a future police state that they are allowing to be created. As facts emerge about the culpability of executives, officials, and individual soldiers, American citizens will have to decide whether they wish for those individuals to be prosecuted. Prosecution would help to restore some of America's credibility, as well as to help ensure that justice prevails in the future, and, it might help American citizens to come together in realizing their own values. Although further investigation and prosecution, as Watergate or Iran/Contra have demonstrated, would be disruptive, the turmoil caused could be mitigated by swift but thorough and unhurried action. The horrors already committed can never be undone but the future will be influenced by the next steps taken.

Leonard Nimoy dies, but Spock continues to live long and prosper.

2015

Nimoy played Spock, the part-Vulcan, part-human crew member of Star Trek from 1964 to 2013.

Science Fiction is a powerful tool for humans to imagine not just possible future scenarios but also to explore what motivates us as a species and what we cherish about Earth.

Although ostensibly about space travel, the Star Trek series addressed issues of diversity, peace, war and justice which it delivered to an American audience grappling with the Vietnam War and the Civil Rights Movement. It was one of the first American TV shows to use a multi-racial cast and Nimoy endowed his half-human character with poise and intelligence.

Although Leonard Nimoy's life comes to its natural end, the influence of Star Trek never will. LLAP - Live long and prosper.

The New Horizons spacecraft flies past Pluto.

In July, New Horizons flies past the Pluto system, sending back the first clear images of these distant and mysterious rocks.

2015 is proving to be a bad year for peat fires in Indonesia.

A combination of extreme drought, El Niño, and careless slash-and-burn land clearing methods have been cause for more than 100,000 active fires in Indonesia this year alone. Environmental and health officials worldwide are concerned with the implications as CO_2 emissions from the fires climb above 1 billion tons.

Though still dwarfed by their level of investment in copper and other resources, Chinese investments in prime African agricultural lands keeps increasing.

Map showing the six economic zones established by the PRC in 2011.

Both Chinese and many African populations are increasing, putting agriculture and the means of feeding these populaces in the spotlight. Most traditional African agriculture focuses on the cultivation of small family plots that cover perhaps a few acres. Recent Chinese investment, however, has built very large mono-crop plantations in the interest of furthering their "20% on 10%" campaign. China boasts that they can feed 20% of the world's population on 10% of the arable land.

Fears exist that decisions by Chinese investors are moving Africa-China relations from strictly bilateral aid-based investments, to something more predatory. If wages on these Chinese-held farms are high enough to stimulate local economies, and if crop yields are high enough, African staple food exports could help stabilize them.

Many African governments face high levels of corruption. The pragmatic nature of Chinese investment bankers, the lack of penalties at home for paying bribes, and the general Chinese cultural attitude toward giving personal gifts and cultivating personal relationships with people you do business with, all enable Chinese firms to conduct business easily.

The Cassini spacecraft detects water on one of Saturn's moons.

Enceladus is a small icy moon in Saturn's orbit. It is proposed that below its icy shell roils an ocean capable of supporting amino acids and other building blocks of life. As it flies through the water plumes, Cassini will be sampling the effluent molecules for elements like hydrogen, which could indicate the existence of underwater incubators of life - Hydrothermal vents.

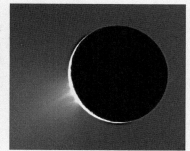

ISIS runs amok through Iraq and Syria.

As al-Maliki's Shiite-controlled government in Iraq has continued to exacerbate sectarian tensions, more and more Sunnis have joined an organization that comes to be known as ISIS. A critical mass of anger and desperation seems to have been reached in the aftermath of the brutal slaughter of many demonstrators at a protest encampment in the city Hawija in 2013. The storming of the Abu Graib prison in July of 2013 releases some 500 hard-line Sunni radicals and changes the atmosphere to one of action. As ISIS soldiers move from town to town, local men join their ranks and government troops seem to evaporate.

The mood is not just of liberation from the Iraqi government abuse, but of anger and power. Following a blend political dogma and Wahhabism (an austere form of Sunni fundamentalism originating in Saudi Arabia), ISIS troops show no mercy and brag of their atrocities. They take over many cities and towns in Western Iraq and roll on into Syria. It all seems to turn to a lust for blood.

Syria has a multi-ethnic population -more than half of whom are Sunni- and is commanded by Bashar al-Assad, an Alawite (which is a Shiite sect). Following his father's death in 2000, Assad assumed the presidency amidst hopes of reform, but he soon imprisoned many leading intellectuals. In 2011 he brutally repressed the peaceful Arab Spring protests and the Syrian Civil War began. Assad is supported by the Shiite government of Iran and by Russia, both financially and militarily.

Syrian government forces, establishing an attack front with the Northwestern city of Aleppo, have displaced thousands. Russian air forces join the Syrian government's attacks in September and coordinate many tactical strikes. The number of citizens fleeing Aleppo jumps quickly to 35,000 in October alone.

Syrian refugees flee the war zone.

Midway through November 2015, estimates of displaced and homeless Syrians total more than 13.5 million; with 7.2 million displaced within Syrian borders and 1.9 in Iraq. This means that more 4.5 million Syrians are traveling abroad fleeing the atrocities at home, creating the largest refugee crisis since World War II. Many are seeking new lives in Turkey and Europe, crossing through the Balkans in huge convoys entirely on foot.

Germany does not close its border and expects the number of asylum seekers to number 800,000 by the end of the year. While many Germans welcome the migrants, some grumble that other nations do not take in their share of refugees. The United States continues to fortify its border with Mexico. The U.S. is also experiencing a new kind of asylum seeker: unaccompanied children fleeing drug gangs in Central American nations.

By trying to understand the cosmos as a whole, it's possible to gain a new perspective of ourselves and our home planet.

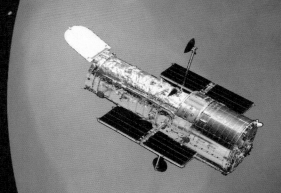

The number of humans on Earth has recently been rising exponentially.

8 billion forecast for 2026

8 billion

World population stood at about 10 million before the advent of agriculture. Since that time, population increased in a fairly linear fashion; the outbreaks of plague in the 6th and 14th centuries caused steep declines but slow, steady growth resumed after these brief episodes. The next billion came little more than a century later and the third followed in just a few decades. We reached 7 billion in 2011. Will we reach 8 by 2026 as most estimates predict?

Earth's biosphere is being damaged by the actions and inaction of its citizens. Taking care of the planet requires the investment of every last one of us. Many who have benefitted from industrialization and material conveniences have been blind to the effects of wasteful practices and global methods of exploitation- but many others have become committed to sustainable lifestyles. Most humans have never shared in material prosperity and eagerly await their chance, having witnessed the wealth of others. Those who discount their own long term future prospects are less likely to work to solve the problems of deforestation and global warming The path to sustainability requires that, through economic and social fairness, everyone have hope in the future.

Bibliography

Andersen T B et al. *The Heavy Plough and the Agricultural Revolution in Medieval Europe*. Univ of Southern Denmark; 2013.

Bennet, Donahue, Shneider, Voit. *The Cosmic Perspective (6th ed.)*. San Francisco: Pearson Addison-Wesley; 2010

Blay, Chuck and Siemers, Robert, *Kauai's Geologic History: A Simplified Guide*. TEOK Investigations; 2004

Brasier, Martin. *Darwin's Lost World: The Hidden History of Animal Life*. New York: Oxford University Press. 2009.

Brown, Cynthia S. *Big History: from the big bang to the present*. New York and London; The New Press; 2007

Bryson, Bill. *A Short History of Nearly Everything*. New York: Broadway Books. 2003.

Castor, Alexis Q (Franklin &Marshall College). *Between the Rivers: The History of Ancient Mesopotamia*; The Great Courses. Chantilly, VA. The Teaching Company; 2006. Multimedia Learning Course.

Chaisson, Eric L. *Cosmic Evolution: The Rise of Complexity in Nature*. Boston: Harvard University Press. 2001.

Chaisson, Eric L. *Epic of Evolution: Seven Ages of the Cosmos*. New York: Columbia University Press. 2006.

Childers, Thomas (University of Pennsylvania). *A History of Hitler's Empire, 2nd ed*; The Great Courses. Chantilly, VA. The Teaching Company; 2001. Multimedia Learning Course.

Christian, David. *Maps of Time: an introduction to Big History*. London; University of California Press 2003

Christian, David. (San Diego State University) *Big History: The Big Bang, Life on Earth, and the Rise of Humanity*; The Great Courses. Chantilly, VA: The Teaching Company; 2008. Multimedia Learning Course

Condie, Kent C. *Plate Tectonics and Crustal Evolution (4th ed.)*. Burlington: Butterworth-Heinemann. 1976.

Condie, Kent C. *Earth as an Evolving Planetary System*. Burlington, MA: Elsevier Academic Press; 2005.

Davis, James C. *The Human Story: Our history, from the stone age to today*. New York, NY: Harper Perennial; 2004

Delsemme, Armand. *Our Cosmic Origins: From the Big Bang to the Emergence of Life and Intelligence*. New York: Cambridge University Press. 1998.

Eliot C LL D. (editor) Harvard Classics: *Wealth of Nations Adam Smith*. (vol. 1, bk. 1, ch. 7.) New York: P F Collier & Son; 1909

Fagan, Brian M (University of California at Santa Barbara). *Human Prehistory and the First Civilizations*; The Great Courses. Chantilly, VA. The Teaching Company; 2003. Multimedia Learning Course.

Falkowski, Paul G. *Life's Engines: How Microbes Made Earth Habitable*. Princeton: Princeton University Press. 2015

Filkin D. *Stephen Hawking's Universe: The Cosmos Explained 1st Ed*. New York: Basic Books; 1997

Fortey, Richard. *Life: A Natural History of the First Four Billion Years of Life on Earth*. New York: Vintage Books – Random House Imprint. 1997.

Francis, Daniel. *A History of World Whaling*. New York: Viking Books. 1990.

FRONTLINE. *Who is Nouri al-Maliki?* PBS. (by Jason Brelow). July 29, 2014

Gaines, Susan M., Geoffrey Eglinton, & Jürgen Rullkötter. *Echoes of Life: What Fossil Molecules Reveal about Earth History*. New York: Oxford University Press. 2009.

Gelvin, James L. *The Modern Middle East: A History*. New York: Oxford University Press. 2005.

Golub, Leon & Jay M. Pasachoff. *Nearest Star: The Surprising Science of Our Sun (2nd ed.)*. New York: Cambridge University Press. 2014.

Goodsell, . *The Machinery of Life (2nd ed.)*. New York: Copernicus Books. 2009.

Gould, Stephen Jay. *The Book of Life*. New York and London: W.W. Norton & Co.; 2001

Green, P. Alexander of Macedon, 356-323 B.c: A Historical Biography. Berkeley: University of California Press, 1991.

Harari, Yuval Noah. *Sapiens: A Brief History of Humankind*. Harper Collins: New York. 2015.

Hardy, Grant (University of North Carolina at Asheville). *Great Minds of the Eastern Intellectual Tradition*; The Great Courses. Chantilly, VA. The Teaching Company; 2011. Multimedia Learning Course.

Hawks, John (University of Wisconsin – Madison). *The Rise of Humans: Great Scientific Debates*; The Great Courses. Chantilly, VA. The Teaching Company; 2011. Multimedia Learning Course.

Hazen, Robert M. *The Story of Earth: The First 4.5 Billion Years, From Stardust to Living Planet*. New York: Viking Books. 2012.

Hazen, M. (George Mason University and Carnegie Institution of Washington) *Origins of Life*; The Great Courses. Chantilly, VA: The Teaching Company; 2005. Multimedia Learning Course

Heilbroner, Robert L. *The Worldly Philosophers: The lives, times and ideas of the Great Economic Thinkers (7th ed)*. New York: Touchstone; 1999

Hilton, Richard P. *Dinosaurs and Other Mesozoic Reptiles of California*. Berkeley: University of California Press. 2003.

Johnson, Norman A. *Darwinian Detectives: Revealing the Natural History of Genes and Genomes*. New York: Oxford University Press. 2007.

Johnson, Steven. *The Invention of Air*. New York: Riverhead Books. 2008.

Jones B. *Discovering The Solar System 2nd Ed*. The Open University, Milton Keynes, UK: John Wiley & Sons Ltd; 2007

Kemp T.S. *The Origin & Evolution of Mammals*. New York: Oxford University Press; 2005

Kimball, Charles (University of Oklahoma). *Comparative Religion*; The Great Courses. Chantilly, VA. The Teaching Company; 2008. Multimedia Learning Course.

Kleveman, Lutz. *The New Great Game: Blood and Oil in Central Asia*. New York: Grove Press. 2003.

Knoll, Andrew H. *Life on a Young Planet: The First Three Billion Years of Evolution on Earth*. Princeton, NJ: Princeton University Press. 2003.

Lane, Nick. *Oxygen: The Molecule that made the World*. New

York: Oxford University Press. 2002.

Lane, Nick. *Life Ascending: The ten great inventions of evolution*. New York & London: W. W. Norton & Co.; 2009

Little, Richard D. *Dinosaurs, Dunes, and Drifting Continents: The Geology of the Connecticut River Valley (3rd Ed.)*. Easthampton: Earth View LLC. 2003.

Long, John and Peter Schouten. *Feathered Dinosaurs: The Origin of Birds*. New York: Oxford University Press. 2008.

Mackey, Sandra. *The Iranians: Persia, Islam, and the Soul of a Nation*.

Margulis, Lynn. *Symbiotic Planet: A New Look At Evolution*. New York: Basic Books. 1998.

Margulis, Lynn, Asikainen Celeste A., and Krumbein, Wolfgang E. (ed) *Chimeras and Consciousness: Evolution of the sensory self*. Cambridge, MA: MIT Press; 2011

Marshak S. *Earth: Portrait of a Planet 3rd Ed*. New York & London: W. W. Norton & Co.; 2008

Martin, Anthony (Emory University) & John Hawks (University of Wisconsin-Madison). *Major Transitions in Evolution*; The Great Courses. Chantilly, VA. The Teaching Company; 2010. Multimedia Learning Course.

McMeekin, Sean. *The Berlin-Baghdad Express: The Ottoman Empire and Germany's Bid for World Power*. Boston: Harvard University Press. 2010.

McMenamin M. *Science 101: Geology*. New York: Collins; 2007

McNeill, William. *Plagues and Peoples*. New York: Anchor Press Books. 1976.

McNeil & McNeil. *The Human Web: A bird's eye view of world history*. New York & London: W. W. Norton & Co.; 2003

McWhorter, John (Professor Manhattan Institute) *The Story of Human Languag.*; The Great Courses. Chantilly, VA: The Teaching Company; 2004. Multimedia Learning Course

Moorehead, Alan. *Darwin and the Beagle*. New York, NY: Penguin Books; 1969

Muesse, Mark W. (Professor Rhodes College) *Relgions of the Axial Age: An Approach to the World's Religions*; The Great Courses. Chantilly, VA: The Teaching Company; 2007. Multimedia Learning Course

Pacey, Arnold. *The Maze of Ingenuity: Ideas and Idealism in the Development of Technology*. London: Allen Lane Books. 1976.

Pasachoff, Jay and Roberta J. M. Olson. *Fire in the Sky: Comets, Meteors, the Decisive Centuries, in British Art and Science*. New York: Cambridge University Press. 1998.

Prothero, Donald R. *Bringing Fossils to Life: An Introduction to Paleobiology*. WCB/McGraw-Hill. 1998.

Randall, Lisa. *Knocking on Heaven's Door: How Physics and Scientific Thinking Illuminate the Universe and the Modern World*. Ecco: New York. 2011.

Reade, John. *Potato: A History of Propitious Esculent*. Yale University Press: New Haven, CT; 2011

Rees, Martin. *Our Cosmic Habitat*. Princeton, NJ:

Princeton University Press; 2001

Rollinson, Hugh. *Early Earth Systems: A Geochemical Approach*. Malden, MA: Blackwell Publishing; 2007.

Roth, Jonathon P. (San José State University). *War and World History*; The Great Courses. Chantilly, VA. The Teaching Company; 2009. Multimedia Learning Course.

Schneider, Paul. *Brutal Journey: Cabeza De Vaca and the Epic First Crossing of North America*. New York: Henry Holt and Company, LLC. 2007.

Southwood, R. *The Story of Life*. Oxford, England: Oxford University Press; 2003

Spier, Fred. *Big History and the Future of Humanity*. Boston: Wiley-Blackwell. 2011.

Stanley, Steven M. *Earth System History Third Edition*. New York, NY: W. H. Freeman and Company; 2009

Steams, Peter N. (George Mason University) *A Brief History of the World*; The Great Courses. Chantilly, VA. The Teaching Company; 2007. Multimedia Learning Course.

Stevens, Scott P. (Professor James Madison University) *Games People Play: Game Theory in Life, Business, and Beyond*; The Great Courses. Chantilly, VA: The Teaching Company; 2008. Multimedia Learning Course

Stow, Dorrik. *Vanished Ocean: How Tethys Reshaped the World*. New York: Oxford University Press. 2010.

Summers, Frank (Space Telescope Science Institute). *New Frontiers: Modern Perspectives on Our Solar System*; The Great Courses. Chantilly, VA. The Teaching Company; 2008. Multimedia Learning Course.

Tsiganis, K. et. al. *Origin of the orbital architecture of the giant planets of the Solar System*. Letters, Nature vol. 435, 26 May 2005 pp. 459-461.

Tyson, N. (Hayden Planetarium and Princeton University) *My Favorite Universe*; The Great Courses. Chantilly, VA: The Teaching Company; 2003. Multimedia Learning Course

Tyson N and Goldsmith D. *Origins: Fourteen Billion Years of Cosmic Evolution*. New York and London: W. W. Norton & Co.; 2004

Ward, Peter and Joe Kirschvink. *A New History of Life: The Radical New Discoveries About the Origins and Evolution of Life on Earth*. Bloomsbury: New York. 2015.

White Andrew D. *A History of the Warfare of Science with Theology in Christendom* Vol 1., Amherst MA: Prometheus Books; 1993

White Lynn Jr. *Medieval Technology and Social Change*. 1962

Wicander, Reed and James S. Monroe. *Historical Geology: Evolution of Earth and Life Through Time (6th ed)*. New York: Brooks/Cole- Cengage Learning. 2010.

Wilson, Edward O. *The Social Conquest of Earth*. New York: W.W. Norton & Company LLC. 2012.

Wrangham, Richard. *Catching Fire: How Cooking Made Us Human*. New York: Basic Books. 2009.

Zimmer, Carl. *At The Water's Edge: Fish with Fingers, Whales with Legs, and How Life Came Ashore but Then Went Back to Sea*. New York: Touchstone. 1999.

Zirker, Jack B. *Journey from the Center of the Sun*. Princeton: Princeton University Press. 2002.

Image Credits

NOTE: Unless otherwise noted, citations stating "Public Domain," are considered to be legally within the Public Domain of the United States copyright law, and no other country. All unmarked images were created by GeoBookStudio team members and are copyright of Wendy Curtis.

10:1 - unknown. "Diatoms." Image. Via Monterey Bay Aquarium, Web.
10:1 - Haeckel. "Diatomeas." Image. [Public Domain] Via Wikimedia Commons. Web.
10:2 - Luterman, Heather Kyoht. "Dilophosaurus wetherilli." Illustration. [CC BY 2.5] Original by Heather Kyoht Luterman. Via WikiMedia Commons. Web.
10:2 - Tamura, Nobu. "Sellosaurus." Illustration. [CC BY 2.5] Original source: spinops.blogspot.com. Modified by Wikimedia User FunkMonk. Via WikiMedia Commons. Web.
10:2 - Tamura, Nobu. "Scutellosaurus." Illustration. [CC BY SA 3.0] Original source: spinops.blogspot.com. Via WikiMedia Commons. Web.
10:9 - ДиБгд. "Illustration of Rhamphorhynchus muensteri." Illustration. 2003. [Public Domain] Original held ДиБгд. Via WikiMedia Commons. Web.
10:9 - Tamura, Nobu. "Rebbachiasaurus." Illustration. [CC BY 3.0] Original source: spinops.blogspot.com. Via WikiMedia Commons. Web.
10:9 - ДиБгд. "Spinosaurus." Illustration. [CC BY SA 3.0] Original by ДиБгд. Via WikiMedia Commons. Web.

12:9 - "The Cave of Swimmers." Image. Original by Science Magazine. Via astrobio.net. Web.
12:16 - Hufstedler, Carla. "20,000 Year Old Cave Paintings, Hyena" Photograph. [Attribution-Share Alike 2.0] Original posted to Flickr. Via Wikimedia Commons. Web.
12:16 - Saura, Pedro (Science/AAASD). "In El Castillo cave." Photograph. Via National Geographic News. Web.

13:14 - "Mongolian Horse, Monarto Zoo, South Australia." Photograph. Via Trevorstravels.com. Web
13:14 - Anon. "Ur Chariot." Image. [Public Domain] Via Wikimedia Commons. Web.
13:15 - Flembles. "Papyrus Ani curs hiero." Image. [Public Domain] Original held by Bridgeman Art Library v. Corel Corp. Via Wikimedia Commons. Web.

14:1 - "GilgameshTablet." Image. [Public Domain] Via Wikimedia Commons. Web. 14C – 6: "國畫 山水." Image. Via tlzd.com. Web.
14:1 - Jurvetson, Steve. "The Santorini Caldera." Photograph. [CC-BY-2.0] Via Wikimedia Commons. Web.
14:2 - Yu, Du. "Spring and Autumn Annals." Photograph of replica. ca. 1938. [Public Domain] Original held by Fujii Saiseikai Yurinkan Museum, Kyoto, Japan. Via Wikimedia Commons. Web.
14:2 - asurbanipal . "Portrait of Cyrus the Great." Image. Via klix.ba. Web.
14:2 - "Sunzi, author of the Art of War". Image. Via Suntzuart.com
14:6 - Klenze, Leo von. "Akropolis." Painting. [Public domain] Via Wikimedia Commons. Web.
14:9 - Bpilgrim. "Asokan Pillar at Vaishali, Bihar, India." Photograph. [CC BY-SA 2.5] Via Wikimedia Commons. Web.
14:9 - WikiUser: Maros M r a z. "Terracotta Army Pit 1." Photograph. 2007. [CC BY-SA 3.0] Via Wikimedia Commons. Web.
14:10 - Veronese, Paolo. "Jesus among the Doctors in the Temple". 1558. Painting. Via 1st Art Gallery. Web.
14:11 - Scrope, G. Julius Poullet. "The Eruption of Vesuvius as seen from Naples…" Painting. October 1822. [Public Domain] Via Wikimedia Commons. Web.
14:11 - WikiUser: AmoreMio. "Hai Ba Trung statue in HCMC." Photograph. September 2009. [CC BY-SA 3.0] Via Wikimedia Commons. Web.
14:11 - Yuan, Jack (Yu Ninjie). "中文: 公元189年时的东汉疆域。" Image. January, 2007. [CC BY-SA 3.0] Via Wikimedia Commons. Web.
14:12 - "4th Century Christ." Image. Via AncientReign.com. Web.
14:12 - Jlascar. "The Church of the Holy Sepulchre-Jerusalem." Photograph. [CC-BY 2.0] Original uploaded to Flickr. Via Wikimedia Commons. Web.
14:13 - Sarkar, Arunava de. "Nalanda Univercity." Photograph. June 1, 2011. [CC SA 3.0] Original held by Arunava de Sarkar. Via Wikimedia Commons. Web.
14:13 - "Nalanda University, India, Ruins." Photograph. [Creative Commons Attribution 2.0] Via Wikimedia Commons. Web.
14:13 - K□ne, Herb Kawainui. "Ancient Polynesians in Outrigger Canoes Coming to Hawaii." Painting. Via bragg.com. Web.
14:13 - VeronikaB (Wikipedia Loves Art participant). "Buddha Bust." Photograph. [CC-BY-2.5] Via Wikimedia Commons. Web.
14:15 - DieBuche. "Map of Expansion of Caliphate." Image. [Public Domain] Original held by The Times Concise Atlas of World History ed. by Geoffrey Barraclough published by Times Books Ltd. Isbn 0-7230-0274-6 pp. 40-41. Via Wikimedia Commons. Web.
14:15 - Yoosai, Kikuchi. "MokoShurai." Image. [Public Domain] Original held by Tokyo National Museum - Dschingis Khan und seine Erben (exhibition catalogue), München 2005, p. 331. Via Wikimedia Commons
14:15 - ~crystalina~. "Koran Cover Calligraphy." Photograph. [CC-BY-2.0] Original uploaded to Flickr. Via Wikimedia Commons. Web.
14: 15 - Stiener, Ariel. "A Full View of the Giant Buddha Statue of Lashan, Sichuan, China." Photograph. June 2005. [CC BY-SA 2.5] Via Wikimedia Commons. Web.
14:15 - WikiUser: Vassil. "Jouesue de polo. Chine du Nord, dynastie Tang, première moitié di 8ème siècle." Photograph. October 2007. [Public Domain] Original held by Musée Guimet, Paris. Via Wikimedia Commons. Web.
14:18 - DannyL. "Flying Money of the Tang Dynasty, circa 841-846 AD." Image. Via Pintrest. Web.
14:18 - "Kneeling Knight, Westminster Psalter, London, c. 1250." Image. Original held by London, British Library ms. Royal 2. A. XXII fol. 220. Via hubert-herald.nl. Web.
14:18 - "Godfrey of Bouillon with Other Crusade Leaders." Image. Via Hist2615 Wikispaces. Web.
14:19 - "Somnath Temple at Night." Photograph. Via sonalitravels.com. Web.
14:21 - "Nalanda University, India, Ruins." Photograph. [Creative Commons Attribution 2.0] Via Wikimedia Commons. Web.
14:23 - DavidYork71. "Arabslavers, 19th-century." Engraving Image. [Public Domain] Original held by Encarta UK. Via Wikimedia Commons. Web.
14:24 - Kāne, Herb Kawainui. "Ancient Polynesians in Outrigger Canoes Coming to Hawaii." Painting. Via bragg.com. Web.
14:24 - Yoosai, Kikuchi. "Mooko Shuurai." Ink on Paper. 1847. [Public Domain] Original held by Tokyo National Museum. Via Wikimedia Commons. Web.
14:26 - Hooke, Robert. "HookeFlea01." Image. [Public Domain] Original held by National Maritime Museum, Greenwich, London. Via Wikimedia Commons. Web.
14:26 - Hooke, Robert. "Hooke-microscope." Image. [Public Domain] Via Wikimedia Commons. Web.

15:1 - WikiUser: Shakko. "Timur, Forensic facial reconstruction by M. Gerasimov. 1941." 2008. Photograph. [CC BY-SA 3.0] Via Wikimedia Commons. Web.
15:1 - Pawliszak, Wacław. "Lucznik tatarski." Image. [Public Domain] Original held by Muzeum Narodowe, Warszawa. Via Wikimedia Commons. Web.
15:2 - unknown. "Fall of the City." Painting. Via ballandalus.wordpress.com
15:3 - "Los Reyes Catolicos." Image. [Public Domain] Original held by Aceros de Hispania. Via Wikimedia Commons. Web.
15:3 - Zeschky, Jan. "Patio de los Arrayanes, Palacio Nazaries, Alhambra, Granada." Photograph. [CC-BY 2.0] Via Wikimedia Commons. Web.
15:3 - Weeks, Edwin Lord. "The Moorish Bazaar." Painting. Via Edwinlordweeks.com. Web.
15:3 - Ortiz, Fransisco Pradilla. "La Rendición de Granada." Image. [Pubic Domain] Original held by Invertirendarte.es. Via Wikimedia Commons. Web.
15:3 - Kemal, Mustafa. "Ataturk Janissary." Photograph. 1913. [Public Domain] Via Wikimedia Commons. Web.
15:5 - unknown. "Cristoforo Colombo in ginocchio davanti alla regina Isabella I." Painting. [Public Domain] Original held by US library of Congress. Via Wikimedia Commons. Web.
15:5 - Prang, L. & Co. "Christopher Columbus arrives in America." Painting. 1893. [Public Domain] Original held by US Library of Congress (Call # cps.3b49587). Via Wikimedia Commons. Web.
15:5 - unknown. "View of the Seraglio Point (Sarayburnu) from Pera…" Painting. [Public Domain] Via Wikimedia Commons. Web.
15:6 - Da Vinci, Leonardo. "Paleodictyon." Sketch. c. 1507. [Public Domain] Via historyofgeology.fieldofscience.com
15:6 - Da Vinci, Leonardo. "Study of horse." [Public Domain] Original held by Web Gallery of Art. Via Wikimedia Commons. Web.
15:8 - "Xiuhtecuhtli." Image. [Public Domain] Via Wikimedia Commons. Web.
15:8 - "Codex Magliabechiano (141 cropped)." Image. [Public Domain] Original held by FAMSI (Foundation for the Advancement of Mesoamerican Studies, Inc. Via Wikimedia Commons. Web.
15:8 - Sauber, Wolfgang. "Murales Rivera - Market in Tlatelolco." [CC BY-SA 3.0] Via Wikimedia Commons. Web.
15:9 - unknown. "The Codex Fejervary-Mayer." 15th Century. Paint on Stone. [Public Domain] Via Wikimedia Commons. Web.
15:11 - Coello, Alonso Sanchez. "Arrival of the Fleet in the 16th Century (1531-88)." Painting. [Public Domain] Original held by Spainthenandnow.com. Via Wikimedia Commons. Web.
15:13 - "Spanish Galleon." Image. [Public Domain] Via Wikimedia Commons. Web.
15:13 - unknown. "Casta painting containing complete set of 16 casta combinations…" Painting. 18th century. [Public Domain] Via Wikimedia Commons. Web.
15:14 - White, John. "Roanoke map 1584." Photograph. [Public Domain] Original held by British Museum. Via Wikimedia Commons. Web.
15:14 - de Loutherbourg, Philippe-Jacques. "Defeat of the Spanish Armada, 8 August 1588." Painting. Via Maritime Museum, Greenwich, London. Web.
15:15 - Dhanraj. "Babur visiting the Urvah valley in Gwalior, Where Idol Statues had Been Cut Out of the Rocks." Illustration. c. 1590. Via Wikimedia Commons. Web.
15:15 - Matham, Jacob. "A Beached Sperm Whale on the Shore near Beverwijk." Engraving. 1601. [Public Domain] Original held by the Trustees of the British Museum (call #AN57681001). Via mercuriuspoliticus.wordpress.com. Web.
15:15 - Shaw, Byam. "The Adventures of Akbar Artillery." Illustration. 1913. [Public Domain] Original published in novel by the same name, authored by Flora Annie Steel. Via Wikimedia Commons. Web.

16:1 - Galilei, Galileo. "Phases of the Moon." Image. [Public domain] Via Wikimedia Commons. Web.
16:2 - Van de Velde, Jan. "1628 Version of Printing Press from 1440." Engraving. [Public Domain] Press invented by Pieter Saenredam. Original held by Geheugen van Nederland. Via Wikimedia Commons. Web.
16:2 - Translators, Early 17th-Century and Evangelists. "The King James Bible." Image. [Public Domain] Original held by the Private Collection of S. Whitehead. Via Wikimedia Commons. Web.
16:2 - Catarinella, Massimo. "Molen de 1100 Roe in de sneeuw, Amsterdam." Image. [CC-BY-3.0] Via Wikimedia Commons. Web.
16:2 - "Peat Extraction ca. 1800." Image. Via Encyclopedia Pictura.
16:3 - unknown. "Two members of the select Solaks guard (Janissary archers) of the Ottoman Sultans." 16th century. Illustration. [Public Domain] Via Wikimedia Commons. Web.
16:3 - Mola, Pier Francesco. "Pirarta saraceno." 1650. Painting. [Public Domain] Original held by Louvre, Paris. Via Wikimedia Commons. Web.
16:4 - Robert-Fleury, Joseph Nicholas. "Galileo Galilei before the Holy Office in the Vatican, 1632." Painting. 1847. Via Lessing Images. Web.
16:5 - Crofts, Ernest. "A Scene from the Thirty Years' War." Painting. Via Principia Dialectica. Web.
16:5 - "Bondi brennandi hus" Image. [Public Domain] Via Wikimedia Commons. Web.
16:5 - Haiworonski, Oleksa. "Crimean Khanate 1600." Image. Via Wikimedia Commons. Web.
16:5 - Ivanov, Sergey Vasilyevich. "Trade Negotiations in the Country of Eastern Slavs." Painting. [Public domain] Via Wikimedia Commons. Web.
16:5 - Ivanov, Sergey Vasilyevich. "At the Guarding Border of the Moscow State." Painting. [Public domain] Via Wikimedia Commons. Web.
16:6 - Karim, Muhammad Mahdi. "Taj Mahal 2012." Photograph. [GNU Free Documentation License 1.2] Original held by www.micro2macro.net and author. Via Wikimedia Commons. Web.
16:7 - unknown. "Dutch in Japan." c. 1609. Illustration. [Public Domain] Original held by Koninklijke Bibliotheek, Netherlands. Via geheugenvannederland.nl. Web.
16:7 - Vingboons, Johannes. "View of New Amsterdam." Image. [Public Domain] Original held by the Atlas of Mutual Heritage and the Nationaal Archief (Dutch National Archives). Via Wikimedia Commons. Web.
16:7 - "Whaling Fleet At Work." Via Berkshire Fine Arts. Web.
16:7 - 清实录. "Battle of Ningyuan, where Nurhaci was injured in defeat." Illustration. [Public Domain] Via Wikimedia Commons. Web.
16:9 - Steenhorst, Paul. "Leeuwenheok's Microscope (replica)." Image. Original held by Museum Boerhaave, Netherlands. Via Museum Boerhaave. Web.
16:9 - Thom, Robert. "Van Leeuwenhoek at Work." Painting. Via ToLearn. Web.
16:9 - Van Leeuwenhoek, Anton. "Animalcules." Image. [Public domain] Via Wikimedia Commons. Web.
16:12 - "Siege Of Vienna By Ottoman Forces." Image. [Public Domain] Original held by the Hachette Collection, Istanbul. Via Wikimedia Commons. Web.
16:12 - Geffels, Frans. "Vienna Battle 1683." Painting. [Public Domain] Original held by Badisches Landesmuseum. Via Wikimedia Commons. Web.
16:12 - Osman, Hafiz. "Name of Allah." Calligraphy. 17th century [Public Domain] Via Wikimedia Commons. Web.

17:2 - Ingersoll. "Meissen-Porcelain-Dancers." Photograph. [Public Domain] Via Wikimedia Commons. Web.
17:2 - Bezur. "Meissen Porcelain Sign 2." Image. [Public Domain] Via Wikimedia Commons. Web.
17:3 - unknown. "Loom with Kay's Flying Shuttle." Photograph. Via http://lisahistory.net/hist104/pw/lectures/indust/kay.gif
17:3 - Antisell, T. "Kay's Spinning Jenny." Image. [Public Domain] Original from "The Handbook of The Useful Arts" (1852). Via From Old Books. Web.
17:3 - "Whaling Fleet At Work." Via Berkshire Fine Arts. Web.
17:3 - Linnaeus, Carl. "Leaf forms from Hortus Cliffortianus." Image. [Public Domain] Original from "Hortus Cliffortianus" (1738). Via WikiMedia Commons. Web.
17:5 - GeraldK. "Cape Ann Earthquake." Image. Via Wikimedia Commons. Web.
17:6 - "Cape Ann Earthquake 1755." Engraving. Original held by National Information Service for Earthquake Engineering, UC Berkeley. Via USGS. Web.
17:6 - Berann, Heinrich. "Atlantic Ocean Floor." Painting. 1968. Via ICA Commission on Map Design. Web.
17:8 - "The Chocolate House." Painting. Via TimeOut Tours. Web.
17:8 - Hohenstein, Anton. "Franklin's Reception at the Court of France, 1778. Respectfully dedicated to the people of the United States." Painting. Original held by the Library of Congress (call number LC-DIG-pga-01591). Via Library of Congress. Web.
17:8 - "Tryworks On Whaling Ship." Image. Via Golden Assay. Web.
17:9 - "Enclosure." Image. Via ECIMM. Web.
17:10 - "Arkwright Water Frame." Image. [CC BY 3.0] Via Wikimedia Commons. Web.
17:10 - Johnson, Layne. "Thomas Jefferson." Illustration. Via Rutgers Prep. Web.
17:10 - Ferris, Jean Leon Gerome . "Writing the Declaration of Independence, 1776." Painting. [Public Domain] Original held by Library of Congress Prints and Photographs Division (Call # cph.3g09904). Via Wikimedia Commons. Web.
17:11 - Streminger, Gerhard. "Wealth of Nations." [Public Domain] Via Wikimedia Commons. Web.
17:11 - Court, Joseph-Désiré "Gilbert du Motier Marquis de Lafayette." Image. [Public Domain] Via Wikimedia Commons. Web.
17:11 - "First Japanese Treatise on Western Anatomy." Photograph. [Public Domain] Via Wikimedia Commons. Web.
17:11 - Zveg, V. (US Navy employee). "Battle Of Virginia Capes." Image. [Public Domain] Original held by US Navy Naval History and Heritage Command: Photo #: NH 73927-KN. Via Wikimedia Commons. Web.
17:11 - Siebold. "Nagasaki Bay." Image. [Public Domain] Via Wikimedia Commons. Web.
17:13 - David, Jacques-Louis. "Portrait of Monsieur Lavoisier and His Wife." Painting. [Public Domain] Original held by Metropolitan Museum of Art (call # 436106). Via Wikimedia Commons. Web.
17:12 - "Volcano of the Revolution." Photograph. Via La Terre du Futur. Web.
17:12 - Wedgewood, Josiah & (either) William Hackwood or Henry Webber. "The Official Medallion of the British Anti-Slavery Society." Image. [Public Domain] Via Wikimedia Commons. Web.
17:14 - Delacroix, Eugène. "La Liberté Guidant le Peuple." Painting. [Public Domain] Original held by Louvre-Lens. Via Wikimedia Commons. Web.
17:14 - "Storming of the Bastille." Image. Via Parables Blog.
17:14 - David, Jacques-Louis. "Portrait of Monsieur Lavoisier and His Wife." Painting. [Public Domain] Original held by Metropolitan Museum of Art (call # 436106). Via Wikimedia Commons. Web.
17:15 - Knapp, H.S. "Johnny Appleseed." Illustration. [Public Domain] Original from "A History of the Pioneer and Modern Times of Ashland County," Philadelphia: J. B. Lippincott & Co. (1862). Via Wikimedia Commons. Web.
17:15 - WikiUser: dougtone. "Historic Slater Mill in Pawtucket, Rhode Island." May 2010. Photograph. [CC BY-SA 2.0] Via Wikimedia Commons. Web.
17:15 - Raleigh, C. S. "The Whaling Schooner Amelia of New Bedford, Massachusetts." Drawing. Original held by NOAA. Via Cool Antarctica. Web.
17:15 - US Patent Office. "Drawing of Eli Whitney's Cotton Gin." Drawing. c. 1795. [Public Domain] Original held by the Textile Industry History Organization. Via Wikimedia Commons. Web.

18:1 - "Général Toussaint Louverture." [Public domain] Original held by NYPL Digital Gallery. Via Wikimedia Commons. Web.
18:1 - "Toussaint L'Ouverture." Engraving. [Public Domain] Via Wikimedia Commons. Web.
18:1 - de Thulstrup, Thure. "Louisiana Purchase, New Orleans." Painting. [Public Domain] Via Wikimedia Commons. Web.
18:1 - "Louisiana Purchase." Image. [CC BY-SA 3.0] Via Wikimedia Commons. Web.
18:1 - Suchodolski, January. "San Domingo." Image. [Public Domain] Via Wikimedia Commons. Web.
18:1 - Dumont, Eugenio Álvarez. "Churruca's Death." [Public Domain] Original held by Museo del Prado. Via Wikimedia Commons. Web.
18:1 - Turner, Joseph Mallord William. "The Battle of Trafalgar." 1806. [Public domain] Original held by Tate Britain. Via Wikimedia Commons. Web.
18:2 - Sagredo, Ramón. "Ejército Trigarante." Painting. [Public Domain] Original held by La Secretaría de la Defensa Nacional. Via Wikimedia Commons. Web.
18:2 - Northen, Adolph. "Napoleons Retreat from Moscow." Painting. [Public Domain] Via Wikimedia Commons. Web.
18:2 - Giggette. "Political divisions of Mexico 1821." [CC BY SA 3.0] Original map by Instituto Nacional de Estadística y Geografía. Via Wikimedia Commons. Web.
18:3 - Bernard, Fred. "Dickens at the Blacking Warehouse." Image. [Public Domain] Original from "The Leisure Hour", 1904, London. Via Wikimedia Commons. Web.
18:3 - Smith, William. "Geological Map Britain." 1815. [Public Domain] Original held by LiveScience Image Gallery by the Library Foundation, Buffalo and Erie County Public Library. Via Wikimedia Commons. Web.
18:3 - "McConnel & Company mills, about 1820." Watercolor image. [Public Domain] Original from A Century of fine Cotton Spinning, 1790-1913. McConnel & Co. Ltd. Frontispiece. Via Wikimedia Commons. Web.
18:3 - Smith, William. "Fossils 2." Engraving. [Public Domain] Original William Smith's guide to classifying rock strata by characteristic fossils, 1815. Via Wikimedia Commons. Web.
18:4 - Hine, Lewis. "Mill Children in Macon 2." Image. [Public domain] Original held by United States Library of Congress's Prints and Photographs Division (Digital ID nclc.01581). Via Wikimedia Commons. Web.
18:4 - "Breaker Boys." Via epubbud.com. Web.
18:5 - De la Beche, Henry. "Duria Antiquior." Watercolor image. [Public Domain] Original held by National Museum Cardiff. Via Wikimedia Commons. Web.
18:7 - Cuvier, George. "Ichthyosaurus communis and Plesiosaurus dolichoderes." Illustration. [Public domain] Original from George Culvier's "Discours sur les révolutions de la surface du globe et sur les changements qu'elles ont produits dans le règne animal," 1834. Via Wikimedia Commons. Web.
18:7 - Van Voorst, John. "A Sketch of a South Sea Whaling Voyage, London." 1839. Via Sothebys.com. Web.
18:7 - "Morse Telegraph Diagram." Image. [Public Domain] Via Wikimedia Commons. Web.
18:7 - "Friedrich Engels, 1840." Photograph. [Public domain] Via Wikimedia Commons. Web.
18:7 - "Industrial Factory." Image. Via High Tech High Blog. Web.
18:8 - Missionary Society, The London. "Preaching from a Wagon (David Livingstone)." Image. [Public Domain] Original held by National Portrait Gallery, London: (Call # NPG D18387). Via Wikimedia Commons. Web.
18:8 - "Chinese Ships in the Opium Wars." Via TimeToast. Web
18:8 - "Child Laborers." Photograph. Via Maxell.syr.edu. Web.
18:9 - "Map of the Gold Regions of California." Image. 1849. [CC BY-SA 3.0] Original held by David Rumsey Map Collection. Via Wikimedia Commons . Web.
18:9 - Nesbitt, G.F. & Co., printer. "California Clipper 500." Image. Ca 1850. [Public Domain] Original held by Robert B. Honeyman, Jr. Collection of Early Californian and Western American Pictorial Material, UC Berkeley,
18:10 - Ramirez, Valentin. "Panorama Dentro." Painting. [Public Domain] Original held by Interior del Museo Panorama. Via Wikimedia Commons. Web.
18:10 - Fenton, Roger. "Roger Fenton's Waggon." Color film copy transparency. [Public Domain] Original held by Library of Congress, Prints & Photographs Division (Call # LC-USZC4-9240). Via Wikimedia Commons. Web.
18:10 - Krassovsky, Nikolay. "Russian Black Sea Fleet after the battle of Synope, 1853." Painting. [Public Domain] Via Wikimedia Commons. Web.
18:11 - Heine, W. "Landing of Commodore Perry, Officers & Men of the Squadron, to Meet the Imperial Commissioners at Yoku-Hama July 14th 1853." Lithograph. 1853. [Public Domain] Original published by Sarony & Co., 1855, held by Library of Congress. Licensed under Public domain via Wikimedia Commons. Web.
Bancroft Library. Via Wikimedia Commons. Web.
18:11 - "Matthew Perry." Woodblock Print. Ca. 1854. [Public Domain] Original held by the United States Library of Congress's Prints and Photographs division (Digital ID cph.3b52813). Via Wikimedia Commons. Web.
18:12 - NASA "Earth's Magneto Sphere and Solar Barrage." Image. Via NASA Heliophysics Division. Web.
18:12 - "Confederate 5 and 100 Dollars by Confederate States of America." Scanned Image. [Public Domain] Via Wikimedia Commons. Web.
18:12 - Barnard, George N. "Whitehall Street, Atlanta, 1864." Photograph. Via Shorpy.com. Web.
18:13 - LaFlaur, M. "Frederick Douglass." Photograph. Via Flickr. Web.
18:13 - Cheney, William H. "Harriet Tubman with Rescued Slaves." Photograph. Ca. 1885. [Public domain] Original held by Bettmann/Corbis Images (call # BE038091). Via Wikimedia Commons. Web.
18:13 - Billings, Hammatt. "Masthead of the 1850 Liberator." Engraving. [Public Domain] Original held by University of Virginia. Via Wikimedia Commons. Web.
18:13 - "Burlaks Walking." Photograph. [Public Domain] Original held by State Historical-Architectural Art Museum and National Park Photofiles, Russia. Via Wikimedia Commons. Web.
18:13 - Harper & Brothers. "Gordon, Scourged Back." Photograph. [Public Domain] Original held by Library of Congress, Harper's weekly, 1863 July 4, p429, bottom. Via Wikimedia Commons. Web.
18:14 - Brady, Matthew. "Confederate Dead in Chancellorsville." Photograph. 3May, 1863. [Public Domain] Original held by National Archives and Records Administration (NARA). Via Wikimedia Commons. Web.
18:14 - Leutze, Emanuel. "Westward the Course of Empire Takes Its Way." Study for Painting. [Public Domain] Original held by the Smithsonian American Art Museum. Via Wikimedia Commons. Web.
18:14 - Kurz & Allison. "The Battle of Chickamauga." Lithograph. Ca. 1890. [Public Domain] Original held by the Library of Congress Prints and Photographs Division. Via Wikimedia Commons. Web.
18:14 - "Picket Station of Colored Troops Near Dutch Gap Canal." Photograph. Nov. 1864. [Public Domain] Original held by Library of Congress (Call # LC-B811- 2553[P&P]). Via Wikimedia Commons. Web.
18:14 - Remington, Frederic. "Smoke Signal." Painting. [Public Domain] Original held by the Amon Carter Museum, Fort Worth TX. Via Wikimedia Commons. Web.
18:15 - "Tarr Farm, The Valley Where it All Began." Photograph. Via Titusville Shale Taskforce. Web.
18:15 - Chiossone, Eduardo. "Meiji Tenno." Conte Illustration. [Public Domain] Originally published in Tenno Yondai No Shozo, Tokyo, Japan: Mainichi Shinbun Sha. Via Wikimedia Commons. Web.
18:15 - Minard, Charles. "Figurative Map of the successive losses in men of the French Army in the Russian campaign 1812-1813." llustration. 1869. [Public Domain] Via Wikimedia Commons. Web.
18:16 - Garneray, Louis Ambroise. "Attacking a Right Whale and Cutting In." Originally from 'The Whale Fishery,' Published by Currier & Ives by Louis Ambroise Garneray. Via Magnolia Box. Web.
18:16 - "Construction of the Suez Canal" Image. ca. 1868. Via Missouri University of Science and Technology. Web.
18:16 - Kane, Paul. "Assinibone Hunting Buffalo." Painting. [Public domain] Original held by the National Gallery of Canada. Via Wikimedia Commons. Web.
18:17 - "Drake's Oil Well Pennsylvania, The Valley Where it All Began." Photograph. Via Titusville Shale Taskforce. Web.
18:18 - "The landing of the Unyo in Korea." Painting. 1877. [Public domain] Original held by National Diet Library, Japan. Via Wikimedia Commons. Web.
18:18 - London Stereoscopic & Photographic Company. "Henry Morton Stanley." Photograph. 1872. [Public Domain] Original held by the Smithsonian Institution Library, Russell E. Train Africana Collection. Via Wikimedia Commons. Web.
18:19 - Gaba, Eric (username fr:Sting). "Colonial Africa 1913 Map." Image. [CC BY-SA 3.0] Original by John Bartholomew & Co. from "Hammond's Atlas of the Modern World," 1917. Via Wikimedia Commons. Web.
18:19 - Renard, Jules Jean Georges (AKA Draner). "Bismarck Partitioning the African Cake at the Berlin Conference." Illustration. Via tlaxcala-int.org. Web.
18:19 - Tenniel, Sir John. "Save Me From My Friends!" Illustration. 30 Nov 1878. [Public Domain] Originally published in Punch magazine, 30 November, 1878. Via Wikimedia Commons. Web.
18:19 - Sambourne, Edward Linley. "The Rhodes Colossus." Illustration. [Public Domain] Originally published in "Punch and Exploring History 1400-1900: An anthology of primary sources," p. 401 by Rachel C. Gibbons. Via Wikimedia Commons. Web.
18:19 - "Zoroaster." Photograph. 1878. [Public Domain] Original held by Swedish National Museum of Science and Technology. Via Wikimedia Commons. Web.
18:20 - "Construction Tour Eiffel." Photograph. [Public Domain] Originally published in "Tour Eiffel: Montage de la deuxième plateforme," 1888. Via Wikimedia Commons. Web.
18:20 - Parker & Coward. "Krakatoa Eruption." Lithograph. [Public Domain] Originally published as Plate 1 in "The eruption of Krakatoa, and subsequent phenomena. Report of the Krakatoa Committee of the Royal Society" (London, Trubner & Co., 1888). Via Wikimedia Commons. Web.

For a more detailed source list of the images and photographs represented in the book, go to:

www.GeobookStudio.org/BiggestPicture

58708270R00190

Made in the USA
Charleston, SC
17 July 2016